China's Population Struggle

CHINA'S POPULATION STRUGGLE

*Demographic Decisions
of the People's Republic, 1949-1969*

H. YUAN TIEN

Ohio State University Press: Columbus

Library of Congress Cataloging in Publication Data

Tien, H. Yuan
　　China's population struggle.

　　Bibliography:　p. 385
　　1. China (People's Republic of China, 1949–　　)—
Population.　2. Birth control—China (People's Republic
of China, 1949–　　)　I. Title.
HB3637.T5　　　　　　301.32'9'51　　　　　　73–1868
ISBN 0-8142-0184-9

In honor of my Parents

Contents

List of Tables

Preface

This book is written for persons who are interested either in population policy in general or in China in particular or in both. But, let it be stated at the outset that it is not a treatise on the number and growth of the Chinese population. That China's population is large and growing is beyond dispute, even though our knowledge of the population size and its rate of increase is far from precise. Whether China's present population is 500, 600, 700 or 746 million, of course, is a question of immediate practical significance. Likewise, whether the population is growing at 2 percent or 1.5 percent per annum cannot but be of long-run import. Available Chinese demographic statistics permit, however, no definitive answers to these questions. In recent years, numerous estimates and projections of China's population size and growth have been made, revised, and re-revised. Some of them are the best possible computer enumerations, displaying statistical ingenuity and demographic sophistication. However, whatever the purposes they serve, they are not population data in the usual sense of the term. Moreover, all of them are based on assumed rates of change in fertility and mortality that still lack empirical confirmation. Thus, rather than expend additional energy and time to conjure up yet another set of estimates and projections of China's population, the present book is devoted to examining China's demographic decisions only. It is policy measures rather than computer print-outs that will ultimately determine population developments in China. An examination of same should also help shatter of the myth of the "yellow peril."

In the summer of 1949, on the eve of the defeat of the Kuomintang (Nationalists) regime, the U.S. Department declared, "The population of China during the eighteenth and nineteenth centuries doubled, thereby creating an unbearable pressure upon the land. The first problem which every Chinese government has had to face is that of feeding this population." In the spring of 1972, on the eve of the twenty-third anniversary of the founding of the People's Republic, Premier Chou En-lai declared, as though in reply, that of the priorities, our first has been the feeding of the population, and in this we have succeeded. During the interval between the two statements, a remarkable feat has clearly been accomplished; this accomplishment contradicts not only many political predictions but also various oft-repeated generalizations regarding the relationship between population and poverty, disease, and disorder. Of the large variety of policy measures that the People's Republic has adopted in the course of its first two decades, a significant number are concerned directly or indirectly with the question of population size, growth, and distribution. This book is about these demographic measures as they were in the process of being made, implemented, deemphasized, discarded, or modified. It seeks to relate their initial and changing determinants. It also attempts to assess their effectiveness and meaning in the context of the immediate past twenty years and, to a lesser degree, to appraise their possible impact on China's demographic future.

This volume grew out of a research proposal that I submitted to the Joint Committee on Contemporary China of the Social Science Research Council and the American Council of Learned Societies. Two fellowship grants from this Committee facilitated the collection of most of the data and their initial analysis. Additional generous support came from the Research Committee of the University of Wisconsin and the

Graduate Research Board of the University of Illinois. I also wish to recognize the immense help of Mr. Charles Mutter who aided in getting together materials for some of the chapters.

Portions of this book have been previously published in *Population Studies, Milbank Memorial Fund Quarterly, Demography, American Sociological Review, Journal of Marriage and the Family, Asian Survey, World Population Conference (1965)*, and *Proceedings* of the 1969 Assembly of the International Union for the Scientific Study of Population. Slight or substantial modifications have been made of these for inclusion in this book. I gratefully acknowledge the permissions of the publishers of the various journals to allow me to do so. I should also thank many friends and critics who read these earlier papers, before and after publication, and communicated their views to me in personal correspondence as well as in informal exchanges at professional meetings.

The preparation of the manuscript was capably handled by Sandy Booth and Barbara Burns. Ms Sarah T. Millett of the Ohio State University Press provided considerable editorial assistance. Ms Janet Hamilton prepared the index with dispatch and professional thoroughness. I sincerely thank them all.

Research for this volume was initially carried out in 1961–62 in Hong Kong. Coincidently, I was able to return to this metropolis in 1972 during the final phase of preparing the manuscript for publication. My second sojourn was made possible by a grant from the Fulbright-Hays Exchange Program. Not only am I grateful for the chance to be back in this part of the world, but also for the opportunity that the grant provided for finishing the last few details in relative freedom from nonacademic struggle in universities. In this connection, I want also to thank Professor Murray Groves and other colleagues in the Department of Sociology at the University of Hong Kong for the courtesy and cooperation that they kindly extended during my year as visiting professor in their department.

Lastly, I must mention the help of my wife, Corinne G. Tien. Not only did she agree with me on the importance of the topic, but she also made many valuable suggestions and otherwise contributed to the quality of the final product.

As the book goes to press, I am looking forward to spending a period of time in the People's Republic of China, to reviewing the organization and interpretation of the facts referred to in this volume with interested persons there, and, as the result of the exchange, to amending the book's deficiencies.

H. Y. T.

Hong Kong
1 October, 1972

China's Population Struggle

Introduction

Chapter one

The problems of population have long taxed the ingenuity and imagination of man. Practical measures to cope with them, for instance, can be found in centuries-old writings of scholars in many parts of the world. Likewise, speculative assessments of the possible determinants and consequences of population trends have also been recorded in volumes of great antiquity. Thus, the history of the making of population policy is long, and its legacy rich. This notwithstanding, only since the emergence of demography as a scientific discipline in modern times has there been a relatively adequate understanding of the factors affecting and affected by population size, growth, and distribution. However, omniscience does not now reign. In the contemporary world, in fact, the formulation of population policy still involves many imponderables; "population policy even at its best must be a relative matter and must deal in approximations."[1] The writing of population policy has been and remains the outcome of periodically definitive, albeit not irreversible, conclusions of the perennial controversies of population numbers, growth, and distribution. And policies,

1. Hope T. Eldridge, *Population Policies: A Survey of Recent Developments,* p. 1.

once formulated, characteristically accentuate rather than settle demographic issues of long standing.

In this connection, no other single issue in demography and population policy has sparked more heated debate than the one centered around Malthus and his principle of population. This controversy is, for a number of reasons, particularly relevant in regard to Chinese population measures in recent years. Not only did Malthus intend his principle to be universally applicable to all peoples, but he also made use of Chinese materials of purported reliability to support his thesis. He outlined China's demographic circumstances as well as future prospects as he saw them at the end of the eighteenth century. In response, there grew up in China a literature based on the repudiation of Malthus by Chinese writers.

A review of the Malthusian controversy in the Chinese context follows, which will also serve to introduce the major dimensions of population policy.

Dimensions of Population Policy

The most recent rejection of Malthus in China followed the establishment of the People's Republic of China in 1949. Like many other post-1949 events in China, this has been hastily or conveniently attributed to the ideological stance of the government. Although interpretation of this kind can be easily documented by reference to numerous forceful official statements on the question of Malthus in Chinese publications in recent years, it grossly oversimplifies the matter. In China, the acceptability of Malthus and his principle of population has been, for quite some time before 1949 as well as afterward, questioned on a number of other grounds.

In 1798, when the first edition of his *An Essay on the Principle of Population* was published, Malthus averred, "The [Chinese] population must be immense. . . . [However,] it certainly seems very little probable that the population of China is fastly increasing."[2] In his view, in China at the be-

2. Thomas Malthus, *An Essay on the Principle of Population,* pp. 24, 25. The immense population of China allegedly was 333 million.

ginning of the nineteenth century and during the preceding
two hundred years or more, a state of demographic saturation
had been reached. The enormous population of China was
seen by Malthus as the result of the "natural tendency of population to increase," which in China was also augmented by
the fertility of the soil and encouragement given to agriculture
and marriage over the centuries. But, under the then existing
circumstances, virtually all of the country's labor force was engaged in the production of food just to sustain the large population at the minimum level of subsistence. In unfavorable
years, famines led to recurrent losses in population. Thus, the
numerical stagnation of the population was believed to have
reflected the operation of the positive checks (i.e., famine, war,
epidemics) to population.[3] Moreover, Malthus also maintained that not only had there been little increase in population but also that in a country "so fully peopled" as China,
further growth in population was not to be expected. He declared, "From the accounts we have of China and Japan, it
may fairly be doubted whether the best-directed efforts of
human industry would double the produce of these countries
even once in *any* number of years."[4]

Furthermore, Malthus asserted, not only was there little
likelihood of any improvement in the food situation, but there
was also not much hope for a change for the better in the lot
of the population through an expansion in manufactures for
foreign commerce:

> An immense capital could not be employed in China in pre-
> paring manufactures for foreign trade, without altering this
> state of things, and taking off some laborers from agricul-

3. Ibid., pp. 206–18. However, according to Malthus, it would be
erroneous to overlook the role of the preventive check (i.e., moral restraint) in the Chinese situation.

4. Ibid., p. 155 (italics added). With respect to China's food problem, Malthus also stated, "In China, the question is not, whether a certain additional quantity of rice might be raised by improved culture;
but whether such an addition could be expected during the next twenty-
five years, as would be sufficient to support an additional three hundred
millions of people" (p. 475).

ture, which might have a tendency to diminish the produce of the country. Allowing, however, that this would be made up and indeed, more than made up, by the beneficial effects of improved skill and economy of labour in the cultivation of the poorest lands, yet, as the quantity of subsistence could be but little increased, the demand for manufactures which would raise the price of labour, would necessarily be followed by a proportionate rise in the price of provisions, and the labourer would be able to command but little more food than before.[5]

This Malthusian prognosis of China's demographic condition certainly is an attempt by Malthus to "empirically" substantiate his principle of population. It cannot be accepted as an accurate reflection of the actual situation. In fact, his principle of population and the suitability of the logical method used to validate it are very much in dispute.[6] Part of the continuing dispute is epistemological in character, but much of it also has a great deal of practical significance. For instance, scholars have been and still are divided on the question of whether poverty is an epiphenomenon of "overpopulation" as Malthus believed. The role of population in relation to poverty is much more than an intellectual issue in China. Within China, a major continuing concern pertains to the possible elimination or reduction of poverty. In Malthusian terms, the probability is that the Chinese are foredoomed to a state of perpetual and static poverty; the only way out would be through a marked reduction of the population by means of increased mortality and the adoption of "moral restraint" im-

5. Ibid., p. 453. Malthus also argued that the laborers "would be in the same or rather worse state than before; and a great part of them would have exchanged the healthy labors of agriculture, for the unhealthy occupations of manufacturing industry" (p. 116).

6. For a comprehensive review of the development of conflicting population theories up to 1900, see E. P. Hutchinson, *The Population Debate: The Development of Conflicting Theories up to 1900.* For a systematic critique of Malthus's logic, see Kingsley Davis, "Malthus and Theory of Population," in Paul F. Lazarsfeld and Morris Rosenberg, eds., *The Language of Social Research,* pp. 540–53.

mediately thereafter. Seeking an escape through a program of deliberate increase of mortality is only a theoretical possibility in the idle manipulation of the demographic equation.' Thus, even if there were no other reasons, the Malthusian diagnosis is sufficiently repugnant to those who are actively seeking an effective end to China's poverty; for it forecloses any improvement in the Chinese situation, regardless of effort. But, Malthus has been declared persona non grata on other grounds in China.

Malthus asserted, as previously noted, that the population of China had been in a state of numerical stagnation for quite some time. However, the implications of this demographic condition are not limited to those contained in Malthus's exposition. Dr. Sun Yat-sen, the founder of the Chinese Republic in 1911, for instance, also reminded the public of it in one of a series of lectures a year or so before his death in 1925. He said, "We Chinese are constantly boasting of our large population [of 400 million] which cannot easily be destroyed by another nation. . . . Gentlemen, do you know when China's four hundred million census was taken?—In the reign of Ch'ien Lung [1734–1795 A.D.] in the Manchu dynasty. Since Ch'ien Lung, there has been no census. In this period of nearly two hundred years our population has remained the same—four hundred millions. A hundred years ago it was

7. Assuming no migration, the demographic equation reads as follows: $P_1 = P_0 + (F - M)$ where: P_0 refers to the population at an earlier date; P_1 is the population at a later date; and F and M refer to the number of births and deaths that occur during the interval. To bring about a population reduction (i.e., P_1 becomes smaller than P_0), mortality must exceed fertility. This can be accomplished by decreasing fertility to a level below that of the current mortality or much lower to take care of any possible decline in mortality. It may also be realized, in theory, by raising the level of mortality to offset present fertility or a lot higher to counteract any increase in fertility. The control of population numbers in contemporary societies follows the first model at least to the extent that it concentrates on fertility reduction as a means of achieving a slower rate of growth of population. No nation is known to follow or even remotely to consider the second model in its population policy decisions, though the practice of genocide against racial, religious, or ethnic minorities was, and may still be, in use in certain nations.

four hundred millions; then a hundred years hence it will still be four hundred million."[8] Dr. Sun went on:

Now compare the rate of increase of the world's populations during the last century: the United States, 1,000 percent; England, 300 percent; Japan, also 300 percent; Russia, 400 percent; Germany, 250 percent; France, 25 percent. . . . What is the significance for China of this rapid growth of other populations? When I compare their increase with China's, I tremble. . . . The reason why other nations cannot for the present seize China right away is simply because their population is yet smaller than China's. A hundred years hence, if their population increases and ours does not, the more will subjugate the less and China will inevitably be swallowed up. Then China will not only lose her sovereignty, but she will perish, the Chinese people will be assimilated, and the race will disappear.[9]

Thus, Dr. Sun rejected Malthus and called for a population increase:

A hundred years ago an English scholar named Malthus, bewailing the world's overcrowded condition and the limited supply of natural resources for its use, advocated a reduction of population and proposed the theory that "population increases in a geometrical, food in an arithemetical, ratio." Malthus's theory appealed to the psychology of the French and to their love of pleasure. . . . A century ago, France's population was larger than any other European country, but because of the spread of Malthus's ideas to France and their reception there, the people began to practice race suicide, and today France is suffering from too small a population, all because of the poisonous Malthusian theory.   China's

8. Sun Yat-sen, *The Three Principles of the People,* trans. Frank W. Price, pp. 23–24. This particular quotation is from a speech Dr. Sun made on 27 January 1924. By August, he not only was concerned with the numerical stagnation of the population, but also spoke of its reported decline in his time: "According to reliable foreign investigations, China at present does not really have more than 310,000,000 people. Several decades ago we had a population of 400,000,000 which means that we have lost 90,000,000. This is a frightful fact that raises a serious problem for our consideration" (pp. 450–51, 487). The reason for the decline was, according to him, "food shortage."

9. Ibid., pp. 22–23, 27.

modern youth, also tainted with Malthus's doctrine, are advocating a reduction of the population, unaware of the sorrow which France has experienced. Our new policy calls for increase of population and preservation of the race, so that the Chinese people may perpetuate their existence along with the . . . races of the world.[10]

Here China's demographic prospects were viewed in relation to those of some other nations. The alarm over the presumed decline in the relative size of the Chinese population probably can *now* be dismissed as having no statistical foundation. The fact of the matter is that such a fear did exist and, in this instance, did lead to the public denunciation of Malthus by one of the most prominent political leaders of China long before 1949.

The unacceptability of Malthus since 1949 has been predicated on additional grounds. These will be discussed later. Here it is sufficient to say that the views of Sun and Malthus are irreconcilably divergent on account of their differential stress on different dimensions of population problems. Overpopulation (in relation to the means of subsistence), according to Malthus, prevailed in China; this constituted the framework within which he explained the existence of poverty there. On the other hand, underpopulation or depopulation (relative to population growth in other nations) provided the terms of reference in which Sun sought to arouse China to the danger of future deterioration of the country's international demographic status or extinction. Because of the differences in their perception of China's population problem, Malthus and Sun necessarily alluded to different corrective measures. Whatever its other significance, therefore, Sun's castigation of Malthus in terms of what he considered to be China's demographic predicament and prospects appropriately demonstrates the many complex issues involved in population policy decisions. If Malthus's view can be termed the poverty-welfare dimension of population policy, Sun's stance is an illustration of what may be called the power dimension. These are the two major dimensions of population policy.

10. Ibid., pp. 24–25.

Population Policy Defined

During the last several decades, an increasingly large number of measures affecting population have been adopted by many governments. An alphabetical list of these measures reads like this: annual-wage plans; artificial insemination; assimilation; child-care provisions; child spacing; conservation of natural resources; contraception; custodial institutions; education; eugenics; euthanasia; family allowances; genetics; governmental subsidies for education, farmers, and veterans; health insurances; housing; immigration laws; insurance, other than health; labor legislation; marriage grants and loans; marriage laws; mental health provisions; nutrition research; public health provisions; recreational provisions; retirement plans; safety legislation; social security programs for families, children, aged, dependent mothers and children, handicapped; standards of living; sterilization; tax allowances; transportation; vocational training and rehabilitation; and wage supplements.[11]

However, though these measures have been adopted either in the face of, or in anticipation of, social problems of frequent occurrence, the existence of social problems per se does not automatically mean recognition and remedial action. "Different countries recognize a varied selection of problems as deserving immediate attention and their social plans will vary accordingly," observed Phelps and Henderson, and "as a rule most countries have adopted a combination of these practical measures which can be identified as their current [social or population] policies."[12] A relationship between the measures and social problems is self-evident. The adoption of the former is contingent upon the *recognized* existence of the latter.

Nevertheless, the demographic impact of the various measures is, in many instances, either not immediately apparent or difficult to ascertain. As a case in point, the effect of some clearly pronatal measures of the 1930s on the birthrates of

11. Adapted from Harold A. Phelps and David Henderson, *Population in Its Human Aspects,* pp. 460–61.

12. Ibid., p. 461.

France, Italy, and Germany is still at issue many years after they were implemented. Quite apart from anything else, the known changes in fertility may have been due to factors other than such pronatal measures. Moreover, in a country where several or many of these measures are applied simultaneously, there is the very real possibility that they can partially or fully neutralize the effect of any one measure. Because of a lack of adequate information or want of appropriate instruments, the difficulty involved in the empirical assessment of any of these measures is considerable.

Of course, even if the demographic effect of these measures of a particular country cannot be readily detected, it does not necessarily mean that they influence population not at all. This leads to a question that is of central importance here: Does the adoption of measures affecting population amount to a population policy?[13] No answer can be given to this question until a definition of population policy is set forth.

In the literature, various conceptualizations of population policy exist, ranging from the most specific to the most general. There are those who consider "the deliberate intent of a (nation) to control its size and/or its characteristics the criterion for judging whether that (nation) has had or now has a population policy."[14] In other words, social measures of a nation that may have a profound effect on its population do not, according to the advocates of this circumscribed view, constitute a population policy unless they are the result of deliberate intent to so modify the population or segments thereof. As has also been pointed out by many, a large variety of measures affecting women, children, the family, immigration, employment, labor mobility, and the like exist in America, yet it still can be said that "the United States has laws affecting population but no concerted population policy."[15] Con-

---

13. The present analysis is "positive" in that it does not specifically consider the implications of inaction through either neglect or a conscious negative approach to population on the part of a government.

14. Warren S. Thompson and David T. Lewis, *Population Problems,* p. 527.

15. Ralph Thomlinson, *Population Dynamics,* p. 395.

sideration of a nation's population policy thus can best be limited to viewing only those measures having specified and explicit demographic purposes.[16]

On the other hand, as Eldridge pointed out, all the elements of national policy that affect demographic trends and patterns are elements of population policy, whether they are "deliberately concerned with population" or go by the name of population policy.[17] Following this comprehensive conceptualization, almost any and all measures devised to cope with social problems can be deemed as having varying degrees of demographic relevance and import. Consideration of measures of population, to paraphrase and extend what Paul Meadows said in this connection, therefore runs the whole gamut of social problems and measures.[18]

At first glance, it would seem that the difference between these two conceptualizations of population policy is simply a matter of emphasis and methodology. The selection of one or the other perspective in an analysis of population policies would be dictated by the purposes of a study. In an indirect comment on the circumscribed view, for instance, Eldridge warned: "But for the purposes of international analysis, it is too narrow a definition. Its application would result in an uneven coverage of many types of legislation, since similar laws may in one country be regarded as demographic policy, in others not."[19] But, the ramifications of these two divergent views far exceed the question of the adequacy of coverage in population policy analysis. They involve, among other things, the controversial issue of the nature of population problems. This dispute has been involved, often implicitly, in two other

16. If, as Joseph J. Spengler observed, those who follow this circumscribed approach to population policy are concerned with what may be called "explicit" population policies, it should be said that they also sometimes dwell upon the importance of measures that exercise similar influence, though not so designed or enacted. See his "Socioeconomic Theory and Population Policy," pp. 129–33.

17. Hope T. Eldridge, *Population Policies*, p. 4–5.

18. Paul Meadows, "Toward a Socialized Population Policy," pp. 193–202.

19. Eldridge, *Population Policies*, p. 5.

questions: (1) Are social and economic problems reducible
to problems of population numbers and growth?   (2) Are problems of population numbers and growth, in fact, social and
economic problems?

The first question, if answered in the affirmative, suggests
that population numbers and growth may be viewed as barriers
to social and economic improvements in the short run and as
nullifiers to them in the long run.   In a conceptual scheme of
this kind (e.g., the Malthusian model), the centrality of population numbers and growth is assumed, wherein corrections of
social and economic problems must await, or are conditional
upon, a solution to demographic problems.

In a brief note, T. Lynn Smith described the objectives of
demographic decisions as follows: "Population policies . . .
[are] designed to get and maintain the kind of population that
is desired, from the standpoints of number, quality, and distribution." [20]   In more elaborate terms, Spengler stated:

> The objectives of population policy must be defined in quan-
> titative, spatial, and qualitative terms.   If the objective be
> quantitative in character, it consists in an increase, or a de-
> crease, or the prevention of any change, in the magnitude of
> a population, or in its rate of growth, or in one or both of
> the two governors of natural increase [i.e., mortality, na-
> tality], or in one or both of the two governers of increase
> (decrease) through migration [i.e., gross emigration, gross
> immigration].   If the objective be spatial in character, it
> consists in a change, or in the prevention of change, in
> the distribution of a population in geographical space.   If
> the objective be qualitative in character, it consists in a
> change, or in the prevention of change, in the qualitative
> composition of the population.[21]

To be sure, in the final analysis, the actual or potential impact of a population policy can be meaningfully expressed only
in demographic terms; what is ultimately affected by it is
nothing other than the population itself.   However, this does
not automatically validate the assertion that social and eco-

20. T. Lynn Smith, *Population Analysis*, pp. 518–19.
21. Spengler, "Socioeconomic Theory and Population Policy."

nomic problems are reducible to problems of population numbers and growth. Both in theory and on empirical grounds, the propriety of this reductionism is questionable. Poverty such as that which exists in *The Other America*,[22] for instance, can be conveniently, but not satisfactorily, attributed to demographic factors, given the affluence of the United States. Moreover, the knowledge accumulated in social demography also serves to undermine this narrowly demographic approach to social and economic problems. With respect to the engineering of a decrease in population growth, for example, Frank Notestein once remarked:

> Contraception is an important means, among others, by which people can control their fertility. Whether they control it depends on the social setting; hence new patterns of behavior are to be established principally by the alteration of that setting. . . . Paradoxically, a reduction of the growth potentialities can be achieved only in terms of increased population in the near future. . . . Fertility decline will come gradually and only after the people acquire new interests and aspirations. These new interests are likely to develop only in a period of rising levels of living, urbanization, widespread education, and growing contacts with foreign culture . . . [and] only a society in which the individual [child or adult] has a reasonable chance for survival in healthy life will develop that interest in the dignity and material well-being of the individual essential to the reduction of fertility.[23]

Thus, it seems preferable to give a positive answer to Question Two rather than to Question One, and to characterize population problems as social and economic problems. Accordingly, the comprehensive definition of population policy is basic to this analysis. Perhaps, most eloquently of all, Alva Myrdal summed up this conceptualization in her *Nation*

22. Michael Harrington, *The Other America*.

23. Frank W. Notestein, "Problems of Policy in Relation to Areas of Heavy Population Pressure," pp. 424–44.

and Family in one sentence: "A population policy can be nothing less than the social policy at large."[24]

Population Policy in Developmental Perspective

The analysis of a nation's population policy could begin with a determination of the relative share of what can be described as therapeutic and prophylactic measures in its makeup. As previously stated, the adoption of measures (which, in aggregate terms, are a nation's population policy) is necessarily preceded by formal recognition of social and economic problems already in existence. Fundamentally, the thrust of such measures is therapeutic, and aimed at the correction, diminution, or erasure of problems in existence. In actuality, the formulation of a nation's population policy may and often does go beyond the mere recognition of existing problems and their redress as such. To the extent that this is true, some component measures of a nation's population policy are also fully or partially oriented toward future problems or anticipated consequences of current events.

However, this therapeutic-prophylactic dichtomy has only limited utility in the analysis of population policy. First of all, dual purposes are often served by one measure. Second, what is regarded as therapeutic at one time may be differently labeled at a later date. Third, analytic criteria for differentiating policy measures along these lines are difficult, if not impossible, to establish. Thus, important as this mode of differential characterization of policy measures is, a more adequate and versatile scheme for analyzing population policies cannot be secured on this foundation.

In table 1, the framework for the present analysis is detailed. Along with some of the elements referred to in the discussion thus far, new elements are added to make it possible for a more fruitful probe into the making, substance, and connotations of China's population policy.

The conversion of "problems" into policy measures can be

24. Alva Myrdal, *Nation and Family*, p. 2.

TABLE 1

AN ANALYTIC FRAMEWORK FOR POLICY ANALYSIS

PROBLEM DESIGNATIONS	STEPS IN POLICY-MAKING	POLICY VARIABLES
I. Existing: (a) Actual (b) Anticipated	1. Recognition of existence of problems	A. Previous Experiences B. Current needs
II. Future: (a) Actual (b) Anticipated	2. Articulation of causes of recognized problems	C. New Experiences D. Changed Circumstances

conceived of, as is outlined in table 1, as a two-step process: (1) recognition of existence of problems, and (2) articulation of causes of recognized problems. Mention of the first has been made several times; nevertheless, three additional points require further comment. In table 1, social and economic problems are classified in terms of the existing-future dichotomy. However, note should be taken of the added designations that so-called existing or future problems can be actual or anticipated. A problem that is *believed* to exist or to be likely to occur can be of as decisive influence on the writing of population policy as a problem whose existence or occurrence is empirically verifiable. Furthermore, the recognition of problems is invariably selective in number and in priority: not all existing and future problems are given simultaneous cognizance; neither are recognized problems rated equal in importance. Finally, the neglect (deliberate or otherwise) of certain problems and the preferential treatment of selected problems may well represent the outcome of the interplay of a large number of policy considerations (variables) *at a given point in time.* These variables can be conveniently placed into two broad categories: (A) previous experiences, and (B) current needs.

"Previous experiences" include historical legacies, ideology, administrative skills, knowledge and information (whether or not true is immaterial), national and international outlook, hopes and fears, and so on, that policy-makers possess or come to inherit at the outset of policy formulation. All or any of these can screen various problems from view or serve to focus attention on some problems. Likewise, "current needs" can also have a similar effect and produce selective recognition and preferential treatment of "problems" at hand and in the foreseeable future. The promotion and maintenance of internal stability and external security, the allocation of available financial and material resources among competing projects, and the sheer circumstances under which policy-makers are confronted with problems are examples of "current needs." Any or all of these happenings and contingencies may make it imperative or expedient to recognize or brush aside certain problems at any given point in time and to concentrate on others.

In the categorization of the policy variables producing selective recognition and preferential treatment of problems, "time" is an implicit element. Whatever problems are recognized preliminary to the adoption of specific measures, and however recognized problems are ranked in priority, neither the selection nor the preference based on "previous experiences" and "current needs" is necessarily for an indefinite duration. Time validates or demolishes previous experiences as well as satisfies or modifies needs; in the course of time, recognition or preference may be withdrawn from some problems and shifted to certain others. As time elapses, moreover, "new experiences" and "changed circumstances" also come to pass. Consequently, there may very well be significant alterations in the selection and preferential treatment of problems over time.

Recognition of the existence of problems per se does not necessarily lead to the adoption of appropriate meaningful measures. In many instances, a problem is recognized and may even be extensively discussed without policy results. Nor does recognition prescribe the character of policy measures adopted to deal with the problem in question. A problem whose existence is acknowledged by all or by a majority of concerned persons is often variously interpreted by different individuals at the same time or by the same people at different times, when the cause or causes of its existence are sought. The kind and contents of measures adopted to deal with a problem hinge directly and squarely on what is accepted as its cause or causes. "Articulation of causes" thus constitutes the second vital step in policy decisions.

By "articulation of causes" is simply meant the explicit or implicit assumption or assumptions on the basis of which policy measures are devised or advocated. These need not be more than "working hypotheses." Nor must they be more than tentative diagnoses of conditions that presumably give rise to the problems in question. Of course, they can be far more than hypothetical or diagnostic propositions. Whatever their essence, they set the terms and tempo of policy measures.

Like the selection and preferential treatment of problems, the character of policy assumptions is defined by a large number of variables ("previous experiences" and "current needs") at any given point in time. Their definition, however, can also undergo extensive revision in emphasis as well as in detail as "new experiences" and "changed circumstances" emerge over time.

All in all, the variables intervening in the conversion of problems into policy measures manifest their influence in two time contexts. They do so in a temporal setting that is inexorably ephemeral and in the flow of time that is continuous. Only in terms of both temporal spaces can the making, contents, and connotations of policy decisions be fathomed. Either alone does not suffice. Analysis and appraisal of what takes place at an earlier time must be tempered by what develops subsequently. No adequate understanding of what obtains over time can be arrived at unless there is also a good knowledge of previous developments. In the present analysis, this perspective is of crucial importance: the People's Republic of China was proclaimed in 1949; its demographic policies necessarily date therefrom. The circumstances (i.e., "previous experiences" and "current needs") that surrounded their inception can only be those that accumulated up to, and prevailed in, 1949. However, by 1969, the People's Republic of China had been in existence for twenty years. Thus, there has been time enough to allow additional factors (viz., "new experiences" and "changed circumstances") to come into play. In short, what is suggested here is that it takes time for a nation's demographic policy to take shape and to develop.

Therefore, in the present book, the analytical approach to Chinese demographic measures is in terms of their *development* rather than static description.

This developmental approach to population policy (which, as stressed previously, is also the social policy at large), however, does not presume logical and practical consistency among all policy assumptions and measures at any given time. Nor does it postulate their inevitable evolution toward coherence over time, though time enhances the possible emergence of the latter. Thus, as Eldridge cogently remarked:

> The body of national policy often contains contradictions and inconsistencies some of which are real and some of which are only apparent; some of which are perhaps necessary and some of which are probably not. These "contradictions" arise partly from the ambivalent nature of the underlying purposes, requiring as it does a certain amount of compromise or balancing. They arise also from a somewhat fortuitous selection of national objectives, *through the interplay of contending interests and pressures within a country.* Finally no small part of them is due to poor understanding of the relationships and connections that exist in the tangled web of social organization and social history. As insight into these relationships is sharpened, the ground is laid for resolving contradictions and developing more intelligent social-demographic policies.[25]

The development of population policy requires time and, as previously noted, also takes place within a system of power or a political context. Viewed in its political context, two additional questions of considerable importance must be clarified if an analysis of a nation's demographic measure is to be of real value. The two questions can be telescoped into one query and simply stated as follows: Whose recognition of problems and whose articulation of their causes do actually prevail and produce concrete results in the dynamic process of policy-making?

Perhaps the same answer applies to both parts of the query. Perhaps there may be different answers. Different persons

25. Eldridge, *Population Policies,* p. 4.

or groups of persons within a nation may recognize the existence of different problems with no overlap. Or, the disagreement pertains only to the causes of an identical set of recognized problems. To the extent that this is the case, and assuming parity among all participating groups in the writing of population policy, the ensuing exchange would produce either no policy results or a policy that is farraginous in composition. In actuality, the preponderance of one or a few groups often is more distinguishable, and they decisively influence the formulation of a nation's population policy. Whether national demographic measures result from mutual concessions among divergent groups or reflect the dominance of one or a few of them, the close affinity between population policies and politics is indicated. In fact, population policies *are* politics. Thus, analysis of a nation's population policy must also include the identity of individuals or groups participating in its formulation.

Plan of the Book

The People's Republic of China enjoys jurisdiction over an area of 3,800,000 square miles. The geographic magnitude of China therefore resembles that of Europe (which is 375,000,000 square miles, including the British Isles and non-Asian portion of the Soviet Union). Had this latter piece of real estate been incorporated into one sovereign state, the hypothetical "European Union" would have had an estimated population of 587 million in 1960. The resemblance between China and "Europe" would also have been expressed in their demographic dimensions as well. In November 1954, the population of China was officially reported to be 582.6 million as of 30 June 1953.

This announcement attracted a great deal of attention at the time, and still excites scholars and others as well as embroils them in heated exchange on the accuracy of the figure. By comparison, curiously lesser concern of a similar character has been shown in actual population data for Europe, the aggregation of which puts Europe's population at a numerical party with the Chinese population. Mention of Europe's teeming millions produces only faint stir, whereas even a passing reference to the Chinese multitude brings forth emotions of all descriptions. This differential effect of two nearly identical population numbers can be variously explained. In scores of cases, it is simply a case of Sinophobia; the cry of the "Yellow Peril" remains loud. On the other hand, genuine concern with the welfare of the Chinese, of course, is the decisive element: whether measured in terms of the total national income or income per capita, China's standing compares conspicuously unfavorably with that of Europe as a whole. But, the lesser impact of Europe's massive population may owe much to the fact that it is divided into more than two dozen separate national populations, whereas China's population is the population of a single sovereign state.

According to United Nations estimates, the population of the world was 2.5 billion in 1950, and increased to just below 3.0 billion by 1960. The reported 1953 Chinese population of 582.6 million thus amounted to more than one-quarter of the global population in 1950, or nearly 20 percent of that in 1960. The possession by one nation of a population of this proportion cannot be but impressive, although the relationships between population, on the one hand, and power or poverty, on the other, still are controversial topics. Inevitably, this has conditioned the perception among many of the nature of the Chinese population problem; it has served to define it, almost exclusively, in terms of the control of population numbers.

In the present volume, however, the control of population numbers will not be taken up at the start. Instead, and notwithstanding its popularity in writings of all sorts, the topic of population numbers will be deferred to the last two of the five chapters (chapters 2 through 6) wherein the framework and contents of China's demographic measures between 1949 and 1969 are traced and interpreted. This arrangement is not at all whimsical, however. In China, given the size of its population in 1949, when the People's Republic of China was established, measures capable of altering appreciably this demographic circumstance would have required a considerable number of years to succeed, even if they had been adopted immediately thereafter. In China, in 1949 and the following few years, the sustenance and employment of its existing population were of paramount importance and, for social, political, and economic reasons, demanded relatively immediate attention. Thus, the organization of the present analysis is, in fact, based on the approximate order of actual events in China since 1949.

Consideration is first given to measures affecting and affected by the existing population in China. Those pertaining to the spatial pattern of the population are dealt with under three separate headings: rural-urban population distribution and redistribution (chapter 2), the stabilization of the urban population (chapter 3), and population transfers and land reclamation (chapter 4). The importance of these measures, however, should not be understood only in terms of the demographic goals implicit in the descriptive titles of the various chapters. They have a great deal to do with the accommodation, feeding, and gainful employment of the existing population.

Chapters 5 and 6 are devoted to examining the beginning, evolution, and implementation of China's fertility-policy decisions. In chapter 7, attention is focused on some of China's social-policy measures that presumably affect Chinese population trends in the longer run. An appraisal of China's overall population policy during the interval covered in the study and other conclusions are presented in chapter 8.

In addition, a number of official statements and selections from other publications are reproduced as appendixes at the end of the book. These are arranged in the same order as that of the several topics treated in the text. Their inclusion is based on two considerations. One is that, as far as China's population policy is concerned, they are the key documents. The second reason is to illustrate the nature and kinds of data on which the present study is based. Apart from information that may some day be collected on the spot to supplement what is contained in the currently available sources, the published items adequately serve the purposes of the present study and include: official documents; directives; speeches by officials at different levels of the administrative structure; popular essays and learned articles in political, professional, and technical journals; and accounts in newspapers and other periodicals of local and nationwide circulation in China.

Although the present analysis covers a period of two decades, 1949 to 1969, only, a few references have been made to the more recent years. Partly, this is due to the availability of information; but principally, this is because there have been no known changes in China's population policy. Though emphasis has shifted and fluctuated, the basic decisions made, tried, and revised before the mid-1960s have remained unchanged.

Rural-Urban Population
Distribution and Redistribution

Chapter two

As things stood in 1949, the government of China inherited a sizeable population whose spatial distribution had been shaped by natural, political, social, and economic forces over many centuries as well as in recent times. Because of this huge and still growing population, the need for limiting population growth has been extensively debated inside and outside of China. But, in the immediate context of internal recovery and development, the sustenance and utilization of the existing population, logically and in the sequence of the actual policy formulation, occupied the first and primary place.

Population growth aside, therefore, decisions must be and have been taken with respect to the ways in which the "hands" may be gainfully employed, and to the distribution of what they produce. Such decisions must inevitably involve the allocation of resources between different uses, e.g., between current consumption and future consumption (capital investment and savings), between investment in human beings and investment in material capital, and so on.[1] However, in reality, policy decisions are complicated by wider considera-

1. United Nations, *Measures for the Economic Development of Underdeveloped Countries*, p. 50.

tions than economic calculation alone. Bowman, in introducing the question of the limits of land settlement, said that
"policies grow chiefly out of political, social, and economic
conditions and situations."[2] In terms of population policy,
Eldridge also said: "Governments are . . . confronted with a
great variety of delicate decisions (whether they are aware of
them or not), decisions which should involve weighing elements of the future against the present, of quality against
quantity, of political freedom against military strength, even
of the international outlook against national outlook. And
although it is axiomatic that a state will not consciously follow
any policy that it suspects might interfere with its survival,
whether in terms of number, importance, power, cultural value,
national pride, or what have you, yet it must again and again
violate some of its interests while serving others."[3]

For China, the question of the sustenance and utilization
of its existing population is, as expected, wedded to its economic and social policies. Broadly speaking, the solution to
the question of the sustenance and utilization of China's existing population lies in the consolidation of, and adjustments
in, the two major spheres of economic activities, nonagricultural and agricultural. It pertains to an expansion of nonagricultural employment opportunities, on the one hand. On
the other hand, it encompasses measures designed to achieve
agricultural reorganization (i.e., the mutual-aid team, agricultural cooperative, advanced agricultural cooperative, and
People's Commune) as well as the continuation of the intensive use of human labor in agriculture and its supporting activities (e.g., irrigation, flood control, and so on) and other rural
nonagricultural pursuits.

The reorganization of agriculture, the requisition of agricultural land for industrial use, the demand for workers in
the expanding nonagricultural sector of the economy, the
search for natural resources, and the need to bring additional
land under cultivation, among other things, all have their
demographic antecedents and consequences. In particular,

2. I. Bowman, ed., *Limits of Land Settlement*, p. 5.
3. Eldridge, *Population Policies*, p. 4.

the active quest for chosen economic, social, political, and military objectives has necessarily had repercussions in the geographically delimited pattern of population distribution. There have been in China since 1949 a wide range of laws, regulations, and programs initiated, tried, and refined in an attempt to adjust the population to the attainment of specific nondemographic objectives and to counter demographic consequences resulting therefrom. Although they may possibly have some indirect effect on population growth in the long run, these measures have, in the short run, been concerned with population distribution and redistribution in China.

The two well-known features of China's population distribution are: (1) according to the 1953 Census over 500 million, or some 87 percent, of the population resided in rural villages; and (2) over 95 percent of the population is concentrated (though unevenly) on about 40 percent of the land area of China lying below an imaginary line drawn from Ai-hui in in Helungkiang to Teng-chung in Yunnan. In terms of agricultural expansion and national security, this uneven distribution led to the adoption of measures aimed at transferring population from areas of high density (or areas of population surplus) to areas of low density. These will be scrutinized in chapter 4, for the scope and purposes of these measures differ markedly from those enacted to regulate the flow of rural migrants to the cities.

Here in this chapter and in the next chapter, the focus therefore will be on only those measures that fall under the two rubrics of rural-urban population distribution and redistribution, and the stabilization of the urban population.

The Quick Urban Entry and Interim Measures

The People's Republic of China was proclaimed on 1 October 1949. Peking, then a metropolis of nearly three million population, once again became the national capital. All this occurred considerably ahead of even the most authoritative estimate in China a year or so earlier. On 20 March 1948, Chairman Mao Tse-tung stated:

We do not contemplate setting up the Central People's Government this year, because the time is not yet ripe. . . . After the capture of one or two the country's largest cities, and after northeastern China, north China, Shantung, northern Kiangsu, Honan, Hupeh, and Anhwei are all linked together in one contiguous area, it will be entirely necessary to establish the Central People's Government.[4]

He had previously also estimated that the overthrow of the Nationalist regime would be carried out in about five years from July 1946. Even though Mao later stated, on 14 November 1948, "As we now see it, only another year or so may be needed to overthrow it completely," the original decision to postpone the establishment of the Central People's Government was not immediately revised.[5] This seems to have been at variance with the scope of the military success, which was already enormous toward the end of 1948. Shenyang, Changchun, and Chinchou in the northeast were entered in quick succession in October and early November 1948. Kalgan, an important transportation and commercial hub in Hopeh, was taken on Christmas Eve in the same year. And, Peking itself and Tientsin were to fall in January 1949.

Changchun (population in 1953: 855,220), Chinchou (352,200) and Kalgan (229,300) are not among China's largest cities, but Shenyang (2,299,900) certainly enjoys this distinction. Their acquisition clearly signified a decisive turning point in the Civil War of 1946–49. But, the import of the 1948 statement on the need to gain control of one or two of the country's largest cities was confined to the then immediate political context. Chairman Mao apparently had in mind cities other than those located in China's northeast; for several other cities in the region (Harbin, Chichihaerh, Mutanchiang, and Chiamussu in Heilungkiang) had already been taken before 1948. Although his statement in 1948 represented a sense of political realism, it also provided a good résumé of the revolutionary movement itself and its locus of power:

4. As quoted in Jerome Ch'en, *Mao and the Chinese Revolution,* p. 308.

5. Ibid., pp. 307–8.

scattered bases of operations in the rural regions of several contiguous and noncontiguous provinces in China Proper.

But, by October 1949, the Nationalists were driven from all major Chinese cities except Canton, Chungking, and Kunming. The physical control of the cities thus was rapidly assumed. However, as the era of rural existence swiftly came to an end, there was scarcely time to make systematic preparations for urban administration. In the previous March, for instance, at the Second Plenary Session of the Seventh Central Committee of the Chinese Communist Party, a special report entitled *The Focus of Work Shifts from Rural Villages to the Cities* was issued, and aptly reflected the situation at the time:

> From the major defeat, in 1927, of the Chinese Revolution to the present, . . . the focus of the revolutionary struggle of the Chinese people was in rural villages. In the villages strength was gathered, villages were used to ring and isolate the cities, and [we] then fought to occupy the cities. . . . History has already proved this strategy as being completely necessary, completely correct as well as completely successful. But, the period during which this tenet was considered appropriate for the execution of our task is now over. From this moment onward, . . . [we] are to enter an era . . . in which the city is to lead the rural villages. . . . The focus of work must be centered in the cities. . . . [We] must endeavour to learn how to administer the cities and how to develop the cities.[6]

An editorial in the *Northeast Daily* gave another sketch of the circumstances during the rapid rural-urban transition:

> Recalling the time of the ten years' Civil War and the War of Resistance against Japan, we did not then possess large cities, large industries, and railroads, relying only on persistent effort of the Chinese Communist Party and the Chinese people in organizing the economic power of agriculture and handicrafts in rural villages for the long and arduous guerrilla war. At that time, we bore the brunt of

6. *Great Impartiality Daily* (Tientsin), 18 Oct. 1949. All Translations of documents, newspaper and magazine articles, speeches, and monographs that were originally in Chinese are by the author, unless otherwise noted.

"Without industry and Without Cities," and sustained a myriad of hardships. In those days we all thought, "If, one of these days, we were ever to have these things, [we] surely would take exceedingly good care of them, make use of them, and rely on them to defeat the anti-Revolutionary rule. . . . Now, . . . unfortunately, in many places there are numerous comrades who have neither adhered to nor paid attention to [this resolution] . . . , chiefly because of the hit-and-run [guerrilla] orientation, subjectivism, and narrow financial viewpoints that evolved under the circumstances of prolonged isolation, rural living, and guerrilla warfare. . . . [They] still look at the cities from the standpoints of guerrilla wars and of rural villages, and still think that the occupation of the cities is only temporary. . . . Hence [there have been] removals of machines and materials, dismantling of parts, . . . damages to factory facilities, etc.[7]

However, the scarcity of time and the relative paucity of experience with urban administration were only two of the visible variables that shaped the range and kinds of urban measures in the early years of the People's Republic. Other major factors included public security in the cities and rural reorganization.

Just prior to the establishment of the People's Republic, more than 600 delegates who represented China's democratic parties, people's organizations, the People's Liberation Army, various geographic regions and national minorities, and overseas Chinese, gathered in Peking for the First Chinese People's Political Consultative Conference in September. A notable result of the conference was the issuance of the *Common Program*, which was "to serve as guiding principles for all levels of governments, national as well as local, and all Chinese people during the reconstruction of China." Its 60 articles covered, among other matters, national economic policy, policy on

7. As quoted in *Chinese People's Liberation Army's Policy on the Entry into Cities*, p. 30. This echoes a directive on the protection of newly recovered cities that the Northeast Bureau issued on 10 June 1949.

minorities, and cultural and educational policies. They contained no reference to population.[8]

But immediately after 1949, the vast countryside with its hundreds of millions of peasants almost instantaneously came under the control of the new government. The cities presumably were made to function with the help of the personnel from the previous regime as were the factories therein. In scope, complexity, and urgency, problems associated with the countryside and peasants were, by comparison, far greater than those connected with the management of the new urban acquistions. Thus, practical considerations, coupled with commitments to change, dictated the extension of agrarian reforms to newly acquired villages. Efforts to restore agricultural production, to redistribute land, and to prepare conditions for the socialist transformation of agriculture claimed the attention of the Party leaders and cadres. The results of these and other exigencies (e.g., China's involvement in the Korean War) seem to have accounted for the relative absence, in the years prior to 1953, of long-range urban policies in general and urban population policies in particular.

In the interim, urban management accented the reinstitution of household registration procedures and apparatus,[9] the reduction of urban unemployment, and the return of refugees of the Civil War to places of origin. But the magnitude of urban problems was recognized. Also, preliminary to the formulation of urban population measures in subsequent years, views were voiced concerning the city in historical perspective and its role in the context of national recovery and construction.

In an editorial in 1949, for example, the New China News Agency warned: "The task and method of social reform in the cities are completely different from those associated with the anti-feudal land reform in the villages. The necessary steps

8. For text, see *Selected Papers on the Founding of the People's Republic of China,* pp. 261–74.

9. See Appendix A for the first set of regulations governing household registration. These are self-explanatory; since they are administrative procedures, they are not directly relevant here.

therefore must also be [taken] with great care. . . . During the war, urban populations, like the people in the villages, must have encountered wartime difficulties in their livelihood. Difficulties of this kind which the anti-Revolutionary rule and the War left behind cannot hopefully be resolved in one morning. All leftistic, measures can only create even bigger and longer difficulties."[10]

But, though the key problem of foremost importance at that stage (i.e., in 1949) of the Chinese Revolution was the problem of the cities, it was pointed out that the urban problem was not merely a practical problem of current significance. It was also a *historical* problem:

Among the many contradictions and antagonisms in human history, the antagonism between the city and the village is of a rather ancient origin. Strictly speaking, the labor power of slaves built the earliest cities. The pattern of the metropolis was determined during the feudal periods. But, modern, large-scale metropolis had to wait the rapid rise of capitalism and the decay of the feudal system. . . . Even though the history of the emergence of the feudal system differed from one nation to another, it directly and indirectly, through the principle of exploitation, gave rise to the foundation of numerous metropolises. . . . Cities owed existence basically to class antagonisms and contradictions. Such antagonisms and contradictions manifested themselves most visibly in the age of capitalism. . . . China will inevitably become an urbanized society because that is an invariant concomitant of a nation's industrialization. Our problems are, on the one hand, how to bring about the downfall of feudalism and erasure of imperialism and, at the same time, how to effectively, quickly, and resolutely accomplish China's industrialization, modernization, and urbanization, and also, how to eliminate the unjust antagonism between the city and the village in the course of industrialization and urbanization.[11]

Of the Chinese cities, Shanghai (population in 1953: 6,240,-

10. *Chinese People's Liberation Army's Policy on the Entry into Cities,* p. 14.

11. *Great Impartiality Daily* (Tientsin), 18 Oct. 1949.

000) is best known internationally. In historical perspective, however, the circumstances that gave Shanghai its worldwide reputation left sharply different imprints on the minds of the Chinese: its national notoriety contrasted vividly with its global fame; Shanghai was regarded as the foremost symbol of foreign domination by the Chinese irrespective of their political affiliations.[12]

But appreciation of Shanghai's actual and potential contributions to China's development was frequently expressed in and after 1949. One such expression, which described Shanghai's past and future roles, appeared a few months after its liberation from the Nationalist regime: "Shanghai's small piece of real estate crowded with some six million people became, after having functioned as a semicolonial public gangway plank, the most favored entrepot of imperialism. . . . But, during the last thirty years, Shanghai also simultaneously developed into the chief arena of national industrial and commercial enterprises, the nation's financial center, and the center of culture and publishing. . . . We can legitimately utilize what had been a base originally developed by imperialism for its own use and transform it into a new source of national industrial and commercial undertaking and the nation's large-scale public-owned and public-operated enterprises under New Democracy."[13]

Nevertheless, also a very short while after Shanghai changed hands, the First Municipal Conference of All People's Representatives of Shanghai unanimously resolved on 3 August: (1) to disperse systematically and step by step (certain) personnel and to remove a portion of the schools and factories to China's interior; (2) to mobilize a great number of Communist party members, cadres, workers, and students to go to the countryside to advance village work; and (3) to encourage

---

12. Cf. Rhoads Murphey, *Shanghai: Key to Modern China*, p. 25–57.

13. *Great Impartiality Daily* (Tientsin), 18 Oct. 1949.

certain (other) schools and factories to move inland. [14] These tasks constituted one of the six major programs that the East China Bureau of the Central Committee of the Chinese Communist Party put before the Conference and urged its adoption. In a report to the Conference, Yao Sou-shih defined some of Shanghai's demographic problems at the time and their causes:

Because Shanghai is the largest city in China and in Asia—and also, because the city's past so-called prosperity was not built on an economic foundation that was independent, autonomous, and wholesome, but on an amalgamated basis of imperialism, the compradore system, and bureaucratic capitalism—we will inevitably encounter many temporary difficulties in our effort to transform Old Shanghai into . . . New Shanghai that will be truly independent and autonomous and will not depend on foreign imperialism. . . . Because no more than three million of the Shanghai's six million people actually take part, directly and indirectly, in productive work, the number of people who do not participate in production amounts to more than three million. To turn such a huge number of consumers into producers, or to evacuate them to the countryside to take part in production, is a very complex and formidable task. But we clearly realize that all such difficulties are but difficulties inherent in victory and development, and can be completely overcome. . . .

To carry out, in a planned way and step by step, the evacuation of personnel and the removal of some schools and factories to the interior, we should, first of all, mobilize a great number of refugees and unemployed masses to return to the countryside to take part in production and to reclaim land for productive purposes in previously Yellow River-flooded areas in northern Anhwei and salt-producing areas in northern Kiangsu. And, we should persuade all refugee landlords as well as those landlords and rich peasants deceived by the enemy to come to Shanghai and the peasants and youths forced by the enemy to migrate to Shanghai, to return to their respective places of origin to participate in production. Even if some of the landlords and rich peasants had once

14. *Shanghai: One Year after Liberation, 1949–1950*, p. 3; and Jung Wen-tso, "The Removal of Shanghai's Factories into the Interior," pp 29–31.

defrauded and bullied peasants, the local governments of the various localities will treat them generously so long as they are willing to repent and return home to productive work. In addition, to alleviate Shanghai's current crowded condition and to reduce the city's burden, we should encourage, whenever possible and necessary, certain schools and factories to move inland in order that they can have a convenient access to food, coal, and raw materials. But, the removal of factories to the interior is a complicated and laborious task. Not only must this be undertaken in accordance with the principle of voluntary decision, but it also must be on the basis of full and careful planning and preparations. Otherwise, it will entail losses and increase difficulties. . . .

[We should] mobilize a large number of the members of the Communist party, cadres and workers and students to go to the countryside to initiate and expand village work. . . . Only by relying on the vast internal market and a sufficient supply of food and raw materials from the numerous villages, can Shanghai and other cities on the south side of the Yangtze [in Kiangsu] really follow the track of wholesome and prosperous growth.[15]

By the end of 1949, according to an article entitled "The Removal of Shanghai's Factories to the Interior" that appeared in March 1950, more than thirty factories were so transferred. The writer of the article asserted, "We ought to admit that the fact that some 60 percent of the nation's light industry is concentrated in Shanghai is itself an abnormal phenomenon as well as a disgrace inflicted on us by imperialism."[16] However, most of the factories involved were in the category of light consumer industry, such as matches, bicycles, pencils, cigarettes, and cotton textile. As for the removal of schools, the only known case was the relocation of a portion of the University of Communications (Chiaotung Polytechnic University), but this occurred several years later, in 1956.

Thus, the actual implementation of the factory- and school-

15. Yao Sou-shih, "Smash the Enemy's Blockade and Struggle for the Development of New Shanghai," pp. 7–11.

16. Jung Wen-tso, "The Removal of Shanghai's Factories into the Interior."

relocation program seems to have been very limited in scope. This can be taken to mean either that the feasibility of its complete realization was severely limited by the many practical difficulties involved in a program of this sort, or that the need for its full implementation was singularly ephemeral, or both. For instance, that the decision to relocate some of Shanghai's factories was prompted, in part, by noneconomic considerations (e.g., the reference to imperialism) bespeaks the role of historical factors in policy formulation. But, in all probability, the very fact that Shanghai returned to national ownership in 1949 served to quickly lessen the intensity of the feelings and attenuate the need for a rapid dispersion of its factories. Of course, a policy of industrial relocation such as that adopted in the autumn months of 1949, may have been questioned on economic grounds. All the evidence that has since become available points to the useful and prominent role that Shanghai has played and is playing in the economic development of China—a role that has been made possible by *not* dismantling Shanghai's factories for relocation elsewhere in the country. The perfunctory evacuation of trained persons from Shanghai in the earlier years thus preserved the integrity of one of China's top corps of technical personnel.

Nevertheless, and quite apart from historical circumstances, there were a number of other factors then current in 1949–50 that apparently gave added urgency to the need for industrial and demographic dispersion. After June 1949, Shanghai lived under the shadow of a Nationalist naval blockade. In February 1950, it was also subjected to attacks from the air. Later, in the same year, a trade embargo was imposed on China, following the outbreak of hostilities in Korea. To offset the effect of these contingencies on Shanghai's economic capability, it was logical to contemplate the possible relocation of factories to places where they could be productive and of persons to areas where they would be safe. However, as previously indicated, the removal of Shanghai's industries appears to have ceased before any larger or heavier industries became involved. Slowly, trade with other coastal cities was restored. There were and are real economic reasons that Shanghai's industrial complex should be left intact and encouraged to grow.

The relocation of some of Shanghai's small industries in 1949–50 also apparently did not directly contribute to the lessening of the crowded conditions in the city, for not all of their employees followed the move. There was evidently no definite program in 1949–50 for the removal of Shanghai's residents. But steps were taken to return to the countryside a large number of refugees who came to Shanghai during the Civil War. Of an estimated 450,000 refugees, some 350,000 were sent back to Anhwei and to the northern part of Kiangsu between July 1949 and March 1950.[17]

During the same period, but for different reasons, governments in other cities also took steps to assist refugees and, in some instances, "residents" to leave urban areas. In February 1950, for example, Peking's Bureau of Civil Affairs dispatched an official mission to Suiyuan and Chahar (these and portions of other provinces were later consolidated into the Inner Mongolia Autonomous Region) in order that plans for the transportation and settlement of relocatees could be satisfactorily concluded. Preliminary preparations to receive migrants apparently had already been under way when the mission arrived. Special agencies were established by both provincial People's governments, land and housing were reserved for the migrants, and credit in kind (i.e., food grain, draught animals, and farming implements) was arranged. Between early March and the commencement of the spring plowing, it was planned that an average of some 400 persons a day would leave Peking by train. By the time this particular relocation project was terminated early in May, some 4,700 persons (1,200 households) were moved to Suiyuan, and 2,400 persons (620 households) to Chahar. In addition, some 340 workers and their families went from Peking to an industrial city (Pen-Chi) in Manchuria. Of those sent to the areas that were to become a part of the Inner Mongolia Autonomous Region, each reportedly received some 5 to 6 *mou* of land

17. *Shanghai: One Year after Liberation,* p. 4.

and a loan of 560 catties of millet. The latter was to be repaid in three years.[18]

The occupational composition of the 7,100 relocatees was officially described in these words: "pedacab drivers, poor municipal residents, a small number of hand-wagoners, and unemployed intellectual elements." This rough breakdown reflected the two chief aims of the relocation project: to reduce the number of pedacab drivers in Peking (who numbered over 30,000 in 1950), and to solve the problems of earning a livelihood on the part of some of the poor city residents.[19]

Similar activities in other cities were also reported. Tientsin, for example, provided passage for some 1,471 persons to go to Chahar during the spring plowing in 1950. They included pedacab drivers as well as unemployed and poor city residents. Likewise, Shenyang (Mukden) relocated over 3,300 persons during the same period within the province and in Heilungkiang and Kirin. Assigned to irrigation projects, lumbering, and farming, more than one-half of the relocatees were persons on the city's relief roll during the previous winter, and had undergone reform through labor in the municipal production and training institution in Shenyang. The People's Government of Kirin distributed to each person a seven-month food-grain and vegetable allowance.[20]

In the context of rural-urban population distribution, the various measures to relocate factories, to resettle war refugees, and to reduce urban unemployment in Peking, Shanghai, Tientsin, and other cities obviously were not without some meaning. But, on the whole, they appear to have had more

18. *People's Daily,* 3 Mar., 7 May 1950. The initial proposal to relocate refugees and others was first made at a conference on civil affairs that the Department of Interior of the Central People's Government arranged in the spring of 1950. But the proposal itself apparently came from Peking's Municipal People's Government. In early March, Peking Employment and Production Headquarters was organized jointly by the Bureau of Civil Affairs, Bureau of Labor, and the Municipal Council of Labor (Union) to supervise the relocation. One *mou* is equal to 0.16 acre; one catty is equal to 1.33 pounds.

19. Ibid.

20. Ibid., 19 June 1950.

regional than national significance. They do not seem to have received sustained support from the Central Government or to have achieved national prominence as in the case of many subsequent demographic measures. They should probably be regarded as interim or emergency measures rather than components of an urban population policy of national scope.

Growth of the Urban Population, 1949-1960

While the various local measures were being implemented, a more significant debate (or a series of debates) at the national level apparently was also under way. Initially it still had to do mostly with the question of geographically dispersed versus geographically concentrated distribution of industrial plants. An indication of its beginning appeared in November 1950:

. . . Most of China's light industry is concentrated in coastal provinces. From both the point of view of national defense and security and the standpoint of closer proximity to raw material and market, this is not very rational. Henceforth, we must develop plans to selectively restore and expand inland industries. The location of any new industry must be at a most suitable place chosen in accordance with careful consideration of all factors, such as resources, transportation, market, fuel, power, labor and its connections with other industries. At the same time, when it is necessary, we ought to encourage and assist the removal of some of the coastal industries to the interior where they will be even more able to grow. . . . After an appropriate period of efforts, the current irrational distribution of industries can be gradually adjusted to become rational.[21]

The debate soon expanded to encompass a large number of issues that, in one way or another, were connected with the then rapidly growing urban population. In a major way, they are part and parcel of the urban dilemma with which every developing or developed nation has had to cope more or less successfully or not successfully at all. They include the prob-

21. Ibid., 3 Nov. 1950.

lems of feeding and housing urban population, transportation, school facilities, health and sanitary provisions, recreation, and city planning. In China, the outcome of the debate is a series of decisions of demographic import. Their specified aim was to regulate or stabilize the urban population size (see chapter 3).

Beside the considerations of national security and uneven distribution of industries, an initial, and probably the most decisive, factor in the development of a massive and comprehensive urban population policy in China was the start of an evidently steady flow of peasants into the cities in the early 1950s. The timing of the first reported in-migration, however, was such that it was not a strictly seasonal movement due to a slackening in employment opportunities in the villages:

Rural surplus labor in not a small number of areas has recently been found moving blindly towards the cities. Most of these peasants have credentials from local People's Governments or removal permits, some taking their families with them. . . . In the Nanwan district in Peking, for instance, between 10 and 23 August [1952], over 800 peasants came looking for work. Most of them came from Tunghsien, Wuchin, Antzu and other counties in the vicinity of Peking. During employment registration in Chungking, unemployed persons were also found coming from Kiangpei, Luhsien, and other places; figures taken from 9–11 September alone gave 35 such persons. Among them were persons who did not want to till their land, returned to the Peasant's Association the land allotted them, and went to Chungking especially to look for work. In Shansi, southern Kiangsu, Sian and Chinhuangtao, similar occurrences have also been found.

This blind movement toward the cities was due mainly to the cadres in some areas [principally district and village cadres] who did not appreciate the spirit of the *Decision on Labor Employment* promulgated by the State Council of the Central People's Government. It was pointed out in this decision: "The development of cities and industry and the development of State construction in various fields will draw large labor forces from the countryside. This work, however, must proceed according to plan in an orderly manner; it is impossible to absorb large numbers in a short period of time. It is therefore necessary to persuade the peasants with great efforts and overcome their inclination towards blind movement to the cities." Some cadres have not seriously studied or grasped the significance of this instruction . . . [and] do not understand that . . . the question of surplus labor in the villages can be solved only gradually as various construction schemes unfold themselves, and that it cannot be solved at one stroke.[22]

These phenomena of in-migration apparently were not restricted to a particular region. Rather they evidently occurred in cities throughout the country and apparently were in response to change in both actual and perceived labor requirements in the urban nonagricultural sector. A local official near Shanghai, for instance, wrote to the editor of Shanghai's *Liberation Daily* in December 1952, urging avoidance of undue recruitment stimulation in Shanghai: "We hold that, in its drive to recruit carpenters from Shanghai, the Chinwei Textile Machines Manufacturing Company of Yutzu *hsien* [county] in Shansi should work through the various Shanghai's agencies concerned [e.g., labor district offices, relief and unemployment associations] to satisfy its needs. It should not employ informal connections and recruit on its own; [otherwise,] it will accent the blind drift of peasants toward the city and add difficulties to the work of labor employment registration."[23] A letter of similar content later appeared in the *People's Daily*: "This year, they [peasants in Feitung *hsien* in Anhwei] heard that the country started to undertake large-scale economic construction projects. Because of this, the number of peasants who poured into the cities increased more than ever."[24]

However, the flow of persons into the cities was not merely stimulated by labor recruitment in the cities themselves. Instances of direct recruitment at the village level were re-

22. Ibid., 26 Nov. 1952. For the text of the *Division on Labor Employment,* see Appendix B.

23. *Liberation Daily* (Shanghai), 12 Dec. 1952.

24. *People's Daily,* 30 Jan. 1953. See also *New China Daily* (Chungking), 5 Apr. 1953.

ported.[25] Nor was it entirely the peasants who were on the move. Among the persons who visited the employment office of Chungking between 18 and 28 February 1953, for instance, a total of 532 came from various districts and villages of some 37 *hsien* and were classified as "poor peasants and hired hands, handicraftsmen, discharged soldiers, landowners and intellectuals, and unemployed wanderers."[26] Another account related that a number of cadres took a very dim view of agricultural production: in one district of Huanghua *hsien* in Hopeh, one-third of the village cadres left to work in the cities, and, also wanting to leave were about 100 of the *hsien*'s 150 teachers specifically appointed to take part in a campaign to erase illiteracy.[27]

Not only were numerous village and local cadres interested in seeking city jobs themselves, but they also failed either to find suitable work for surplus laborers locally after the village land reform or to refrain from writing letters of introduction at the request of departing peasants and others, thus contributing to the outflow from the villages.[28]

In very rough statistical terms, one salient demographic consequence of rural exodus is indicated in table 2. The urban proportion of the total population increased to over 14 percent in 1957 from 10.6 percent in 1949. Though the upward shift in percentage points is relatively unimpressive, the net gain in absolute numbers is 35,350,000 in less than a decade. Thus, a boom in China's urban population in the 1950s evidently followed the increased and expanding stream of cityward migration.[29]

25. *New China Daily* (Chungking), 5 Apr. 1953; and *People's Daily,* 20 Apr. 1953.

26. *New China Daily* (Chungking), 5 Apr. 1953.

27. *People's Daily,* 25 Apr. 1953.

28. Ibid., 30 Jan. and 25 Apr. 1953; *New China Daily* (Chungking), 5 Apr. 1953.

29. One contrary view was that "comparison of the expected and reported increase in the population of [China's] cities between 1953 and 1956 suggests that natural increase contributed substantially more to urban growth than did migration. In several cities natural increase

Appropriate figures cannot be procured to document the trend of the Chinese urban population growth subsequent to 1957, but some hypothetical approximations could be produced by extrapolation from the data for 1949–57. However, as in the case of almost all demographic projections, the results of such statistical manipulations are difficult to interpret and, in the light of actual empirical data that eventually become available, can be quite absurd. In all likelihood, the degree of absurdity is greater the longer the time span such projections are made to cover. On the one hand, demographic trends and patterns can be and often are altered by unforeseen circumstances in the long run. On the other hand, in the case of China, knowledge of the factors affecting the course of its urban population change even in the short run is rather insufficient. As a case in point, there is yet no full explanation of the nonregularity of the growth of urban population in China between 1949 and 1957 (table 2 and also see below). Comprehension of the nonlinear character of the recent urban population growth in China is made difficult by the limited amount of statistical information that is available. The quality itself of the available statistics also is not unimpeachable. As can also be seen in table 2, the urban proportion of the total population has not been consistently greater from one year to another. Small losses in percentage points are evident in two of the years (1954–55 and 1956–57). Explanation of these will be attempted later in this chapter. What is of more immediate concern here is the fact that, although the urban proportion of the total population increased by one-half of one percent between 1949 and 1950 and by four-tenths of one percent between 1953 and 1954, the annual increment in all other

---

exceeded total growth, implying a net loss of population by migration. Actually these years witnessed the restriction of rural-to-urban migration and the expulsion of migrants from some of the larger centers during 1955. Still, the magnitude of natural increase was so great [usually in excess of 3 percent per year] that it is doubtful whether migration could have exceeded natural increase even had not restrictions been imposed" (Morris Ullman, *Cities of Mainland China: 1953 and 1958*, p. 14).

TABLE 2

URBAN AND RURAL POPULATION OF CHINA, 1949–1957

(Absolute Figures, in Thousands, Refer to Population at End of Year)

		URBAN†		RURAL	
YEAR	TOTAL*	N	%	N	%
1957	656,630	92,000	14.0	564,630	86.0
1956	627,800	89,150	14.2	538,650	85.8
1955	614,650	82,850	13.5	531,800	86.5
1954	601,720	81,550	13.6	520,170	86.4
1953	587,960	77,670	13.2	510,290	86.8
1952	574,820	71,630	12.5	503,190	87.5
1951	563,000	66,320	11.8	496,680	88.2
1950	551,960	61,690	11.1	490,270	88.9
1949	541,670	57,650	10.6	484,020	89.4

*SOURCE: 1949–56: "China's Population from 1949 to 1956," *Statistical Work*, no. 11, 14 June 1957; 1957: *People's Daily*, 14 November 1957. But the total population was placed at 642,000,000. See Wang Kung-wei, "How to Organize Agricultural Labor," *Planned Economy*, no. 8, 1957.

†Including population living in market places and towns in the suburbs of urban places, but excluding population living in villages of such suburbs.

four periods was reportedly identical, being seven-tenths of one percent yearly. This may have been, in reality, coincidential. The need to establish or verify the good character of Chinese urban population statistics is, nevertheless, apparent. Thus, no production of urban population projections for China will be made.

Measures Relating to Rural Exodus

It may well have been also true that compared with natural increase, the volume of migration into the cities was the smaller component of urban growth in China during this period. But demographic observations of this sort can be misleading unless the socioeconomic import and other ramifications of the cityward migration, however small, are expressly noted. A quantitative answer may eventually be given to the question of whether or not migration exceeded natural increase in Chinese cities during the 1950s. But the answer must be qualified by the fact that demographic processes are not entirely discreet phenomena. To the extent that in-migrants are young and fecund persons from rural areas, internal migration contributes to urban growth in two different ways (see below,

p. 49). Furthermore, even if population increments through in-migration are identical with, or less than, those from natural increase in numerical terms, they have profoundly different social and economic repercussions. Jobs, houses, transportation and recreational conveniences, and other physical amenities are immediately required by in-migrants on arrival; whereas, for a number of years, babies need only be fed and sheltered.

These immediate requirements of in-migrants should then, and did soon, constitute the core problems that were to receive massive and comprehensive attention in and out of the official circles. But at the very beginning, interpretations of the fact that some of the peasants and other rural and small-town residents were on the move stressed the possible adverse impact on agriculture and industrial development more than the urban ramifications as such. Also discernible in the dialogue on the consequences of the cityward migration was an immensely large amount of political sensitivity that it generated. This sensitivity was displayed by means of an old generalization in the philosophy of Chinese political economy: "When the masses dwell in villages, order prevails; when the masses flock to the cities, disorder ensues."[30] At the very least, expressions of concern, coupled with specific policy directives during the years in question, were clearly indicative of a substantial demographic expansion of the cities throughout China.[31]

---

30. *Great Impartiality Daily* (Tientsin), 10 May 1953. The quotation is from Kuo Ting-lin, a scholar-official who lived during the Ching dynasty.

31. However, this overall gain should not be taken to mean simply the acquisition of additional population, via natural increase or migration or both, on the part of these established urban areas since 1949. Reclassification of previously rural territory has served to enlarge the urban portion of the population, though no migration of any kind occurred, on the one hand. On the other hand, according to one recent report, "newly built" towns total 167 in China up to 1960. Presumably, migration was of fundamental import in the emergence of these new "urban" areas. See the speech of Liang Ssu-cheng during the second session of the Second People's Congress. Mr. Liang is a well-known

However, this recent urban in-migration should not be lumped together with "peasant flight" from the land in traditional China or even with that of as late as the 1930s and 1940s on account of natural and man-made calamities. The earlier exodus decidedly was in the form of expulsion of peasants in scattered directions. In isolated instances, post-1949 rural out-migration may have been a repetition of similar movements in the past; but new elements, such as the onset of industrialization and improved and expanded transportation networks, have been introduced into the situation, serving to attract peasants and others into cities. The most powerful stimulant of the outflow was of obviously urban origin rather than rural conditions as such. Notwithstanding, or perhaps because of, this apparently rising magnetism of the cities, a relative stability of the rural population continued to be emphasized as the economic pillars of Chinese society remained rooted in the villages. Thus, as during the period of locally initiated interim urban population measures, a considerable stress was understandably placed on agricultural and village occupations. The *under*employment of the peasants was declared to be the principal cause of their out-migration, and the negligence of local cadres a chief contributing cause. In the words of the Office of Social Affairs of the Ministry of Interior:

> The nation will soon begin large-scale economic construction; we will certainly concentrate our strength first on industrial development. But agricultural development is equally important. If the development of agrarian economy fails to keep up with the requirements of industrial development, it will affect the progress of industrial construction. Cadres of People's Government of all levels should grasp this

---

architect, and an excerpt of his speech is printed in the *People's Daily,* 11 Apr. 1960. In this speech, Mr. Liang put the number of cities in China at "over 2,100." Of these, 167 are the newly built urban places. The others include 124 urban places that have been much expanded or redeveloped, some 180 urban places *(chen shih)* that have been given the administrative status of municipality, and the more than 1,700 "county seats" *(hsien chen).*

point and should know that the present labor employment scheme is to reduce unemployment. Surplus laborers in the villages are not unemployed persons: they have land and food. Rural surplus labor moves blindly towards the cities at present because their latent capacity for labor is not being utilized. . . . The correct solution to this problem lies principally in the development of agricultural production, which should be coordinated with subsidiary production, and in organizing peasants to participate actively in the development of mutual-aid and cooperation, in accordance with various rural economic constructions. Cadres of People's Government at various levels should dissuade and prevent peasants from moving blindly towards the cities, on the one hand. . . . On the other hand, they should solve the question of rural surplus labor by sponsoring small-scale irrigation works, encouraging afforestation, initiating repair of village roads, developing freshwater fisheries and subsidiary occupations including handicraft industry, advocating preliminary processing of rural products in the villages, and exploring markets for these products. Next, the area of cultivation should be increased, and planned resettlement for reclamation of land should be undertaken. In this, semieducated persons in the villages should be absorbed and trained, so that they may take part in cultural, educational, medical, and health work and offer elementary technical guidance on afforestation and animal husbandry. In this way not only will outlets for rural surplus labor be effectively found, but the rural economy will be pushed a step further.[32]

These words make clear the scope and orientation of China's demographic concern during the early 1950s. It was focused on the question of population *distribution*, and, with regard to the stabilization of urban population, was framed in terms of the retention of the rural population. A more vivid recapitulation of this was given by the South-Central Military Administrative Committee when it quoted an old proverb: "People living on the mountains must get their subsistence from the mountains; those near the water must obtain their

---

32. *People's Daily*, 26 Nov. 1952: " 'We should dissuade peasants from blindly moving toward cities,' declared the Office of Social Affairs, the Ministry of Interior." For similar directives and pronouncements, see *Yangtze Daily* (Wuhan), 23 Oct. 1952.

livelihood from the water."[33]   Rural surplus manpower was not to be exported to the cities, but should be utilized on or near the land.

Obviously, some rural migrants had already found their way into the cities; prevention of the exodus could pertain only to the possible stoppage of future movements. Meantime, systematic efforts were begun to return in-migrants to the villages. A dispatch from Peking stated:

Following the directive of the State Council of the Central People's Government on "Persuading Peasants from Blindly Moving towards the Cities," the People's Government of the Municipality of Peking has already, as of 5 May, mobilized to return to home villages more than 9,500 peasants [who had blindly drifted into the capital] to take part in agricultural production.

In order to handle the return of some 10,000 of such peasants . . . to their villages to participate in productive work, the People's Government of Peking and other concerned agencies jointly set up, on 18 April, a Bureau of Mobilization of Peasants to Return to the Villages. Personnel were drawn from the Bureaus of Labor and Civil Affairs of the People's Government, and North China Administrative Committee, and People's Government of Hopei assigned [additional] persons to assist in the task. In this drive to mobilize peasants to return to the villages, [the Bureau] paid special attention to thought-mobilization work. Some peasants who failed to find employment in the city were afraid of facing people in the village if they went back; some peasants reckoned that, as the construction projects in the city just began, they would find work after a while, even though they were unable to do so immediately. Other peasants who, having been in the city for quite some time, had already exhausted their funds, could not go home because of lack of travel money. Under these circumstances, the Bureau of Mobilization of Peasants made very patient efforts to educate the peasants and notified various local People's Governments to send cadres to Peking to persuade them to go home. It also provided varying amounts of travel money to the peasants who were really without means. . . .[34]

33. *Yangtze Daily* (Wuhan), 23 Oct. 1952.

34. *Great Impartiality Daily* (Tientsin), 10 May 1953.

Thus, quite unlike the days when individual municipal governments made plans on their own to return refugees of the Civil War to their homes in rural areas, the question of population distribution received both direct and active notice of the Central People's Government. The incipient out-migration of rural residents drew the attention of those at very high levels in the government to its possible economic, social, and political consequences and led to the adoption of remedial measures of national applicability. The Ministry of Interior of the Central People's Government gave direct support to Peking's project to return peasants to the villages in 1953. Its Bureau of Social Affairs had previously put forward a lengthy statement on the prevention of rural exodus in November 1952. On 17 April 1953, the State Council of the Central People's Government itself issued a directive on dissuading peasants from blindly moving toward the cities. In it, it defined the responsibility of the *hsien* (county), *chu* (district), and *hsiang* (village) governments in the following words:

1. In cases where letters of introduction have been indiscriminately furnished the peasants, the *hsien, chu,* and *hsiang* governments involved should mobilize those whom they recommended, to find jobs in the cities or, if unable to do so, to go back home.

2. In cases where peasants desirous of migrating to the cities to find work, but are not in possession of official documents attesting to their actual employment in factories, mines, and construction companies, the *hsien, chu,* and *hsiang* governments shall not issue certificates of introduction.

3. The *hsien, chu,* and *hsiang* governments should patiently dissuade the would-be migrants from going to the cities, explaining to them that industrial development in the cities is only at its start, that the existing labor force there exceeds demand, and that their blind migration would adversely affect agricultural production.

4. In cases where additional workers are required for urban construction, the *hsien, chu* and *hsiang* governments

will do the recruiting in a planned and organized manner upon official notification.[35]

Changing Urban Patterns

The magnitude of the recent population growth in Chinese urban areas indeed may be far from being reflected in available statistics. Nor is it unlikely that the various decrees and campaigns designed to stem post-1949 rural exodus have fallen considerably short of the mark. All evidence indicates that the urban portion of the total population of China has been markedly augmented since 1949. A significant, though quantitatively imprecise, gap existed between the stated role of the *hsien, chu,* and *hsiang* governments in the prevention of rural out-migration and the actual population mobility during the past two decades. All the while a reduction in urban mortality evidently also occurred. This, coupled with the flow of rural in-migrants, has given additional impetus to natural increase in the cities. Whatever the short-term impact of the preventive measures on rural-urban migration may have been, the long-term stabilization of China's urban population could hardly be secured by these means. The introduction and acceptance of methods of fertility control seem imperative in this regard. However, both in design and in timing, as will be shown in chapter 6, measures to promote planned parenthood in China trailed policy developments in the area of rural-urban population distribution. Initial demographic decisions of the early 1950s reflected principally the urban population circumstances inherited from the Civil War years of 1946–49 and prior decades as well as the emergent rural-urban population movements stimulated by the far-reaching changes in both the cities and villages alike. These are the focus of the next chapter. Here it appears appropriate to outline some basic changes in China's urban pattern in the years since 1949.

35. New China News Agency (hereafter cited as NCNA), 17 Apr. 1953. See also *People's Daily,* 20 Apr. 1953. For the text of the directive, see Appendix C.

The total number of urban places in China has been variously reported in different publications. This variation owes chiefly to the differences in the definitions of urban places. If, as in the case of Ullman's report on Chinese cities, the urban category is constructed to include places with less than one thousand inhabitants, China can be said to have, as of June 1953, a total of 5,568 urban places.[36] Of these, some 11.1 percent are reported to be under 2,000 population each. Those having less than 1,000 inhabitants number 193. In all, about one and one-quarter million people resided in these 820 mini-urban places, giving an average size of 1,500.

Given their numerical salience, the importance of the mini-urban places in future urbanization in China cannot be minimized. Their role will be greatly enhanced if conscious and effective steps are taken to foster industrial dispersion rather than giant concentrations of manufacturing and processing enterprises in and around a small number of metropolitan centers. Nonetheless, even though they constitute not an insignificant portion of China's urban places, only a modicum of the national population is shown to reside in these mini-urban places. Their omission from the present consideration of urban growth in China seems amply justified. Their exclusion also stems from an interest in conceptual clarity and meaningful contrast between the present and future levels of urbanization in China. At the present stage of China's industrial development, the great majority of its population still is engaged in agricultural and closely related pursuits. On the basis of the official definition of urban place, a portion of the population of administratively delineated "urban" areas belongs to this occupational category. As administratively delimited urban areas can be modified by fiat, the size of "urban" population may be enlarged (or, in rare cases, reduced) on paper, in the absence of migration or occupational shift from the agricultural sector to the nonagricultural sector of the economy. Impressive gains in population, for instance, accrued to the municipality of Peking in the early 1950s as a result of a series of annexations of a number of adjacent

36. Morris B. Ullman, *Cities of Mainland China: 1953 and 1958.*

counties of largely rural character.[37]   It would be misleading to lump this together with the principal thrust of urbanization of the immediate past and in the decades ahead; the influx of population that is a concomitant of developing employment opportunities in the urban nonagricultural sector positively merits separate treatment on methodological and theoretical, as well as practical, grounds.

As a significant portion of the population in places with even 20,000 inhabitants or more consists of rural residents engaged in agricultural pursuits, population figures for smaller urban places undoubtedly must have included a still larger number of similarly situated persons.   It is possible that, in some instances, as much as 50 percent of the population could be employed in agriculture.   According to Paragraph B of Section 1 of the *Criteria Established for the Demarcation of Rural and Urban Areas*, which the State Council adopted on 11 November 1955, residential areas with 2,000 inhabitants or more are designated as either *chen* (city) or *cheng* (town) if more than 50 percent of the population are in nonagricultural occupations (see Apendix D).   But even a rough estimate of the occupational distribution of the mini-urban places (i.e., under 2,000 inhabitants) is beyond realization at present.

Under the circumstances, it seems realistic to focus attention on the larger urban places only.   Not only are estimates of nonagricultural population available for 420 urban places with 20,000 inhabitants or more, but there are also statistics of varying quality that show the extent and pattern of population growth in 95 municipalities[38] between 1938 and 1958.

37. For a list of known changes in areas of municipalities between 1953 and 1958, see ibid., pp. 42–44, Appendix D.

38. The designation of certain urban centers as municipalities is not a new practice.   Municipalities were also the administrative units during the rule of the Nationalists, and were either placed under the direct supervision of the central government or designated as provincial municipalities.

According to the "Decision of the Establishment of Municipalities and Towns" adopted at the eleventh meeting of the State Countil on June 1955, municipalities are the leading administrative units of the provinces, autonomous districts, and autonomous regions.   Cities or

In practical terms, moreover, during the last two decades, expressions of official concern and their translation into concrete measures have been stimulated primarily by many observed and anticipated consequences of population trends in the larger urban places having the administrative status of municipality.

As of June 1953, as is shown in table 3, a total of more than 61.7 million persons resided within the administrative boundaries of the 420 larger urban places. But some 10 million of the residents are estmiated not to have belonged to the nonagricultural category. Thus, following a definition that is based on both residential and occupational criteria, China's urban population in cities with 20,000 or more inhabitants is shown to have been about 51,313,000, or a little less than 9 percent of its 588 million in 1953. However, the distribu-

TABLE 3

ESTIMATED TOTAL AND URBAN POPULATION IN MUNICIPALITIES AND
OTHER URBAN PLACES WITH 20,000 INHABITANTS OR MORE,
BY SIZE OF PLACE, JUNE 1953

(Population Figures in Thousands)

	NUMBER		TOTAL POPULATION		URBAN POPULATION	
	Urban Places	Municipalities	All Places	Municipalities	All Places	Municipalities
1,000,000 or more	9	9	21,020	21,020	17,474	17,474
500,000–999,999	16	16	11,279	11,279	9,377	9,377
200,000–499,999	28	28	8,492	8,492	7,060	7,060
100,000–199,999	49	49	7,201	7,201	5,986	5,986
50,000–99,999	71	50	5,497	3,925	4,570	3,263
20,000–49,999	247	12	8,236	437	6,846	363
Total	420	164	61,725	52,354	51,313	43,523

SOURCE: Adapted from Morris Ullman, *Cities of Mainland China: 1953 and 1958*, p. 10, table D.

towns with 100,000 inhabitants or more may be designated as municipalities. Municipalities may also be established in population clusters with less than 100,000 inhabitants, if they are important industrial or mining bases, the sites of provincial government agencies, relatively large hubs of commodities exchange, or essential cities or towns in distant frontier areas, and provided that there is real necessity (see Appendix D).

tion of this population is tremendously uneven among the urban centers in question. More than one-third of this population segment is concentrated in the nine urban places with 1,000,000 or more inhabitants. The magnitude of the concentration is even more impressive if consideration is limited to the 164 urban places that are also municipalities. The 1953 urban population (17.5 million) in the nine leading municipalities amounted to more than 40 percent of the urban population (43.5 million) in all municipalities.

In other words, as of 1953, a significant number of the municipalities (62 out of 164, to be exact) had fewer and, in some cases, considerably fewer than 100,000 population each. Some of the cities in the size-classes 50,000 to 100,000 and 20,000 to 50,000 may and probably will, in time, grow demographically and in other ways. The 164 municipalities[39] are located principally in China's northeast and in its coastal provinces. A small concentration of municipalities in Szechwan Province is the most notable exception. A few municipalities are in the frontier provinces and regions such as Kansu, Tsinghai, the Inner Mongolia Autonomous Region, Singkiang Uighur Autonomous Region, and Tibet. Most of the municipalities in the last group had, as of 1953, fewer than 100,000 inhabitants each.

The 102 municipalities in the size-class 100,000 and more are ranked according to population in 1938, 1948, 1953, and 1958.[40] Information, however, is not available for all the municipalities over the entire period, e.g., data are available for only 86 municipalities in 1938. Thus, the number of municipalities actually ranked varies from one year to another. Nevertheless, the overall pattern—that is, that the relative rankings of a sizable number of the municipalities have been significantly elevated by substantial population increments over the years—is unlikely to be affected even if data can subsequently be secured for the unranked municipalities. The degree of association between the sizes of the various munic-

39. See Appendix E.
40. Ibid.

ipalities on two different dates can be shown by the employment of Kendall's Rank Correlation.[41]

As would be expected, a high degree of stability in the demographic ranking of the municipalities obtained between 1953 and 1958. But the large magnitude of the coefficient (.901) cannot be unequivocally attributed to the brief time interval involved in this instance. To the extent that the 1958 population data are extrapolations to midyear 1958 of the 1953 data, the impressive size of the coefficient may, indeed, be no more than a statistical artifact. However, the 1938 and 1948 data are derived from sources that are independent of each other and of the 1953 data. Thus, greater confidence can be placed in the conclusion that the rank change of the municipalities up to 1958, was genuinely remarkable, whether it is measured from 1938 (.595) or from 1948 (.744). Even if an allowance is made for population increases from territorial annexations, many of the comparatively smaller municipalities in 1938 advanced by leaps and bounds in population during the twenty-year period and in prominence relative to other municipalities. A significant number of them achieved new places in the urban hierarchy ten or more steps higher than those in the earlier year of 1938. This criterion "ten steps or more" is somewhat arbitrarily established. With a few minor exceptions (e.g., Wenchow, Chenchiang, and Chanchiang), all municipalities gained population between 1938 and 1958. The use of this criterion is simply to draw up a list of the municipalities that realized very notable gains in population, which, in turn, enabled them, in a short lapse of time, to surpass other municipalities in the same size-class in 1938. This list (table 4) is of considerable utility in the present analysis of China's urban population trend and policy, to which we shall return a few paragraphs later.

41. Coefficients of rank correlation between population sizes of municipalities, 1938–1958:

	1938	1948	1953	1958
1938	....	.767	.637	.595
1948	....	....	.738	.744
1953	....	....	....	.901
1958	....	....	....	....

TABLE 4

RANK CHANGE OF MUNICIPALITIES, 1938–1958

MUNICIPALITY	1938		1958	
	Rank	Population	Rank	Population
Sian	24	218,000	11	1,368,000
Taiyuan	35	170,000	14	1,053,000
Fushun	26	215,000	15	1,019,000
Kunming	33	184,000	16	900,000
Anshan	55	120,000	18	833,000
Tangshan	45	146,000	19	812,000
Lanchow	54	122,000	22	732,000
Chichihaerh	63	97,000	25	704,000
Shihchiachuang	42	194,000	28	623,000
Kirin	50	132,000	30	583,000
Kueiyang	46	145,000	31	530,000
Loyang	73	73,000	33	500,000
Paotow	76	70,000	34	490,000
Penchi	79	66,000	36	449,000
Chinchou	59	105,000	38	400,000
Hofei	66	94,000	40	360,000
Huhehot	65	94,000	42	320,000
Tatung	77	70,000	54	243,000
Chiamussu	75	71,000	58	232,000
Chinhuangtao	83	47,000	61	210,000
Nanchung	82	55,000	62	206,000
Liaoyuan	85	32,000	74	177,000

SOURCE: Adapted from Morris B. Ullman, *Cities of Mainland China*: 1953 and 1958, pp. 35–36, table 3.

The number of steps that a municipality could advance within the ranking order, of course, depended on its position in 1938. It is impossible for any one of the ten leading munic-ipalities in 1938 to ascend ten steps or more in the hierarchy, for there is no room at the top; but it is not impossible for them to be evicted from this exclusive top ten position. In fact, two of the ten leading municipalities were demoted to lower ranks between 1938 and 1958, viz., Tsingtao and Hang-chow (table 5). The former is, in the words of Shabad, "the product of Western colonization in China.[42] A seaport with a sheltered deepwater harbor, Tsingtao possesses a narrow in-dustrial base, but rather attractive beaches. Hangchow, also a coastal city, has no useful harbor and is better known for its natural charms, which attract a great number of tourists and

42. Theodore Shabad, *China's Changing Map*, p. 115.

TABLE 5

TEN LEADING MUNICIPALITIES OF CHINA, 1938-1958*

(Rank According to Population)

MUNICIPALITY	1938	1948	1953	1958
Shanghai	1	1	1	1
Peking	2	3	2	2
Tientsin	4	2	3	3
Shenyang	6	6	4	4
Chungking	9	7	5	6
Canton	5	4	6	7
Wuhan	3	8	7	5
Harbin	[12]	10	8	8
Nanking	[15]	5	9	10
Tsingtao	7	9	10	[12]
Dairen	10	[15]	[14]	9
Hangchow	8	[14]	[17]	[20]

*This list includes more than ten municipalities because of changed rankings of the leading municipalities between 1938 and 1958.

vacationers. Tea, silk, and silk cloth are Hangchow's traditional and famous products.

In terms of both geographic location and economic character, the two municipalities, Harbin and Nanking, which displaced Tsingtao and Hangchow from their position among the top ten, belong to a different league. Both Harbin and Nanking are inland cities. The former, again in the words of Shabad, "is the product of the railroads."[43] The transportation hub of northern Manchuria, Harbin is also the region's leading food-processing center and produces electrical goods, power generators, measuring instruments, and cutting tools. Traditionally, Nanking has been of more political and cultural than industrial importance. It is known, however, that the second bridge ever spanned across the Yangtze is located in Siakwan, a northern suburb of Nanking, and Nanking also now has a number of chemical industries.

That Harbin and Nanking grew faster than the two coastal cities of prestigious rather than "substantial" repute seems not to have been accidental. This juxtaposition and that of the various other municipalities listed in table 4, provide some

43. Ibid., p. 228.

prima facie evidence of the emergence of three distinct, though related, patterns of urban growth of nationwide importance. Eldridge defined urbanization as "a process of population concentration. It proceeds in two ways: the multiplication of points of concentration and the increase in size of individual concentrations."[44] Of the twenty-two municipalities that ranked higher on account of population growth in 1958 than in 1938, none is a new point of population concentration. Nor have most of them emerged from obscure origins. The history of each of them goes back centuries and if reconstructed in detail would require several volumes. They were, at one time or another or continuously, regional centers, provincial capitals, or even the seat of the imperial court. As such, they were the locus of administrative, religious, and cultural establishments and power and were intimately tied to China's agrarian economy. Some had already grown to impressive size long before 1938. But their recent surge in population is unprecedented in the history of urbanization in China. In the majority of the cases, the magnitude of increase was fivefold or more in two decades or less. And the source is decidedly not traditional agriculture and related activities. Its main impetus is the development of heavy and light industries occurring after 1949.

Second, all but one of the twenty-two municipalities (Chinhuangtao) are inland cities (table 4). In view of their location only a short distance from the sea, Tangshan and Chinchow could be classified as "coastal cities." Not only are the great majority of these cities *not* coastal cities but almost all of the other cities that advanced in rank between 1938 and 1958 are also inland urban centers (see Appendix E). Many coastal cities did register population gains during this same period as did a number of the urban places along China's main waterways. On the whole, their relative ranking dropped, even though a few (e.g., Shanghai, Tientsin, and Wuhan) have retained their positions and prominence in the urban hierarchy.

44. Hope Eldridge, "The Process of Urbanization," p. 311.

Third, recent urbanization in China contrasts with a past pattern of land use along the frontier region. Historically, extensive use of settlers to dig and seed the ground was long synonymous with land reclamation, particularly in connection with schemes for assisted migration to the frontier provinces. To be sure, land reclamation in the border provinces was resumed after 1949 (see chapter 4). But, at the same time, recent migration to these areas has also been and probably is increasingly of a different character, particularly in the case of China's northeast. The fact is that, like Harbin, more than a third of the twenty-two municipalities listed in table 4 are in this last named region. These are Fushun, Anshan, Chichihaerh, Kirin, Penchi, Chinchow, and Chiamussu. The populations of these places increased from 50 percent to 500 percent in one decade between 1948 and 1958. Thus, apart from its agricultural potential, the capacity of at least China's northeastern frontier to absorb population has evidently been greatly enhanced by the nation's efforts to develop it industrially. One additional piece of evidence of this is that two of the provinces (Heilungkiang and Kirin) reportedly grew by 75 percent and 54.5 percent, respectively, in the more recent fifteen years between 1953 and 1968. In another inland frontier region (Inner Mongolia) where the municipalities of Paotou and Huhehot are situated, population increased by 86 percent during the same period.[45] Thus, a significant portion of China's urban development is in the northeast, in other border areas, and in the interior. The unfolding opportunities in these still relatively sparsely populated areas can and must be seen not in agricultural terms only but rather in terms of industrial expansion and urban growth.

45. See Appendix E.

The Stabilization
of the Urban Population

___

Chapter three

As China continues to industrialize, it is imperative that assessments of its demographic future be put in an urban perspective. A predominately agricultural and rural society, China's transformation obviously entails a sustained process of industrial and urban growth. In a short-term perspective, it should be stressed that demographic adjustments in response to increasing investment in industry and agriculture are likely to be imperfect, particularly in the face of rapid population growth. Urban in-migration retards industrial development, on which agricultural expansion rests, if it diverts substantial funds into housing projects and other urban amenities; and the concentration of unempolyed persons in the cities can have grave social and political consequences, on the one hand. On the other hand, rural out-migration checks agricultural development, on which industrial development depends, if it deprives villages of their educated persons; and the quantity itself of all departures can also adversely affect orderly procedures in farming. Thus, in China, as elsewhere, the rate, volume, and character of demographic exchange between the rural and urban areas are problems of transition. As such, and like international immigration, national governments (China included) have become increasingly involved in the management of internal migration. In this connection, there are problems of tactics of immediate significance, which are subject to debate and variable decisions. The focus of this chapter is the urban debate and decisions in China since the early 1950s.

The Urban Debate

As shown in the last chapter, the main thrust of the various policy directives in the early 1950s was to prevent the outflow of rural residents. City residents of *urban* birth were not visibly included in the discussion. Nor were they affected by the measures that the incipient in-migration of rural residents ushered into existence. As a matter of record, and in spite of the known reservations about rural out-migration, city growth itself was not deplored at the time. On the contrary, a number of positive statements on future and post-1949 urban development were made:

Sian (New China News Agency, 5 January 1953): one of the most ancient Chinese cities has advanced by leaps and bounds during the last year or so. . . . Newly built or repaired streets [paved roads] number more than 30. . . . Bus routes were added or extended. A new water works outside the Western gate can supply some 5,000 tons of water daily to 300,000 residents. Public water faucets or stations were installed in densely populated areas where there are no piping facilities. Within one year, the municipality built and repaired some 20,000 kilometers of sewage mains. . . . making it possible to improve environmental sanitation conditions. The so-called "Muddy district" of the city's northern section now has a new look. A well-equipped workers' hospital, a modern nursery, and an 800-apartment workers' dormitory [Production Village] was built there. Some 400 families have already moved into their new homes. Similar workers' dormitories total 10 in the whole city. . . . The People's Government of the Municipality of Sian has also made preliminary decisions on new suburban development: the western suburb will be turned into an industrial area, the southern suburb a cultural and educational area, and the western suburb a residential area for workers. Urban road network will be extended to the suburbs, so that the commercial, industrial, and residential areas can all be connected together. Following these urban developments, Sian has become more and more prosperous. The municipal population has increased since the liberation from 500,000 to 700,000.[1]

Peking (*China Constructs*):   Professor Liang Ssu-cheng [vice-chairman of the Municipal Plan Committee of Peking and Head of the Department of Architecture, Tsing Hua University] said, "April 21, 1953, is Peking's 800th anniversary since it was first made the nation's capital. . . . At present, a 15–20-year plan is being drawn up to expand and develop Peking into a great political and cultural center and, at the same time, a highly industrialized metropolis. . . . The population of Peking will increase from its current 2,500,000 to 4,000,000 or 5,000,000, and the territory of the municipality from the present 24 square kilometers to 173 square kilometers, or seven times. . . . The Municipal Plan Committee has already outlined the steps involved in this systematic expansion: up to now, most progress has been made in sanitation work, which is the first of the four tasks.   The second task pertains to municipal transportation, the third housing, and the fourth long-term planning. . . . The eastern and southern suburbs will be zoned as industrial areas. . . . Since Peking often has northern and western winds, smoke and dust will not be blown into the central city in order to keep it clean.   The scenic western and northern suburbs, where many cultural and educational institutions are now located, will be further developed. . . . Tienanmen Square, the heart of Peking, will be enlarged 100 percent, around which a number of government buildings will be built. . . . The area near the Railway Station at Chienmen will be designed a commercial area. . . . During the past three years, newly opened roads amounted to some 75 kilometers, which is two-thirds of all new roads built during the thirty-eight years between the overthrow of the Manchu dynasty and the liberation of Peking. . . . Peking now has twice as many electric tramcars as before the liberation.   Buses increased by more than 14 times. . . . During this initial period, many houses were also built.   The emphasis has been the construction of dormitories for the workers.   Residential housing and repairs and construction of schools and government offices are the next emphasis.   All in all, during the last three years, newly built and repaired housing units number 130,300.

1. *Great Impartiality Daily* (Hong Kong), 6 Jan. 1953.

But, in comparison with Peking's future development, this is only a very small beginning.[2]

Lanchow (New China News Agency, 1 September 1953): Situated on a river plane of an elevation of 1,500 meters at the upstream of the Yellow River, Lanchow has since the Ch'in (221 B.C.) and Han (206 B.C.–220 A.D.) been our nation's northwestern transportation center and the chief exchange market between China Proper and the various nationalities minorities in Kansu, Tsinghai, and Sinkiang. After the completion of the Tienmen-Lanchow Railroad, the highway network with Lanchow as its center continues to expand in the northwestern direction.... Along with the extension of the Lanchow-Sinkiang Railroad westward, Lanchow will hereafter become the nerve center of the northwestern transportation system and an industrial base area. Near the Lanchow Railroad Station, which was still a vacant lot just a year ago, new buildings with space of 10,000 square meters have already been completed. Many factories in the suburbs are in the process of expansion and redevelopment. Lanchow Electric Power Company has just finished its construction projects for the current year, enlarging its generating capacity by 100 percent.[3]

There can be little doubt that extensive renovation and new construction were carried on in numerous Chinese cities in the early 1950s. However much actual or potential accomplishment may have been inflated in these reports, some useful and specific data on urban development are disclosed. In addition, they probably give a good depiction of the mood of the country at that time, juxtaposing a proud view of the actual achievements and a positive vision of China's urban future.

A somewhat more detailed account in August 1954 tallied urban progress throughout the nation as follows:

During the five years from 1950 to 1954, the state devoted a total of more than ¥100,000,000 to the construction of public utilities and the improvement of environmental sanitation in the cities. According to the statistics reported by some twenty cities at the end of 1953, more than 1,900

2. Ibid., 13 Apr. 1953.
3. *Wen Hui Daily* (Hong Kong), 1 Sept. 1953.

kilometers of water pipes were added as were more than 1,400 kilometers of sewage mains. Buses, tramcars, and trackless trolleys increased by approximately 2,000 units in each city. Just in the year of 1952 alone, some 5,000,000 square meters of residential space were made available to workers in five cities [Peking, Tientsin, Shenyang, Anshan, and Shanghai]. Numerous polluted wells, canals, and rivers in and near Peking and Tientsin were thoroughly cleansed in order that millions of laboring masses can have a comfortable and immaculate environment in which to live.[4]

Of course, China's urban record of the early 1950s could be tangibly depreciated if the measuring rod employed were the enormity of its immediate urban needs. However, China's efforts to renew and develop its cities must not be considered apart from the overall situation and some particular policy decisions at the time. Generally, the aim of urban development was to aid industrial development. Specifically, cities were grouped into three categories based on the degree of immediate relevance to industrialization.

In concrete terms, efforts must be concentrated in the development of new industrial cities where important industrial projects are located. Such cities previously had no industrial foundation. Now that large-scale modern industries are being erected, the construction of public utilities and facilities typical of modern cities must be undertaken to complement them. Cities in this category necessarily are the central focus in our urban development work. Next are the modern cities that have already acquired a certain industrial base. The present plan is to augment the existing factories and to build new factories in these cities. Cities in this category must be placed second in our nation's urban development scheme, and be redeveloped and expanded in accordance with industrial growth. As regards several large cities and most medium and small cities where industrial construction is minimal during the First Five-Year Plan (1953–1957), new projects are, basically speaking, not to be undertaken, even though such cities still possess many unjust conditions inherited from the old society and, in a number of ways, cannot satis-

4. *People's Daily*, 11 Aug. 1954. (¥1=U.S. $0.40.)

fy the material and cultural needs of the people. In these instances, only maintenance and repair work can be allowed.[5]

No list is available of the cities in each of the three categories. From the previous analysis of urban growth, it is possible to name some of the cities in the first category. But it is the close link between urban development and industrial development that merits greater attention here. By this criterion, cities were treated differentially. However, the import of this policy decision goes beyond the treatment that individual cities as such received. The fortune of individual cities was also the country's fortune, for the policy decision was made at the highest level and in the national context. The question concerning the geographic distribution of industry and the establishment of new industrial bases was extensively discussed in China. The outcome was recorded in China's First Five-Year Plan:

> The abnormal concentration of our industry in a few areas and in the coastal cities is irrational both from the economic point of view and in respect to national defense. The geographic distribution of our new industrial capital construction must conform to the long-term interests of the state, and take account of conditions at different stages of our development. It must follow the principle of appropriately distributing our industrial productive forces over various parts of the country, locating industries of consumption, and complying with the need to strengthen national defense, so as to change gradually the irrational distribution of industry and develop the economy of backward areas.
> In order to change the irrational distribution of industry, we must build up new industrial bases, but the utilization,

5. Ibid. However, Mr. Sun Ching-wen, director of the Urban Construction Bureau of the Department of Building, reported that the First National Conference on Urban Construction made a fourfold classification of cities. In addition to the three categories just described, a fourth group of cities was distinguished consisting of those medium and small cities where no new industrial projects were being constructed. It is difficult to differentiate these from those in the third category so far as public utilities and environmental health work are concerned (*People's Daily*, 12 Aug. 1954).

reconstruction, and extension of existing industrial bases is a prerequisite for the establishment of new industrial bases.

Whether we are reconstructing and extending existing industrial bases or building new ones, we must avoid over-concentration; a suitable distance should separate enterprises one from another. A proper relationship should also be observed in the building of large, medium, and small enterprises.

The First Five-Year Plan makes the following basic arrangements for the geographic distribution of industrial capital construction:

1. The industrial foundation already established in the Northeast, in Shanghai, and in other cities must be rationally utilized and made full use of it in order to accelerate our industrial construction. The most important thing is to complete the major part of our industrial base in the Northeast centered on the integrated iron and steel works in Anshan so that it will be better able to give technical support to the building of new industrial bases.

In addition to the important reconstruction of the integrated iron and steel works in Anshan, reconstruction work will also be undertaken at other existing industrial enterprises in the Northeast such as the coal mines in Fushun, Fuhsin, and Hokang, the iron and steel works in Penhsi, the machine-building works in Shenyang, and the power installations in Kirin.

2. The building of new industrial bases like those in north, northwest and central China must be actively pushed ahead so that two new industrial bases centered on the integrated iron and steel works in Paotow and Wuhan can be established during the period of the Second Five-Year Plan.

3. A start must be made with part of the industrial construction scheduled for Southwest China along with active preparation of conditions for the building of a new industrial base there.

Accordingly, as these basic arrangements for industrial capital construction are carried out, by the time the Second Five-Year Plan is fulfilled on the basis of the completion of the First Five-Year Plan, our country will have giant industrial bases in the Northeast, North, Northwest, and central China. This will greatly transform the economic life of a vast area of our country, and since this new geographic distribution of industry is based on the growth of heavy industry, it will eventually transform the whole nature of the original distribution of industry in China.

Besides the arrangements for the location of heavy industry outlined above, the First Five-Year Plan also makes new and more rational arrangements for the location of new light industrial enterprises [mainly textile enterprises]. This will to a certain extent remedy the former concentration of light industry in the coastal cities and transfer it to the interior where it will be near to sources of raw materials and areas of consumption.

To satisfy the needs of the interior, gradual steps should be taken to move certain transportable industrial enterprises from the coastal cities to the interior.[6]

Quite obviously, this pronouncement contained as well as affirmed the several major assumptions that various municipal and regional authorities had previously (i.e., since 1949) employed in the formulation of interim measures aimed at industrial and population dispersion. The First Five-Year Plan itself was drafted by the State Planning Commission (Li Fu-chun, chairman) under the direction of the Central Committee of the Communist Party of China and Chairman Mao Tse-tung. And it was endorsed on 30 July 1955 by the First National People's Congress at its second session, before its formal publication. Thus, the status of these earlier policy assumptions was significantly elevated and authoritatively ratified. This ratification was also accompanied by reference to fresh starts on the industrial and urban fronts.

The pronouncement on industrial development was no longer premised on the need to restore China's industrial facilities. It emphatically pointed to the direction and location of future and ongoing industrial projects. This new departure evidently stemmed from the development that by the end of 1952, China had largely completed the restoration phase of her national construction. Soviet assistance for industrial construction had already been successfully negotiated. Consistent with this was the earlier disclosure in 1954 that cities were to be distinguished on the basis of their assigned place

6. *First Five-Year Plan for Development of the National Economy of the People's Republic of China in 1953–1957*, pp. 40–42.

in the industrial developmental scheme. Accordingly, selected cities in the Northeast and some inland provinces were to receive preferential treatment during the First Five-Year Plan.

Also consistent with this policy of preferential treatment of such "key cities" was another provision in the First Five-Year Plan: "The development of the public health and medical services plays a significant role in improving the people's well-being. . . . In developing health and medical services *priority must be given to improving the work in industrial areas*, in areas where capital construction is in progress, and in forest areas, and sanitation work in rural districts must be gradually improved."[7] The demographic implications of this provision need no elaboration. And its implementation, coupled with industrial construction, evidently had considerable impact on the population of the cities involved, as has been shown in the last chapter.

Yet, in either the pronouncement on industrial development itself or other points of the First Five-Year Plan, no direct reference was made to demographic matters. The item that came closest in this regard pertained to manpower utilization: "We must improve the distribution of labor power and step by step establish a proper system for this work. An annual plan for replenishments of labor power must be mapped out by each enterprise, on the basis of its production and man-power plan. The various sections of departments that require replenishments of labor power should, in the first place, secure them from surplus personnel in their respective departments or trades [including private enterprises]. If this cannot be done, the organizations in question must not blindly go ahead enrolling additional workers or staff members they need, but the central or local labor offices must assume the responsibility for making the necessary adjustments or arranging transfers."[8] To the extent that "replenishments of labor power" entail the introduction of migrants from outside the cities, this admonition amounted to an implicit acknowledgement of the possibility or probability of a too rapid urban population growth.

7. Ibid., pp. 199–200.
8. Ibid., p. 192.

This reading of the statement is reinforced by another excerpt from the dialogue on urban conditions in China in 1954:

> During the First Five-Year Plan, a large number of our nation's new industrial areas are to be built on the foundations of old cities. Therefore, . . . we must give exhaustive consideration to the question of how to best combine the development of new industrial areas and the reconstruction of old cities simultaneously. This consists principally of two aspects: one is the problem of employment and occupational change of old cities' existing labor power, and the other is the utilization of old cities' existing material base, such as physical plants, housing units, and various public welfare amenities. [But], there are comrades who, in their consideration of urban expansion, frequently overlook these factors. They either have yet to consider, or have given little thought to, a greater utilization of old cities' existing consumer population, unemployed persons, and housewives in industrial construction projects. Instead, they believe that all or most of the personnel and workers needed to expand or build industrial enterprises can only be transferred from without. Thus, they unavoidably overestimate the extent of urban population growth, inappropriately increase the nation's investment in workers' housing and other public welfare amenities, and bring certain difficulties to the construction of new industrial areas. At the same time, they make it impossible for old cities' existing consumer population to find employment or to shift into new types of employment. Therefore, when the scope of expansion of new industrial areas is being examined, we must endeavor, in a pragmatic way, to investigate and analyze the composition of the existing urban population, to consider the possibility of absorbing current labor power in the city, and to maximize the utilization of hidden potentials of old cities. . . . We must be against the kinds of thought and practices that accent unrealistic and highly inflated estimates of population growth rates and blindly attempt to create large-scale cities.[9]

More specifically, as was revealed in an earlier article on urban construction, some of the plans for large-scale cities were predicated on an initial population of more than one mil-

9. *People's Daily,* 22 Aug. 1954.

lion and an area of several hundred square kilometers.[10] Judging from the size of some existing cities in China, urban population projections of this magnitude would not seem purely visionary. However, the fact was that mention of such plans, then being drawn up for several new industrial cities, was invariably coupled with admonitions phrased in terms similar to those in the last quotation. Undoubtedly, there were those who had genuine reservations about the emergence of additional large-scale cities in China. To them, past conditions in the slums of Shanghai, Tientsin, and numerous industrial metropolises in western countries could have served as a vivid reminder of what might arise in cities under development. Perhaps there were also others who, for these and other unspecified reasons, were opposed to large-scale cities as such and in whose opinion cities of this kind were incompatible with the Chinese way of life.

If this opposition based on a simple desire to preserve Chinese cultural traditions was ever present, it was not resolutely registered, and little evidence can be found to substantiate its existence. Nor was it likely that possible recurrence of slums per se constituted a major deterrent. Large-scale cities were explicitly resisted on other, and quite diverse, grounds. Some material and immediate difficulties, for instance, were seen in the cost, coordination, and care involved in too rapid implementation of the various proposals for erecting them. But the most decisive consideration appears to have been how cities could most properly be developed in China:

The growth of modern cities depended on and followed the growth of industrial development. Our urban construction must bear obedience to the demands on the industrial front, and proceed in accordance with industrial construction. Of course, there will be cities that are to be developed to serve chiefly educational, cultural, and recreational purposes. But, cultural, educational, and recreational cities must also be developed in response to the demands of industrial construction. Therefore, regardless of whether the redevelopment of old cities or the construction of new cities

10. Ibid., 7 Jan. 1954.

is being undertaken, we must endeavor to adjust the scope of urban development to the geographic distribution of industry in the nation as a whole. First of all, in order to positively guarantee industrial construction and the livelihood of the laboring people, we must proceed to redevelop and construct important industrial cities in a concentrated manner and step by step. As regards to cities where little or only some industrial construction is being attempted, strict observance must be made of the national strategy of developing selected cities; in such cities work ought to be done only to maintain their present conditions. Proper development of [such] cities is possible only after the development of important industrial cities has been successfully concluded as a result of the nation's concentrated efforts. Even so, in the course of their construction, the development of the selected cities must, under necessary and possible circumstances, be limited to some "key points." We must absolutely avoid trying to accomplish everything at once and making disconnected efforts.[11]

Quite clearly, what the statement sought to discourage was not large-scale cities as such; their eventual emergence was implicitly acknowledged. Rather, it advised against urban construction on a grand scale under China's *present* circumstances. It called for great restraint in undertaking urban construction projects that were unrelated to, and exceeded, the need of the industrial development. Gradualism and realism were the two discernible themes. However, these probably were of more tactical than strategic significance. China's urban strategy evidently consisted in building a firm economic base of emerging large-scale cities and in dispersing them throughout the country.

Quite obviously, this dispersal of industrial cities was not and could not be a matter of scattering cities randomly. It entailed almost exclusively the dispersal of new or old industrial plants to *existing* cities where industrial enterprises were nonexistent or negligible and where circumstances were relatively favorable. Thus, as a matter of policy consideration, urban construction became synonymous with, or a component

11. Lan Tien, "Urban Construction Be Undertaken in Accordance with the Principle of Economy, Utility, and Beauty."

part of, industrial construction in the evolving urban policy of China. In the words of the director of the Bureau of Urban Construction, "New China's cities are to be in the service of socialist industrialization, and of the laboring people and the working class."[12] The terms of reference of urban construction thus were largely devoid of demographic particulars, save the encouragement that greater utilization be made of manpower already in the cities. But this proscription on labor recruitment from without had to do more with current urban conditions than with future urban growth. It was consistent with the policy to foster an orderly development of cities. Its aim was to alleviate and prevent urban congestion rather than to preclude large-scale cities forever:

> Urban construction is a matter of long-term [one hundred years] planning, and the scope of possible urban development must be examined in the light of the nation's plan for industrial development. That is, . . . a unified plan must be established in order to fulfill current needs and, at the same time, to assure long-term advantages. . . . Appropriate [land] areas must be set aside to meet developmental needs in the distant future.[13]

As a matter of record, the State Council formally allowed extensive annexations by China's two leading municipalities a few years later in 1958. Shanghai acquired the land areas (1,280,000 *mou*) of three adjacent *hsien* and an additional population of 650,000; the population of Greater Shanghai reached just below the 8 million mark.[14] The territory of the municipality of Peking doubled in 1958, as a result of the annexation of five contiguous *hsien* and one municipality; its total land area increased from 45,400 square kilometers to 87,700 square kilometers. Peking's total population jumped to 5,200,000 from 4,060,000. These consolidations of previously separate political units into giant municipalities are pregnant with meaning.

12. *People's Daily,* 12 Aug. 1954.
13. Ibid.
14. NCNA (Shanghai), 21 Mar. 1958. (1 *mou*=0.16 acre)

The proclamation to enlarge Peking pointed to some of the advantages that would consequently accrue to Peking's residents. For instance, the flow of vegetables, meats, and other food supplements to the city's retail outlets would be more regular and abundant as sources of supply increased and were integrated into one marketing area centered on Peking. But the extension of municipal authority into adjacent areas also greatly enhanced Peking's freedom and ability to make long-range plans and to expand various construction projects.[15]   To some extent, adjustments in municipal boundaries in the case of Peking, Shanghai, and other cities undoubtedly were made in response to, rather than in anticipation of, population growth.   Nevertheless, given the direction of change, some very propitious circumstances have been created under which regional megalopolises seem certain to emerge and can be systematically planned.

Thus, China's strategy for urban development was not mapped out to place a ceiling on cities' eventual size demographically and territorially.   Rather, as it was wedded to her strategy for industrial development, urban construction, for tactical reasons, was to be contingent upon the progress in industrial construction.   The exhortations that the rate and scope of urban construction be so managed during, if not beyond, the First Five-Year Plan (1953–57) were in support of the strategy of city-building through industrial development. Presumably, they were to prevent an excessive flow of material and monetary resources into urban construction projects that could or would otherwise be used to erect industrial and related facilities.   Schemes for urban construction at variance with this strategy were duly criticized in the press and other public media:

. . . At the present time [1955], there remain defects and errors in urban construction work. A number of cities, in drawing up plans [for urban construction], overestimated the increase in population. On the basis of the preliminary plans of some 21 cities, population estimates still exceed, by some 10 percent, those calculated on the basis of the

15. NCNA (Peking), 20 Mar. 1958.

industrial units already fixed by the state. The planning criteria adopted by certain cities are too high: the average [per capita] space alloted to residential use is too large, [planned] streets are too wide, and [projected] public squares too big. If urban construction work were to proceed according to these criteria, it would be necessary to demolish and remove many existing dwelling units, railroads, airports, warehouses, and so forth.[16]

Apart from personal ambitions on the part of some officials, the sources of these defects and errors were readily said to include poor organization, inadequate skill and data, and insufficient experience in urban planning work. Nevertheless, within the short span of time of a little more than a year during which urban construction work was first discussed mostly in nondemographic terms, the urban debate in China began to acquire a demographic dimension late in 1955:

> Hence forth, an important aspect of urban construction work that awaits solution is the prudent estimation of the scope of expansion of the urban population. The size of the population of a city will directly affect the construction cost in that city. If the population is large, the scope of the total plan of the city will have to be extensive; the expenditures for public buildings and public utilities must be vastly increased. Therefore, when a city fixes the range of its short- and long-term population increase, it must correctly calculate this in accordance with the national economic plan. The extent of demographic expansion in an industrial city must especially be made to correspond to the scope of its industrial construction. After the range of demographic expansion has been determined, *it must make every attempt to institute tight population control,* and systematically place surplus labor power and prevent peasants from blindly drifting into the city.[17]

The stabilization of the urban population thus remained the current policy goal, albeit not in static terms. But unlike the situation a few years earlier, urban residents themselves were

16. "Strengthen Urban Planning Work and Reduce Urban Construction Cost," *People's Daily,* 23 Nov. 1955.

17. Ibid.

rapidly being involved in the various efforts to realize this dynamic goal. The continuing drive to stabilize the urban population was buttressed by specific measures instituted within the cities to complement those adopted to prevent or retard the out-migration of rural residents.

Urban Population Decisions

Components of urban population growth are fertility, mortality, in-migration, and out-migration. In China, strong and systematic efforts have been made to reduce mortality in the city and countryside alike, making possible a great surge in population growth throughout the nation. Thus, the stabilization of China's urban population at a fixed size or a controlled rate of growth clearly involves the introduction of fertility limitation, for it is unlikely that a deliberate program to restore the death rate to its previous high levels would be instituted. But the benefits of fertility control are not immediately realizable. In the short run, therefore, measures designed to regulate urban population growth are necessarily limited to manipulating the remaining two components of urban growth, in-migration and out-migration.

Thus, to the extent that the urban natural increase exceeds population replacement needs of the cities or their capacity to absorb it, the out-migration of residents of urban birth becomes imperative if the urban population is to be maintained at a given size, or its growth slowed. So far as this out-migration is concerned, inducements and persuasion are needed in order to overcome possible reluctance to relocation among the residents involved, and decisions must be made as regards the criteria for selecting would-be out-migrants. Moreover, outlets must be found to receive them. Possible outlets include: (1) existing rural villages, (2) new rural settlements, (3) new cities, and (4), in the case of residents from large urban centers, smaller towns and cities.

So far as in-migration is concerned, steps may be taken to return those who have found their way into the cities. The removal of the in-migrants again involves the application of inducements and persuasion as well as decisions as to their selection and destinations. The transfer of resident in-mi-grants to new rural settlements and new cities represents a policy alternative as does the return of the in-migrants to their villages of origin. Of course, all efforts to transfer in-migrants would be futile if fresh flows of in-migration are not restrained or stopped altogether. The need for preventive measures is thus clearly indicated, and these include: (1) vigorous super-vision of travel facilities, (2) imposition of travel restrictions, and (3) programs and measures to promote the retention of rural population, the largest reservoir of potential urban in-migrants in China.

Some of the steps taken to curtail the out-flow have already been referred to earlier. So have some of the actual efforts to return to villages of origin those who had migrated into urban areas. Of particular importance were the various pronounce-ments and decisions on labor recruitment from outside the cities, as repeated references were made to them in the debate on urban construction and growth in China. They thus de-serve further attention.

In April 1953, when the State Council first sought to check rural out-migration at the *hsien, chu,* and *hsiang* levels (see Appendix C), it specifically made labor recruitment for urban and industrial construction projects a responsibility of the *hsien, chu,* and *hsiang* governments: "In cases where addi-tional workers are required . . . , the *hsien, chu,* and *hsiang* governments will do the recruiting in a planned and organized manner upon official notification." It further specified:

> In order that manpower can be allocated and regulated ac-cording to plan, workers may not be arbitrarily recruited in the countryside. Nor may posters for indiscriminate re-cruitment be publicly displayed. All enterprises in the cities should notify the local labor departments of their needs, giving the number of workers required, precise project plans, and date of start of work.[18]

All these were to replace the direct, separate, and unsystem-

18. Article 7 of the State Council Directive of 17 April 1953 (see Appendix C).

atic hiring practice then in use, and constituted some of the key provisions of a developing centralized scheme for labor recruitment. On the whole, the 1953 directive reportedly served its purpose; for a while "the blind influx of peasants into the cities was stopped." [19]   However, a resumption of rural out-migration followed shortly thereafter. Noncompliance with the 1953 directive in some places and among some local cadres, industrial and construction enterprises, and peasants was cited as the main cause in another directive issued in March 1954. The 1954 directive reiterated much of what was said in the earlier document, but it differed in two important ways. It authorized local governments to take stern measures to stop random recruitment of workers in the villages. Whereas the Department of Interior alone was involved in the previous attempt to restrain rural exodus, the Department of Labor joined with it in 1954 to keep the flow within bounds.[20]

This deployment of additional obstacles to uncoordinated labor recruitment and, hence, to rural out-migration in 1954 was followed by still others in the same year and in 1955. Rules governing arrivals and departures were detailed in the *Organic Regulations of Public Security Precincts* (31 December 1954), under which a removal permit should be secured by any and every person if his absence from his place of domicile was to be more than six months. Specifically:

A. In case of departures from one *hsiang* or *cheng* [hamlet] to another within the same *hsien*, application for removal permit should be filed with the *hsiang* or *cheng* people's committee before making the move. The fact will be recorded in the register of departures.

B. In case of departures from one *hsien* to another, application for removal permit should be filed with the *hsiang* or *cheng* people's committee before making the

19. *People's Daily*, 15 Mar. 1954. Joint Declaration on Continuing Implementation of the Directive Advising Against Blind Influx of Peasants into Cities, the Ministry of Interior and the Ministry of Labor, Central People's Government. See Appendix F.

20. Ibid.

move. The *hsiang* or *cheng* people's committee should either issue the permit, or pass the application on to higher authorities concerned for action. In the latter instances, removal permit will be issued by the agency to which the application has been referred.

All removal permits were to be centrally printed by the Ministry of Public Security.

The other measures put into effect in 1955 included: the establishment of a permanent system for registration of persons (2 July 1955), the creation of urban street offices and urban residents' committees (31 December 1954), and the institution of grain-rationing in China's cities and towns (25 August 1955).[21]

Also established under the *Organic Regulations of Public Security Precincts* were police substations in *hsien* (counties) and *shih* (municipalities) in 1955.[22] However, apart from participating and assisting in local welfare work, public security precincts were no longer to be involved in civil affairs as they had been for some time in the past. But they continued to be in charge of household registration; in fact, this particular function has largely been handled by *local* public security (police) stations in China since 1949. Several municipal authorities initially drew up their own regulations governing household registration and placed the work in the hands of police precincts.[23] All these were later declared void and superseded by the *Provisional Regulations Governing Urban Household Registration.*[24] With the approval of the State Council, these were issued by the Ministry of Public Security of the Central Government in July 1951. Operating procedures were left to regional, provincial, or municipal public security organs to work out in accordance with the spirit

21. For the texts of the various regulations governing population registration, urban street bureaus, urban residents' committees, public security precincts, and food-rationing, see Appendixes G, H, I, J, and K.

22. See Appendix G.

23. For a typical version of these regulations, see *People's Daily,* 17 Nov. 1949.

24. *People's Daily,* 26 July 1951.

of the *Provisional Regulations*, but a uniform model of household registration was promulgated for the entire country.

Basically, six categories of households were distinguished in 1951: residential households, industrial and commercial households, transient households (hotels, and so on), boat households, temple households, and alien households. A "household" included all the persons, regardless of number and types of relationships, who shared a common household head, resided together, and ate and slept in the same dwelling unit. Separate households could be established when members of the same family lived in several dwelling units, used separate cooking and eating facilities, were located at a distance from one another, or when financially independent families resided in the same dwelling unit. Each household was required to be in possession of a household register in which the names and other particulars of all the persons of the household were entered. Whenever change in the household composition occurred, the head of household had to have the matter recorded in the register at the local public security office. Specifically, five types of change were to be so reported: births, deaths, arrivals, departures, and "miscellanies" (marriage, divorce, separation, consensual marriage, persons missing and found, adoptions, acknowledgments of paternity or maternity, hiring and discharge of workers, opening and closing businesses, household head replacement, and occupational changes).

Household registration procedures included the reporting of all births within one month of occurrence, deaths within 24 hours (or immediately if deaths were sudden or due to unknown causes and communicable diseases), arrivals (moving into the household) within three days, and departures before the fact. Removal certificates were issued to persons intending to move out of the jurisdiction of one police precinct into another, and persons who moved into a different household were required to submit such certificates or other appropriate documents. Samples of standardized forms, certificates, and so on used in household registration were issued by the Ministry of Public Security of the Central People's Government, from which copies for local use were to be made by provincial and municipal public security organs.

However many other functions local police precincts were given charge of, household registration itself constituted a tedious task of major proportion. The fact that numerous other functions were also assigned to urban public security precincts was brought out in December 1954, when police precincts were divested of their civil functions: "For a period in the past, because urban public security precincts were also responsible for a number of civil functions, they have not been able to devote all their power to the maintenance of public peace and order. And, because of their own [police] duties, public security precincts have not been able to spare much effort to systematically investigate and understand the administrative policies, conditions, and problems involved in civil affairs. This has limited the development of civil administration." [25] Nevertheless, household registration work was not then, and so far as is known, has not since been transferred out of local police precincts.

But with the issuance of the 1954 *Organic Regulations of Public Security Precincts*, a step in the direction of greater specialization in urban administrative apparatus was made. Also implicit in the regulations was the removal of local police precincts from the direct supervision of the Ministry of Public Security of the Central People's Government; they were termed "the district offices of the municipal or county public security bureau."[26]   A further step was taken in June 1955, when the State Council issued its *Directive on the Establishment of a Permanent Population Register.*[27]   Article 1 of the directive reaffirmed that household registration work be managed, as before, by public security precincts in cities and towns.   But where there were previously no public security precincts, the work would be handled by *hsiang* and *chen* people's councils in villages and hamlets.   The urban population register thus was expanded into a national system of registration of persons.   Along with this change, the administration of the system in the nation was placed in the hands of

25. Ibid., 2 Jan. 1955.
26. See Appendix G.
27. See Appendix J.

the Ministry of Internal Affairs and the civil-affairs departments of the people's councils of the *hsien* level and above.
The 1955 Population Register differed little from the 1951 *Provisional Regulations Governing Urban Household Registration* in respect to the registration of birth, deaths, arrivals, departures, and so on.[28] However, it contained more detailed procedures for applying for removal certificate before relocation:

> . . . When the whole family or an individual changes its or his/her permanent address, the head of the household or the individual concerned should comply with the following provisions before making the move.   In the case of a change of permanent address within the same *hsiang* or *chen* being reported to the *hsiang* or *chen* people's council, the change will be recorded as a change of address only, and no out-migration application need be made.   In the case of moving from one *hsiang* or *chen* to another within the same *hsien*, the out-migrant should apply to the *hsiang* or *chen* people's council for a removal certificate, and his departure should be registered accordingly in the register of departures by the *hsiang* or *chen* people's council.   In the case of out-migration from one *hsien* to another, the *hsiang* or *chen* people's council should issue, or arrange with the appropriate office of a higher level to issue, the person a removal certificate and register his departure in the register. When a person is absent from his place of domicile for more than six months, he should complete the out-migration procedure. . . .

Along with the registration of births, deaths, arrivals, and other related demographic matters, the 1955 Population Register would logically yield the most complete and rather current data on the size, growth, and distribution of China's population.[29] But the implementation of the 1955 directive on

28. A major exception in the reporting of deaths was the change from "within 24 hours" to "within one month."

29. Article 4 stated: "Statistics on persons registered shall, for the time being, be collated once a year.   Places of *hsiang* and *chen* level should submit reports on population changes during the previous year to *hsien* every February.   The *hsien* should report changes in population to the province every March, and the provinces should so report to the Ministry of Internal Affairs every April.

household registration appeared only partial, probably mostly in urban areas. Personnel and orientation were visibly insufficient to translate it into a wholly successful operation, and political and demographic events soon induced the return of the administration of household registration to the Ministry of Public Security. On 9 January 1958, the Standing Committee of the National People's Congress gave its approval to the *Regulations of the People's Republic of China Governing Household Registration.*[30]

The 1955 National Population Register would have been an impressive source of demographic data, but its importance in regard to the regulation of internal migration probably should not be exaggerated. Judging from subsequent reports and letters that appeared in local newspapers, considerable delay in the issuance of removal certificates was common. However, this often meant hardship and other inconveniences for the individual *after* he had already changed his place of residence.[31] The 1955 National Population Register was, at

---

"In the case of places under the jurisdiction of *hsien* where the registration of persons is handled by public security stations, at the time when places of *hsiang* and *chen* level make their reports, the public security stations should report the changes in population figures in places under their jurisdiction to the *hsien* public security bureau, which will in turn transmit same to the *hsien* civil affairs bureau. At the time when the *hsien* forward their reports to the province, the municipal public security bureaus should report the changes in population figures in their municipalities to the municipal bureaus of civil affairs, which will in turn transmit same to the provincial department of civil affairs. In the case of municipalities under the direct control of the State Council, the public security bureaus should report the changes in population figures to the bureau of civil affairs for transmission to the Ministry of Internal Affairs before the end of April every year."

30. See Appendix L. According to Article 3, "household registration shall be in the charge of the public security organs," and nowhere in the regulations is a reference to their reporting of changes in population to the Ministry of Internal Affairs and bureaus of civil affairs at lower levels.

31. See *Brilliance Daily* (Peking), 7 Dec. 1955; *Chianghai Daily* (Hsining), 6 Dec. 1956; *Hunan Daily* (Changsha), 9 Dec. 1956; and *Kiangsai Daily* (Nanchang), 16 Feb. 1957.

best, a rather cumbersome mechanism for stabilizing urban population from without the cities.

To return to the measures put into effect within the cities early in 1955, suffice it to say that two types of urban organizations emerged as a result of their adoption. Characteristically, neither urban street bureaus nor urban residents' committees were initially conceived of as population measures designed to affect urban growth. As it was revealed at the time of their formal establishment, they were tried experimentally in some seventy cities during the preceding two years or so, in order that the basic urban administration could effectively serve economic development. More specifically:

> As the country enters the period of socialist construction, the duties of the basic political power are daily becoming heavy and complicated. Along with the rapid expansion of the various urban construction enterprises, new circumstances and new problems often and continuously arise in connection with social welfare, compensation and pension, peace and safety, culture, education, sanitation, settlement of disputes, and work relating to women. To do well in these areas will not only serve to enhance the daily life of the people but will also be in direct coordination with and support of socialist construction. This requires that the basic urban administration strengthen its relationship with the masses, extensively enlist the masses to participate in the nation's management work. . . .[32]

Urban street offices were the precincts of the urban people's government, and were to perform certain routine daily administrative functions affecting the people directly, such as marriage registration and the issuance of certificates. "And, in order to strengthen the basic urban administration, it is necessary to rely on the positive support of the great masses and to better organize urban residents." Urban residents' committees were formed to consolidate into one structure all previous residents' organizations. "Because of its limited jurisdiction, a residents' committee can easily understand the circumstances and problems of each household, easily

32. *People's Daily*, 2 Jan. 1955.

comprehend the demands of the residents, and . . . organize the residents into undertaking joint efforts to solve various problems of livelihood, production, and study and to promote the welfare of the residents." [33]

The jurisdictional boundaries of urban street offices were to coincide with those of public security precincts, and those of urban residents' committees corresponded to the jurisdiction of the household registration beats of the public security precincts. As a general rule, all municipalities of 100,000 inhabitants or more (whether or not such municipalities had *chu* divisions within them), were to establish urban street offices. Their establishment was optional in municipalities of between 50,000 and 100,000 population, depending on administrative work requirements. Urban street offices were not to be set up in municipalities of less than 50,000 inhabitants. The chief officer and his staff (three to seven persons) of the urban street office were appointed by the municipal people's committee. [34]

More detailed specifications were given in the *Organic Regulations of Urban Residents' Committees*. In consideration of residential patterns of the inhabitants and jurisdictional boundaries of household registration beats, urban residents' committees should be so set up to cover from 100 to 600 households each. Each residents' committee was to organize the households under its jurisdiction into "residents' units" of 15 to 40 households each, but the total number of such units under any residents' committee should not exceed 17. The residents' committee would be made up of 7 to 17 committee members, one of whom would be elected as chairman. Each residents' unit was entitled to elect one committee member, who ordinarily would also serve as the unit leader. If, however, he should be elected the chairman or vice-chairman of the residents' committee, the residents' unit would elect another

33. Ibid.

34. See Appendix I. Of the three to seven full-time staff members, one would be especially concerned with matters relating to women. When necessary, a deputy chief officer would be added. All officers would be compensated by the municipal people's committee.

unit leader. In addition to the chairman, there would be from one to three vice-chairmen on the residents' committee, one of whom would be in special charge of matters affecting women residents. All members were elected for a one-year term, but reelection was apparently possible. Operating expenses of residents' committees and living allowances for the committee members were to be borne by the people's committees of the provinces or municipalities under the direct supervision of the Central People's Government in accordance with scales to be fixed by the Ministry of Interior. Solicitation of funds in any form from residents was explicitly disallowed, except in connection with public welfare activities. Fund-raising of this kind required the concurrence of residents themselves and approval of the appropriate people's committee, and had to be conducted on a voluntary basis.

The functions of the residents' committee included:

1. The promotion of matters relating to the welfare of the residents;
2. the transmission of opinions and requests of the residents to the local people's committee and its subordinate agencies;
3. the mobilization of the residents for law and order, and in response to the Government's appeals;
4. the active guidance in matters concerning public security; and
5. the arbitration of disputes among the residents.[35]

Unlike a number of other organizational innovations in China since 1949, information about either the street offices or the residents' committees since their establishment has been rather scarce. Reports and other published materials on such other developments as the agricultural producers' cooperatives and the People's Commune can be readily found in a large variety of sources. Perhaps urban street offices and urban residents' committees were only innovations in urban administration and welfare, whereas the cooperatives and People's Commune represented elements in the revolutionary transfor-

35. See Appendix H.

mation of Chinese society. Relatively little publicity would appear necessary in the institution of the former; the scope and importance of the latter changes could not but command greater publicity. The existence of the residents' committees, however, has been vividly verified. One 1962 account tells of the range of their activities in one Chinese municipality:

> Within every block of houses there will be found numerous dormitories in which single men and women live, groups of them sharing a common room with several double-deck bed-steads, which they tend communally. The single and the married workers living away from their parents' homes eat all their meals in the messroom of their organization, but at home they need hot water for washing and drinking, and for this they depend on the thermos flask and the nearest hot water depot. Many families living in the neighborhood also have the same dependence on the hot water depot as the percentage of households with gas installation is negligible.

.   .   .   .

> Every early morning, before the rush to catch a public bus for the early morning shift in factories begins, and in the fall and winter it is still quite dark and the streets are deserted, one meets numerous women with babies in their arms. These are working wives hurrying to creches to leave their babies for the duration of the working day. Among them are factory and office workers, trolley bus drivers and conductors, teachers, nurses and doctors. They do not live with the family of their husband or in their own parents' families since they married, but independently with their husbands in a rented room, or in a room in married people's quarters provided by the organization in which either the husband, or the wife, or both of them work.

> The creches and the hot water depots are two of the many services provided or supervised by the residents' committees.

> The principal tasks of the residents' committees are looking after public hygiene; they help the welfare clinics where the babies get their inoculation, instruct in first-aid work, participate in sanitation and cleansing work; there are subcommbittees for law and order, for welfare, for women, for culture, and, a very important one—for mediation in matrimonial and family disputes, and disputes among inhabitants of the same tenement or locality. The commit-

tees are appointed collection agents for public utility services, for house rent, for the milk supply company. Thus, on the one hand, the residents' committee serves the state or municipally operated concerns. On the other hand they make it easier for residents to pay their bills, practically on their own doorsteps and at any time.

The committees also act as receiving and paying agents of the People's Bank of China for the keeping of savings accounts by the residents. Supplies of vegetables and other country produce, milk by the state-owned dairy, are frequently delivered to the committees and the latter arrange for distribution within their locality. In addition, they operate kindergartens, junior schools, lending libraries, communal kitchens, barber shops, provide babysitters, nurses, and look after the children when parents are incapable of doing so themselves because of either sickness or work.

The residents' committees, of which all the larger cities in China have a great many, are all selected by the residents themselves, and though not part of the structure of local government, they supplement and aid the latter by keeping it in touch with the whole body of residents.[36]

Thus, within a short period of time, the residents' committees seem to have assumed an increasingly vital role in Chinese urban life. However, as the evidence is limited, the diverse functions of the residents' committees in the above instance may not actually be performed by all such committees throughout the nation. But the evidence is overwhelming in that the residents' committees are the small, albeit crucial, cogs in the giant urban administrative apparatus. All of the functions alluded to in this report and in the *Organic Regulations of Urban Residents' Committees* have to do with the basic amenities, conveniences, and comfort of city-dwellers. As such, the committees constitute an ameliorating agent of urban living.

It is possible that such services as babysitters, infant care, and kindergartens exert a pronatal influence in the urban milieu, but this is highly conjectural. A more plausible link between the urban residents' committees and urban population size would be in the area of migration. Identification of

36. Our Shanghai Correspondent, "Tinker, Tailor . . . ," p. 511–12.

in-migrants presumably would be less difficult in a well-organized urban setting, particularly in view of the strategic role of the residents' committees in the distribution of foodstuffs.

A few months after the establishment of the urban residents' committees, a system of grain-rationing in cities was promulgated on 25 August 1955. Under a directive of the State Council, individual allotments of rice, wheat, and miscellaneous grains would be fixed on the basis of types of work, age, and dietary habits.[37]

The implementation of the ration directive was the responsibility of the people's committees of the provinces, autonomous regions, and municipalities under the direct supervision of the central government; they were instructed to do so some time between 1 September and 30 November 1955. Given the scope of the task, the residents' committees and residents' units had to be relied upon to put the scheme into

TABLE 6

RATION SCHEDULE (25 AUGUST 1955)

(Monthly Allowance in Catties*)

TYPE OF WORK AND AGE	RICE CONSUMPTION AREAS		WHEAT AND COARSE GRAIN CONSUMPTION AREAS	
	Range	Average	Range	Average
Extraordinary physical labor	45–55	50	50–60	55
Heavy physical labor	35–44	40	40–49	44
Light physical labor	26–34	32	29–39	35
Employees of various governmental agencies, organizations, public and private enterprises, store clerks, and other brain workers	24–29	28	27–32	31
Students (college and high school)	26–33	32	29–36	35
General residents and children over 10	22–26	25	24–28	27½
Children, 6 to 10	16–21	20	18–23	22
Children, 3 to 6	11–15	13	12–17	14
Children under 3	5–10	7	6–11	8

*1 catty = 1.33 pounds.

37. Article 5 of the 1955 *Directive on Temporary Methods of Handling Fixed Grain Supply in Cities and Towns.*

effect in the cities in short order. Calculation of grain-ration would be in terms of households, and members of a household were assessed individually according to the ration schedule by the residents' committees, residents' units, and other related agencies. The same procedure applied to in-migrants from areas not included in the grain-rationing scheme, i.e., from rural areas. Thus, in addition to the requirements of a removal certificate from the place of origin and of registration at the place of destination,[38] in-migrants were also required to present themselves to the residents' committees of the areas into which they moved. Because the determination of grain-rations to which in-migrants would be entitled rested largely with the residents' committees, the significance of the committees in the stabilization of the urban population would seem self-evident.

In a lucid discussion of the timing of the institution of grain-rationing, Dwight Perkins concluded that the scheme was introduced for pragmatic reasons. It was, in part, indicative of a desire to reduce purchases of grain in the countryside in order to pave the way for the start of cooperatives in Chinese agriculture. More importantly, it was an anticipatory action designed to forestall any large rise in the price of grain in the cities where increases in population and per capita purchasing power accompanying the accelerated pace of industrial construction were judged likely in 1956. The resulting rise in grain prices would have been politically and economically undesirable. Nonetheless, he listed restriction of movement as a factor leading to the adoption of the rationing scheme.[39]

38. Article 6 and 9 of the 1955 *Directive on Grain-Rationing in Cities.* See also the previous review of the 1955 Population Register.

39. Dwight H. Perkins, *Market Control and Planning in Communist China,* pp. 184–94. For some of the assessments of the anticipated increases in the demand for grain in cities, see *Great Impartiality Daily* (Peking), 27 July 1955; *People's Daily,* 3 and 4 Aug. 1955. Urban grain consumption apparently had been increasing faster than population because of a rise in purchasing power (*Daily News* [Shanghai], 10 Aug. 1955; *People's Daily,* 24 Aug. 1955). Prevention of waste and pressures on the transportation network were cited in connection with the need for grain-rationing in cities (*People's Daily,* 3 Nov. 1955).

But the view that the urban residents' committees and other closely allied measures (e.g., household registration and grain-rationing) were an urban population stabilizer would be strongly fortified if two additional questions are answered in the affirmative. These are: Were they intended to be measures of urban population stabilization? Did they actually serve to stabilize China's urban population?

As previously indicated, the 1955 Population Register probably did not leave a major impact on the out-migration of rural residents. But the evidence does not allow a precise answer to the question of whether it was intended to be a mechanism for regulating population growth. As it was established to secure residential and migration data, it could have, at least potentially, aided the stabilization of the urban population. The same probably can be said of the urban residents' committees, for they were in an excellent position to gain an intimate knowledge of entry and departure of persons in their respective areas.

However, knowledge of residents per se does not and cannot constitute an effective step in the stabilization of the urban population. Nor is it correct to equate household registration with restrictions on geographic movement. The urban residents' committees were vested with little power to deny entry to persons moving into their areas or to enforce their departure after arrival, and their role in the grain-rationing scheme was to help administer rather than police it. Nor is there much truth in the belief that "individual movements were restricted . . . by the inability of an individual to obtain food coupons unless his move had been approved by the cadres involved." [40] Food coupons issued in accordance with the 1955 scheme were of two different kinds: those honored only in designated local stores, and those redeemable with proper cash payment in stores anywhere in the nation. Article 7 of the 1955 directive on grain-rationing stipulated that "urban residents who travel to, or eat in, other places can either bring personal grain or, within the quota of fixed supply, exchange personal food cou-

40. Perkins, *Market Control and Planning in Communist China*, p. 192.

pons for local or national food coupons." Article 13 stipulated that "rural residents who go back and forth between cities and villages can bring personal grain or, in accordance with the *Provisional Measures for the Unified Purchase and Supply of Grain in Rural Districts*, exchange [personal grain] for local or national food coupons." Thus, freedom of movement probably was affected by grain-rationing only in a very tangential way.

Moreover, not all the determination of individual rations in the cities was placed in the hands of the residents' committees. Employees of government agencies, organizations, enterprises, schools, and college and high school students were classified by their own units (Article 6). Workers recruited outside the centralized employment system presumably were not deprived of grain-rations because their employers apparently were able to intervene in their behalf.[41]   And not all rural residents who out-migrated did so only after having scrupulously met the requirements of the 1955 household registration system.   Thus, whatever its other immediate effects on the supply and price of grain, it is highly improbable that grain-rationing greatly augmented the power of the government over the movement of individuals.

In Shansi Province, for instance, the national government allotted, in 1953, to its cities and towns a total of one billion catties of grain.   By June 1957, the total population of large and small cities had increased to 2,518,000 from 1,400,000 in 1952, *not counting some 88,000 seasonal laborers*.   The grain allotment had to be raised to 1,560,000,000 catties.[42]   Admittedly, not all the increase in Shansi's urban population occurred after the institution of grain-rationing, or was attributable to the in-migration of persons from rural and other

41. See the discussion of the 1958 directive on household registration below; also, *People's Daily*, 24 Nov. 1956. The State Council issued another directive on grain supply in cities on 21 Nov. 1956. In an editorial in support of the directive, it was implied that many workers participating in economic and defense construction work had no food coupons in their possession.

42. *People's Daily*, 26 Aug. 1957.

urban areas. But subsequent to the institution of grain-rationing, instances of a sharp rise in population on account of migration remained frequent and impressive:

Shanghai: In May 1956 the number of permanent residents in the city was over 6,020,000 [not including 60,000 temporary residents]. Since June 1956 the population rose abruptly and, by the end of November, permanent residents already numbered more than 6,280,000 [not including 240,000 temporary residents]. In addition, there are about 60,000 persons in the city who have not registered.[43]

Hsiamen (Amoy): Large numbers of peasants have blindly infiltrated into Amoy City from the adjacent *hsien*. According to the latest statistics, since the second half of 1956, apart from a small number who had returned to the countryside, there were still 4,187 of them in the city. The peasant and intellectuals who have infiltrated into the city admired city life and thought that with the completion of the Yingtan-Amoy Railroad, municipal construction would be greatly expanded and so came here to find work. . . .[44]

Tientsin: The Tientsin Municipal Public Security Bureau reports that from 1956 to October 1957, a total of 205,000 peasants came to the city—of whom 100,000 were women. Only 1,700 of the latter took up jobs as day nurses. 12,000 got jobs as temporary workers, 8,000 as permanent workers, and 4,000 became unskilled peddlers. The other 77,000 are either old and disabled, or under 18 years of age, or loafers.[45]

Shangtung, Honan, Anhwei, and Kiangsu: Between the end of the last fall and this summer according to incomplete accounts, some 570,000 rural residents have blindly drifted into the cities. In Shangtung, Honan, Anhwei, and Kiangsu, there have been some 110,000 peasants blindly migrating into the cities between last fall and the first part of October this year.[46]

43. *Liberation Daily* (Shanghai), 26 Dec. 1956.
44. *Hsiamen Daily* (Amoy), 22 Jan. 1959.
45. *People's Daily,* 16 Dec. 1957.
46. Ibid., 19 Dec. 1957.

Shanghai: The number of permanent residents has increased from 6,070,000 in June 1956 to 6,860,000 in October 1957; and the number of temporary residents from 60,000 to 340,000. Of the total increase [1,120,000], some 300,000 are from natural increase, and 820,000 from net migration.[47]

Presumably, reports of the increases in both permanent and temporary population in these several instances were based on relatively current data. Thus, household registration functioned to provide some information about urban population growth via migration. As previously stated, formal rationing served to prevent a rise in the price of grain in the cities, even though both the demand for grain and wages increased. However, with regard to the stabilization of the urban population, it is inescapably evident that the impact of these various measures should not be exaggerated, even though there was an outward consistency in the relationship of the *means* to the goal. Perhaps, a few other means could be fashioned that would prove more effective. Nevertheless, it is legitimate to ask whether or not the stabilization of the urban population itself is an attainable goal.

Continuing Efforts To Order Urban Growth

Questions about the attainability of relative stability in urban population size are, needless to say, crucial to the formulation of China's demographic decisions as well as any assessment of their merits. Where a goal itself is unattainable, no effective means can be found; and, of course, the effectiveness of the means employed to attain a specific goal can hardly be shown unless the goal has been realized. But the argument here is not and need not be tautological. Inasmuch as the stabilization of a country's urban population necessarily requires direct and indirect intervention in the national demographic processes, its attainability can be appropriately determined in terms of the overall context in which relevant demographic phenomena occur.

47. *Wen Hui Daily* (Shanghai), 6 Jan. 1958.

TABLE 7

URBAN–RURAL DIFFERENTIALS IN PER CAPITA CONSUMPTION:
SELECTED CONSUMER GOODS

(Yearly consumption in Catties*)

	URBAN		RURAL	
	1949	1956	1949	1956
Grain	394	404	280	432
Vegetable oils	5.3	12.8	1.7	3.8
Pork and meat products	10.5	14.0	6.9	7.7
Salt	14.0	17.0	8.0	11.0
Sugar and candies	2.6	7.7	0.3	1.7
Cotton cloth and cloth products†	27.4	61.8	6.9	20.0

SOURCE: Tien Lin, "Comparison of the Last Seven Years to the Last Century," NCNA, 7 July 1957. (*New China Bi-Monthly,* no. 113, pp. 158–60.)
*1 catty = 1.33 pounds.
†In *chih,* 1 *chih* = 14.1 inches.

The figures in table 7 are some preliminary statistics released by the Statistical Bureau in 1957. Taken at face value, they show that urban-rural differentials in per capita consumption persisted and, in two instances, widened somewhat. Even though a rise in per capita consumption also occurred in both the urban and rural sectors of the nation, the average urban resident obviously enjoyed more material advantages. And the material advantages to which urban residents had easy access were not limited to these consumer goods. In an article entitled "Urban Population Must Be Controlled," the apparent irresistability of cities was explicitly conveyed:

Why has the urban population increased so rapidly? . . . The *third* reason was that large numbers of people in the countryside infiltrated into the cities. Some had gone to the urban areas to work as temporary workers or to visit relatives but had remained away from the rural areas permanently. Some have found work as governesses. Some were not content with agricultural work and wanted to get work in the cities. There were also workers in the cities who had been given to the idea of letting the state take care of everything. They thought that since the family lacked labor power in the countryside and as they themselves had to send remittances home to support their dependents anyway, they might as well move their families to the city, where they can have recourse to relief in the event of difficulties. In many agencies and enterprises, when the workers give birth to children, the children can be taken care of at the creches from the time they are 56 days old up to the time they enter the primary school. This means a saving of both trouble and money. Some factories charge nominal rental and utilities fees for the dormitories of their workers, and in some cases these services are even supplied free of charge. These systems make the workers feel that it is more advantageous for their families to be moved to the city than to remain in the rural areas. And so their dependents are being moved to the cities in large numbers. In one factory in Nanking, because the rents charged the dormitories of workers were too low, of the 199 workers' families, 108 had been moved into the city vacating their former dwellings or reletting them to others. In the State-Owned No. 1 Cotton Mill of Peking, during the past year, more than 800 dependents of its workers moved from the countryside to the city, and among them 200 persons have not yet obtained proper household-registration papers or have registered only as temporary residents. From 1950 to the end of 1956, about 150,000 persons from the rural districts came to Peking to look for employment, while the original workers and residents brought to the city another 200,000 dependents. There are normally about 150,000 temporary residents in the city.[48]

Thus, short of a significantly more equitable distribution of material and other advantages, the out-flow of rural residents would be unlikely to diminish. Even if that should be achieved in the long run, the attractiveness of the cities would be unlikely to diminish. In the short run, and for a variety of economic and social reasons, China's urban population continued to grow. Consequently, several other measures were introduced in the years from 1955 through 1958, and among them were both direct sanctions and indirect persuasions to check urban population growth.

In December 1957, the Ministry of Public Security was instructed to establish checkpoints at key places in the railroad

48. Sun Kuang, "Urban Population Must Be Controlled," *People's Daily,* 27 Nov. 1957. The first and second reasons were said to be (1) a reduction in urban mortality and an increase in births, and (2) "appropriate increments" in workers and staffs of production and construction enterprises.

network. Unauthorized out-migrants were to be promptly assisted back to villages of origin.[49]

Following a recommendation made by a deputy at the third session of the Standing Committee of the Second National Political Consultative Conference in March 1957,[50] the Standing Committee of the National People's Congress endorsed, on 16 November 1957, the *Provisional Regulations Governing Home Leaves and Wages of Workers and Employees*.[51] A system of annual leaves thus was inaugurated, enabling qualified urban cadres and workers to visit with relatives in the countryside and presumably lessening the propensity of the latter to migrate into the cities. Its key provisions read as follows:

> Of the workers and employees of the state-operated, state-private jointly operated enterprises and firms, state agencies and people's organizations, those who have completed one unbroken year's service and who, living apart from their fathers, mothers, or spouses, cannot visit them during public holidays, will be, in principle, allowed home leave once a year. The length of the leaves shall be from two to three weeks, depending on the distance involved.[52]

The regulations governing home leaves were to encourage workers and employees to leave their families in the countryside, and also to encourage the family members of workers and employees who had come to the cities to return to the countryside.[53] Furthermore, according to Minister of Labor Ma Wen-jui, of the 24 million workers and employees in the na-

---

49. Joint Directive of the Central Committee of the CCP and the State Council on *Prevention of Blind Exodus of Rural Population,* 18 Dec. 1957.

50. *People's Daily,* 18 Mar. 1957.

51. *New China Bi-Monthly,* No. 122 (25 Dec. 1957), pp. 95–96. These were promulgated in the name of the State Council. See Appendix M.

52. Ibid.

53. NCNA (Peking), 16 Nov. 1957.

tion, approximately 6 million were believed to be living away from their parents or spouse or both. Many of the parents and spouses frequently visited their children and husbands or wives in the cities, creating additional difficulties in urban housing, transportation, and so on.

Though provisional in 1957, these regulations apparently have since been neither revised nor supplanted. In fact, their coverage has been considerably extended as a consequence of usage and administrative interpretations. Though applicable originally to workers and employees in the several broad categories listed above, the Labor Protection Bureau of the Ministry of Labor, in 1962, offered a far more specific list of organizations covered by the 1957 provisions. These include: "state-operated and public-private jointly operated industrial establishments, communications and transportation agencies, capital construction units, commercial and financial organizations, and other administrative organs and subsidiary units; agricultural, forestry, water conservation, geological, meteorological, surveying, cultural and educational, health, and scientific research departments financed by the government; State organs, organs run by democratic parties and people's organizations in general." [54]   The regulations adopted in 1957 to deflate out-migration from rural areas of parents and spouses of urban workers and employees thus were subsequently extended to benefit workers and employees *outside* the cites.

The most unequivocal evidence of this transformation of the 1957 provisions into a general fringe benefit came in the form of an answer that the Bureau gave to the question: "Are cadres sent down *to the countryside* to take part in field work entitled to home leave?"   Although stipulating that leaves of such cadres be taken during slack farm seasons so as not to interfere with agricultural production, the Bureau stated that all cadres who fulfilled the conditions for home leave are en-

54. "Some Questions Concerning Workers' Home Leave," *Daily Worker,* 19 Dec. 1962.   In all, the bureau answered some 34 specific questions about the 1957 regulation governing home leave.

titled to do so.[55] Presumably, some such cadres go to visit their families *in the cities*.

However, the transformation of the 1957 regulations into a general welfare measure represented not at all a compromise on their original objective, i.e., to stabilize the urban population by way of a reduced flow of rural residents into the cities. Workers and employees who left their parents and spouses in the villages or whose parents or spouses returned to home villages have not been deprived of annual leaves. Rather, the change in coverage to increase cadres sent down to the countryside reflected another major development in China's efforts to stabilize her urban population. Previously, and for the several years prior to 1955, the emphasis of the various measures (the 1957 regulations included) was almost exclusively on the retention of rural residents. As one of two sources of urban growth is located within the cities themselves (i.e., natural increase), this proved insufficient. Even if the outflow of rural population could be largely curbed, urban growth can still be at a somewhat higher rate than that of increase in employment opportunities in the nonagricultural sector or the rate of construction in urban housing, educational facilities, and so on in the short run. The extension of the privilege of annual leave to "cadres sent down to the countryside" grew out of a fresh ingredient in the broadened effort to stabilize China's urban population. This new component consisted in the assisted out-migration of city residents of urban birth to established villages or rural areas selected for agricultural reclamation and settlement projects,[56] supplementing the measures devised to retain rural population.

55. Ibid. (italics added). The conditions for home leave include one full year's service without interruption, not living with parents or spouse or both, and unable to visit them on public holidays because of distance. In case husband and wife are both workers and working in two different places, only one of them is entitled to home leave.

56. Part of these efforts involved population stabilization in individual cities rather than the national urban population as such. For instance, as will be described later, Shanghai sent a number of technically trained personnel to other cities. The net effect on the total national urban population was nil, but the population of the cities involved was affected.

Previously (i.e., in the months immediately following the conclusion of the Civil War in 1949), several municipal authorities were independently involved in the relocation of refugees. Shortly thereafter, the Central Government initiated and sanctioned nationwide efforts to return rural in-migrants to the villages. However, though the stabilization of the urban population remained the fundamental goal in all these efforts, the assisted out-migration of residents of urban birth to rural areas differed from the other two types of urban population measures in three critical ways. First, in addition to those whose relocation was in agriculturally developed areas, a significant number of the out-migrants initially served as pioneers, and their places of destination were in China's frontier provinces. Second, beyond the mere fact that persons of urban birth were directly involved, a portion of the urban out-migrants were also technically, or otherwise, trained individuals. Third, along with its role in the stabilization of the population of cities of origin, urban out-migration carried positive ramifications for economic development in areas of destination as it involved the geographic redeployment of persons with at least minimal educational attainment (see chapter 7). In keeping with the policy of urban population stabilization, the extension of the home-leave privilege to urban expatriates also constituted an inducement to their relocation to places where they were needed.

Before turning to population transfers in China, a few other comments about the 1958 *Regulations Governing Household Registration* are in order. As their promulgation restored the administration of household registration to the Ministry of Public Security, its minister, Lo Jui-ching, quoted an earlier directive of the State Council as saying that rural exodus could be stopped through "strict household control." [57]   In his words, "The perfection of the household registration work is . . . a necessary condition for realizing this objective." More specifically, as he explained,

Paragraph 2 of Article 10 of the *Regulations* states: "A

57. For the text of the directive, see Appendix L.

citizen who wants to move from the countryside to a city must possess an employment certificate issued by the labor bureau of the city, a certificate of admission issued by a school, or a removal certificate issued by the household registration office of the city of destination, and must apply to the household registration office in his or her permanent place of residence for permission to move out and fulfill the removal procedures." Why this regulation? Because, as things stand at the moment, the flow of rural population into the cities has assumed a serious proportion. Some organs and enterprises fail to carry out diligently the policy of *reducing* the urban authorization and arbitrarily write to the countryside asking for [removal] certificate. Some units, instead of assisting the Government in persuading persons, who found their way blindly into the cities, to return to the countryside, allow them to live permanently in the cities. . . . This serves to aggravate the chaotic conditions and causes many difficulties to construction plans and normal life and order in the cities. As a result, some cities are overburdened with problems of mass transit, housing, supply, employment and education. At the same time, the massive flow of labor power from the countryside retards the expansion of agricultural production and construction and adversely affects agricultural production and, by the same token, the socialist construction as a whole.

In a long-term perspective, our guiding principle of socialist construction is to simultaneously develop industry and agriculture on the basis of the preferential development of heavy industry. Both industrial and agricultural production must follow the unified plans of the state. This being the case, both the urban and the rural labor power should be systematically organized according to the requirements of the socialist construction so that the urban labor is not blindly increased and the rural labor power is not blindly exported. Besides, the urban labor power at the moment already exhibits a superabundance while rural production with its great potentiality can accommodate massive labor power. It is for this reason that the government is mobilizing cadres and graduates of primary and middle schools and universities to take up work in the countryside and in mountainous regions, and one can well understand the necessity for stopping the exodus of the rural population.

Further, those who blindly move into the cities from rural areas will encounter hardship in life when they cannot find jobs. Some will wander about the city's streets, and a small segment of them, falling unwittingly to the tricks of undesirable characters of the society, will even commit larceny and fraud and disturb the urban social order.[58]

This explanation most directly, and for the first time, connected household registration with planned distribution and redistribution of China's population. It reflected the evolution of the premises, scope, and thrust of the relevant decisions. Further, it specifically pointed to the assisted out-migration of urban residents, giving it a dual role in the continuing effort to stabilize the urban population. The out-migration of urban residents was invoked as a reason for rural residents not to leave the countryside, whereas its actual realization obviously also meant some real reduction in the urban population. The interdependence of China's urban and rural demographic circumstances was made explicit. Thus juxtaposed, and in the context of national construction, the character of the interrelationship between the two dimensions was also subtly altered. Early accounts of, and decisions on, the out-migration from villages often stressed the need to find suitable jobs locally for rural surplus manpower and a gradual solution to the question of surplus manpower *in* the villages. China's demographic reservoir was her countryside, from which workers needed to carry out industrial development could and should be systematically drawn. In the last delineation, however, not only was the capability of the villages to make use of rural manpower favorably affirmed, but their capacity to absorb additional population from *without* was also positively postulated. China's cities became, as it were, a source of its surplus manpower.

This seemingly anomalous characterization of China's cities, however, was not a simple exercise in hyperbole. It was an acknowledgment both of their transmutation dictated by demographic events of post-1949 years and of the great economic and social costs generated by the rapid urbanization of the same period:

58. Lo Jui-ching, "Explanations of the Regulations Governing Household Registration."

[From] the end of 1949 to 1956, the staff of government organizations, public-private owned enterprises and industries jumped from 8 million to 24 million. A large segment of the additional workers and employees had come from villages. For every one of them, there was a number of dependents who flocked into the city with him. The migration turned especially heavy when wage adjustments fattened the workers' pocketbooks. Drawbacks in the wage and welfare system, liberal relief benefits and other subsidies, exceptionally low house rentals and medical charges, and children's schooling facilities in the cities have been some of the other factors inducing the rural exodus. It is estimated that during the period of the First Five-Year Plan alone, approximately 8 million persons flocked into cities. . . .

. . . As a result, the number of dependents make up 60 percent of the population of [more than 15 of the cities investigated by the National Planning Commission and other agencies].

The influx not only has turned persons involved from producers into sheer consumers, but also has emasculated the rural labor force, and brought new difficulties to cities, particularly newly established industrial cities. In the case of housing, the State Statistics Bureau reported, on the basis of an investigation conducted in 99 cities in September 1956, that 1.1 million workers had applied for government dormitories, and estimated that this figure would reach a total of 2.5 million if new city residents were included. And, on the assumption that some 60 percent of the workers wanted family accommodations, the state would have to build houses for 1 million bachelors and for 1.5 million families at a total cost of ¥4,488,000,000 to ¥5,615,000,000. This would be equal to 70 to 86 percent of our national industrial investment in the year before last. . . . If [this] colossal sum were to be so spent, we might as well shelve our five-year plans and forget about socialism. Take food supply for another example. On the basis of an annual per capita consumption of 400 catties of grain, we would have to increase our supply by 1.8 billion catties of grain to take care of an annual addition of 4.5 million persons to our urban population. . . . [Also] since the institution of wage adjustments that increased the purchasing power of workers for vegetables, meats and other foodstuffs, long queues have appeared in front of shops. Coal consumption has also been on a steady increase. The State Statistics Bureau reported that in 1956, urban residents used up 23,320,000 tons of coal, being 11,460,000 tons more than they consumed in 1952. . . . In addition, transportation facilities, hotels and taverns, department stores, hospitals and amusement halls, lagging behind population growth, are crammed to overflowing.[59]

The demographic antecedents of the transformation of China's cities were clearly authentic, and the economic and social consequences profound. Quite apart from the influx of rural migrants and their dependents, it was reported that "the high rate of natural multiplication of our 89 million urban population generates an estimated addition of some 2 million annually to the labor force for whom employment must be found. . . . [And], there are still unemployed persons left over from old society. Thus, in the cities the number of persons desirous of employment exceeds that of jobs available, resulting in a labor surplus. . . . The principal way to [resolve this] will be to have them participate in agricultural production on the basis of an overall arrangement and appropriate regard for all. For, only the vast rural region can absorb the ever-increasing labor force." [60] Parenthetically, this last reference also presaged the emergence of the People's Communes a few months later. Whatever their other social and cultural functions, the promotion of large-scale and divergent projects in the countryside such as big irrigation works, more intensive farming, and initiation of subsidiary as well as primary industrial undertakings, was to induce labor shortage in many communes.[61]

But, from 1955 to early 1958, the assisted out-migration of urban residents gradually expanded in magnitude and, as previously indicated, was cited as a major reason for restrictions as well as voluntary restraint on internal migration in the explanations of the 1958 *Regulations Governing Household Registration.* There arose in China a question of possible

59. Chang, Ching-wa, "Why Must We Reduce Urban Population," *Daily Worker* (Peking), 4 Jan. 1958.

60. Ibid.

61. *People's Daily,* 12 Mar. 1959.

conflict between citizens' freedom of domicile and change of residence and the restrictive provisions in the *Regulations*. The minister of public security asserted:

> It is true that certain restrictive provisions in the Draft Regulations come into conflict with the acts of a few persons who blindly move about only to serve their own interests to the neglect of the state and collective interests. But such a conflict does not amount to restriction on the citizens' freedom of domicile and change of domicile. This is because freedom stipulated in the constitution is a guided freedom instead of a state of anarchy; it is a freedom of the broad masses of the people instead of a personal, absolute freedom of a few. . . . Thus, to restrict the irrational "freedom" of a few to move about blindly is precisely intended to protect the real freedom of the broad masses of the people. . . .[62]

Mention of the constitutional issues involved in China's urban demographic decisions is only to emphasize the complex nature of population policies, and the fact that such issues were aired was itself of significance. But, pragmatically speaking, such constitutional issues were resolved not long after the establishment of the 1958 Household Registration System and the start of sponsored population transfers from the cities. Notwithstanding the administrative restrictions and the call for voluntary restraint on internal movements, the efforts to stabilize the urban population have been only relatively successful. The growth of the urban population has continued, owing to the fact that freedom of domicile and freedom of movement have been continually exercised in fact.

However, it should also be said that even though the growth of the urban population has continued, one can imagine what the situation might have been in Chinese cities had there been no efforts of the kinds described above and in the next chapter. Nowhere have there been reports that indicate that the conditions so clearly visible in such cities in India as Bombay, and especially Calcutta, also prevail in Chinese cities. The

62. Lo Jui-ching, "Explanations of the Regulations Governing Household Registration."

substance of China's demographic problems and that of India's are not dissimilar. In policy terms, China differs from India in that it has chosen to resolve its urban population dilemma in a positively different manner. It seems that China has managed to achieve a comparatively orderly urban expansion under the circumstances.

Furthermore, the relationships between the cities and the countryside have undergone change in recent years in China. Most symbolic of the transformation has been the demolition of city walls that set them apart from the surrounding rural districts. A substantive modification in the symbiosis has involved the relocation of city residents of urban birth to near and far places beyond the city limits. This out-migration of urbanites obviously is a fresh departure in historical perspective, and, perhaps, has been of some importance in the new context of recent urban population growth. Yet, part of the impetus behind this transfer of population, particularly in connection with land reclamation and border settlement, is of ancient origin. This and related developments will be taken up in the next chapter.

Population Transfers
and Land Reclamation

Chapter four

In a publication before 1949, Fei Hsiao-tung, the Chinese sociologist, espoused the thesis of earthbound village China, and illustrated it with the following anecdotes:

At its foundation, Chinese society is village-oriented and earthbound. . . . Those so-called rustic villagers . . . really constitute the foundation of Chinese society. Even though to use the term "soil-odor" to characterize them seems to be somewhat contemptuous, the word "soil" nevertheless is most apt. . . . Villagers are inseparable from the soil. Because they live in villages, tilling of the soil is the universal way of livelihood. On this Far Eastern continent of ours, in very ancient times, some unknown primitive land-cultivating peoples probably once lived. How they lived is only a matter of curiosity to us. But, on the basis of the current state of affairs, the great majority of the continent's population eke out a living by plowing through mud and water in the field. . . . The basins of the three rivers have all been turned into agricultural use. Furthermore, it is said that every son who migrated from his agricultural native land to the frontier region invariably very faithfully maintained the tradition of directly seeking a livelihood from the soil. Recently, I met an American friend who just returned from a trip to Inner Mongolia, and who [remarked] to me in an incredulous tone: after reaching the most suitable pastoral grassland, those who had gone from China proper still dig up the dirt and plant seeds. Each and every family carves out a small square lot and starts planting. The whole situation seems as though they bored themselves into the soil and saw no other way of using a piece of land! I also remember a story told me [by my former teacher] that as far as Siberia, wherever they settled and regardless of the climate, the Chinese always planted some seeds to find out whether or not it would be possible to cultivate the land. From this standpoint, our people certainly appear to be indivisible from the soil. A glorious history that rose from the soil naturally is constrained by the soil, and, at present, can not seem to be able to elevate itself to the sky.[1]

Fei's caricature of the behavior of rustic villagers (peasants) was, in this instance, based on secondhand information. But his thesis sounded both cogent and persuasive. However, the unspectacular approach to soil utilization that allegedly was in the monopoly of Chinese peasants, in fact, transcended rural China. For quite some time, in minds of officials and scholars alike, land reclamation along China's northern frontier was also synonymous with extensive use of settlers to dig and seed the land. A recent discussion of the development of the Heilungkiang-Sungari River region, for instance, was a poignant demonstration of this.

The discussion was contained in one of a series of specially edited volumes on the economic geography of Sinkiang, Inner Mongolia, Heilungkiang-Sungari River region, and the western section of the middle course of the Yellow River that the Science Publishing House of Peking published in 1956 and 1957. Included in the published volumes are a large variety of data on climatic conditions, soil composition and fertility, vegetation and forest cover, livestock, mineral resources, agricultural and industrial output and potentials, population size and density, urban growth, and transportation and communication facilities. In addition, past reclamation achievements and failures were also summarized. Based on field surveys at

1. Fei Hsiao-tung, *Earth-bound Village China*, pp. 1–2. Translated from the Chinese edition by the author (italics added).

various times in 1952 through 1957, under the auspices of the Chinese Academy of Science, these publications filled, at least somewhat, one of the gaps in the existing knowledge of China's northern frontier. In the volume on the Heilungkiang-Sungari River region, the prospects of the area as a possible outlet for agricultural settlers were assessed:

Planned transfer of population to increase the quantity of labor power is the pivotal component of the scheme for the overall development of the region's natural resources. Since liberation, in the course of the nation's large-scale economic construction, the state has already given attention to the development of the natural resources of the region. First of all, [it considered] the question of the reclamation of wasteland and expansion of agricultural production. During the last several years, the state has, according to plan, settled migrants from inside of the Great Wall in vast numbers in the region to undertake reclamation work.

According to the preliminary investigation of the Land Use Administration of Heilungkiang, there are approximately 2,850,000 hectares of arable wasteland in the region [or 42,750,000 *mou*], of which individual tracts of 500 hectares or more each comprise some 2,400,000 hectares. These wastelands are contiguous, humus rich, topographically flat, and convenient for large-scale reclamation and cultivation. Of the wastelands, some 1,000,000 hectares can be planted immediately following drainage or minor adjustments. Seen in the perspective of land resources, more than 1,000,000 persons may be settled if each settler is given one hectare of land. This would leave still unexploited some 1,500,000 hectares of grassland. It thus can be seen that so far as population transfers are concerned, the region possesses immense potentials.

In the past several years, the government has already achieved many results in the matter of organizing and placing settlers. It has also acquired a great deal useful experience and learned many lessons. According to the settlement plans of various local governments and projections of natural increase, the region's population will approximately double itself between 1955 and 1967. We believe that in the course of the overall development of the Heilungkiang valley that will start in the not too distant future, a large increase in the region's labor power can be totally realized.[2]

Thus, even if Fei's characterization of the Chinese peasant is unassailable, he seems to have overlooked the fact that the peasant's vision of land use paralleled that of the presumably more sophisticated. If the peasant was a prisoner of circumstances of past centuries, the effect of the circumstances evidently permeated Chinese society as a whole. As the circumstances proved lasting, they continued to affect policy outlook and decisions. In practice, heavy reliance on settlers has also been an integral part of post-1949 efforts to reclaim land in the border regions, though there have been significant innovations in organization and in other aspects of land reclamation projects. The purposes of this chapter are to document these efforts and to indicate continuing as well as changing significance of China's border provinces for the nation's demographic future.

Border Settlements in Historical Perspective

Of all the epithets heaped upon Chinese peasants, the term "spatially immobile" probably has the least empirical basis. Over the centuries, their migrations have been impressive in size and in distance. Beyond China's geographic boundaries, the presence of the Chinese people has been deeply felt and relatively well chronicled in near and far lands throughout the world. But knowledge of internal movements is statistically rather imprecise, to say the least, save a few instances in the present century. Rural poverty made acute by excessive exploitation in the hands of the gentry-scholar-official class, natural calamities, and so on drove many off the land. Civil strife and military devastation caused depopulation in sections of the countryside, which in turn provided room for the influx of peasants from the more congested areas. China's defeats at the hands of the Mongols, the Manchus, and others

2. Wei Chuan et al., *The Economic Geography of Heilungkiang and Sungari River Valley*, pp. 39–40.

also set in motion population redistribution in a south and south-westward direction. Thus, whatever the specific causes were at a particular juncture in time, tens of millions of peasants abandoned birthplaces out of desperation and sought a livelihood in other parts of the country and in the cities.

However, not all population movements in China were the direct results of dire circumstances. In the past, officials in disfavor and convicts were often deported to China's southern and southwestern provinces. Though only an insignificant number of persons were involved in this type of enforced migration, there were numerous government-sponsored reclamation and settlement projects in these provinces that absorbed settlers in substantial numbers.[3] In Yunnan, for example, colonies of military personnel and civilians were established in the Ming dynasty (1368–1644) as a measure of border security. Various other settlement schemes have also been attempted since the Ming in Yunnan and in adjacent provinces in response to British and French penetration into Tibet, Burma, and Indochina. This use of military and civilian settlers to secure China's frontier has been far more ancient, frequent, and extensive in such northern regions as Inner Mongolia, Sinkiang, and the northeast.

Shortly after the first unification of China in 221 B.C., soldiers were employed to fill the area on the southern bank of the Yellow River in Suiyun (now a part of the Inner Mongolia Autonomous Region); the Great Wall was completed to bolster defense against invasion from the north. During the Early Han dynasty (206 B.C.–8 A.D.), an aggressive military policy of "offense in order to defend" was successfully pursued, which also entailed agricultural settlements along the border. But, in addition to garrison troops, poor civilians were also transferred by the government to buttress the frontier. However, none of these and similar efforts of later years produced permanent peace. In fact, during the half-millennium before China's northern regions were again secured under the Ming late in the fourteenth century, the Mongols regrouped and reestablished themselves there and went on to conquer not only

3. Cf. Tang Chi-yu, *China's Reclamation and Cultivation,* chap. 3.

China but also parts of Europe. Some 250 years later on the eve of the collapse of the Ming itself, several hundreds of thousands of Chinese apparently had been settled in South Manchuria, and opened up more than 3 million *mou* of land. Again, the pacification and dominance of the area immediately to the north of the Great Wall provided the impetus for Chinese activities in the region.[4] Thus, for the most part, population transfers and land reclamation were repeatedly undertaken in pursuance of the perennial goal of filling up China's border regions, which was political and military in character.

During the Ching (1644–1911), Manchuria and Inner Mongolia were alternately open and closed to migration. In the latter region, legal prohibition was imposed from 1740 to 1897, though several migration bureaus were established at the beginning of the Ching to promote agricultural reclamation. Settlers were also excluded from Manchuria from 1669 to 1857. The initial encouragement to reclamation and settlement was to safeguard the border against incursions into China proper. The exclusion of settlers was to minimize the subversion of the indigenous economy and culture (Manchuria was the ancestral home of the Manchu rulers) and to keep the population in ignorance of ways and means potentially more dangerous to the Manchu regime (Inner Mongolia sheltered the once powerful Mongols). But migration to both Inner Mongolia and Manchuria never really stopped. Impoverished peasants continued to infiltrate the paper barriers, particularly in times of famine and other disasters in North China. The formal end of the exclusion policy came in the waning years of the Ching.

In essence, pressure of events, expedience, and external menace combined to produce the policy reversal in late Ching. Manchuria was reopened to settlers partly as the result of: (1) the start of the construction of the South Manchuria Railway by Imperial Russia and the British-enforced creation, in North China, of five additional entrepots under the terms of the Treaty of Tientsin (1858); (2) increased insecurity and devastation in North China following the Taiping and Moslem

4. Cf. T. C. Lin, "Manchuria in the Ming Empire," p. 2–43.

Rebellions; and (3) the growing need for additional revenue to finance military operations to suppress the rebels. Several areas in the eastern section of Inner Mongolia were opened to settlers in 1898 in the face of possible occupation and exploitation by the Chinese Eastern Railway, then under the control of Imperial Russia. Western Mongolia was thrown open for agricultural settlement in 1902.

The reversal in policy eventually went far beyond the mere removal of the legal ban against migration. Government-sponsored reclamation projects temporarily flourished just before the downfall of China's last imperial dynasty. Positive encouragement was actually given to settlers.[5] Though military personnel were involved in some of the settlement projects, civilians predominated in the stream of migrants to Manchuria.

Thus, in both Manchuria and Inner Mongolia, the policy swung like a pendulum. But in Sinkiang and in the provinces adjacent to it in China's northwest, a more consistent tactic was employed from the beginning of the Ching. This region was never officially closed to settlers, though actual circumstances and distance of the area effectively deterred a large-scale influx of migrants. Over the centuries of the Han, Tang, Sung, and Ming dynasties, repeated attempts were also made to penetrate forcefully into, or to trade with, the area. During the Ching period itself, possible use of soldier-settlers to

5. Cf. Tang Chi-yu, *China's Reclamation and Cultivation.* Toward the end of the Ching, the imperial authorities adopted three different methods to assist the settlement of Manchuria. (1) Cultivable land was offered to civilian settlers in one-hundred *mou* lots at four strings of coins each (with a maximum of ten lots per settler). Those who were unable to purchase the land could pay an annual rent of 600 *wen* (cents) per lot. (2) State-owned wastelands could be assigned to settlers to develop. No tax would be levied during the first five years; the rate for each hundred *mou* of land would be 650 *wen* thereafter. Those whose reclaimed land exceeded several thousand *mou* would pay the rate for a specified number of years and would become full owners of the land. (3) Settlers who were willing to go to areas that were less fertile and had a severe winter climate were exempt from rates of any kind and entitled to a subsidy of 32 *liang* (1 *liang*=1.33 oz.) of silver per person.

occupy Sinkiang's strategic places was discussed as soon as it was pacified in the first quarter of the eighteenth century. In Sinkiang (meaning "new territory"), however, in addition to security and trade considerations, the notion that newly re-claimed land would serve to alleviate land shortage in China proper had a role in the enactment of measures to establish paramilitary settlements. Family members of banished con-victs of civilian background were allowed to accompany them to the northwest. Moreover, from 1726 onward, in several northern provinces, direct recruitments of the unemployed and the poor for land reclamation projects in the area were re-peatedly made. In a number of instances, Moslems were ex-clusively involved on account of the region's religious char-acteristics. But, because of the distance and severe climatic conditions, the number of permanent settlers never was large —probably in the neighborhood of 250,000 in 1842. Renewed political hostilities and the Nien (Moslem) Rebellion of 1866–73 caused many of them to flee from Sinkiang and Kansu. A resumption of reclamation activities followed the restoration of peace, which again required the use of soldier- and convict-settlers as well as bona fide civilians till the end of the Ching.

Thus, during the Ching, as in previous centuries, the main-tenance of security and border peace constituted the main policy tenet throughout, though tactics varied. But in the course of the Manchu rule, an unprecedented demographic growth also happened. The total population of China proper doubled in a century (1751–1851) and passed the 400 million mark some time after 1841.[6] A demographic dimension perforce was added to official thinking in regard to the sparsely popu-lated border regions. However imprecisely formulated at first, this demographic calculation was gradually made explicit, and the concept of man-land ratio incorporated into the overall policy framework for coping with China's population problem in the early years of the Republican period (1912–49).

6. John D. Durand, "The Population Statistics of China A.D. 2–1953," pp. 209–57.

Frontier Land Reclamation to 1949

The developing policy framework into which demographic particulars were incorporated received definitive endorsement from persons in some influential quarters in China very shortly after the establishment of the Republic in 1912. The first piece of agrarian legislation was, for instance, entitled "Regulations Concerning the Reclamation of National Wasteland," which was promulgated by the Peking government in March 1914. Fourteen administrative districts for reclamation were created; two for the northeast, two for the northwest, one for Sinkiang, and so on.[7] The reclamation of land came to be viewed as a necessity, and became so linked to the problem of population. As Dr. Sun Yat-sen asserted:

> From the standpoint of the principle of citizens' need, population transfers, at present, are the major problem among all urgent matters. In China, the number of soldiers who should be cut currently exceeds one million. The number of people is large, which land is needed to support. In both instances, colonization is the best solution.[8]

Contemporary elaborations of this theme were numerous. One such exposition read as follows:

> In China's southeast, population density has just reached a zenith point. . . . This high demographic concentration is a both auspicious and worrisome phenomenon; it is precisely the troublesome part of the problem of distribution in the land tenure system. Even though the ancient scholars said that what is distressing is not scarcity but inequity, whether inequity [in land holdings] exists is only a matter of concern before the establishment of an [equal] land tenure system. Once it had been instituted, although disparity would no longer be present, the knottiest problem would actually be the scarcity of land.
> Therefore, to meet this problem of "scarcity," coloniza-

7. Jefferson D. H. Lamb, *The Development of the Agrarian Movement and Agrarian Legislation in China*, p. 123.

8. Sun Yat-sen, "Colonization of Mongolia and Sinkiang," as quoted in Chen Deng-yuan, *China's Land System*, p. 441.

tion and reclamation are a most potent medicine. . . . The amount of land is limited by nature, and cannot be increased [along with population growth]; hence, the transfer of surplus population to empty space is a must in the reorganization of the land tenure system.[9]

However, this loosely defined notion of border land reclamation that was in vogue remained largely untranslated into concrete measures, though actual migration to the northeastern provinces persisted and swelled according to statistics kept by the South Manchuria Railway Company. But the migratory movement to this region did not apparently benefit all parties concerned because definite measures for the establishment of a positive social policy of land acquisition and settlement were wanting.[10]

Nonetheless, the movement to Liaoning, Kirin, and Heilungkiang eventually reached an impressive magnitude and, in some years, rivaled the volume of immigration into the United

TABLE 8

NUMBER OF CHINESE MIGRANTS TO MANCHURIA, 1912–1930

(In Thousands)

YEAR	NUMBER	YEAR	NUMBER
1912	10	1922	32
1913	13	1923	342
1914	9	1924	385
1915	13	1925	473
1916	24	1926	567
1917	31	1927	1,051
1918	26	1928	1,089
1919	30	1929	1,046
1920	28	1930	748
1921	25		

SOURCE: 1912–1922, *Manchuria Yearbook* (English); 1923–1930, *Reports* of the Social and Economic Committee, Nankai University. Reproduced from Chi-yu Tang, *China's Reclamation and Cultivation*, pp. 26–27.

9. Chen Deng-yuan, *China's Land System*, pp. 433–41.

10. Franklin L. Ho, "Population Movement to the Northeastern Provinces," pp. 346–401.

States in the period just before World War I. Table 8 gives a rough account of the trend from 1912 to 1930.

Along with the increase in volume, the composition of migrants also underwent alterations. The early migrants characteristically stayed only a brief period and were not accompanied by their families. The character of migration began to change in the late 1920s; permanent settlement developed as women and children became more numerous among the migrants. But, more important, the shift from seasonal migration to permanent residence stemmed from the fact that more farmers and farmhands migrated with their families. From such provinces as Hopeh, Shantung, and Honan (which, for quite some time, furnished the bulk of the migrants to the region), they came in large numbers to settle on the land. Previously in this century, migrants found work principally in mines and forests and on the railroads and wharves. The extension of the transportation network made possible land reclamation in areas that had been inaccessible. On numerous occasions, railways and steamship companies offered reduced fares to migrants and transported them in highly congested carriers, helping to inflate the flow.

Very roughly speaking, from 1923 to 1930, some 5.7 million persons went to China's northeastern provinces. Of these, a large number of them may be operationally defined as "assisted migrants." They were the refugees transported at the initiative and expense of charitable or relief organizations. Others made the move unassisted. But the difference between the "assisted" and "unassisted" migrants was rather superficial; it was no more than a faintly discernible difference in the degree of destitution. To insist on the distinction would be in supercilious disregard of the circumstances that contributed to the spurt of migration in the late 1920s. A brief recapitulation of these is provided by two keen reporters close to the scene:

War and famine have lately aggravated the social and natural handicaps of existence in Shantung. The traditional attachment of the Chinese to their ancestral soil, which tends to make them somewhat reluctant to migrate, can no longer triumph over the unbearable misery and poverty. The latter, more than any other single factor, accounts for the magnitude of the migration movement since 1927. Shantung is noted for the frequent occurrence of famines, due primarily to drought, floods, or the ravage of locust pests. . . . The famine in 1927 affected 56 districts or *hsien* in Shantung and 20,861,000 or 60 per cent of the entire population of the province. The famine in 1928 . . . was more intensive than that of the previous year, though not so widespread. In a number of districts affected by the famine, 60 percent to 70 percent of the population was in destitution, with crop harvests . . . less than 10 percent of the normal. The situation was made worse by the constant ravages of soldiers and bandits who infested the entire province and took away whatever the famine-stricken people might still have possessed.

.   .   .   .

. . . Indeed, the effects of the famine in Shantung, aggravated by the merciless ravages of bandits, soldiers, and tax collectors, left most of the villages and rural districts in a dreadful plight. Thus, reported a foreign relief worker in 1928, on his visit to a village that was "a fair sample of the conditions in all Western Shantung":

> In some cases children and even wives have been sold for traveling expenses, the aged left behind to shift for themselves, while the men have gone to other parts where times are better. In other cases the women, children and old people have simply been left to get along as best they can, and the strong able-bodied men have gone. In still other cases, whole families have left in a body. Between 80 percent to 90 percent of the people remaining are living on chaff and cotton seed. . . . Many have already died of starvation, and others are on the verge of it. Funerals are held almost every day. People are unable to sell their land at any price, and the same is true of any furniture or other belongings which they may have. The only thing they are able to sell is women and children. Boys are selling for something like $10; girls for $10 to $30, while young women bring as much as $100 or more.

All that has been said of Shantung applies, to a less degree, to Hopeh and Honan.[11]

11. Ibid., pp. 361–63.

Thus, peasant-refugees and assisted migrants alike were the victims of identical circumstances in home provinces. It was true that numerous migrants from Honan were dispatched in groups by the Honan Relief Commission in Peking, "which gathered the destitute from all parts of Honan, furnished them with provisions, free transportation, and necessary protection on the way, and through previous arrangements, distributed them to the landlords upon their arrival in Manchuria." But much of the migratory movement was unorganized; in large numbers, peasants from Shantung and Hopeh migrated on their own. After arrival, assisted migrants and peasant-refugees alike again were confronted with identical circumstances: they remained the victims of insufficient capital and inadequate implements for farming, high interest rates, insecurity, heavy taxation, inflation, and ignorance of local currencies of diverse and fluctuating value.[12]

Toward the end of the 1920s, proposals were officially drawn up to aid the reclamation of the northeast.[13] But all this was done in vain, for Japan invaded and annexed the three provinces in 1931.

During the entire Republican period (1912–49), as previously indicated, various reclamation bureaus were created in Sinkiang, Tsinghai, Kansu, and Ninghsia to foster agricultural settlements. But achievements were spotty and transient. The War of Resistance against Japan (1937-45) halted all plans to settle additional civilians in these provinces. Though Sinkiang and Ninghsia absorbed, on an ad hoc basis, a number of flood victims and refugees from famine from Honan in 1942–44, their relocation was an account of relief expediency rather than due to demographic presumptions about the border regions. Given its extremely limited volume, the movement itself was also of little demographic significance.

Furthermore, knowledge of the carrying capacity of all the border regions was scanty; little systematic reconnaissance of the extent, quality, and distribution of reclaimable land took place during the Republican period. Twentieth-

---

12. Ibid., pp. 390–401.
13. Tang Chi-yu, *China's Reclamation and Cultivation*, pp. 20–21.

century efforts to explore their agricultural potential was truncated by political and military contingencies of the 1930s and 1940s. In demographic terms, therefore, the border provinces appeared in the 1950s as fresh and virgin territories as in the earlier decades. As previously indicated, the exploitation of their fertility initially was seen, at least, partly in terms of a massive introduction of settlers at the beginning of the People's Republic of China.

Recent Border Politics and Settlements

Of course, China's borderlands have never spelled romance only, however much agricultural and other potentials there may be. Shaped like an arched belt across the top of the country, Sinkiang, Inner Mongolia, and the northeast provinces are the points of direct contact with the Soviet Union and the People's Republic of Mongolia. Now, as in the formative years of the Chinese People's Republic, the politics of the border regions has remained a major policy impetus. To a very large extent, post-1949 border settlements, particularly in Sinkiang, were initially sanctioned on security rather than demographic or economic grounds, as had been done in past centuries.

In fact, a few years before the publication of the various volumes on the economic geography of Sinkiang and other provinces, steps had already been taken to reclaim land in this northwestern region. They were the most recent measures in the long series of similar attempts to secure the border. Pressure of events apparently resurrected the practice of converting soldiers into part-time farmers. Known as the Ili Incident and the Peitashan Incident, two open clashes occurred in the Sinkiang region in 1944–45 and in 1947, respectively, just before the establishment of the People's Republic.[14] These and other incidents along the Sino-Soviet border and inside the region itself are reminiscent of the long

14. Cf. Chou Tung-chiao, "The Peitashan Incident, Sino-Mongolian Border, and the Sinkiang Question," p. 3–10; *People's Daily*, 6 Sept. 1963.

series of externally instigated or assisted rebellions that threaten the territorial integrity of China. As before, they served to stimulate government-sponsored migration to the area.

But, the crucial question is whether border security and other considerations sustained a migration that, in recent years, is quantitatively greater than previously. The number of people involved is the only measuring rod of immediate demographic significance. This is not an easy question to answer, but a review of recent demographic changes in Sinkiang should provide some clues to it.

The population of Sinkiang nearly doubled in thirteen years, if the data in table 9 are accepted at their face value. This would mean an average rate of increase of about 4.2 percent per annum, which is more than twice the annual rate (2%) of the nation as a whole. Thus, migration presumably played an important part in the recent population growth in Sinkiang. But it is difficult to say how large a role migration actually had in this rapid increase, and it is also nearly impossible to describe who the migrants were, except in very general terms. Thus, only an overall assessment of past and future demographic developments in Sinkiang is presently possible, particularly in relation to the question of land reclamation and agricultural settlement, because the essential information is in short supply.

In his review of the available population data of Sinkiang, Freeberne came to favor a rate of migration of about 250,000 per year between 1953 and 1962. His reasons are as follows:

Han Chinese numbered between 200,000 and 300,000 in 1949. The Chinese claim that the minority population has increased by 22.5% since 1949, so that there were possibly about 2.6 million Han by the end of 1962. . . . The number of Han Chinese in 1953 [was] still only 300,000, in which case the increase must have occurred between 1953 and 1962, at the rate of about 255,000 a year. This estimate probably hides a marked upward, if fluctuating, curve in the number of Chinese immigrants, starting from a relatively low base of considerably less than 255,000. . . . The Chinese repeated the claim of a population of 7 million, first made in October 1962, in April 1964,

and again in October 1965, but obviously the population
has not remained static during the last three and a half
years. . . . In any event, especially *in view of the general
development and strategic importance of the area*, the
present population of Sinkiang is probably more than 8
million, and may be considerably higher as a result of un-
disclosed Han immigration.[15]

Freeberne's estimates of past (1953-62) and recent (1963-
66) migration to Sinkiang thus are implicitly based, in a
large measure, on nondemographic assumptions concerning
the strategic importance of the area. The validity of this assumption can be readily and fully granted. But, in the face
of it, a great deal of caution also is in order. In the absence
of an equation whereby the assumption can be converted into
population estimates, it would be easy to inflate both its short-
and long-term demographic implications. Similarly, the same

TABLE 9

GROWTH OF THE POPULATION
OF SINKIANG, 1949-1962

YEAR	POPULATION
1949	3,700,000*
1953	4,873,608†
1954	5,144,700‡
1955	5,200,000§
1956	5,300,000‖
1957	5,640,000#
1958	5,800,000**
1959	6,000,000††
1962	7,000,000‡‡

SOURCE: Adapted from Michael Freeberne, "Changes in the Sinkiang Uighur Auton-
omous Region," *Population Studies* 20, no. 1 (July 1966):105.
*Chang Chih-yi, "Land Utilization and Settlement Possibilities in Sinkiang," *Geo-
graphic Revew* 39 (1949):57-75.
†Midyear population based on the 1953 Census.
‡Year-end figure from Hu Huan-yang, *Ti-li Chih-shih*, no. 9 (1957):390-91.
§Wang Wei-ping and Hu Ying-mei, *The Sinkiang Autonomous Region* (Peking: Com-
mercial Press, 1959).
‖August 1956. *K'o-hsueh Hau-Pao* (*Science Pictorial*).
#*Ten Great Years* (Peking, 1960), p. 11.
**Sinkiang Jih-pao* (Urumchi), 29 September 1958.
††Or "about 6,000,000," ibid., 13 March, 1 November 1959.
‡‡NCNA, Urumchi, 25 October 1962.

15. Michael Freeberne. "Changes in the Sinkiang Uighur Autonomous Region," *Population Studies* 20, no. 1 (July 1966): 103-24. Reprinted by permission.

can be said of the relationship between migration and the "general development" of the area. In fact, Freeberne himself was fully aware of the possibility that his estimates may have been too high. He noted this in a footnote:

Clearly the above calculations are based on highly unsatisfactory and inadequate information. For example, the statement that the total minority population increased by 22.5% suggests that the minorities increased from about 3.5 million in 1949 [itself a suspect base year] to roughly 4.4 million. This estimate does not agree, however, with an NCNA report dated 2 June 1962 which gave Sinkiang's total minority population as " over five million people." If this last figure is the more accurate, then the number of Han Chinese in Sinkiang would be less than 2 million, which means that the estimates of Han migration given above are too high. For instance, an NCNA [Urumchi] report dated 20 September 1965 stated that the eleven non-Uighur and non-Han Chinese minorities accounted for 13% of the population. With the Uighurs totalling 67%, on this basis the Han Chinese make up only 20% of the population, or approximately 1,400,000 of the 1962 total population of 7 million, or more than 1,600,000 if the 1965 total is over 8 million, as suggested; these figures indicate an average yearly increase in the numbers of Han Chinese of at least 100,000, less than half the estimate above.[16]

Thus, according to fragmentary data from press releases and other sources, the number of Han Chinese (i.e., migrants) could have varied, as of 1962, from a net maximum of 2.6 million to a net minimum of 1.4 million. In the perspective of China's total population, this discrepancy of 1.2 million would seem small, but the practical significance of the difference is enormous. Whether the volume of migration to Sinkiang be-

16. Ibid., p. 106 n. 8. In a summary report that appeared in *People's Daily* on 2 December 1958, only 60,000 settlers went to Sinkiang. Consistent with this is a recent reference that according to a Chinese geographical atlas corrected up to 1962, only about 10 percent of the 5,640,000 people living in Sinkiang are of Han nationality, and they are mostly from the provinces of Hopeh, Shantung, and those to the west (see *Far Eastern Economic Review* 48, no. 12 [17 June 1965]: 538).

tween 1953 and 1962 was closer to the larger estimate or to the lower one bears directly on the question of the speed and scope of demographic change in relation to the area's development.

The years 1953 to 1962 saw the implementation of China's First and Second Five-Year Plans. During the period of the first plan (1953-57), the projected increase in the number of workers and employees in various enterprises and government agencies was 4,220,000; but the actual growth was at a somewhat higher rate, reaching an annual average of 1.1 million persons. Though the Second Five-Year Plan called for a slightly larger overall increase, it envisaged an annual average of only 1.4 million, or a total of 6 to 7 million additional personnel.[17] For the ten-year period as a whole, some 11.5 to 12.5 million workers and employees were added to the work force under the state plans. It would seem highly improbable that some 21 percent of the projected and real increase were involved in the development of Sinkiang alone. For this and other reasons (see below), the number of migrants to the area therefore could not have been nearly as high as 2.6 million.

The development of Sinkiang was, for reasons of cost and political considerations, likely to have also included use of a number of workers and employees recruited locally from among the various nationalities within the region. This must have limited the number of employment opportunities available under the state allocations so far as migrants were concerned. Unless assisted and promised jobs, few migrants would have come. The distance between Sinkiang and sources of potential migrants is long, even though they have been linked by a new railway. As is well known, some major determinants of previous migrations to Sinkiang and other border provinces were war, natural disaster, and so on in China's northern provinces. During the years in question, however, relative peace and prosperity obtained in the areas of origin, which undoubtedly must have constituted real disincentives to out-migration. Furthermore, industrial development in

17. Wu Ching-Chao, "A New Treatise on the Problem of China's Population," p. 8.

Sinkiang appears most unlikely to have absorbed 2.6 million workers and employees in addition to locally qualified persons. Otherwise, more than 40 percent of its economically active population would have been in nonagricultural employment; and Sinkiang would have become the most developed region of all China. The proof of this is nowhere to be found.

Two other possibilities can legitimately be suggested to account for the supposedly "heavy" migration to Sinkiang: the bulk of the migrants were in agricultural employment, or a large number of them were the dependents of employed migrants. But a careful reading of available exhortations to stimulate migration to Sinkiang found little evidence of encouragement of family migration. Instead, it was the migration of youths free of family responsibilities that was being encouraged. As Freeberne himself put it,

> the press and radio appeal[ed] to socialist awareness, patriotism and the spirit of adventure in encouraging youths to [migrate] to Sinking, but the harsh environment caused an initial backwash of population. In consequence advance parties were established to prepare the way, as in the case of demobilized army units, whose members with families in the eastern province *might* send for them after an interval of a year or so.[18]

Some of the discharged soldiers undoubtedly did send for their family members and thus helped to increase the flow of migrants into Sinkiang. The evidence is very sketchy on this point, however, making it implausible that a substantial number of the migrants were in the category of dependents.

Neither is it likely that agricultural development is Sinkiang has absorbed more than a limited number of migrants, even though considerable progress has been made in agriculture. Settlement of historically nomadic peoples, improvement and extension of irrigation systems, and the establishment of state farms have added immensely to agricultural production and population of the area. Only the last two types of activities involved "migrants," almost exclusively in the form of organ-

18. "Changes in the Sinkiang Uighur Autonomous Region," p. 117.

ized units of discharged and active military personnel. Known officially as the Sinkiang Production and Construction Corps, its officers and men developed and are operating 149 state farms in the region. Some 10 million *mou* of land are mechanically cultivated by the members of the corps.[19]

Not only has new agricultural land been costly to develop, but considerable expense also appears to have been required to maintain or retain settlers, even though they are military personnel. An account of Sinkiang's soldier-settlers' experience provides a partial indication of the extent of investment from 1949 to 1956:

> Among the military units in Sinkiang, a very special circumstance prevails. Almost every one of the soldiers has a saving from ¥5,000,000 to ¥6,000,000 [old currency]. A principal source of this saving was a bonus of ¥4,000,000 that each soldier received from the Central Government in 1953. The Central Government, in consideration of the hardship sustained by members of Sinkiang's military units, their participation in productive work to create a great deal of wealth for the country, and their help in the resolution of many national difficulties, gave each soldier a production bonus of ¥4,000,000 as a reward. Soldiers of the various units that were stationed in Sinkiang and joined in the revolution or subsequently entered Sinkiang in 1949, were all qualified to receive the bonus if they had been with their units in 1950, 1951, and 1952. Since 1953, bonuses have been determined on the basis of production record. In addition, at present, each soldier receives a supplementary allowance of over ¥100,000 each month. Ordinarily, each person can save from ¥50,000 to ¥60,000 every month. . . . When a careful auditing was done, it was discovered that during the last several years, production returns actually have not been as large as what the state supplied to each individual.[20]

Nonetheless, agricultural production of Sinkiang has been considerably augmented since 1949. To some extent, this has come about through the settlement of the region's nationali-

19. *People's Daily,* 16 Apr., 31 July 1960; and *Peking Review,* 8 Nov. 1963.

20. Chu An-ping, *The Manan River Reclamation District* p. 96.

ties in villages scattered in the various reclamation districts, but large-scale farming performed by members of the Sinkiang Production and Construction Corps has been a leading factor. Besides managing its own mechanized farms, the corps also has completed major irrigation projects and aided the diffusion of technical and other information essential to agricultural improvement.   These are soldier-farmers or ex-soldiers at work.

One early reference to this conversion of soldiers into part-time farmers[21] (and "extension agents") was contained in a progress report on China's northwest on the eve of the First Anniversary of the People's Republic in 1950.   After outlining the conditions in China's five northwestern provinces (Sinkiang, Kansu, Ninghsia, Chinghai, and Shenhsi), Peng Te-huai, the then military commander of the northwest, concluded that there is a vast amount of land in China's northwest where migrants could be employed to reclaim the land, along with an expansion of livestock-raising and industrial construction. He specifically mentioned that, on instruction from Chairman Mao, several hundreds of thousands of soldiers had been channeled into agricultural production during the preceding year. Along with disbanded soldiers from the nationalist armies, they opened up a total of over 2 million *mou* of wasteland and supplied or restored irrigation to some 3.7 million *mou* of land.[22]   These figures pertained to what took place in the *five* northwestern provinces as a whole.   It is impossible to say how many of these soldier-farmers were in Sinkiang itself.

The introduction of units of the People's Liberation Army into the latter area began in October 1949.[23]   At the time, there were two known military contingents inside the region: the Fifth Army (the Nationality Army) made up of some four regiments of local troops (and their auxiliary units) involved in the 1944 revolt against Ili and its adjacent districts, and the Twenty-second Army Group of former Nationalist soldiers

21. As distinguished from later soldier-*settlers*.

22. Peng Te-Huai, "Report on Work in New Northwest during the Last Year," pp. 1233–36.

23. Ibid.

stationed in Sinkiang. Both were incorporated into, and later identified as units of, the People's Liberation Army. It is also impossible to say how many additional soldiers were sent to Sinkiang late in 1949. According to a work report of the chairman of the Provincial People's Government of Sinkiang, the People's Liberation Army borrowed and purchased a total of some 64,322 *tan* of grain during a period of a little over four months in 1950.[24] Calculated on the basis of an individual monthly ration of 45 catties, there would be approximately 35,000 officers and men in *all* the units of the People's Liberation Army in Sinkiang at the time. In the same report, it was said that they had planned to reclaim a total of some 600,000 *mou* of wasteland in 1950, but that under the present circumstances, they would be able to exceed this goal by another 150,000 *mou*.

However, it was most unlikely that all of the soldiers were mobilized for reclamation and related activities early in 1950. Sinkiang was then not yet wholly pacified; the various recently introduced units probably were more occupied with pacification than anything else.[25] Thus, the efforts to reclaim land and to otherwise aid agriculture appear to have mainly involved resident former Nationalist soliders and those recuited from within the region. The aims were to make them agriculturally self-sufficient and to prepare conditions for an overall increase in the region's agricultural production. Various massive irrigation projects were begun in connection with the latter purpose. In the then immediate context, therefore, the significance of the participation of soldiers in agricultural and related work was decidedly local. Land reclamation was not a mechanism for settling bona fide migrants from outside the region. In 1949 and 1950, at least, the diversion of military personnel to agricultural production also may have simply represented a continuity in policy and practice of the more

24. *Hsin Hua Monthly* 2, no. 4:764–68. (One *tan*=100 catties, or 133 lbs.)

25. Peng Te-huai, in his report, characterized the role of the Fifth Army and the Twenty-second Army Group as "rendering assistance to the units sent to Sinkiang."

immediate past. Local agricultural self-sufficiency had been the goal of the Chinese Communist party before 1949, when its armies and cadres were actively engaged in land reclamation, cultivation, and so on in the Shensi-Kansu-Ninghsia Border Region and other areas under its de facto jurisdiction.[26]

The accomplishments of the Sinkiang Production and Construction Corps have been variously told. In his report entitled "Sinkiang's Great Achievements in Agriculture, 1949–1959," Saifudin, the then first secretary of the Sinkiang Uighur Autonomous Region Committee, stated:

> By 1958, a total of 220 state farms and ranches have already been established in the entire Region. Of these, 178 are mechanized farms. State farms and ranches possess more than 13,000,000 *mou* of land, which amount to more than 30 per cent of the land under cultivation in the region. More than 6,000,000 *mou* of land have been actually planted, constituting nearly 20 per cent of the region's planted area. They also have over 2,900,000,000 catties of grain, 200,000,000 catties of cotton, and quantities of animal products. Moreover, the state farms have played an important role in the socialist transformation of agriculture as well as in the demonstration of advanced agricultural techniques and management methods to the peasants.[27]

But, there has been no report on the number of persons in the various detachments of the corps. The figure of eight divisions has been cited in press dispatches as the number of military units stationed in the region. A liberal estimate would be between 150,000 to 200,000 men. Moreover, apparently not all of the 178 *mechanized* state farms belong to the Sinkiang Production and Construction Corps. A 1963 report revealed that the corps was in charge of a total of 149 mechanized farms, of which 85 were developed between 1958 and 1961. Of the 11 million *mou* of arable land in its possession, some 7.2 million *mou* were actually planted in 1963. Thus,

26. Chao Kuo-chun, *Agrarian Policy of the Chinese Communist Party*, pp. 61–62 and passim.

27. In *China's Agriculture*, No. 214 (8 Oct. 1959), pp. 19–23.

at the time of Saifudin's report in 1959, the Corps could have developed only some 100 or so of the 178 mechanized farms. In any event, before 1958, the number of state farms run by the corps was 64, according to the 1963 disclosure.[28]   Thus, though the social, political, military, and agricultural significance of the state farms may be readily granted, they are of limited demographic import before 1958, and probably have remained so since then.   They are clearly not major outlets for a surplus agricultural labor force in other parts of China.

Neither have civilian migrants become the main component part of a viable agricultural scheme in Sinkiang.   Harsh climatic and soil conditions demand efforts and resources far beyond what peasants can muster on their own.   The high cost of land reclamation in the region has been alluded to earlier. Following the long history of clashes among the various nationalities, and amid the politically still volatile circumstances, measures of security for peasant settlers entail additional expenditure.   It would also be most uneconomic to divide reclaimed land into small lots and distribute them to peasants for individual farming.   That would be in total disregard of the extent to which large-scale farming is suited to the terrain, and has contributed to its more efficient utilization.   All these and other factors have apparently combined to bring about the formal decision to establish the Sinkiang Production and Construction Corps in 1954.[29]   Though soldiers took part in agricultural production in Sinkiang almost as soon as the People's Republic was proclaimed in 1949, the formalization of their role implicitly reflected a negative assessment of the viability of large-scale peasant settlement projects.

Military participation in Sinkiang's agriculture in general

28. *People's Daily,* 9 Aug. 1963.   Consistent with this is the statement that, as of 1955, there were 73 military *and* locally controlled state farms in Sinkiang (*Sinkiang Daily,* 7 Sept. 1955).   They accounted for only 5 percent of the total planted area in Sinkiang as a whole.

29. Wang Chi-lung (director, Political Department, Sinkiang Production and Construction Corps), "Strive to Strengthen Further the Solidarity of All Nationalities in Building a New Sinkiang," p. 4.

and in the development of state farms in particular was originally prompted by nondemographic considerations only. As
approved by the State Council at its fourteenth meeting, a
major policy aim of the Sinkiang People's Government was
that "every military unit in Sinkiang must . . . positively
carry out preparation for greater production, turning all soldiers into fresh labor troops in the development of New Sinkiang."[30] This dual role of the garrison troops in Sinkiang
has recently been amplified by a general in 1965 as follows:
"With rifle in one hand and spade in the other, the officers
and men . . . safeguarded the security of the frontiers of the
motherland and helped in the socialist construction by engaging in agriculture during the past few years."[31] It should be
pointed out that when these words were uttered in 1965, the
national concern with the northwestern corner of the country
had undergone a profound change during the preceding decade and a half. Events "unheard of in the relations between
socialist countries" have taken place, and include "the en-
ticed and coerced [movement, from Sinkiang, of] several tens
of thousands of Chinese citizens into . . . the Soviet Union" in 1962.[32] Thus, unlike in the years immediately after
1949, the manifestations of concern are no longer premised
on the circumscribed basis of agricultural production. The
political realities of the northwestern portion of China's inner
frontier, coupled with its climate and soil conditions, continue
both to inspire and to frustrate attempts to bring about large-
scale agricultural in-migration.

On numerous occasions in the past, the belief that the northwest possesses vast space where migrants may possibly be used
to undertake reclamation, has been voiced. A high official
recently reiterated this view in 1964:

China has sufficient space. . . . We have rich mineral resources, and we have gigantic quantities of land which can

30. *People's Daily,* 6 Sept. 1963.

31. NCNA, 2 Jan. 1965. This is from a speech by General Tao
Chih-yueh at the first session of the Third People's Congress.

32. *People's Daily,* 6 Sept. 1963.

be cultivated. Take the northwest of China. There is, for one example, the province of Sinkiang. Only 6 million people live there, but Sinkiang could easily provide space and food for 50 million people.[33]

An in-migration of 40 million people was rumored after the publication of this statement, which is traceable only to a Western source.[34] Sinkiang's space and agricultural potentials are immense and appear capable of providing food for a population several times its present size; but the volume of recent migration to Sinkiang has been exaggerated. Developmental needs, strategic importance, and open space (Sinkiang's land area: 600,000 square miles) of the region are only too easily translated, on paper, into migration estimates. All things considered, between 1953 and 1962, the annual average number of migrants probably could have exceeded 100,000 by a very small margin. There is no evidence that a deluge of migrants has since poured into the region.

Nor will large contingents of civilian settlers be needed in the rural districts of Sinkiang, because the development of agriculture is being accelerated by mechanical means. Of course, civilian migration has been substantial relative to Sinkiang's population, and will be likely to continue. But when all the evidence is in, the flow of migrants probably has been mainly to augment the region's urban population rather than to populate the vast space.

33. From the report of an interview that Hugo Portisch, editor of the Vienna newspaper *Des Kurier,* had with a high Chinese official believed to be the foreign minister in 1964, printed in *New York Times,* 7 Aug. 1964. Note the conspicuous discrepancy between the figure of 6 million in the 1964 statement and the reported population of 7 million in 1962 (table 8). This may have been simply an error in recall during the interview.

34. *Sunday Express* (England), 11 Oct. 1964, as quoted in Freeberne, "Changes in the Sinkiang Uighur Autonomous Region," p. 122. Note the difference of 44 million between the reported population of 6 million and Sinkiang's presumed capacity to accommodate 50 million people. The rumored in-migration of 40 million may have been based on a careless reading of the 1964 statement referred to in the previous footnote.

Planned Migration and Agricultural Settlement: The Northeast

Sinkiang obviously is not a microcosm of China. Whatever land reclamation has occurred there represents, in part, the outcome of interplay of the unique circumstances inside the region itself. These have, as has been shown, permitted the settlement of only a limited number of migrants *on the land*. Additional evidence of this is an account in 1957 that, between 1949 and 1955, only about 600,000 persons were settled on reclaimed land in the country *as a whole*.[35] The record thus is far from distinguished, and the salience of the annual average of some 100,000 settlers is also considerably diminished by the possibility that as many as 40 percent of them could have been resettled within their respective provinces of origin.

In 1956, in contrast, a great deal more land reclamation was accomplished. A total of 725,000 persons were involved in the various resettlement projects throughout the nation (of whom at least 40 percent, or 292,000, to be exact, were *intra*-province settlers).[36] In all probability, however, not more than 50,000 were bound for Sinkiang.[37] Thus, the bulk (433,000) of the agricultural settlers in 1956 went to places such as the northeast, the southwest, Inner Mongolia, Hainan Island, and other northwestern provinces (i.e., Kansu and Ninghsia). This nearly fourfold increase from the yearly average of the 1949–55 period obviously reflected an acceleration in *inter*province population settlement. Behind the change of pace of reclamation, as will be shown later, lay the demographic consideration that was *not* directly involved in the planning and implementation of pre-1956 efforts to reclaim

35. Chiao Yu, "On the Problem of Resettlement and Reclamation."
36. *People's Daily,* 28 Dec. 1956.
37. *China Youths Daily* (Peking), 7 Sept. 1956. According to this report, a total of 45,000 youths from Honan Province went to Sinkiang in 1956. They constituted the full contingent of the Honan Youth Volunteers Land Reclamation Brigade, and were assigned to units of the Sinkiang Production and Construction Corps. Their arrival received much publicity in local and national press. No comparable attention was given to any other groups of volunteers from other provinces, which is taken as an indication of their numerical insignificance.

wasteland. But it had a major role in what took place in 1956: not only would planned migration, it was said, bring additional arable land under cultivation but it would also modify what has long been viewed as an imbalanced distribution of China's population. The upshot of this was the first explicit trial of the practicality of using the border provinces as a possible safety valve for population pressure in areas of high density.

Of course, Sinkiang offered a test, of sorts, of the feasibility of extensive land reclamation and population redistribution within China. But the geographic and political circumstances there are stacked, as it were, against successful settlement of a substantial number of settlers. Thus, it would seem only fair to look elsewhere in China for more fitting lessons of demographic accommodation by means of land reclamation under comparatively less harsh conditions. This consideration eliminates Kansu and Ninghsia, both of which resemble Sinkiang climatically and in other ways. The topographic and ethnographic features of the southwest (e.g., Kwangsi, Kweichow, Yunnan, and Tibet) are likewise formidable. The insular character and sphere of Hianan Island precludes a large dose of demographic infusion. Except in districts where massive irrigation sustains limited agricultural activity, Inner Mongolia is predominantly pastoral territory. Thus, the present attention is logically shifted to the northeast (Heilungkiang, Kirin, and Liaoning), where once in the present century peasants were able to settle in large numbers. The region's hospitality is above question.

Planned migration and agricultural settlement in the northeast gained momentum in 1956, as China embarked upon an elaborate program of land reclamation. This was part and parcel of the *National Programme for Agricultural Development, 1956–1967*. It was envisaged that "in the twelve years starting from 1956 the area cultivated by state farms should be increased from the 1955 figure of over 13 million *mou* to about 100 million *mou*. Wherever conditions permit, land

reclamation should be carried out by organized new settlers."[38]
Before describing the extent, forms, and lessons of actual
reclamation and settlement in China's northeast, it is essential to mention the fact that the Soviet Union had revived,
about two years earlier, its efforts to transfer population to
settle in such areas as Kazakhstan, the Altai, Novosibersk,
Omsk, and Vladivostok. The first four places are part of West
and Central Siberia and situated just at the top of Sinkiang,
and the last is almost a stone's throw from China's northeastern region. The last major effort to colonize and develop
these Russian areas occured in the 1930s.[39] Perhaps, in a very
real sense, the resumption of land reclamation activities by
the Soviet Union may have been a determinant of China's
decision to promote planned migration in the mid-1950s.

The revival of Soviet efforts was initially made in the context of agricultural development. In September 1953, the
Central Committee of the Communist Party of the Soviet
Union adopted, as a matter of great urgency, a set of priorities
for agricultural expansion. In connection with this, the Soviet
Premier Nikita Khrushchev made a special representation at
another plenary session of the Central Committee in March
1954. As a result, a formal and lengthy decree was issued on
further increasing the country's production of grain and on
putting virgin and idle lands into cultivation. Broad in geographic scope, it specified that

> an important and readily available source for increasing
> grain production quickly is the expansion of grain sowing
> by employing virgin and idle lands in Kazakhstan, Siberia,
> the Urals, the Volga region and some parts of the North
> Caucasus. . . . And that successful development of idle
> and virgin lands will depend primarily on correct selection
> of skilled executive, engineering-technical, and agronomical
> personnel and their assignment to the new land areas, and
> that . . . organized recruiting and sending of workers to

38. *National Programme for Agricultural Development, 1956–1967*,
p. 16.

39. Cf. I. Bowman, ed., *Limits of Land Settlement* (New York:
Council on Foreign Relations, 1937), pp. 156–65.

the areas of new land development must be viewed as ful-
filling an important task of the Party and government, as
a great patriotic undertaking.[40]

A resolution adopted late in March 1954, by the USSR
Council of Ministers and the Central Committee again affirmed the principle of organized recruiting of personnel to
staff newly formed state farms, and approved "the initiative
. . . of the Young Communist League Central Committee and
local YCL committees in organizing the sending out of 100,000
equipment operators from among YCL members and young
people as volunteers to work on Machine and Tractor Stations and state farms developing new lands."[41] A detailed
schedule of financial assistance to persons who would migrate
to regions with virgin and idle land was drawn up in July 1954,
together with arrangements for credits for housing and livestock and exemptions from agricultural taxes and compulsory
deliveries of farm and animal products.[42] It was hoped that
in 1956 the area sown to grain and other agricultural crops
on the newly developed lands would reach 28,000,000 to
30,000,000 hectares.[43]

In October 1954, *Pravda* stated optimistically:

> More than 300 new state farms will be formed on virgin
> and idle lands in the steppes of Kazakhstan, Siberia, the
> Urals and along the Volga. More and more new detach-
> ments of patriotic Soviet volunteers are going to the
> regions where lands are being developed. . . . The USSR
> Ministry of State Farms and local Party and Soviet agen-
> cies receive hundreds of letters from soldiers, sailors and
> sergeants in the reserves who are requesting work on the
> new state grain farms on virgin and idle lands. Thousands

40. "Central Committee Decree on Virgin and Idle Lands—I," pp.
1–6.

41. "Party, Government Decree on Virgin and Idle Lands," pp.
11–14.

42. "On Procedures for Resettlement and Special Grants to Citizens
Moving to Collective Farms Developing Virgin and Idle Lands," p. 23.

43. "Expanding Grain Production on Virgin and Idle Lands," pp.
4–5.

of former soldiers will soon be going to the new state farms.[44]

On 7 January 1955, speaking to a group of young people in Moscow, Khrushchev exhorted:

Comrades! It is a fine thing that you have decided to set off to develop the virgin lands and by your efforts reinforce the volunteers already working there and represented by speakers at this meeting. When we talked about these virgin lands last year, they seemed farther from Moscow than today. At that time few Muscovites had visited the distant regions of Kazakhstan and the Altai and, consequently, few had a specific, clear idea of those lands.

It is different now that thousands of people have gone to the virgin lands, have been there, have set to work there in fitting fashion. . . . I would like to share my impressions with you, Comrades. As you know, last year I had occasion to visit the virgin lands in Kazakhstan, the Altai and Novosibirsk and Omsk Provinces. I have lived a long time, and I spent my childhood in the Ukraine. I know its riches. As it seems to me that it would be hard to find rich soil in the Soviet Union than exists in the Ukraine! But, Comrades, the soil of Kazakhstan and the Altai is much richer! . . . But these blessed lands were left to the rabbits until recently and wild goats roamed here. It is high time that we set about developing the virgin lands. . . . There are underpopulated and in some instances entirely unpopulated districts here. But, with your active support, with the support of all our young people, this difficulty will be overcome.

It is a fine thing that it is young people who are going to the virgin lands. All those who come are working directly in production. You know that many have come to wilderness where housing has not yet been built and necessary articles of everyday life are lacking. It is easier for a young man or girl to bear these temporary difficulties than a large family. . . . Evidently things [are] not so gay. . . . But people are working there, unfrightened by the difficulties. . . . And we will not abandon this land after a year or two. We must settle on it firmly, once and for all. For this it is desirable that you marry there.

44. "Reservists Go to Virgin Lands," p. 28.

What is a married person? It means that the person wants to build a family, to settle firmly in a new place. And he who founds a family is a good citizen. The more people we have, the stronger will our country be. Bourgeois ideologists have invented many cannibalist theories, including the theory of over-population. They think about how to reduce the birth rate and the growth of population. Matters are different among us, Comrades. If we were to add 100,000,000 to our 200,000,000, it would be too few! . . . The lands in the East of our country are rich. We must go eastward beyond the Altai. What lands there are in Krasnoyarsk Territory! . . . Whatever you sow on this soil grows, and grows well. Yet this soil is still very little used. . . .

And, as Lenin said, Vladivostok, far as it is, is a city of ours! Maritime Teritory has inexhaustible possibilities for development of agriculture and particularly animal husbandry. Grasses grow in this territory as in the jungle, yet we still send meat, butter and other dairy products there. This must be corrected.

·   ·   ·   ·   ·   ·   ·   ·   ·

In a word, we must develop the empty lands in the East and settle down firmly on those lands.[45]

Khrushchev's exhortations to Soviet youths followed his visit to China and to Kazakhstan and other virgin territories for the first time in October 1954. What he saw and heard must have profoundly impressed him. By the same token, what he subsequently said cannot but have left a definite impression on those who read it in print. In one stride, he expanded the goal of organized population transfers to areas of virgin and idle lands beyond the original aim of "meeting the growing need of our country's population for consumers' goods and providing the light and food industries with abundant raw materials, within the next two to three years, on the basis of socialist industry's mighty growth."[46] Khrushchev escalated it into a call for demographic expansion to populate virgin

45. "Khrushchev's Speech to Young Settlers of New Lands," pp. 12–13.

46. "Party, Government Decree on Virgin and Idle Lands," p. 11.

and idle lands: "If we were to add 100,000,000 to our 200,000,000, it would be too few!"

Even before Khrushchev's speech to would-be settlers in January 1955, the magnitude, fervor, and particulars of the Soviet campaign to populate areas immediately north of Sinkiang undoubtedly had received close examination in China. The full text of Khrushchev's talk was instantly translated and reprinted in the February 1955 issue of *New China Monthly*, which was then the official gazette but also contained selected major announcements and events of foreign origin.[47]   As previously indicated, the Sinkiang Production and Construction Corps was formally promulgated in 1954, and its work (measured in terms of the number of state farms alone) accelerated soon thereafter.[48]

On 16 January 1955, just nine days after Khrushchev's speech, *China Youths* published an article drawing the direct attention of its readers to what he advocated. Entitled "Take Part in Labor, Go to Places Where the Country Needs You!", the article declared:

> The speech of Comrade Khrushchev not only benefits Soviet youths, but is also of great educational value for Chinese young people. . . . It reminds us of the border regions of our own motherland [such as] Hainan Island, . . . the vast and limitless landscape of Chihsi *Hsien* of Heilungkiang, [where the Soviet Union helped us to form the Friendship State Farm] . . . Sinkiang, . . . Yunnan, Kwangsi, . . . ; the development of all these places awaits us, and our motherland needs young men and women to gradually migrate to these places to open up mountains and to clear land, according to the state plan, and to develop these areas. We should warmly adore this beautiful soil of our motherland, and be prepared at all times to respond to the call of our country to go there to participate in their development. Now, like the youths of the Soviet

47. *New China Monthly,* 28 Feb. 1955, pp. 170–72.

48. See also various dispatches of NCNA from Urumchi: 15, 27 January; 2 August; 15 October; and 11 December 1956. *People's Daily,* 25 Dec. 1955.

Union, New China's youths are also marching toward the border regions in a steady stream.[49]

As shown in chapter 2, some urban residents were relocated immediately after the conclusion of the Civil War in 1949 to places in Inner Mongolia and Heilungkiang. Also, persons were assigned to the border areas to meet the need for qualified personnel in administration, survey, and development. However, these were not a part of the national decision of 1955 to institute planned migration in conjunction with land reclamation projects. Given its timing, this decision may have been, at least partly, either an attempt to emulate, or a reaction to, the varied efforts by the Soviet Union along the border between the two countries. In any event, from the mid-1955 onward, reports on young volunteers who went to the border provinces quickly turned into a flow in China.[50]

Many of these reports include reference to specific numbers of migrants going to the northeast, to Sinkiang and other border provinces. But, because of their unsystematic character and overlapping coverage, it is impossible to estimate from them the volume of migration to specific areas between the initial decision and the commencement of a relatively organized program early in 1956. However, these reports provide a sufficient documentation of the main thrust, components, and consequences of China's post-1949 land reclamation and planned migration projects.

In the background of land reclamation in the recent past was the explicit calculation that the territory of China consists of 15 billion *mou* of land, of which a little over 1.6 billion *mou* were under cultivation in the early 1950s; and according to preliminary estimates, China still has some 1.5 billion *mou* of arable land, which nearly equals the area then under the plow.

49. *China Youths,* No. 153 (16 Jan. 1955).

50. For example: *China Youths Daily* (Peking), 8 Feb., 6 Aug., 1 Sept. 1955; *People's Daily,* 26 Aug., 12 Sept. 1955, 18, 26 June, 12 Sept. 1956, 20 Jan. 1957; *Brilliance Daily* (Peking), 14 Oct. 1955; *Daily Workers* (Peking), 9 Aug. 1956; *Changchow Daily,* 1 Nov. 1956; and *Southern Daily* (Kwangchow), 26 Nov. 1956.

Of these, relatively good wastelands are reported to amount to some 44 million *mou*.[51] Thus, from the standpoint of land resources, the primary and long-term aim of land reclamation is reasonable. Potentially arable land exists in large quantity, even if the figures should prove only approximately accurate.

Within the ultimate limit of the available land, and in the short run, it is the rate and methods of reclamation that command attention. In all, it was announced early in 1955 that the Department of Agricultural Affairs had decided to survey some 111,500,000 *mou* of large tracts of flat and fertile land in fourteen provinces in three years.[52] According to one report, a total of some 48,825,000 *mou* of wasteland would be reclaimed in Heilungkiang alone. In preparation for this task in this one province, special classes were set up in 1954 to train up to two thousand surveyors by 1957.[53] But in the First Five-Year Plan, both the immediate goal and longer-term estimates were lower than the above figures. Only a total of some 38,680,000 *mou*, according to this plan, were to be reclaimed in the nation as a whole. The survey of another 100 million *mou* of wasteland would also be completed during the same period, together with the arrangements for the reclamation of some 40 million to 50 million *mou*. The latter would pave the way for reclamation projects during the Second Five-Year Plan (1958–62).[54] Thus, if the lower figures are accepted, the rate of planned reclamation would be around 9 million *mou* per annum over the entire ten-year period. The actual achievements during these years turned out to be of about this magnitude.

However, relatively little was specifically said about the methods of reclamation in 1954 and the early part of 1955. What was stated pertained to the possible employment of mechanical means to open up and cultivate new lands. An example of this was the establishment of the Friendship State

51. *Southern Daily* (Canton), 7 Dec. 1955; *People's Daily,* 6 Mar. 1956; *Brilliance Daily* (Peking), 3 Mar. 1956.
52. NCNA (Peking), 5 Jan. 1955.
53. *People's Daily,* 21 Nov. 1954.
54. *Southern Daily* (Canton), 7 Dec. 1955.

Farm in Chihsien *Hsien*, Heilungkiang, which was formally announced late in 1954. This occurred after a period of planning and negotiations with the Soviet Union, which initially provided, free of cost, all the required mechanical implements. The total area of the farm was 326,200 *mou*, which it was estimated would, in 1956 and the following years, have an annual yield of: food grain (66,120,000 lbs.), beets (33,000,000 lbs.), milk (12,000,000 lbs.), fresh beef (1,200,000 lbs.), pork (1,420,000 lbs.), eggs (781,000 lbs.), and sundry vegetables and fruits.[55] The accent was clearly on the scope and output of the project. Its capacity to absorb settlers was given no play in the announcement.

In fact, immediate large-scale population transfers appear to have been discounted at first because of the suitability of the land for mechanized farming and in view of the practical difficulties involved in mass migration. In a reply addressed to "numerous discharged soldiers, peasants, intellectuals, cadres, and students . . . [who had written to suggest] that the government institute assisted migration and land reclamation projects," the *People's Daily* cautioned in June 1955:

> In the course of our nation's economic development, to transfer people to reclaim land is an important and necessary step. It will have a major impact on the expansion of agricultural production and the output of food grain. In our nation's northeast, northwest, and southwest, land is vast, population density low, and soil rich. These circumstances are particularly suited to moving people to undertake reclamation. Therefore, the suggestion . . . is correct. At present, the government has already begun to give attention to this task, and is making preparations for some test runs. For instance, this spring, in order to assist agricultural expansion in the northeast and to alleviate the hardship of the people whose livelihood has been affected by conservation and reservoir projects along the banks of the Yellow River and elsewhere, the provincial government

55. For a description of the farm before it was actually created, see Ho I-tsun, "Make Arrangements for the Establishment of the Friendship State Farm." The first shipment of Soviet equipment arrived in January 1955 (NCNA [Peking], 5 Jan. 1955).

of Shantung relocated more than 12,000 households totalling 55,000 persons. These people joined agricultural production in various places in Kirin, Heilungkiang, and Inner Mongolia. Population transfers of this kind can serve to adjust the relationship between village manpower and land on both sides of the Great Wall and to aid peasants' production. This work hereafter will be carried on according to plan and by steps.

But, large-scale population transfers in connection with land reclamation are a complex, delicate, as well as cumbrous, task. There must be beforehand sufficient planning in all aspects. They should not be initiated carelessly. Therefore, large-scale population transfers and land reclamation should be undertaken only under supervision and planning so as to meet the nation's needs. They should also be instituted only when conditions permit. *At the moment, there will be many difficulties if we should launch large-scale population transfers to reclaim land in a hurry.*[56]

Similar statements on the desirability of planned migration also were hedged by the inclusion of explicit reminders of the difficulties involved in the dispatch of a large number of migrants to reclaim land. This was not inconsistent with the objective of land reclamation that could be realized by mechanical means—a fact that seems to have been implicit in the establishment of the Friendship State Farm. However, at about the same time, owing to a combination of circumstances, planned migration began to gain an increasingly positive endorsement in the mass media and official publications.

Some of the circumstances surrounding this development have already been alluded to earlier in this chapter, which include similar projects on the Soviet side of the border. Three other main categories of relevant events were:

1. A variety of measures were adopted to stabilize the urban population in the mid-1950s. A component of this policy was the relocation of city residents to the countryside.

2. Along with agricultural development, and in keeping with the goal of a stabilized urban demographic growth,

56. *People's Daily,* 19 June 1955 (italics added).

efforts were made to retain people in the villages.   This
entailed the finding of outlets for unemployed and under-
employed farm laborers and their assisted migration to
areas of low population density.
    3. During all this time, the advocates of family planning
as a public policy imperceptibly gathered and worked behind the scene.   Their view eventually prevailed to the
extent that an energetic drive to promote fertility control
opened early in 1957.

In the last two chapters, an analysis of the first two sets of
events has been given. The third item will be treated in the
two chapters that follow. Taken in sequence and as a whole,
the progession of these related happenings reflected the then
developing expression of concern with the distribution and
growth of China's population. As shown in the last chapter,
the year 1955 was the beginning of public discussions of the
country's demographic affairs. In terms of organizational efforts and publicity, it also was a pivotal moment in the shift
to an accelerated program of planned migration both as an
instrument of land reclamation and as an end in itself.
    The preliminaries of the impending acceleration were trans-
acted in an exchange of formal statements between five youths
of Peking suburbs and the first secretary of the China Youths
League in August 1955. The Peking Municipal Committee of
the Youths League also was an active participant from the
outset.[57] The exchange ran like this:

    From the youths to the Committee: "When we learned
    that more than one thousand million mou of wasteland of
    our country are dormant, and as the Party and nation are
    summoning us to begin reclamation, we wish we could
    immediately rush to the border regions, command the black
    dirt to turn itself over, forbid it to grow wild grasses, and
    demand it to produce foodgrain! Why is it that such good
    earth is not able to serve socialism?"[58]

    From the first secretary to the youths: "Comrades, you
    are going to Heilungkiang to undertake reclamation there.

57. China Youths Daily (Peking), 16 Aug. 1955.
58. Ibid.

Why must we make efforts to reclaim wasteland at this time? The reason is that our motherland still requires increased food production. Some say, 'Our country's food supply remains insufficient, and actually very tight.' This is correct. But, why is it still tight? This is not because our country's food production has decreased. But, because of the continuous elevation and improvement in the livelihood of the people, the demand has increased. Therefore, we have to adopt various methods to increase food production in order that we can satisfy the growing requirements of the people. What methods must we adopt in order to raise food production? The Central Committee of the Party told us three main methods: (1) to speed up the expansion of the agricultural producer cooperatives, which is at present the chief method; (2) to push improvements in farming techniques, which is a method requiring a great deal of effort; (3) to positively undertake land reclamation, which is the most promising method. . . . Comrades, the young people of the Soviet Union are able to establish Communist Youths cities on the idle land of the Far East. Why can the youths of Peking not erect a Peking Youths Farm on the prairie of Heilungkiang? We believe that our country's young people will not just construct one farm. They will build hundreds of thousands of farms all across the 1,500,000,000 *mou* of the vast wasteland."[59]

Following the exchange, teams of young volunteers for land reclamation were organized in various provinces throughout the country.[60] They were the forerunners of the substantially enlarged movement in 1956. However, as stated in the above exchange, the accent of the drive in late 1955 still was on land reclamation rather than on planned migration. The latter remained a means of augmenting the supply of cultivable land. But this soon gave way to an encouragement to planned migra-

59. Ibid., 1 Sept. 1955. This is from the text of a speech by Hu Yao-pong, the First Secretary of the Central Committee of the China Youth League, at a farewell gathering of Peking Young Reclamation Volunteers.

60. For example, such teams were organized in Shantung, Hopeh, Yunnan, Tientsin, and Canton: see *China Youths Daily,* 23 Sept., 12 Nov. 1955; *Tientsin Daily* (Tientsin), 19 Oct. 1955; *Southern Daily* (Canton), 7 Dec. 1955; and *China Youths Daily,* 14 Mar. 1956.

tion per se. As the decision to initiate large-scale planned migration was finally made, a change also occurred in the descriptions of the principal forms of land reclamation:

1. In keeping with the production plans of the agricultural producers' cooperatives [the APC's], the masses are to be mobilized to gradually make use of all small pieces of scattered wastelands near the cooperatives. The APC's that have surplus labor power may organize and dispatch reclamation brigades to compartively more distant places where they can establish branch cooperatives. When the new cooperatives are able to realize the same income as the old cooperatives, they can be separated from one another. The advantages of this approach are that it entails low expenditure, achieves quick results, and is most acceptable to the masses.

2. The second method is the transfer of population to reclaim wasteland. *For a quite long period of time to come, this is to be the chief method.* There are many instances of population transfers and land reclamation in our country's history. . . .

3. To expand and establish state farms according to plan, in places where there are large contiguous tracts of wastelands suitable for mechanized cultivation.[61]

As is evident in the above description, the first form of reclamation either was merely of local significance or, in some cases, pertained only to intraprovince resettlement projects. It has no relevance for the present assessment of planned migration and land reclamation in the northeastern provinces. Accordingly, attention is focused on the activities in the second and third categories. It should be clear at the outset that, given the identical goal, the difference between these two forms of land reclamation is chiefly in terms of labor- and capital-intensive exploitation of land resources. The difference, however, is fundamental because of its obvious demographic im-

61. Wang Feng-tsai, deputy chief of the Bureau of Land Utilization, Department of Agricultural Affairs, described these three methods in a broadcast early in 1956, which was reprinted in a volume entitled *Explanatory Statements on National Programme for Agricultural Development (Draft), 1956–1967,* pp. 61–62 (italics added). See also *People's Daily,* 6 Mar. 1956.

plications, particularly in view of the emphasis on planned population transfers as the chief method of reclamation for a quite long period of time to come.

Planned migration during this period appears to have been of two main types:

1. The shift of whole families (households) to border areas of low population density, where they were to join existing agricultural cooperatives. Each cooperative was to absorb three, five, or no more than a score of families so relocated. These families were to become members of the cooperative and, along with its old members, reclaim and cultivate small lots of wasteland with a short distance of the cooperative.

2. The dispatch of selected settlers, in organized groups, to areas of virgin land where they were to erect new villages, form new advanced agricultural cooperatives, and cultivate comparatively large pieces of reclaimed land made available by the state with the aid of modern farming equipment. Because living conditions in such reclamation areas are invariably primitive, only young settlers were sent at the initial stage to make preparations for production and eventual permanent family settlement.[62]

The meaning of the shift to a demographic emphasis in planned migration was a substantial rise in the number of interprovince settlers. As shown in table 10, between 1949 and 1958 a grand total of 1,380,000 persons were resettled on land in the northeast, northwest, and Inner Mongolia. The annual average was about 60,000 during the years 1949–55, but the yearly number of interprovince settlers rose sharply to an all-time high in 1956. In that year alone, 433,000 migrated.

However, the volume of migration diminished somewhat in 1957 and 1958, the last two years for which there are available statistics. There is little evidence that planned migration continued at all or was anywhere near the 1956–58 level after 1958. The General Office of the Department of Agricultural Reclamation, for instance, announced in June 1958 that "at

62. Ou Yu, "On the Question of Population Transfer and Land Reclamation."

TABLE 10

NUMBER OF SETTLERS, 1949–1958

YEAR	PROJECTED		REPORTED	
	Intra-province	Inter-province	Intra-province	Inter-province
1949–1955	...	...	[240,000]*	[360,000]*
1956	...	...	292,000	433,000†
1957	...	...	...	[217,000]‡
1958	300,000§	370,000§	...	[370,000]‡
Total	300,000	370,000	532,000	1,380,000§

*Chiao Yu, "On the Problem of Resettlement and Reclamation." Of some 600,000 settlers during these years, some 40% could have been intraprovince settlers. If so, only 360,000 persons could have been resettled in the border regions.

†People's Daily, 28 December 1956.

‡Estimated on the basis of the reported information for the period as a whole and for the years 1949–55 and 1956. It is assumed that the number of interprovince settlers in 1958 was the same as the projected figure of 370,000.

§People's Daily, 21 April 1958 and 2 December 1958. Of these, 140,000 were to be the family members of the settlers in 1956 and 1957. They were destined to go to Heilungkiang, Kansu, Tsinghai, and Inner Mongolia.

present, many *state farms* are in the process of major expansion, and are generally in need of additional labor power. . . . The key reclamation projects of the Department of Agricultural Reclamation are in the region east of Mishan and Chiamussu in Heilungkiang. There are approximately over 60 million *mou* of wasteland. During the period of the Second Five-Year Plan, some 20 million to 30 million *mou* will be reclaimed according to plan in the Heilungkiang region. Therefore, the amount of labor power requirement is comparatively large." However, rather than issue a general call for volunteers to go to the reclamation areas, the department established three circumscribed guidelines:

1. Of the youths unable to find employment or to continue schooling, those who volunteer for border reclamation work must be centrally handled by local people's governments and labor departments. So long as it does not contradict the principle of planned assignment and organization of labor power, volunteers can participate in reclamation work after they receive the introduction from the labor departments and the consent of the Department of Agricultural Reclamation. In principle, employed youths, continuing students, and members of the agricultural cooperatives will not be accepted. However, they may be absorbed on an individual basis if they have the consent of their respective units and the departments concerned,

and the approval of the labor departments for the reassignment.

2. The qualifications of reclamation volunteers are: clear political standing; male or female youths between 18 and 35 years of age; free from diseases; able to endure hardship; industrious; and willing to work and settle permanently in the border areas.

3. When young people request permissions to take part in reclamation, they may get in touch with local labor departments. After the local labor departments have given their consent, they can then directly approach the provincial departments of agricultural reclamation or the Department of Agricultural Reclamation. In making the trip, they must complete household registration and food-ration transfer procedures, and be in possession of sufficient sleeping gear and clothing. *In principle, they must provide their own travel expenses.*[63]

The new guidelines contrast markedly with the projections and purposes of yesteryear. Early in 1957, the case for large-scale resettlement and reclamation projects was put in the following terms:

Although the land of China is very vast and there is plenty of virgin land, the density of the population is very unevenly distributed. In the northeast and the frontierland of the northwest, the land is sparsely inhabited. Take Heilungkiang for example. In this province, there are on the average 11.7 *mou* of arable land per capita. If all the virgin land can be opened up, the arable land in the province can be doubled. Tsinghai, Kansu, and Inner Mongolia also have plenty of virgin land, but the population in these places averages below 15 persons per square kilometer.

On the other hand, some of our country's regions are very densely populated and there is insufficient arable land. For instance, in places along the coast and the middle and lower reaches of the Yangtze and Yellow Rivers, there are between 200 and 600 people to one square kilometer of land. According to the 1955 statistics of Shantung, the

---

63. *People's Daily,* 30 June 1958 (italics added). See also Hsu li-che, deputy chief of the Bureau of Settlers, Department of Agricultural Reclamation, "Letter to Young Friends."

province has a population of more than 50,000,000, but there are only about 130,000,000 *mou* of arable land. Therefore, there are less than 2.1 *mou* of land per person. In some barren alpine districts, even less arable land is available. From this standpoint, not only are resettlement and land reclamation a practical problem in the building of socialism, but they also have a theoretical foundation: this is the rational deployment of socialist agricultural productive power,—i.e., the deployment of labor power, the balancing of population density, and the readjustment of land [and man] ratio, in order to expand agricultural production. It is said that in the course of our country's socialist industrialization, we need to rationally deploy industrial productive power [which is precisely the problem of industrial distribution]. If so, then, in the process of agricultural development, there is a need to rationally readjust the phenomenon of imbalanced population distribution involving low and high man-land ratios. This will not only positively contribute to the expansion of agricultural production and an increase in grain output, it will also carry extremely important implications with respect to the promotion of balanced development of political, economic, and cultural conditions in all places throughout the nation.[64]

Thus, in view of the new prospectus of 1959, the orientation of planned migration seems to have undergone subtle yet material modifications since its acceleration in 1956. Undoubtedly, the accelerated program itself served to compound the difficulties that are generally associated with migration to the frontier regions:

Because some difficulties were encountered, and certain maladjustments developed in last year's planned migration projects, a minority of the cadres lost their confidence in this work. They have become weary and afraid of planned migration, tying their own hands and feet, avoiding migrants, and not daring to assume the initiative.[65]

However, it was also pointed out that in 1956, planned migration has, indeed, not been blemished. But the in-

64. Chiao Yu, "The Problem of Resettlement and Reclamation."

65. "The Chief Tasks in the Migration Work for 1957," *Brilliance Daily,* 6 Feb. 1957.

adequacies in question do not negate the achievements. Besides, the achievements actually predominate. . . . An increasingly positive inclination toward reclamation and production has been manifested among the migrants; and the number of them who are determined to settle down for good in the reclamation areas is steadily growing. Tens of thousands of their relations have already come or are in the process of going to the reclamation districts. Only a very few of the migrants returned to their places of origin on account of the temporary difficulties that they encountered. This is an indisputable proof of the complete feasibility of using settlers to reclaim wasteland. The claims that planned migration has failed and that settlers are not digging in for an extended stay in the reclamation areas are clearly incorrect.[66]

Thus, the fundamental cause for the changed mood seems to be unlikely to have been the practical difficulties that the greatly expanded program generated. In all probability, the shift stemmed from the debate over what was the appropriate mode of land reclamation, which developed subsequent to the implementation of the decision to expand the scope of planned migration.

The debate was phrased, at least in part, in demographic terms. But it was chiefly centered on the issue of how best to reclaim land:

In view of the circumstances during the last several years, reclamation of wasteland [as a means of augmenting arable land] should not be treated with indifference. Along with the expansion of industrial construction and the relentless growth of population, reclamation of wasteland will become more and more imperative. Of our nation's 600,000,000 population, more than 500,000,000 are in agriculture. With respect to the expansion of agricultural production, this unique feature of "demographic abundance and land shortage" of our nation makes possible the adoption of the practice of fine tilling and careful cultivating, the improvement of planting methods and farming technique, and the full exploitation of the soil, in order to increase the yield per unit of land, on the one hand. On the

66. Ibid.

other hand, this is also a weak spot in agricultural production. According to recent statistics, during the four years 1953–56, a total of some 66,000,000 *mou* of wasteland were reclaimed. Notwithstanding this achievement, the per capita arable land has actually decreased because of the continuous growth of population. It dropped from 2.85 *mou* per person in 1952 to 2.68 *mou* in 1956, registering an average reduction of 0.2 *mou* per person. Clearly, if no suitable efforts are made to reclaim wasteland to extend the acreage under cultivation, the continually growing requirements [of our nation] will not be met solely through increased yield per unit of land.

. . . Our nation has vast amounts of wasteland. Not only must the country increase arable land, but it also must develop new areas of cotton and grain production. In view of the nation's economic strength, how to utilize the scattered small pieces of wasteland as well as various large tracts of wasteland is an important question that requires research.

On the basis of past experience, insofar as small lots of wasteland are concerned, the reliance on the masses is a method that is economic and gives quick returns. From 1953 to 1956, more than 40,000,000 *mou* of land were reclaimed by this means, or an annual average of a little over 10,000,000 *mou*. Will it still be possible from now on, to not require state investments and to continue to rely on the masses to reclaim wasteland? This is wholly possible. . . .[67]

The two reasons for this were: (1) agricultural cooperativization permits the unified allocation of labor power, and (2) it also allows the unified management of the previously fragmented lots of land, following the elimination of field boundaries. However, the reliance on the masses to reclaim land could not be viewed as a chief method in the long run; for there is a fixed limit to the amount of land that could be so reclaimed. Nor was it feasible in Heilungkiang, Sinkiang, and other areas where large tracts of virign land exist and where the population is sparse. Accordingly, "the nation must devote a certain sum of money to establishing state farms."[68]

67. Chao Hsueh, "On the Question of the Reclamation of Wasteland."

68. Ibid.

In 1956, some 433,000 settlers migrated and reclaimed 6,520,000 *mou* of wasteland. The greater portion of their travel, living, and production expenses and the cost of housing construction was borne by the government, and loans from the government made up the remaining smaller part of the resettlement expenditures. According to *incomplete* statistics for 1956, the total outlay was ¥110,000,000 for the relocation of these 433,000 migrants. The government thus invested about ¥17.00 per *mou* of the land thus reclaimed. As shown in table 11, the experience in the establishment of state farms in various parts of the country indicates that the cost per unit of reclaimed land (¥32.00 and upward) was much greater than that of the land reclaimed by settlers. According to official reports, up to the end of 1956, a total of 454 large state farms were organized on newly reclaimed land, in which 13,620,000 *mou* were under cultivation.[69] Thus, the average cost per *mou* of land reclaimed by settlers appears to have been far less than that of the land opened up by mechanical means (i.e., state farms).

TABLE 11

RELATIVE COST OF LAND RECLAMATION

(State Farms Only) *

LOCATION	COST PER MOU†
Heilungkiang, Kwangtung, Kwangsi	¥ 32.00‡
Middle and Lower Yangtze Valley	33.00
Coastal areas	35.00
North China	53.00
Kansu, Sinkiang	50.00-67.00
Average	¥ 45.00

SOURCE: Adapted from Chao Hsueh, "On the Question of the Reclamation of Wasteland."
*Exclusive of investment in land improvement and irrigation work outside the state farms, and based on actual expenditure during the First Five-Year Plan.
‡ 2.355 = U.S. $1.00.
†1*mou* = 0.16 acre.

By the beginning of 1958, additional data became available. A reassessment of the relative cost of land reclamation, however, resulted in a strong case for state farms:

69. **Ibid.**

1. From the standpoint of state investment: the cost
per *mou* of the land reclaimed by settlers ranged from
¥26.00 to ¥28.00 in the case of migrants from Shantung
to Heilungkiang, to ¥50.00 for migrants from Honan to
Kansu, and to ¥65.00 in the case of migrants from Shanghai to Kiangsi. . . . Both this and the investment in state
farms [see above] are inclusive of the cost of irrigation
work outside the reclaimed areas. But also included in
the cost of state farms are investment in livestock raising,
processing plants, and afforestation projects, which are not
included in the figures for the settlement of migrants.
Secondly, the production tools of state farms all are tractors, combines, trucks, and other large-scale modern farming implements; whereas, settlers are principally equipped
with animal-driven and small implements. In actuality,
however, if the government had not established tractor
stations to frequently assist in the plowing of land, it would
have been difficult for settlers to undertake production. If
the state investment in tractor stations is included in the
cost of land reclamation by settlers, at least ¥10.00 will
have to be added to the cost of the land so reclaimed. In
fact, the cost of land reclamation by settlers is *higher* than
that of the investment in state farms.

2. From the standpoint of returns: on the whole, in the
new villages established by settlers, the recent arrivals will
not be able to master, within a certain period of time, some
of the peculiar natural conditions in the newly reclaimed
areas. At the same time, among the settlers, there are
often a number of them who had not previously participated in agricultural production. Therefore, within a
certain period of time after the formation of new villages,
they are unable to acquire agricultural production skills
fast enough. As a consequence, rapid increase in productivity is being adversely affected. The situation is entirely
different in the case of state farms, which possess advanced
scientific technique and equipment. Therefore, after their
establishment, the volume of agricultural production is, on
the whole, higher than that of agricultural cooperatives. . . .

3. From the standpoint of the production of commercial
crops: state farms are socialist agricultural enterprises of
all the people. Apart from what they need for their own
consumption, they return to the government all of the rest
of the grain, cotton, and animal products that they produce. Therefore, the proportion of commercial crops is
very high, ordinarily reaching more than 70 percent. In

the case of settlers who erect new villages and organize agricultural cooperatives, they follow the system of collective ownership. All of the grain, and other crops, that they produce are to be allocated by peasants themselves. In addition, newly reclaimed land by settlers is exempt from agricultural taxes for 3–5 years. Therefore, the volume of commercial crops is very much lower among them than among state farms, and is also less than that of the ordinary agricultural cooperatives. According to statistics, the amount of commercial crops among the ordinary agricultural cooperatives is about 30 percent of what they produce.

Furthermore, not only is the superiority of state farms evidenced in the volume of commercial crops, but its superiority also is in terms of the [large] profits transferred to the government. On the basis of an analysis of the experience of the state farms that earned a profit, the initial investment in state farms can generally be recovered within 3–4 or 5–10 years. From now on, as the level of management standards is gradually raised, the recovery of investment can be realized within still shorter periods.

As regards state investment in the settlement of migrants in new villages, however, it is impossible to calculate the number of years that may be required to recover it. Moreover, within 3–5 years, because of their exemption from agricultural taxes, the state cannot gain but little profit.

4. From the standpoint of site selection: the settlement of migrants in new villages generally requires superior economic circumstances, i.e., quality land, favorable weather, abundant water supply, numerous opportunities for subsidiary [nonfarming] occupations, convenient transportation, not too distant from old villages, and so forth. But, because of the possession of strong organization and technical strength, the selection of sites for state farms can be made on the basis of much less stringent criteria. . . .[70]

"According to the above comparisons, it is evident that during the period of the Second Five-Year Plan, the chief way to reclaim large tracts of land is to establish [additional] state farms."[71]

70. Hsiao Yu, "The Reclamation of Wasteland and the Increase in Arable Land," pp. 21–24.

71. Ibid., p. 24.

Consequently, the role of settlers in land reclamation was quietly adjusted. Though planned migration was not discounted, it was to continue in the form of individual placement in existing agricultural cooperatives. During the period of the Second Five-Year Plan, settlers would reclaim some 15,000,000–20,000,000 *mou* of wasteland, or 3,000,000–4,000,000 *mou* per annum.[72] This represented a 50 percent reduction from the projected rate of land reclamation in 1955, and amounted to only about one-third to two-thirds of what was actually reclaimed by settlers in 1956.

As noted earlier, the Department of Agricultural Reclamation issued new and more circumscribed guidelines for planned migration in June 1958. By the end of 1958, encouragement to migration also explicitly emphasized the role of migrants in the industrial, cultural, and medical development of the frontier regions rather than agricultural expansion. Furthermore, it sought to direct the flow of potential migrants to Sinkiang and Inner Mongolia rather than to China's northeast.[73] To this extent, it echoes a statement in 1956, that one aim of planned migration to the border areas was to enable minority populations to develop economically and culturally.[74]

So far as Heilungkiang and its adjacent provinces are concerned, state farms rather than mass settlements have had a predominate role in reclaiming and cultivating virgin land. Between October 1954 and October 1963, 36 large-scale mechanized state farms emerged in the lowlands of the Sungari and Ussuri Rivers. With the aid of more than 5,700 standard tractors (e.g., 15 horsepower) and 930 combine-harvesters, some 100,000-plus persons made arable a total of 6 million *mou* of land.[75] On the plane between the Great and Little Khingan Mountains and north of the Sungari, another 75 large-scale state farms were established together with several hundred new villages. There the members of

72. Ibid.

73. *People's Daily*, 2, 13 Dec. 1958.

74. Ibid., 6 Mar. 1956.

75. Ibid., 4 Aug. 1963. These farms are located in Paochin, Huyao, Mishan, Fuynan, and other *hsien*.

more than 100,000 households live and work. Over 20 percent of the land is farmed entirely by machine, and another 30 percent partially so cultivated.[76]

The importance of Heilungkiang and other border provinces obviously has remained undiminished so far as China's external relations are concerned. On the other hand, the development of their agricultural and industrial potentials has significantly expanded their place in China's economy. To the extent that this has entailed and will stimulate further in-migration, the change is of both short- and long-term demographic import. As shown in the last chapter, urban growth has been extraordinarily substantial in these areas during the last twenty years: old established cities have become truly industrial metropolises, and towns of lesser standing have attained full urban status. The prospects are for even greater urbanization.

Not that all land resources have been exploited agriculturally, for they evidently have not. As of 1963, the extent of actual reclamation in the border regions was far below the amount of wasteland that would be made arable in Heilungkiang along. Heilungkiang is estimated to have had some 1 billion *mou* of wasteland in the early 1950s.[77] Also, state farms accounted for many of the achievements described above; the number of settlers directly and indirectly involved in the projects appears to have been comparatively small. It was certainly not what was considered possible at the start of the recent planned migration scheme. In fact, as previously indicated, the use of settlers in connection with land reclamation was discouraged toward the end of 1958, after it had been emphatically endorsed in 1955. The changes of opinion

76. *Great Impartiality Daily* (Tientsin), 7 May 1963. This area is bisected by Nun Kiang, a main tributary of the Sungari. In all, there are more than 300 state farms in Heilungkiang. Of these, 111 are wholly or partly mechanized. Some 40,000 machine and technical personnel operate over 480 agricultural machine stations and related research, repair, and supply departments (*People's Daily*, 26 Sept. 1962).

77. *People's Daily*, 17 Jan. 1958.

and practice are concretely recapitulated in the following two contrasting quotations:

> Our country's population is large, and labor power abundant. In the provinces where population density is high, but land scarce, the masses have long requested that arable land be extended. In Shantung, Honan, and other provinces, migration and land reclamation are the traditions through the ages. If the government and party leadership at the various levels will only rely on the organizational strength of agricultural cooperativization, adapt to the demands of the people, and diligently exert themselves in this work, land reclamation by the masses will be smoothly expanded.[78]

> During the last few years, the responsible departments have already undertaken, in several areas, to transfer population and organize groups of youths to participate in land reclamation in distant districts. In order to encourage a positive attitude toward reclamation among settlers, and to help them build homes and start production, the government has provided some financial and material assistance. . . . But, because most wastelands are located in the frontier regions, there have been, at present, no satisfactory solutions of the problems of irrigation, transportation, and so forth. Large-scale planned migration and land reclamation are difficult to pursue. . . . Therefore, there is no need for any efforts to generally organize youths in all places throughout the country to join in land reclamation in the border regions.[79]

This changed view of planned migration is especially interesting in several other contexts. In a statement published early in 1957, the difference between the program of assisted migration of the 1950s and past population shifts was articulated:

> Resettlement and reclamation frequently took place in the history of China. Toward the end of the Ming dynasty and at the beginning of the Ching dynasty in particular, the people who left Shantung, Hopeh, Honan, and Shansi

78. Ibid., 6 Mar. 1956.
79. Ibid., 24 Mar. 1958.

to take up reclamation work in the northeast and north-west numbered several hundred thousand and even several million every year. Spontaneous and unorganized movement of population formed the salient feature of settlement and reclamation in the history of China. The causes were war, famine, foreign invasion, imperialist aggression, and feudal rule. The peasants were obliged to go elsewhere to find land to make a living. As the old saying goes, "Villages become the seat of calamity because the people are unable to bear the heavy taxation." This was what made the emigration of the peasant compulsory.

Resettlement and reclamation in New China are fundamentally different in nature from the spontaneous movement of population during the different periods in history. Resettlement and reclamation are sponsored in China today for the purposes of accelerating the realization of socialist industrialization, the development of agricultural production, and the betterment of the material and cultural life of the people. They are carried out in an organized and planned manner. They constitute a specific requirement in the *National Programme for Agricultural Development* and an important measure for developing China's national economy.[80]

In a fundamental sense, the difference throws much light on the question of the viability of large-scale planned agricultural settlements in the border areas. What took place in past eras undoubtedly was, in a large measure, a consequence of severely adverse circumstances in China's established agricultural regions. In the case of the northeast, nineteenth- and early twentieth-century migration also followed the development of the modern transportation network. Apart from the migrants who went to work on the newly introduced railroads, wharves, industrial production lines, and in the mines, peasants rapidly took up land of relatively easy accessibility. The range and intensity of reclamation more or less coincided with the factors of geography, technology, and economy. The remaining virgin lands are located in more remote districts, the settlement and cultivation of which have entailed heavy expenditures for equipment, ir-

80. Chiao Yu, "The Problem of Resettlement and Reclamation."

rigation, drainage, road construction, and so on in recent years. The suitability of the land for large-scale mechanized farming is also well known. This last fact, coupled with the cost, difficulties, and uncertain outcome of assisted migration, makes it evident that large-scale population transfers are neither a necessary nor a viable component of land reclamation efforts in the border areas. Advanced technology permits the use for agricultural purposes of more distant (and hence more expensive) land; but it remains true that, notwithstanding the planned character of the recent projects, geography and economy still are two major deterrents to the introduction of a massive number of settlers.[81]

Accordingly, a restraint was reimposed on planned migration. As restated in 1958, "to undertake planned migration in order to adjust [China's imbalanced] population density is not an urgent matter at the present time. So far as the question of the transfer of urban population to areas of reclamation is concerned, our experience during the last several years is that because the great majority of city residents have neither the habit nor the skill necessary for agricultural production, they should not participate in long-distance migration and reclamation work. They can, after apprising themselves of suitable opportunities, gradually move to nearby villages to take up physical labor and production."[82]

Of course, this departure from the policy of planned migration as a chief means of land reclamation did not demote the place of the border areas in China's economy. On the contrary, the exploitation of their mineral and other resources and their industrial growth have transformed the various regions into even more vital parts of the national life. Nor did it mean an end to land reclamation in the border areas. The role and relative success of state farms in the development of their agricultural resources are still receiving continual acclaim. But, the volume of earthbound migration from outside is, for the above reasons, most unlikely to be large.

81. In a different context, W. D. Forsyth made a similar observation; see his *The Myth of Open Spaces,* chap. 6.

82. *People's Daily,* 24 Mar. 1958.

The Lessons

The fact is that nowhere in Chinese publications have there been even roughly scientific estimates of the population-carrying capacity of China's borderlands.   In this regard, a principal difficulty seems to lie in the fact that the relationship between land settlement and land reclamation is a highly variable one.   Here lies also the important question of intensive agriculture versus extensive agriculture.   Where mechanical means are employed in reclamation work, the number of people needed per unit of land reclaimed would be small; conversely, other things being equal, a greater number of people would be required in the absence of power-driven implements. But would it be sound to transfer a large number of people and to give each of them a small piece of reclaimed land?   Or, would it be preferable to assign the reclaimed land to large-scale agricultural and allied uses with the aid of extensive mechanical equipment?

To a very large extent, some definitive, and perhaps lasting, answers have already been given to these questions.   The results of post-1949 planned migration enjoined the government from continuing large-scale planned migration both as a means of land reclamation and as a remedy for imbalanced population distribution.   Thus, it would be superfluous to calculate, even crudely, the capacity of the frontier wasteland to absorb population.   But such an attempt to define the limit of settlement has relevance insofar as a degree of demographic optimism regarding the border regions may still persist.   An estimation of this kind requires an expenditure of energy that is infinitesimal in comparison with the cost of any future revival of large-scale planned migration that it may help to prevent.

In the four years 1953-56, as previously noted, a total of 66 million *mou* of wasteland were reclaimed throughout China. Notwithstanding this considerable achievement, the per capita arable land has actually decreased partly because of the continuous growth of population.   It dropped from 2.85 *mou* per person in 1952 to 2.68 *mou* in 1956, an average reduction of nearly 0.2 *mou* per person.[83]   The decrease is also attributable, in part, to the construction of new factories, the expansion of transportation and communication facilities, the territorial growth of the cities, housing developments, and the erection of dams and hydroelectric plants.   All of these projects required space; to the extent that they encroached upon arable land, population displacement inevitably followed.   According to one official estimate, between 1949 and early 1958, over 20 million *mou* of land were requisitioned by the government in connection with various development projects.[84]   Thus, of the 66 million *mou* of reclaimed wasteland from 1953 to 1956, almost one-third merely served to replace the amount of land taken out of cultivation.   In other words, only 46 million *mou* of arable land were added to the total area under cultivation at the end of this period, or at an average of 11.5 million *mou* per year.   This achievement is slightly higher than the rate of reclamation envisaged in the First and Second Five-Year Plans.   But, as just noted, this rate of reclamation was not sufficient to offset the effect of population growth and the changed pattern of land use in and near the cities.

It was planned that during the First Five-Year Plan (1953-57), a total of some 40 million *mou* of wasteland were to be reclaimed.   During the same period, preparations would also be made for the reclamation of an additional 40 million to 50 million *mou* of wasteland during the Second Five-Year Plan (1958–62).[85]   In sum, the goal of planned reclamation was 40 million *mou* every five years.   According to preliminary statistics, of the some 1.5 billion *mou* of arable wasteland, 440 million *mou* are reported to be relatively good land.   At the planned rate, it would take a total of at least ten five-year plans, or fifty years, to reclaim all good wasteland.

In 1956, in the border regions, 433,000 settlers reclaimed some 6,520,000 *mou* of wasteland, or 15 *mou* per settler.   On

83.   Chao Hsueh, "On the Question of Reclamation of Wasteland."
84.   *People's Daily,* 7 Jan. 1958.
85.   Ibid., 6 Mar. 1956; *Brilliance Daily* (Peking), 3 Mar. 1956; and *Southern Daily* (Kwangchow), 7 Dec. 1955.

this basis, if only settlers were employed, the reclamation of the 440,000,000 *mou* of relatively good wasteland would give spatial accommodation to some 30 million persons. Of course, should each settler be allowed only 3 *mou* of reclaimed land, which is about the average individual share of land under cultivation in China proper, it would be possible, on paper, to settle a total of 140 million persons on these lands. This figure is equivalent to the estimated increase (2 percent per year) in the population of China during a period of ten years. However, as only 433,000 persons were actually resettled in 1956, it would take approximately seventy years to organize the migration of 30 million people, if it should be physically possible and financially profitable to accomplish even this limited objective. At an annual rate of growth of 2 percent, a population doubles itself in only 35 years. Even if the implementation of planned migration could be accelerated to a rate, say, four times that of the 1956 record, it would still take nearly two decades to resettle 30 million persons, or, it would take more than eighty years to relocate 140 million settlers, assuming that tiny fragments of 3 *mou* of reclaimed land would be assigned to each person. The utility of the policy of planned migration thus would be likely to be minimal in the face of a continuous population growth.

Furthermore, it also does not seem either sound or desirable to duplicate the pattern of labor-intensive agriculture prevailing in China proper in reclaimed areas. As Wilbert Moore observed, in a different context, "measures designed to alleviate pressures without changing traditional patterns [or even re-creating them] are likely to represent a short-sighted policy."[86]

Paradoxically, therefore, the years 1955, 1956, and 1957 saw simultaneously substantial gains in reclamation and the limits of land settlement in the border areas. The 1964 statement that "Sinkiang could easily provide space and food for 50 million people" should be read with an added

86. Wilbert Moore, "Utilization of Human Resources Through Industrialization," in *Demographic Analysis,* eds. J. Spengler and O. D. Duncan, p. 531.

accent on food rather than on space.[87]   In Heilungkiang
where the climatic, topographic and political factors are more
favorable than those of other frontier provinces, numerous
state farms have been established to undertake capital-intensive exploitation of the land.   The evidence underscores
the impracticability of labor-intensive farming in these
areas.   Now that this is demonstrably so, the earth ethos
that has long been associated with the settlement of border
areas should be materially revised.   The unfolding opportunities in these still sparsely populated areas can and must
be seen *not* in agricultural terms only, but rather in terms
of industrial expansion and urban growth.[88]

87. The reference to space was made, in all probability, to refute
repeated allegations outside the country that China's demographic circumstances would require spatial expansion beyond the existing boundaries.

88. Though *China's Agricultural Reclamation* resumed publication
in April 1964, after an interval of several years, no similar drive to reclaim wasteland along the frontier has taken place. Judging from the
titles of its articles (as the journal itself is not available), the contents
of this publication are largely technical in nature.

The Control of Population Numbers: Politics and Ideology

Chapter five

Numerous demographic, social, economic, political, and military circumstances were behind the various measures adopted in China in the 1950s to stabilize the urban population, to retain the rural population, and to render assistance to migrants to the border regions. All these decisions pertained to population distribution and redistribution. Their interrelatedness can best be indicated by reference to a major argument in favor of planned migration and land reclamation: "It is said that in the course of our country's socialist industrialization, we need to rationally deploy industrial productive power [which is precisely the problem of industrial distribution]. If so, then, in the process of agricultural development, there is a need to rationally readjust the phenomenon of imbalanced population distribution involving low and high man-land ratios. This will not only positively contribute to the expansion of agricultural production and an increase in grain output. It will also carry extremely important implications with respect to the promotion of balanced development of political, economic, and cultural conditions in all places throughout the nation."[1]

1. Chiao Yu, "On the Problem of Resettlement and Reclamation."

Specifically, in one discussion of this issue of imbalanced distribution of population, it was said that the northwestern region and other border provinces of China are only sparsely inhabited by minority populations (non-Han Chinese) and are characterized by a low level of cultural development. It was asserted that, after a period of planned migration and land reclamation, these areas would become prosperous and their cultural development would advance at the same pace as in other parts of the country.[2] In his assessment of food resources and population, Sun Chin-chih also called attention to this lopsided demographic pattern: "Our nation has at least 100,000,000 hectares of arable but uncultivated wastelands. The absolute majority of these lands are on the northwestern side of a line drawn from Heiho in Heilungkiang to Tengchung *Hsien* in Yunnan. The main bulk of China's 600 million people are on the southeastern side of the line. There can be no question that along with the development of New China's industrial and transportation facilities, these wastelands will be brought into full use, and can accommodate a large number of people."[3]

This last assertion also made abundantly clear the intimate connection between population size and population distribution. However, the recent experience has shown that, whatever the economic, social, political, and military returns have been, planned migration has been of little significance in the demographic context. Notwithstanding the earlier views regarding the capacity of the border areas to absorb population, virgin lands in these places are unlikely to be future outlets for demographic surplus from China's traditional agricultural regions. In view of the enormous population size, planned migration and land reclamation offers, at best, only some temporary relief of a very limited scope. The management of Chinese population affairs necessarily requires efforts beyond planned redistribution of the population. Given the close connection between population size and population distribution, it is not surprising, as the record shows, that the ques-

2. *People's Daily,* 6 Mar. 1956.
3. Sun-chih, *Food Sources and Population Growth,* p. 15.

tion of population numbers gained a measure of visible attention amid the adoption and implementation of the various
measures affecting population distribution.   Though only in
restrained terms at first, this reference to population size and
growth soon culminated in a nationwide campaign to promote
planned parenthood and provoked a simultaneous debate of
the many issues under the general rubric of the control of population numbers.

Incomparably greater in scope and implication than either
the urban dispute or the planned-migration discussion, this
fertility controversy began innocuously in September 1954,
although, following quiet deliberation, regulations governing
contraception and abortion had been approved a year earlier.
It centered around two categories of issues: (1) those having
to do with the definition and acceptability of fertility control
as a national policy, and (2) those having to do directly with
the propriety and sufficiency of specific means of conception
and birth limitation.   In actuality, of course, actions and expressions of conviction with reference to one set of the issues
exerted impact on the proceedings in the other arena or vice
versa.   However, rather than compound the entanglement of
the circumstances surrounding the whole controversy, events
in the second category will be sorted out and treated in the
pages of the next chapter.

Here in this chapter, the focus is the inception, orientation,
and direction of the birth control campaign, and the influences
shaping it.   The treatment is structured in terms of both the
political setting and ideological milieu in which the policy
took root and evolved in China.   Although ideology is a pervasive determinant of national decisions with respect to birth
control the world over, population policies are also politics,
and are necessarily and intimately tied to individuals who participate in this oldest form of human drama, politics.   As such,
the particulars of China's campaign to promote birth control
must be accounted for chronologically, the arguments and
counterarguments concerning it canvassed, and its connections
with other policy developments appreciated.   Only then will
it be possible to place the campaign in perspective and to indicate its long-term implications

In Years Past

China's population remained below 100 million before the early years of the eleventh century. It was not until the mid-eighteenth century that it passed the 200 million mark, and the population again doubled itself in the one hundred years that followed. Thus, in terms of either timing or level of growth, this rate of demographic surge resembled that of Europe between 1750 and 1850. There the population increased from 144 million to 274 million in one century.[4] In Europe, amid the rapid increase, Thomas Malthus (1766–1834), drawing upon earlier writers, wrote *An Essay on the Principle of Population* in 1798. Extensive and heated debate ensued, especially after the emergence of Neo-Malthusianism. A synthesis of the Malthusian doctrine and the more liberal view (advanced by the utilitarians) of sexual relationships other than that for the procreation of children as the sole legitimate object of the act, Neo-Malthusianism "insisted that over-large families were a cause of poverty, that restraint of late marriage was an overheavy burden to lay upon people at large, and that some artificial checks might regulate the size of families to economic bounds and enable the conception of children to be checked." This was a short step from recognizing Malthus's natural checks to population.[5] The advocacy of this led to the harassment and prosecution by public and ecclesiastical authorities of its various proponents in England, the United States, Australia, and elsewhere.[6] In spite of this, or because of it, knowledge and practice of family limitation spread as the movement for promoting contraceptive tech-

4. Inclusive of Europe and Asiatic USSR. The population of the area "European settlement" grew from 157 million to 335 million between 1750 and 1850. See United Nations, *The Determinants and Consequences of Population Trends,* p. 32–33.

5. F. H. Amphlett Micklewright, "The Rise and Decline of English Neo-Mathusianism," pp. 32–33.

6. Cf. ibid., David V. Glass, *Population Policies and Movements in Europe,* and H. Y. Tien, *Social Mobility and Controlled Fertility,* pp. 15–17.

niques gained adherents in the course of social and economic transformation.

Interestingly enough, the parallel demographic acceleration in China produced an intellectual development of a like kind there at about the same time when Malthus articulated his principle of population growth. Hung Liang-chi (1744–1809) quite independently formulated his law of population growth. Published in 1793, five years earlier than that of Malthus, Hung's view is:

. . . When peace reigns for more than a hundred years, the duration may be called a long one. And yet there are inescapable dangers. Take the population question. Population will in 30 years have increased five times and 10 times in 60 years. Within a matter of a hundred years it will have increased twenty-fold. Let us take a single family as our unit of calculation. Suppose that a single man who will become the great-grandfather or the great-great-grandfather possesses 10 rooms and 100 *mou* of land. When he gets married there will be two in the family. The two in the family will find the 10 rooms, the 100 *mou* of land more than adequate for their needs. Let us suppose, however, that the man has three sons. Now in the children's generation the father and his three sons, each with his spouse, constitute a group of eight. With eight in the family there is no overlooking the desirability of servant help. So now there will be no less than 10 people in the family. With 10 people living in 10 rooms and feeding on 100 *mou* of land, we know that their lodging and board will only just be sufficient. When the sons bear sons and they acquire wives there will be no less than 20-odd people in the home even taking possible deaths into account. With over 20 people living in 10 rooms on 100 *mou* of land we know even if they tighten their belts and live most modestly, that shelter and land will not be sufficient. When grandsons beget great-grandsons and great-grandsons beget great-great-grandsons the population will have swollen to 50 or 60 times the size we started with in the first generation. In other words, a single family of the first generation will have multiplied relentlessly into 10 families. In our sample, of course, there will be families of low fertility as well as families of high fertility. Probably the extremes cancel one another out. Someone will probably tell me that by the time we have reached great grandsons, new previously vacant land and houses will be just double, three times, or at most five times the original, whereas the population has increased 10 or 20 times. In other words, the amount of land and the number of houses will always be deficient compared with the size of the population. The number of families will always be excessive.

What, too, about the added factor of human greed? One may possess a house big enough for 100 persons. Another family may own land enough for 100 families. Small wonder that everywhere men die of hunger and cold, in wind, storm and frost, and of the dew in the morning.[7]

Suffice it to say that the views of Hung and Malthus are similar in some respects. But, there are also obvious differences between them. Hung specifically mentioned, for instance, an unequal distribution of wealth as a cause of poverty in addition to the geometric progression of population itself. That he employed the family as the unit of calculation to emphasize his observations is another difference that should be of interest to the student of the sociology of knowledge. But, above all is the differential impact their writings had on the demographic and related events in subsequent years. In contrast to Malthus's controversial legacy, Hung's career ended with his death shortly after his population essay was published. He produced neither intellectual heirs nor scholarly

7. As translated in Leo Silberman, "Hung Liang-chi: A Chinese Malthus," *Population Studies* 13, no. 3 (March 1960):262. Reprinted by permission. A copy of the original text can be found in Chen Chang-hen, *On the Population of China,* 8th ed., Addendum I. The first edition of Chen's book was printed in 1918, and was based on the author's doctoral dissertation submitted to Harvard University in January 1917. Chen included a discussion of Hung's essays in the 8th edition of his book following the publication of an article by Chang Yin-lin in a Chinese journal in 1926 (see footnote 8 below), and later reprinted it in another volume entitled *The Three People's Principles* (Shanghai: Commercial Press, Ltd., 1930), pp. 35–38. In the text the sentence "And yet there are inescapable dangers" does not appear. Also the original essay is written in the present perfect tense. Apart from these minor variations, this is a most competent translation.

adversaries. It was apparently not until 1926 that his writings were first resurrected and reprinted in China.[8]

Chen Chang-hen was also elated by Hung's exposition, and honored him enthusiastically:

> The above population view of Hung Liang-chi actually coincided, without previous arrangement, with those of Malthus, the first ancestor of demography in the west. Even though Malthus's thesis was comparatively more detailed and more articulate, . . . he merely relied on and synthesized from the writings of earlier population theorists; whereas Hung pioneered a new path single-handedly and was dependent on none.[9]

However, all this is somewhat beside the main point as Hung left behind a theory that depicted demographic processes in far more fateful terms than that of Malthus. On the possible remedies of population increase, Hung observed rhetorically:

> Does Heaven know a remedy? Flood and drought, plague and pestilence are what nature offers us as remedies, though the percentage that die in natural calamities rarely exceeds one- or two-tenths of the population.
>
> Do emperors and state officials possess remedies? They can see to it that there is no uncultivated land and no unused labor in the realm. When land is reclaimed they can move people on to it to cultivate there. In case of flood, drought and plague they can open granaries and allow the treasury to relieve the masses. But that is all there is as

---

8. Silberman's translation was prepared from an appendix to Chen Ta's *Population Problems* (Shanghai: World Press, 1933). But this was not the first reference to Hung's work in the literature after his death. See Chang Ying-lin, "Hung Liang-chi and His Principle of Population," *Eastern Miscellany* 23, no. 2 (25 Jan. 1926):67 ff. In addition to the attention paid to it by Chen Chang-hen in 1928 (see footnote 7 above), Chang Ying-lin's resurrection of Hung's writings stimulated a number of discussions by other writers in the 1930s. Cf C. F. Lung, "A Note on Hung Liang-chi, the Chinese Malthus," pp. 248 ff., and Wu Pai-shi, "The Population Theory of Hung Liang-chi," pp. 241–43.

9. Chen Chang-hen, *On the Population of China*, Addendum I, pp. vi-vii.

to the remedies that could possibly be put into effect by the emperor and the state officials.

In short, in a long reign of peace, the emperor and his officials can neither stop human reproduction, nor are the measures they do dispose of adequate to provide the people with sustenance—no more at least than what we have started.[10]

Although Malthusianism sounded no less ominous, it advocated at least "moral restraint" (delayed matrimony) as an alternate to the natural checks to population growth. Intellectually, Hung broke new ground, but he neither breached the etiquette surrounding sex and reproduction nor broached the subject of birth limitation. The fact that Hung established no dialogue with his contemporaries could have been due, in part, to his failure to mention any solution that had a semblance of practicality.

As a matter of fact, the resurrection of Hung's monologue was—ironically enough—an unanticipated sequel to the Chinese exposure to Malthusianism and Neo-Malthusianism in general and to the idea of moral restraint in particular. In the Preface written for Chen Chang-hen's *On the Population of China* (1st edition, 1918), Tsai Yuan-pei[11] commented reflectively:

Ours is a country which is fond of moralizing. While Neo-Malthusian artificial means of birth limitation are not without their corrupting effects, they are also not without merit. These are the methods in circulation in Europe and America. Our nation's moralists are exceedingly fond of exhorting unreasonable views. As soon as they hear isms of this kind, they immediately cover their ears and dash away, thereby sacrificing the portion of the saying that may be acceptable to their ears. This book rejects unnatural means means of limiting births, but promotes Malthus's principle of abstinence and modern natural method [i.e., the rhythm

10. As translated in Silberman, "Hung Liang-chi: A Chinese Malthus," p. 262.

11. Tsai Yuan-pei was a leading scholar and participant in an earlier literate revolution in China and served, among other positions, as chancellor of Peking University late in the 1910s and the early 1920s.

approach] of birth restriction. Therefore, it should elicit the reader's sympathy.[12]

In this context, it seems that a public exposition per se of possibly or probably adverse consequences of population growth would be less controversial than either an advocacy of specific means to curb it or the combined advertisment of both the consequences and the means. In any case, the fertility debate in China evidently commenced only after the importation of a mixed package of Malthusianism, Neo-Malthusianism, and kindred techniques for restricting reproduction.[13]

As in the West, there were in China those who congregated under the banner of Malthusian pessimism, while others professed anti-Malthusian optimism.[14] Initially, as noted above, an advocate of delayed marriage only, Chen Chang-hen later argued for the adoption of other methods of conception control (i.e., conventional contraceptives for the general population coupled with a program of planned sterilization of those whom he termed as "unhealthy" elements, but not including induced abortion), and for a "reproductive revolution" in China.[15] Chen vehemently critized those in the opposite camp:

In China, those who maintain an optimistic view [on population] are especially numerous at the present time. This is due to the fact that such people are blind to various realities. . . . [They do not comprehend that while increased production permits a stable and good life for a time], this enjoyment is, I am afraid, unlikely to last very long, and that major upheavals will again occur. . . . Mr. Wang Chin-chow, . . . a representative of the optimistic

12. Chen Chang-hen, *On the Population of China*, pp. 418, i–ii.

13. This should not be construed to mean that there were no contraceptive practices of an indigenous character. Nor should it be taken to imply a total ignorance or the nonexistence of delayed marriage or nonmarriage in China.

14. For a monumental work on the history of these two opposite schools of thought outside of China, see E. P. Hutchinson, *The Population Debate*.

15. Chen Chang-hen, *On the Population of China*, chapters 10 and 11.

school, also said, "The population question is merely a question of providing food. After the implementation of the Principle of People's Livelihood [i.e., one of Dr. Sun Yat-sen's Three People's Principles], the so-called population question will cease to exist." . . . But, we feel that Mr. Wang's conclusion depicts China's population problem in rather too simplistic and easy terms. Of course, people deem food an imperative necessity, and there is nothing better than when all the people can have much to eat. However, as the people have much to eat, lewd thoughts that arise from fullness of food and the comfort of warm clothing will engulf them all. It is certain that they will strive "to add sons and increase grandsons, and [to follow the adage of] the more the better." The result of this will assuredly be a recurrence of disequilibrium between "rice" and "rice-eating people." Consequently, "there will once more be great disturbances under heaven." Moreover, Dr. Sun Yat-sen's Principle of People's Livelihood is not exclusively devoted to the problem of food. Nor, furthermore, is the population problem just a problem of food.

Also, Mr. Tsai Pu-chin, too, is a representative of the optimist clique. He said, "Whether or not there is a population surplus is at present not a problem in China. We can disregard it. However, there are many persons who mistakenly viewed poverty as a phenomenon produced by overpopulation. If they use their heads to dispassionately consider it, they will see the still more general cause of poverty. This general cause is the imperfect economic system. When the economic system is no good, it will produce economic inequities; and only under the conditions of economic inequity will poverty be produced in society. This is what is meant by the saying that what is distressing is not scarcity, but inequity. In present-day China, the problem of the people's livelihood is due, not to population, but to the absence of improvements in the economic system which has been traditionally followed during the several thousands of years." . . . We can ask some counter-questions: The peasants who constitute approximately 85 percent of China's total population labor diligently all year round. Can we doubt that they do not work hard enough to increase food production? Furthermore, is it not true that peasants are unable to improve farming because of scarcity of arable land and a severe shortage of capital? Are not this scarcity of land and the concomitant shortage of capital the unique features of overpopulation? Is it really correct to assume that the general cause of China's poverty is its defective economic system? If we were to equalize great poverty and small poverty, would we be able to transform everyone into a very rich or somewhat rich person? Is it really true that our nation's poverty, inability to compete with foreigners, and lower level of productivity all have stemmed from the imperialist aggression and oppression? We are being invaded and oppressed by the imperialist powers. But, are there not many internal causes which encourage invasion and oppression from without? . . .

And, Mr. Wen Kung-chih, the author of *China's Population Problem*, also concluded. "In order that the Chinese can forever live in the world and do not have to face the prospect of extermination, [we] should not delay in seeking ways to increase the population." He also stated, "Our nation's population will certainly grow to more than 1,000,-000,000 after one hundred years. Moreover, there will be no problem of overpopulation. Nor will there be any lack of material goods. And, the state of the nation and the livelihood of the people will also not be as difficult as today. It will be possible to gradually realize the rule of harmony and equality for all people."

. . . But we feel that before the population problem of a nation or of the entire globe is satisfactorily resolved, the attainment of a world of harmony and equality is fundamentally an impossibility. What the situation was like in prehistoric times requires no elaboration here. Since recorded history, mankind has journeyed nearly 10,000 years. But, why has there not been a world of harmony and equality at present [or in the past] here in China or abroad? Why is it that the more than two thousand-year-old Confucius's dream world of harmony and equality is as far from realization as the distance between heaven and earth? We raise these two questions not at all because we harbor doubts as to whether the Three People's Principles are the path that we must follow to reach the world of harmony and equality. Rather, we only regret that Dr. Sun Yat-sen did not live long enough to complete his discourse on the Principle of People's Livelihood and to let us see his full scheme in this regard. Not only have his "comrade-readers" not been able, in accordance with his teaching, to extend by analogy his work and to remedy omissions thereof, but they have also not been able to infer or learn from the limited instructions. For the most part, they all suffer

from what Tao Yuan-ming[16] termed as the disease of "recit-
ing books eagerly but seeking no thorough comprehension,"
and are affected with what Mr. Dai Chi-tao[17] called the ail-
ment of "reading one sentence and shouting one slogan."[18]

Thus, what followed the arrival in China of Malthus and
company was a polarization of opinion among scholars, politicians, and others. The ensuing controversy was clearly not
limited to the question of the acceptability of specific means
to reduce fertility. It escalated, in a short order, to a population debate centered around the relationship between population and poverty and the issue of population growth in relation to national survival and power. It revealed a number of
very basic disagreements about China's economic and social
ills, particularly the role of population therein. As it expanded, it also engulfed the personalities, philosophies, and ideologies of the participants. What transpired was, indeed, a cause
célèbre in the politics of population.

But, the debate was inconclusive. Advocacy of birth control
continued outside the government in the 1920s and 1930s.
The visit of Margaret Sanger to China (1922) attracted considerable publicity. However, few policy measures were
adopted on the national level, although Malthus and contraception were described in relatively favorable terms in some
government-approved high school and college textbooks in
civics. Not only was there no definitive policy in regard to
population numbers, but the divergence of opinion also persisted. The resurrection of Hung Liang-chi meant little to
the great majority of the people. In the early 1940s and at
the time of the collapse of the Nationalists in 1949, moreover,

16. A famous scholar who lived from 365 to 427 A.D., Tao was admired for his refusal to crook his backbone in front of a superior officer
in order to stay in the lowly paid position of magistrate and for his
fine writings, especially an allegory that depicted a Utopia amid chaos
in Chinese society.

17. A prominent member of the Kuomintang (the Nationalists),
Dai held various ministerial posts in the government and served as
the president of the Control Yuan (a modern adaption of the imperial
censorate).

18. Chen Chang-hen, *On the Population of China*, pp. 38–41.

proponents of birth control remained external to the privy council of the state.[19]   In fact, both in and out of China, few governments took steps to reduce fertility before the 1950s.[20]   The controversy reached a standoff in China before the War of Resistance against Japan.

However, in the early 1950s a new chapter was written in China on the control of population numbers.   Though its prologue contained no dramatic statements, it gave rise to an epic campaign to promote birth control in China to be followed by another round of verbal exchange between Malthusian pessimists and anti-Malthusian optimists.   The ebb and flow of this renewed demographic debate will be chronicled in the following sections.

The Innocuous Beginning

Events in the birth control campaign in China can be conveniently divided into four phases. A speech by Shao Li-tzu on 18 September 1954 at the First National People's Congress has been generally, and erroneously, taken to be the beginning of the first phase of the birth control campaign. Shao was a deputy to the Congress and also had held high positions in the previous regime.

The inception of the campaign to promote birth control was much more innocuous than this widely publicized speech of 1954.   In an editorial in the *People's Daily* more than two and one-half years later in March 1957, it was disclosed that the State Council (the highest administrative organ in China) had already, in August 1953, quietly instructed the Ministry of Health to help the masses to control reproduction and had also approved the Ministry's revised regulations governing

19.   Furthermore, a powerful voice in favor of population growth was none other than that of Generalissimo Chiang Kai-shek (see his *China's Destiny,* trans. Wang Chung-hui [New York: Macmillan Co., 1947]).

20.   India did so only in 1951, and as late as 1959, the president of the United States, Dwight D. Eisenhower, made it very clear that the problems of the control of population numbers was not a matter for governmental concern.

contraception and induced abortion.[21]   The original regulations, therefore, must have already existed for some time, and the actual work to revise them must also have begun before that date.   The other significant point here is this: the introduction of birth control programs was not, as has also been generally assumed, simply a reaction to the consequences, real and imagined, of the fact that the 1953 population of the People's Republic of China was nearly 600 million; the action by the State Council in 1953 preceded the announcement of the census result in 1954 by some ten months.

To be sure, the census confirmation of the size of the large and growing population undoubtedly furnished a great deal of support to the person or persons who apparently had already made some small headway in introducing a de facto change in the situation.   Who were they?   Available information suggests that Shao Li-tzu was one of them, or could have been alone in this endeavor.   He was then a member of the State Council, serving apparently in a non-Communist capacity.   But, there were other non-Party members on the Council at that time.[22]

Although Shao Li-tzu certainly played an important role in the birth control campaign, the platform from which he openly advocated its necessity in September 1954 seems to have been picked accidently, as the National People's Congress then met for the first time and provided a stage that had not previously existed.   The significance of his speech lies in the fact that it anticipated much of what was said subsequently in the birth control campaign.   Shao introduced the subject in language that discredited Malthus and argued for birth control in terms of the welfare of mothers and children during the transition to socialism.[23]   He said:

It is a good thing to have a large population, but in an environment beset with difficulties, it appears that a limit

21. *People's Daily,* 5 Mar. 1957.

22. See *People's Handbook* for 1953.

23. The speech was delivered on 18 September 1954 and immediately printed in *Brilliance Daily* (Peking), 19 Sept. 1954.

should be set. The provision of the Constitution [Article 96] to place mothers and children under the protection of the state is encouraging enough. But if a child continues to be born to a mother every year even if she is no longer medically fit or when her burden has already proved to be too heavy for her, even if we disregard the sufferings of the mothers, it is no easy job for the state to place all the mothers under its protection. Lenin pointed out [in an article entitled "The Working Class and Neo-Malthusianism"] that the working class had no place for Neo-Malthusianism [whose supporters seek to spread, by means of the contraception theory, the poisonous effects of the Malthusian theory on population], but he also said: "This in no way prevents us from drastically discarding all laws seeking to punish abortion and the propagation of medical theories on contraception." In China, the question of abortion can be left alone, but [as a matter of urgency], medical theories on contraception must be propagated while contraceptives should be supplied and practical guidance on contraception given.[24]

However, this was not the first time that the question of population numbers was directly and specifically singled out for debate. In August 1949, in categorical terms, the U.S. Department of State, in its White Paper on *United States Relations with China*, injected the demographic question into the then evolving political and military situation:

The population of China during the eighteenth and nineteenth centuries doubled, thereby creating an unbearable pressure upon the land. The first problem which every Chinese government has had to face is that of feeding this population. So far none has succeeded. The Kuomintang attempted to solve it by putting many land-reform laws on the statute books. Some of these laws have failed, others have been ignored. In no small measure, the predicament in which the National Government finds itself today is due to its failure to provide China with enough to eat. A large

24. As quoted in "Communist China—The Population Problem," *Current Notes on International Affairs* (published by the Department of External Affairs in Canberra, Australia) 29, no. 11 (November 1958):713–26.

part of the Chinese Communists' propaganda consists of promises that they will solve the land problem.[25]

In reply to the above statement, Chairman Mao Tse-tung outlined, so far as is known, for the first time his view of population on 16 September 1949:

> Of all things in the world, people are the most precious. Under the leadership of the Communist Party, as long as there are people, every kind of miracle can be performed. . . . We believe that revolution can change everything, and that before long there will arise a new China with a big population and a great wealth of products, where life will be abundant and culture will flourish. All pessimistic views are utterly groundless.[26]

Specifically and directly, he took up the questions concerning the presumed relationship between overpopulation and revolution, and China's ability to support its population.

> Do revolutions arise from overpopulation? There have been many revolutions, ancient and modern, in China and abroad; were they all due to overpopulation? Were China's many revolutions in the past few thousand years also due to overpopulation? Was the American Revolution against Britain 174 years ago also due to overpopulation? . . . Each time the Chinese overthrew a feudal dynasty it was because of the oppression and exploitation of the people by the feudal dynasty, and not because of any overpopulation.

> It is a very good thing that China has a big population. Even if China's population multiplies many times, she is fully capable of finding a solution; the solution is production. The absurd argument of Western bourgeois economists like Malthus that increases in food cannot keep pace with increases in population was not only thoroughly refuted in theory by Marxists long ago but has also been completely exploded by the realities in the Soviet Union and the Liberated Areas of China after their liberation.

25. United States Department of State, *United States Relations with China*, pp. iv–v.

26. *Selected Works of Mao Tse-tung*, 4: 454.

In places like Shanghai, the problem of unemployment, or of feeding the population, arose solely because of cruel, heartless oppression and exploitation by imperialism, feudalism, bureaucrat-capitalism, and the reactionary Kuomintang government. Under the People's Government, it will take only a few years for this problem of unemployment, or of feeding the population to be solved as completely as in the northern, northeastern and other parts of the country. . . . [In short,] . . . revolution plus production can solve the problem of feeding the population.[27]

The thesis that people are the most precious of all things in the world would remain the leading premise of numerous subsequent pronouncements on the control of population numbers. For instance, it so underscored an article in the *People's Daily* of 25 April 1952. In this article, birth control was also characterized as "a means of killing off the Chinese people without shedding blood."[28] Thus, not only did the highly categorical declaration in the 1949 White Paper provoke an immediate response from China, but it also could have been a catalyst for the renewed castigation of Malthus and Neo-Malthusianism that followed. The exchange is another vivid demonstration of the fact that population policies are also politics.

Notwithstanding its external genesis, Mao's rejoinder could not have been without domestic impact. Whatever its original purposes, once enunciated it amounted to a double-edged sword that also served to cut the internal policy framework. The 1952 reiteration of Mao's view in the *People's Daily* may have been simply to dampen quiet efforts to transform the then de facto acceptance of birth control practices into a formal policy. As just noted, regulations governing contraception and abortion were innocuously *revised* by August 1953. Shao's speech therefore should probably be regarded as the beginning of the second phase of the birth control campaign.

27. Ibid., pp. 452–53.
28. *People's Daily,* 25 Apr. 1952.

The Open Advocacy

Whether Shao spoke out on his own or was the spokesman for himself and others similarly inclined on the birth control issue seems immaterial. In either case, the seed of the birth control campaign that followed originated among person or persons outside the Party. For this and other reasons (see below), its open acceptance was necessarily gradual, and eventually came in February 1957, some three and one-half years after the adoption of the 1953 measures by the State Council. The delay seems to have emanated from a prolonged search for agreement on either the rationale of birth control or the form of family-planning programs or both. The practicality of birth control had already been conceded in the 1953 move.

One salient indication of the absence of agreement lies in the more or less completely silent treatment accorded to birth control in the pages of the *People's Daily*. From August 1953, when the State Council first took action, to the end of 1956, only a handful of items on the subject were given space, none of which was of any consequence. Apart from a few short articles in *China's Women* and *China Youths* (both of which have a nationwide circulation) in 1955,[29] news about birth control appeared mostly, and infrequently, in newspapers in major provincial capitals and in Peking and Shanghai.[30] This scanty coverage contrasts sharply with those on rural-urban migration and on border settlement projects during the years in question. Other signs of the disagreement included the positive reactions to the results of the 1953 Census. An article in the *People's Daily* (1 November 1954) that discussed the implications of the population count, for instance, played up the theme "Six Hundred Million People—A Great Strength for Socialist Construction."

29. See *China Youths*, no. 4 (16 February 1955):39–40; *China's Women*, no. 4 (28 April 1955):27; and *China's Women*, no. 5 (28 May 1955):28.

30. This is based on the author's examination and classification of over five hundred news items on birth control that appeared in Chinese newspapers in the course of the birth control campaign.

Nevertheless, by September 1954 the search for a policy rationale appears to have been tentatively fruitful. The advancement of maternal and child welfare was made the fundamental raison d'être of birth control as was articulated by Shao in his public speech in September 1954. This formulation was evidently acceptable, and received a formal endorsement in the Party's chief journal, *Study*, a year later on 2 October 1955:

> In giving publicity to notes on methods of birth control, our newspapers and magazines had not been inspired by the belief that we were overpopulated. On the contrary, they did so having in mind that our country had been at one time a colonial or semicolonial country and one that was semifeudalistic and under imperialist rule so that economically, socially, culturally, and in regard to general amenities we have been rather backward. . . . Viewed from the standpoint of individual families, the fact that there are too many children in a family unduly increases the burden of the parents and adversely affects their work, their study of political doctrines, and their general livelihood. Similarly the children's education may be profoundly affected. In view of the above, in order to lessen the difficulties currently facing us, to protect maternal health, and, finally, to ensure that the next generation may be brought up better, we are not at all opposed to birth control. At the same time the publicity given by certain newspapers and magazines to methods of birth control is also necessary as well as proper.[31]

In this same article, the author simultaneously termed the Malthusian theory of population as "the most reactionary among the theories of the social sciences in capitalist society."[32] A more direct expression was voiced by another author, Chao Ching, in an article entitled "A Critique of Recent Reactionary Population Theories in China."[33] He stated,

31. Yang Ssu-ying, "On Malthusianism," pp. 24–25.

32. Ibid.

33. Chao Ching, "A Critique of Recent Reactionary Population Theories in China," pp. 26–32.

The reactionary population "theories" of the Malthusian and Neo-Malthusian schools had long been, by means of voluminous booklets and journals and through extensive use of university lecture halls, diffused in Old China. They spread a sense of pessimism among the Chinese people [particularly among youths and students], blurred their view of the power of imperialism and domestic reactionary elements, and openly abetted anti-Communist, anti-people, and anti-revolutionary activities in imperialist and domestic reactionary circles. Not only had a number of our nation's well-known scholars been deeply influenced by such reactionary "theories", but they had also once served as active propagandists of the Malthusian "views" and made utmost efforts to disseminate such reactionary thought among the people. Although, since liberation, these comrades have for the most part progressed politically, few have up to the present time thoroughly audited the effects of such reactionary population "theories."[34]

Specifically, he indicted, among others, Wu Ching-chao, Chen Chang-hen, Chen Ta, and Liang Sou-ming as the leading culprits in this regard since the 1930s. These persons were also to figure prominently in the fertility controversy in 1957 and the following several years.

On Wu Ching-chao: "Reactionary population theorists not only rendered the population problem as the most basic one of all social problems, but also were mad enough to term 'China's huge population numbers' as the chief enemy of [viable] livelihood. . . . Beveridge, the imperialist reactionary scholar, once maintained that China should, at best, have not more than 30,000,000 people. Among China's reactionary population theorists, there were also persons who agreed with this proposal."[35]

On Chen Ta: "Imperialist elements have always used 'population surplus' in defense of their aggressive wars. Following the 18 September incident, Japanese imperialism undertook [further] armed aggression against China. Reactionary politicians of Japan, the United States, England,

34. Ibid., p. 26.

35. Ibid., p. 28. (See also Wu Ching-chao, "Land Distribution and Population Accommodation"; and "Capital and Population during Industrialization," pp. 10–12.)

Germany, and France all explained such aggressive acts of Japan in terms of population pressure in Japan. . . . Among China's reactionary population theorists, not only were there persons who agreed with this view, but they also openly advocated . . . 'that in order to recover the four lost provinces, there is no dispute that we must be prepared militarily. But, the more basic problem lies, not in military preparations, but in population reduction.' "[36]

On Chen Chang-hen: "At the time when the Kuomintang reactionary elements stepped up their 'military encirclement' and 'cultural encirclement', reactionary population theorists also discarded their 'scholarly research' disguise, and publicly displayed their hostility against China's working class and peasant masses, particularly the Chinese Communist Party. A reactionary element, Chen Changhen, in his *The Three People's Principles and the Population Question,* openly demanded that 'the poor sacrifice some of their right to life,' and made explicit his own class position and stated that 'for the most part, all eugenists are much concerned about the rich and intellectual classes' right to live,' not that 'of the poor and uneducated classes.' "[37]

On Liang Sou-ming: "Another propagandist of reactionary population theories . . . , in his discussion of China's need to maintain an 'optimum population,' specially pointed out that peasants constitute the majority of the national population, and, therefore, expressed the hope that Yen Yang-chu, Liang Sou-ming, and others would, through their 'village construction movement' and 'peasant' organizations [which are actually landlords' peasant-suppressing organizations], undertake the task of reducing the peasant population. And, Liang Sou-ming and associates have, in fact, included the problem of population control among the tasks of 'village construction.' "[38]

Chao also reiterated: "Of all things in the world, people are the most precious. Under the leadership of the Communist

36. Ibid., p. 28. The 18 September Incident referred to was the beginning of Japan's occupation of China's three northeastern provinces in 1931 (see Chen Ta, *The Population Question,* p. 430).

37. Ibid., p. 28 (see Chen Chang-hen, *On The Population of China,* p. 93).

38. Ibid., p. 29.

Party, as long as there are people, any miracle known to men can be performed."[39]

Thus, the transition to an open advocacy of birth control in China in 1954 must have been preceded by a rather spirited debate behind the scenes. The shift may also have been facilitated by some tacit commitment on the part of its proponents to the welfare premise on which it would be based. The repudiation of Malthus and Neo-Malthusianism was trenchantly phrased. The indictment of Wu Ching-chao, Chen Ta, Chen Chang-hen, and Liang Sou-ming in 1955, however, was far from a true bill since all of them continued in their posts until much later when new circumstances intervened. But, it amounted to an implicit enjoinder to them and others, as well as an explicit proscription of the terms of the policy preamble. It probably also gave assurance to those who, for ideological and other reasons, were opposed to, or unsympathetic with, the idea of making birth control an official function.

The publication of these vigorous criticisms of the various Chinese scholars once again demonstrated the murkiness of the issues centered around Malthus and Neo-Malthusianism. This circumstance was later recalled by Ma Yin-chu (who was to become the most distinguished advocate of planned parenthood in 1957–60): "In 1955 . . . . I drafted a speech concerning the population question [New Population Theory], . . . and planned to deliver it at the 1955 session of the National People's Congress. Before doing so, I submitted it to the Chekiang [province] subcommittee for discussion. At the meeting of the subcommittee, all but a minority of the members either refrained from expressing any opinions, or disagreed with my views. There were people who asserted that my statements were the same as Malthus's. There were also people who asserted that, though my phraseology differed from that of Malthus, the essence of my thought was of the same persuasion. Although their opinions were not acceptable to me, I felt that they were given in good will. On my

39. Ibid., p. 31.

own initiative, I therefore withdrew the draft of the speech and waited quietly for the time to ripen enough for its presentation to the whole Congress."[40]   Ma made the contents of the speech known to the public on 31 March 1957.[41]

However, more important was the fact that planned parenthood was made a public concern in 1954, amid strong reservations about its propriety and potential benefits.   A small number of relevant articles, as has been noted above, were published, beginning in the early months of 1955.   Other significant developments (which came to light a couple of years later) were: (1) "following the symposium on the problems of birth control called by Comrade Liu Shao-chi on 27 December 1954, the Second Bureau of the State Council directed the responsible officials of the government departments concerned to form study groups on the question of contraception, [and] to put forth a number of methods to promote birth control."[42]   And, (2) the Central Committee of the Chinese Communist Party, which, in fact, is the highest policy-maker in China, followed with instructions in March 1955:   "Under the present historical circumstances and in the interest of the nation, the family, and the new generation, our Party seconds [the proposition] that reproduction be appropriately restricted."[43]

Nevertheless, some manifestations of contrary views persisted.   At the Second Plenary Session of the Chinese People's Political Consultative Conference in February 1956, for instance, Chen Po-ta, a highly placed theoretician of the Party, proclaimed, "There is no sign of overpopulation in China, . . . [and] China can provide room for at least another 600 million people."[44]

40. Ma Yin-chu, "New Population Theory," pp. 297–317. A revised version of this speech later appeared in *New Construction,* no. 11 (7 November 1959) : 52–53.

41. *Brilliance Daily* (Peking), 4 Apr. 1957.

42. *People's Daily,* 5 Mar. 1957.

43. See Wu Ching-chao, "A New Treatise on the Problem of China's Population," p. 8.

44. NCNA, 2 Feb. 1956.

Shortly thereafter, however, Premier Chou En-lai added his name to the list of persons in favor of planned parenthood. In his report to the Eighth National Congress of the Communist Party of China on 16 September 1956, Chou declared, "To protect women and children and bring up and educate our younger generation in a way conducive to the health and prosperity of the nation, we agree that a due measure of birth control is desirable."[45] However, Li Teh-chuan, the minister of health, devoted only two sentences to birth control in her report to the 1956 National People's Congress and placed it far behind such other pressing issues as the control of plague, malaria, and schistosomiasis and the establishment of health clinics as the local level.[46]

There were, of course, compelling reasons for this preoccupation with death reduction. But, here a more pertinent question is: Did the order of priorities also reflect, in substance, a deliberate procrastination in the initiation of fertility control activities on an extensive scale? This would seem unlikely to be the full story in view of the several positive endorsements of the policy. Resource allocations and time required to devise means to implement it could well have been responsible for the sluggish pace. Following his 1954 speech, for instance, Shao Li-tzu repeatedly raised the issue of birth control at both the 1955 and 1956 sessions of the National People's Congress. But, the focus of his concern was no longer on policy justifications. He urged, in 1956, the testing of contraceptive recipes collected from among practioners of traditional medicine, the acceleration of birth control propaganda, and the relaxation of restrictions on the use of conception-prevention techniques, particularly sterilization. Instead of limiting either vasectomy or salpingectomy to couples with six or more children, Shao recommended that sterilization be permitted after the birth of three or four children if both the husband and wife give the consent for one of them to undergo the op-

45. Chou En-lai, *Report on the Proposals for the Second Five-Year Plan for Development of the National Economy,* p. 99.

46. Li Teh-chuan, *The Complete Report,* pp. 143–50.

eration.[47]   About a year later, the Ministry of Health announced that sterilization would be allowed without reference to family size.[48]   Thus, in all probability, the lack of agreement on the propriety and sufficiency of specific means of fertility control and the ways of their dissemination could have, more than anything else, accounted for the apparently low place accorded planned parenthood in the Minister's report in 1956.   As stated earlier, issues of this kind will be taken up in detail in the next chapter.

But, by the end of 1956, the case for birth control seems to have been sufficiently accepted, and its rationale defined.   The best evidence of this was a speech that Mao Tse-tung delivered at a meeting of the enlarged Supreme State Council on 27 February 1957.   More than 1,800 delegates were invited to the gathering, including Chang Pai-chun and Ma Yin-chu who also spoke at the meeting and who would emerge as two of the leading personalities in the ensuing fertility controversy.[49] Published later under the well-known title *On the Correct Handling of Contradictions among the People*, the demographically relevant portions of Chairman Mao's speech read as follows:

> In drawing up plans, handling affairs or thinking over problems, we must proceed from the fact that China has a population of 600 million people.   This must never be forgotten. . . . Now, why should we make a point of this? Could it be that there are people who still do not know that we have a population of 600 million.   Of course, everyone knows this; in actual practice some are apt to forget it and act as if they thought that the fewer people and the smaller their world the better. . . . I hope these people will take a wider view and really recognize the fact that we have a population of 600 million, that this is an objective fact, and that this is our asset.   We have this large population.   It is a good thing, but of course it also has its difficulties. Construction is going ahead vigorously on all

47. These recommendations were contained in Shao's speech in *The Complete Report,* pp. 372–75.

48. *People's Daily,* 23 May 1957.

49. *New China,* no. 7 (1951):1.

fronts; we have achieved much, but in the present transitional period of tremendous social change we are still beset by many difficult problems. Progress and difficulties—this is a contradiction. However, all contradiction not only should, but can be resolved. Our guiding principles are overall planning, all-round consideration, and proper arrangements. No matter whether it is the question of food, natural calamities, employment, education, the intellectuals, the united front of all patriotic forces, the national minorities, or any other question—we must always proceed from the standpoint of overall planning and all-around consideration for the whole people; we must make whatever arrangements [that] are suitable and possible at the particular time and place and after consultation with all those concerned. On no account should we throw matters out of the back door, go around grumbling that there are too many people, that people are backward, and that things are troublesome and hard to handle. . . .

[The number of births each year was indicative of] great progress made in medical service and the general rise in living standards, especially in the countryside, and of the faith people have in the future. But this figure must also be of great concern to us all. . . . The increase in grain harvest for the last two years has been 10 million tons a year. This is barely sufficient to cover the needs of our growing population. . . . It is estimated that at present 40 percent of our youth have not been placed in primary schools. Steps must therefore be taken to keep our population for a long time at a stable level, say, of 600 million. A wide campaign of explanation and proper help must be undertaken to achieve this aim.[50]

This articulation in and by itself disclosed little that had not been said about the need for planned parenthood. The conjunction of this speech with the utterances by others and

50. Mao Tse-tung, *On the Correct Handling of Contradictions among People,* pp. 46–47. This last paragraph in the above quotation, however, does not appear in this translation. It was contained in an advanced version of the speech in circulation in Warsaw, Poland, in June 1957 (see the *New York Times,* 13 June 1957). For an indirect confirmation of this speech, see Shao Li-tzu, "Comments on Planned Reproduction." He quoted Chairman Mao as saying "there is a need to promote fertility limitation, and to control population numbers in accordance with plan."

other developments, however, reinforces the conclusion that a sufficient consensus (and, perhaps, preparations) had already been secured on the structure and course of the campaign to promote fertility planning throughout the country. In this sense, it was a ribbon-cutting pronouncement rather than a ground-breaking act.   In fact, in no way was it at variance with the welfare approach to family planning that had obviously been gaining support.   This welfare-based approbation of fertility control was initially outlined in Shao Li-tzu's speech of September 1954.

There can be no doubt that the public endorsement by Chairman Mao Tse-tung of fertility limitation added much to the impetus of its implementation.   But, it should be noted that the approval itself was also accelerated by such demographic events as improved mortality conditions at the time. More importantly, it came at a time when, as has been detailed in chapters 2, 3, and 4, the various measures to stablize the urban population, to retain rural residents, and to encourage migration to the border regions had been put to test for several years.   The accumulated knowledge of population dynamics was considerable.   And, in the larger context of population numbers, the outcome of such efforts must have been highly instructive and influential in the timing of Chairman Mao's public sanction of fertility limitation.

Thus, on the question of the acceptability and definition of planned parenthood, a pragmatic compromise was reached on the basis of practicality and a give-and-take exchange.   Thus, however circumscribed, the welfare-oriented argument in favor of family limitation was irrefutably clear and clean.   Under the circumstances, it was almost an instance of demographic serendipity that should have satisfied family-planning advocates everywhere: in substance, it was of both nonpartisan simplicity and unpretentious persuasiveness.

Of course, a legitimate question is: Was the resultant accommodation achieved at an all too deliberate speed?   This is not easy to answer.   India, which became independent in 1947, was among the first governments to adopt an official population policy, and did so in 1951.   Judging from this, China would seem slow.   But, the Indian Government made no substantial allocation of funds for family-planning programs until 1957.[51] On the other hand, as late as 1959, the problem of population control was deemed a nonmatter for official concern by President Eisenhower. And, persons have recently been and may still be prosecuted for giving contraceptive aid to married and unmarried women alike in a number of states in the United States, where, moreover, less than half the counties offer birth control facilities.[52] Thus, the rapidity with which the shift was made in China stands out well in a comparative perspective, particularly in view of the great leap that was clearly involved in the change: in attitude, it was an immense movement from the 1949 statement (and its subsequent reiterations and elaborations) that "of all things in the world, people are the most precious under all circumstances."

The Auspicious Moment

Early in March 1957, less than two weeks after Chairman Mao's speech, at the meeting of the third session of the Second National People's Political Consultative Conference, no fewer than twenty-eight representatives spoke out on birth control. Li Teh-chuan, the minister of health, delivered her longest and most informative speech in public in favor of planned parenthood (see below). And, Shao Li-tzu once more defined the need for fertility limitation:

> The correct explanation of fertility limitation is in terms of planning childbearing. A modern individual can have plans for living, study, and work. He must also plan his reproduction [family]. If reproduction is without plan, childbearing will be likely to be too early, too fast, too close, and too frequent [many]. This will be burdensome

---

51. Cf. Moye W. Freymann, "Population Control in India," *Marriage and Family Living*, pp. 53–61. A budget equivalent to about 1.3 million dollars was set aside during the First Five-Year Plan period (1951–56). The Second Five-Year Plan allocated the equivalent of about ten million dollars for the initiation of a truly nationwide family-planning action program.

52. See *New York Times,* 28 May 1969.

for himself, prove detrimental to children's nurture and education, and make it impossible to manage family affairs in a suitable manner. It will necessarily upset one's living, study, and work plans, and indirectly affect the nation's plan for economic construction as well as its other plans.[53]

The other twenty-six speakers voiced their views either individually or in joint statements. Of these, at least twenty-two were medical doctors and health workers. They and others generally confined their remarks to such issues as marital postponement, induced abortion, sterilization, and ways of disseminating contraceptive information and devices. But, as will be shown in the next chapter, their involvement was, consciously or otherwise, based on more (or less) than professional considerations. In any event, all the speeches were carried in full in the *People's Daily*,[54] even though two notably different notes were inserted in this round of public discussion of fertility control. These went far beyond the welfare thesis. In her report, Li Teh-chuan sought, at least in passing, to place the question of population numbers in the context of man-land ratio. She stated, "Our 500 million peasants had an average land holding of only three *mou* per person. Now that the population has increased, they average only a little more than two *mou* of land."[55]

But, this man-land note was only lightly struck in comparison to the more firm play of another key by Chung Hui-nan, the superintendent of Peking's People's Hospital. Chung gave a most impassioned assessment of China's ability to provide employment for the tens of millions of persons thus projected and to accommodate them through land reclamation. His conclusions were as follows:

1. According to the report of Vice Premier Li Fu-chuan, only a little more than one million workers [persons] will be able to find employment each year in our country. But, the rate of population growth is 2–3 percent. This is to

53. *People's Daily,* 20 Mar. 1957.
54. Ibid., 17, 18, 19, and 20 Mar. 1957.
55. Ibid., 8 Mar. 1957.

say that if we make no attempt to restrict reproduction, there will be, from now on, more than 10 million persons who will have nothing to do each year.

2. Land reclamation is a very important task in our national economic construction. But, the amount of wastelands and the speed of reclamation nonetheless are limited. During the First Five-Year Plan, only 70 million *mou* of land can be reclaimed, and the rate of reclamation may possibly be somewhat greater during the Second and Third Five-Year Plans. But it is estimated that our nation now has under cultivation about 1.8 billion *mou* of land [counting multiple-cropping areas]. Of these, some 100 million *mou* of cultivated land generally suffer from natural calamities of all sorts each year. Thus, the net area that is productive amounts to approximately 1.6 billion *mou*. Even if the yearly additions of reclaimed land are included, it will still be impossible to satisfactorily meet the need of the population at its present rate of growth. Therefore, if reproduction is not limited, not only will the standard of living of the people not be improved, but it may also become lower than the current level.[56]

In contrast, on 7 March 1957, the *People's Daily* published an editorial entitled "It is Proper that We Appropriately Restrict Reproduction":

In recent years, our nation's population has been increasing approximately at an annual rate of 2.2 percent, surpassing that of any other nation in the world. At the same time, our nation's industrial production has increased at an average of about 10 percent per year, and agricultural production at an annual rate of around 5 percent. Precisely because our industry and agriculture increase a lot faster than population, the level of living of our people has been assured of improvement year after year. But, if the growth of population is at a somewhat slower pace, then the improvement in the level of living of the people will be quicker. This is an obvious principle. . . . We favor [the suggestion] that reproduction be appropriately restricted—this is fundamentally different from Malthusianism. The basic argument of Malthusianism is that life necessities can never increase as fast as population. Our country's realities have already proved the fallacy of this

56. Ibid., 17 Mar. 1957.

argument. But to point out the error of Malthusianism is not to say that early and closely spaced childbearing is beneficial and necessary.[57]

Chung Hui-nan entitled his assessment "It Is Necessary that We Restrict Reproduction According to Plan," and also warned that

> Some one has made a preliminary estimate that if we would have to support only 500 million people, our nation's productive capacity would suffice and enable them to enjoy fine clothing and abundant food. As it is impossible for China's population to be reduced to 500 million, we have no recourse but to control reproduction. If we would manage to keep the population below 700 million within fifteen years, and positively fulfill our nation's economic construction plans, then in 1972 the whole people would be able to have a good life of fine clothing and abundant food. The key to this is whether or not young people can wholeheartedly carry out Chairman Mao's perspicacious instructions, regarding planned restriction of reproduction.[58]

The distinction between "it is *necessary* to restrict reproduction" and "it is *proper* to restrict reproduction" is both subtle and serious; for, therein lies an implicit divergence of opinion based on demographic optimism and demographic pessimism. And, it was a distinction with a difference. Chung also made his pessimism explicit; the chief reason for China to adopt a policy of planned fertility limitation was, he asserted, "the too rapid growth of its population. This has given rise to important problems of national concern: (1) it severely restricts the elevation of the level of economic and cultural life of the people; (2) it prevents the attainment of a perfect and happy family life; (3) it hinders the realization of careers by young people; (4) it jeopardizes the health and work capability of youth; (5) it adversely affects the coming generations with respect to food, clothing, education, culture, and health; and (6) it produces or accentuates the problems

57. Ibid., 7 Mar. 1957.
58. Ibid., 17 Mar. 1957.

arising from a shortage of school facilities and unemployment."[59] Coupled with his warning on the consequences of rapid population increase were some most undiluted remarks echoing Malthus:

> If this year the number of babies should be 23,310,000, . . .
> then each year thereafter the population would be larger,
> and the total number of children born would be still larger.
> It would be just as astonishing as the rate of accumulation
> of high compound interest on loans. The proverb "Two
> in the first generation means a thousand in ten genera-
> tions" (1, 2, 4, 8, 16, 32, 64, 128, 256, 512, 1024) is there-
> fore not without foundation.[60]

The aforementioned annual number of babies was derived from the reported birth rate of 37 per 1,000 for China as a whole. Using this as the point of reference, Chung presented the set of population projections shown in table 12.

TABLE 12

PROJECTIONS OF CHINA'S POPULATION FOR SPECIFIED PERIODS

(In Millions)

	ANNUAL RATE OF INCREASE		
PERIOD	2%	3%	4%
1956	630	630	630
1961	700	730	770
1966	770	850	930
1971	850	980	1,130
1974	.......*	.......*	1,260
1976	930	1,140	.......*
1980	.......*	1,260	.......*
1992	1,260	.......*	2,520
2004	.......*	2,520	.......*
2010	.......*	.......*	5,040
2028	2,520	5,040	10,080
2046	.......*	.......*	20,160
2052	.......*	10,080	.......*
2064	5,040	.......*	.......*
2100	10,080	.......*	.......*

SOURCE: Adapted from Chung Hui-nan, "Birth Control and Later Marriage."
*Not given in the original table.

59. Ibid.
60. Ibid.

The inclusion of Chung's projections here is not intended to serve any scientific purposes. Rather, they are reprinted to underscore the fact that the framework of the fertility discourse was being rapidly transformed in the early months of 1957. As Chung expressed it, the need for birth control was no longer confined to the original arguments of Shao Li-tzu, who emphasized its necessity exclusively in terms of the welfare of mothers and children. Chung also pointedly invoked the Malthusian threat in his argument (i.e., as he put it, "the observation by Malthus that population, when unchecked, increases in a geometrical ratio, is correct").[61] This was indeed an important turning point in the recent birth control movement in China. This and similar expressions also reopened the old quarrels centered around the demographic versus institutional interpretations of China's poverty and related predicaments.[62]

In the same month of Chung's speech before the Political Consultative Conference, Wu Ching-chao (whom Chao Ching labeled a reactionary population theorist in 1955) espoused, in a long article in *New Construction*, the view that the reduction of the Chinese birth rate from 37 per 1,000 to 17 per 1,000 was a requisite for success during the transitional period of socialist construction. This espousal was predicated upon his appraisal of the capacity of the economy to absorb additional workers under conditions of high labor productivity (i.e., taking into account the cost of technical training and sophisticated mechanical equipment). He calculated this on the basis of ¥13,000 per worker in 1954, and ¥78,000 per worker in 1967; in either case, approximately one-fifth to one-fourth of the total national income would be used to finance such an expansion. The increase would be the equivalent of a six-fold rise in cost built into technical advancements in the course of industrialization, as was evident in the Soviet Union during its five five-year Plans. Wu also assumed that China's national income would go up six times between 1954 and 1967 (i.e., from ¥78,000,000,000 to ¥468,000,000,000). By

61. Ibid.
62. See footnote 15.

his computation, therefore, only between 1.3 to 1.5 million workers could be accommodated annually between 1954 and 1967. Wu went on to say:

> The present rate of natural increase of our population is 2 percent, which means a yearly increase of 12 million persons in a total population of 600 million. Even if [only] half of this number would require employment, we would have six million persons to place in the national economy. . . . Here is precisely where the problem lies.[63]

He then listed three possible solutions to this problem, two of which he immediately discounted himself. One was to continue the existing production arrangement of two tiers of technical sophistication (i.e., highly efficient and comparatively backward categories). However, Wu maintained that not only would this division be financially burdensome for the state but it would also inhibit both an increase in labor productivity and a decrease in production cost. Furthermore, given this differentiation, workers in the lower tier would want to transfer to the upper sector, and a labor redundancy would be created therein. Citing reports of the State Statistical Bureau and a 1957 resolution of the Central Committee of the Communist Party to support his thesis, Wu went on to say that "we must on no account increase the number of workers at the expense of labor productivity." Thus, the perpetuation of this dual pattern of production would be no solution, not to mention the fact that "there has as yet been no satisfactory plan by which we can within the shortest possible time eliminate the technically backward sector of the national economy."[64]

Nor, in Wu's view, should China adopt India's approach to economic development: "The primary purpose of India's investment policy is apparently not to rapidly raise the technical level of its national economy, but to provide employment

63. Wu Ching-chao, "A New Treatise on China's Population Problem," pp. 5-6. A summary of this article was published in *People's Daily* on 5 March 1957.

64. Ibid., p. 6.

for as many people as possible. There is a marked difference
between this strategy and that of ours. That is, on the basis
of its investment policy, India cannot hope to build, within a
very short period of time, a large industrial foundation on
which to accomplish the task of industrialization."[65] Not
only would this not serve to eliminate the backward sector of
the economy but it would also contradict China's decision to
give priority to heavy industry. In any event, Wu quoted
Nehru as saying: "Countries such as India absolutely do
not require a still larger population, and it would be better
if the population is smaller."[66]

Accordingly, Wu urged the immediate adoption of positive
measures to reduce the birth rate. This would complement
the efforts to raise the nation's technical level. In his words,
"The rate of reproduction should be curtailed, so that the
number of persons demanding employment would be reduced
gradually, and that after several Five-Year Plans, it would
be possible for our country to achieve a comparatively proper
'mix' of manual labor [manpower] and machine power."[67]

This last point was derived from what was manifestly a
variant of the concept of optimum population that Wu set
forth in his discussion:

> To carry on production there must be labor power [man-
> power.] But, modernized production does not depend on
> manpower only. Manpower must be united with the means
> of production before it can become capable of generating
> maximum effects. The means of production is "mech-
> anized labor" [machine power]. Therefore, there occurs
> the problem of ratio between manpower and machine
> power. If there is a properly blended ratio, production
> can then rise rapidly. Otherwise, if the ratio is poorly
> balanced [i.e., either there is too much manpower and too
> little means of production, or there is too much means of
> production and only limited manpower], production will
> not reach the highest degree.[68]

65. Ibid., p. 7.
66. Ibid.
67. Ibid.
68. Ibid., p. 4.

Wu asserted that "the ratio between manpower and machine power in China is imbalanced. Our present dilemma is that we do not currently possess sufficient means of production to put to use the existing manpower in the most rational, economical, and effective way."[69] Therefore, China could ill afford the diversion of funds away from projects that make for higher technical level of the working people. Such a diversion would be the consequence of high fertility, even though he acknowledged that man is the source of wealth. This is because, Wu declared,

> the young infant possesses no labor power; he cannot create, but consumes wealth. Not only does he not create any wealth in the year he is born, but he will also remain a consumer in the following ten or more years. He will not be able to take part in production until after he is 15 years of age or older. . . . If the present birth rate [i.e., 37 per 1,000 population] is maintained, then there will be 22.2 million babies from the 600 million population each year. On the other hand, if China could manage, by means of effective propaganda on birth control and through adequate supply of contraceptive apparatus, to cause the birth rate to decline to that of western European nations before World War II (i.e., 17 per 1,000), then there would be only 10.2 million babies in a population of 600 million. The difference between these two figures is 12 million. . . . From his birth to the age of 15 when he is able to work, a person would require a total of ¥1,500, assuming that the annual average cost of his food, clothes, education, medical expenses, and so forth is ¥100. In a socialist society, this amount will be borne, in part, by his family and, partly, by the society. Of the 12 million babies, 10 million can probably survive to the age of 15, under the current mortality conditions. If the expenditures on the children who die before 15, are disregarded, the 10 million children reaching that age would cost a grand total of ¥15,000,000,000. If this ¥15,000,000,000 were spent to equip the laboring people, how much more would their technical level be lifted?[70]

69. Ibid.

70. Ibid., p. 3.

In conclusion, Wu specifically noted that "aside from such generally stated considerations as the health of mothers and infants, the care and education of our children, and the prosperity of our people, the reason we promote birth limitation is that we want to bring our production in line with the basic economic law of socialism and the requirements of the law of development according to ratio and plan, so that we will be able to smoothly fulfill the general task of the transitional period and to accomplish without too exhausting efforts the basic economic task in the future." However, he also admitted that "in the course of industrialization, the large rural population carried over from the old society is certain to show mounting labor redundancy. As to how to accommodate this manpower, [I have not] advanced any solution. This is a matter that requires further discussion."[71]

Thus, like Chung Hui-nan, Wu went considerably beyond the welfare argument in favor of birth limitation. In essence, Chung, Wu, and others (see below) sought to establish, either directly or by implication, the dominant impact of population numbers on society's economic standing and development. Their elaboration of the necessity of birth limitation quite evidently made use of the scare of actual and projected scarcity of land and advanced means of production. Also revived were such other analytically useful but practically elusive ideas as the concept of optimum population and the consumer-versus-producer characterization of human beings. In effect, under the then prevailing circumstances, their words were tantamount to a redefinition of the problem of population numbers in more purely economic terms. Moreover, their admonition to curb reproduction stemmed from a basically pessimistic stance; and, as such, it ran counter to the optimism of the day. This encounter was signally sharp, and became ever sharper as time went on. The issue was joined when Wang Ya-nan replied to Wu's article in May 1957.

Wang Ya-nan, president of Hsiamen (Amoy) University, composed his "Marxist Population Theory and China's Population Problem" in the spring of 1956, and had it published in

71. Ibid., p. 9.

the *Hsiamen University Gazette*. He subsequently wrote a preface for the edition printed by the Science Publishing Company in the fall of that year. The purpose of his original treatise was to advance the argument that only under new social circumstances could China's centuries-old problem of large-scale unemployment be gradually solved; and, part of the argument was a "thorough refutation of the falsehoods of Malthusianism and Neo-Malthusianism."[72] The main aim of the preface was to present his view on fertility limitation; Wang expressed the view that "our current promotion of fertility limitation should not be thought of as a course of action in keeping with the Malthusian viewpoint. It must be decisively deemed a measure based on Marxism."[73] What prompted Wang to preface his original essay with his opinion on birth limitation was the fact, as he stated, that "shortly after the publication of my essay, birth control propaganda and appeals began to unfurl throughout the nation. Many friends and readers asked that I give my opinion on the birth control question, and I myself also felt it necessary to amplify and clarify my own view."[74] This recollection reinforces the previous conclusion that the basic policy decision regarding planned reproduction had already been reached some months before Chairman Mao Tse-tung alluded to it early in 1957. It was probably made some time during or after the spring of 1956.[75]

Specifically, Wang Ya-nan wrote in reply to the following questions: "Why is it that we still promote birth limitation when on the basis of new socialist relations of production it is possible to rationally and effectively orchestrate production power and manpower, and eliminate unemployment? Does the promotion of birth control prove that population

72. Wang Ya-nan, *Marxist Population Theory and China's Population Problems,* pp. 41–42.

73. Wang Ya-nan, "Further Considerations of Marxist Population Theory and China's Population Problems," p. 16.

74. Ibid.

75. It may be recalled that the Ministry of Health's "Directive on the Contraceptive Task" was issued in August 1956.

surplus still exists, and that our new socialist relations of production do not provide a total solution to the problem of unemployment? Does it constitute an implicit acknowledgement that population surplus inevitably occurs in any society as a law of nature?"[76] Wang's answer consisted of:

1. Population problem originates in social system and arises from the contradiction between the means of production and the relations of production in a particular society. Societies that differ in the mode of production have different laws of population and different population problems. Therefore, the paths to their solution also vary on account of diverse concrete historical circumstances. In all societies of private ownership, the population problem manifests itself as the problem of the laboring population. Even though at an initial stage some such societies may also experience a shortage of workers, they generally show their surplus in the form of unemployment, hunger, poverty. . . . This also demonstrates, at the same time, that a sharp contradiction exists between the relations of production and the corresponding means of production in such societies. Accordingly, the road to the solution of this contradiction can only be that of transforming the existing system of relations of production arising from private ownership or exploitation.

2. This is to say that as the population problem is the evil consequence of the system of private property, the elimination of the system of private property ought to have completely eliminated the population problem. But, here we should make one distinction: the elimination of the system of private property can only erase the population problem that it generates, . . . but [it] does not root out population problems in general. So long as society exists, it is impossible to avoid the contradiction between the relations of production and the means of production. What is different is that, after the elimination of private ownership, the contradiction between them is no longer an antagonistic contradiction. Therefore, the population problem that issues from contradictions of this kind is naturally not a problem between hostile classes but an internal question among the people. For this reason, the

76. Wang Ya-nan, "Further Considerations of Marxist Population Theory and China's Population Problems," p. 16.

solution is not contingent upon a basic change in the relations of production. Rather, it rests on still more rational arrangements of the existing manpower and production materials that are in accord with the essential requirements of these relations of production.

3. The basic contradiction in our society is the contradiction between the advanced social system containing the socialist relations of production and backward means of production. A contradiction of this kind defines not only the character of our population problem but also its components. What does this mean? The social system of China that has gradually evolved and developed since liberation belongs to the advanced socialist model. Because of this, it has been able, within a period of only several years, to ameliorate very quickly the long-accumulated wounds of the working people and their conditions of unemployment, hunger, poverty, and cultural privation. But, the social and economic structure of the semifeudal and semicolonial period permitted only a very limited expansion of the means of production. At the same time, the universal poverty and the extraordinarily low standard of living that resulted from the long-term plundering and exploitation by imperialism and feudalism, demanded after liberation that the state allocate large sums of manpower and materials to stabilize and improve the people's livelihood in the form of tax reduction and exemption, transfers of supplies, loans, work relief, and direct subsidies. On account of this, the large number of people who required aid appear to constitute a burden during the national construction, and become an obstacle to both the quick acceleration of social productivity and the rapid increase in the standard of living under the socialist system. Hence, to solve the new population problem resulting from the contradiction between the advanced social system and backward means of production, it becomes necessary to appropriately restrict consumption, by which accumulation may be correspondingly augmented. Or, it may be necessary to appropriately limit the production of consumption materials and to find a solution through the corresponding priority given to the creation of production materials. Appropriately restricting consumption by way of suitably limiting the production of consumption materials is, in fact, to require the appropriate limitation of our excessively large population, which has also been growing rapidly since liberation. Population is, indeed, the source and safeguard of wealth. But, before people can transform potential wealth into

actual wealth, they will require not only a rather long
period of nurture and education but also sufficient production materials. Both these requirements are difficult to
satisfy in our society before there is a significantly large
expansion of the means of production.

4. In our society, the aim of the birth-limitation measure
that we have now temporarily adopted is to create conditions for the rapid elevation of labor productivity on the
basis of a highly technical foundation. This is also to
create conditions for obtaining still greater benefits for the
people in the long run. The goal of the birth control
measure is different, and its subjects are also dissimilar.
When bourgeois scholars sound the alarm of overpopulation, they stress that there is not enough food to supply all
the people in society, on the one hand. On the other hand,
they evidence no contradiction at all in concluding that
population surplus occurs only among the working people.
Therefore, apart from the fact that they practice birth
limitation in pursuit of pleasure, they ask in unison that
the burden of birth limitation be borne by the working
people only. . . . But the propaganda of our birth control
movement is directed at the whole people. Every one of
us who has acquired socialist consciousness will, on account
of our national construction, impose on himself the contraceptive task in order to reduce the burden on society
and on himself. This is the reason why we say that our
population problem and the question of birth limitation
are internal questions among the people.[77]

Accordingly, Wang concluded that "at least for some time
to come, and before our means of production have greatly expanded, we should take all possible steps to limit the rapid
increase in population in order to reduce the load during construction. Doing so will benefit not only national construction
but also the people's livelihood; making such efforts will also
be in accord with both the long-term and current interests of
the people."[78]

One could detect and specify a number of close parallels
between Wang's discussion of the birth control issue and that
of Wu Ching-chao, apart from the identical course of action

77. Ibid.
78. Ibid., p. 17.

to which they both subscribed. But, this would be an exercise in which their words would be taken out of the context of their respective articles. It would also serve to divert attention from the thrust of their arguments and the policy impact, which they so obviously had in the days of their utterances. More importantly, the policy significance of what Wu and Wang said lies, paradoxically, not in the areas of agreement. Rather, their disagreement proved crucial in the political context of population policies.

In addition to calling for adherence to the Marxist principle concerning fertility control, Wang also specifically disassociated himself from Wu Ching-chao, even though he credited Wu for having cleansed himself of his past Malthus-based views. Wang declared, "If it is said that, in my thesis, the emphasis is to demonstrate that the persistent problem of unemployment in Chinese society can only be resolved under new relations of production, then the aim of his [Wu's] article is to stress that even if it would not be difficult to solve the problem of unemployment under new social circumstances, it is imperative that birth control be promoted if we are to rapidly increase labor productivity and transform this agricultural country of ours into an industrial nation."[79]

The issue of population numbers once again was joined as the exchange unfolded.

The open advocacy of birth control thus was being quickly transformed into an all-out dispute centered around the role of population in the present and future economic well-being of the country. References to Hung Liang-chi (the Ching scholar who expounded a natural principle of population in 1793) reappeared, which paid tribute to him for having contributed to demographic theory and followed a progressive stance in his time.[80] But, in the days of the Hundred Flowers

79. Ibid., p. 16.
80. *Chekiang Daily,* 23 Mar. 1957. The earlier reference to Hung was in the 1920s (see footnote 7).

in the spring of 1957,[81] far greater space was actually allotted to contemporary writers of diverse political backgrounds and intellectual standing. Prominent among these were Fei Hsiao-tung, Chen Chang-hen, Chen Ta, and Ma Yin-chu. The *Wen Hai Daily* (Shanghai), the *Brilliance Daily* (Peking), and the *Great Impartiality Daily* (Peking) were the three leading papers that provided the most extensive coverage of their views. The editorial staffs of these papers were either nonpartisan or closely affiliated with minority political parties (e.g., the China Democratic League to which Fei Hsiao-tung and Wu Ching-chao belonged). It may be recalled that the *Brilliance Daily* was the first paper to publicize Shao Li-tzu's original speech concerning fertility limitation in 1954.

As previously noted, Ma Yin-chu, another leading figure in the birth control campaign, prepared a speech on the population question for delivery at the 1955 session of the National People's Congress. But, he held it back for possible presentation at a more opportune moment. On 31 March 1957, Ma finally made the contents of the speech known to the public,[82] following the national decision to foster planned reproduction. The occasion was the opening session of the Committee on Contraceptive Techniques Instruction of the Chinese Medical Association.[83] Ma subsequently repeated the speech amid renewed opposition to public dissemination of contraceptive information and devices (see below), at the fourth session of the National People's Congress on 3 July 1957.[84] This speech and other writings of his were later included in a book that Ma himself edited, and a version of the

81. "Let A Hundred Flowers Bloom; Let a Hundred Schools Contend," was an old Chinese saying. It originally refers to the large number of contending schools of philosophies and so forth in the days of the Spring-Autumn period in Chinese history (722–421 B.C.).

82. It has been erroneously reported that Ma first revealed his view at the National People's Congress on 3 July 1957 (see *Brilliance Daily*, [Peking], 4 Apr. 1957).

83. *Brilliance Daily*, (Peking), 3 Apr. 1957.

84. Ma Yin-chu, "New Population Theory," pp. 297–317.

speech also appeared later in the *New Construction*.[85] Entitled "New Population Theory," this particular speech drew considerable criticism from those who disputed the rhetoric, logic, and substance of Ma's argument in favor of population control.[86] In it, Ma declared that Malthus was correct in his view of the geometric increase of population, though he was wrong in maintaining that means of subsistence only increase in an arithmetic ratio. He also saw population growth as the main obstacle to improved standard of living, to rapid accumulation of funds for industrialization, and to the elimination of unemployment and underemployment. On some of these points, Ma's reasoning paralleled that of Wu Ching-chao.

Most of the criticisms of Ma Yin-chu were voiced in the twenty months after April 1958, and he was able to reply to his critics on two occasions, the last of which was in January 1960.[87] Ma was not relieved of his post as president of Peking University until much later on 26 March 1960. His book was published, as just noted, in 1958. Furthermore, at the July 1957 session of the National People's Congress, Shao Li-tzu expressed his basic agreement with Ma's "New Population Theory,"[88] amid the then developing quarantine of the rightists, such as Wu, Fei, and Chen Ta. Shao himself, responded positively to the call to separate the rightists from others,[89] and may have acted either to salvage the campaign or forestall the turning tide against birth control as a national policy. There were clear signs of its possible retrenchment.

85. *New Construction*, no. 11 (7 November 1959):52–53; and Ma Yin-chu, *My Economic Theory, Philosophical Thought, and Political Standpoint*.

86. For an account of this and other criticisms of Ma, see Kenneth Walker, "Ideology and Economic Discussion in China: Ma Yin-chu on Development Strategy and His Critics," pp. 113–33.

87. Ma Yin-chu, "My Philosophy and Economic Theory," pp. 51–55; and "To Repeat My Request," pp. 5–7.

88. Shao Li-tzu's speech delivered before the First National People's Congress, 4th Session, Peking, 1957 (see *The Complete Report*, pp. 880–81). Shao was never adversely affected by all these developments, and passed away, at age 86, in December 1967.

89. Ibid.

Thus, it does not seem tenable that Ma Yin-chu and his advocacy of strong governmental programs of population control could have been involved in the 1957 move against the other prominent proponents of birth control.

The early months of 1957 were, by all standards, a most auspicious time for birth control. Efforts to promote family limitation reached an all-time high, and had the public endorsement of high officials. As previously noted, in March 1957, Li Teh-chuan, the minister of health, delivered her most vigorous speech in favor of birth control, in sharp contrast to a two-sentence reference to the matter in her report to the 1956 National People's Congress. At the July 1957 session of the People's Congress, however, Li was even more curt than she was in 1956, covering birth control in only one sentence in her presentation.[90] Behind this lowered voice was, so far as can be ascertained, a political backlash that was apparently brought on by what may be characterized as "agument overruns" on the part of Wu, Fei, and others during the auspicious months of 1957. The repercussions of this and other developments were acrimonious.

The Acrimonious Repercussions

What Chung and Wu said about the question of population numbers has already been summarized. To complete this account of the unfolding events that preceded the slowing of birth control activities in China, the role of the other major participants must be specified.

Late in the same month of the publication of Wu's lengthy article in the *New Construction*, Chuan Wen-tien, a professor of economics at Nankai University followed up with a most direct move to expand the frame of reference in the *Great Impartiality Daily* (Peking):

In recent years few persons have publicly discussed China's population problem. Mr. Shao Li-tzu has advocated the

90. Li Teh-chuan's speech delivered before the First National People's Congress, Peking, 1957 (see *The Complete Report,* pp. 749–55).

need for contraception, but mainly in terms of "the physical and psychological well-being of mothers" and "the happiness of young people." We are in agreement with this proposal. But, our view is that since the issue of contraception has been raised, the problem of population cannot help but be involved.[91]

Chuan also explicitly based his case on the concept of optimum population: "Any society that does not have a certain quantity of population will not be able to increase its productivity. In areas where population is relatively sparse, the greater the increase in population, the more rapid expansion of social productivity. But, the reverse cannot be maintained; [it does not follow that] under all circumstances, population growth will always facilitate an increase of productivity."[92] The key points of his exposition were as follows:

1. From the standpoint of man and his labor, production can be increased only in two ways: (1) through an expansion of the volume of labor power, and (2) through an increase in the rate of labor productivity. Accordingly, "if labor productivity remains unchanged, and if only the quantity of manpower increases, the average production per capita will not be even one-half point greater than previously, though the total of social production will be larger under the circumstances. Four divided by two equals two; six divided by three still is two. . . . If the quantity of manpower does not change, and if only labor productivity is raised, the result will be wholly different. . . . Four divided by two equals two; six divided by two is three. . . . Therefore, we must follow the [second] path."

2. When population is too large and increases at a rapid rate, it will adversely affect the rates of increase in both labor productivity and the people's living standard. The amount of increase in the total output of mechanical equipment will be neutralized by a simultaneous population growth and the accompanying expansion of available manpower. Moreover, in agriculture, when there is a sufficient

91. *Great Impartiality Daily* (Peking), 22 Mar. 1957.
92. Ibid.

amount of labor power, any subsequent increases will require the utilization of inferior lands. For this reason, the speed of increase in the average rate of labor productivity in agriculture cannot help but be correspondingly slowed.

3. Our nation has already a population of 600 million. That is to say, in relation to economic, cultural development, or whatever, there is an immensely abundant hidden manpower. . . . There is absolutely no need for our nation to increase its manpower or population. So long as we can continually raise labor productivity at a high speed, then our transition to the communist society of "each according to his needs" will certainly not be delayed even thirty seconds because one fewer person is added to the population."[93]

The thrust of Chuan's agrument differed little from that of Wu Ching-chao: "the basic economic law of socialism not only requires us to raise labor productivity [through which to elevate the level of living], but also commands us to accomplish this at top speed. In order to reach this top speed, we must appropriately limit the growth of population." But, he took issue with Wang Ya-nan and his fellow-advocates in a plainer fashion than Wu had; as Chuan stated, "in any event, [while] under socialist system there is no fear of overpopulation and rapid increase of population, this is not equivalent of requiring a very great demographic expansion."[94] And, in addition to calling for open discussion of China's population problem, Chuan also sought to connect the outcome of the national economic development plan to demographic research:

In sum, the ratio between population and all aspects of the national economic plan must be suitably balanced. If not, as the whole national economy expands according to ratio, population will remain the only loophole in, and be out of balance with, and outside of, the plan. Then, will it be really possible to claim that the unified national economic plan is actually a perfect and integral plan? How will it be

93. Ibid.
94. Ibid.

possible to smoothly implement it?   Of course, it will be very difficult.

Therefore, we must master the size of the current population. Also, we must ascertain the sex, age, marital status, and cultural composition of the population and the birth and death rates. These tasks are not an easy matter as the demographic circumstances undergo changes all the time. A further problem is: not only must we ascertain the quantity and composition of the current population, but we must also grasp the number and makeup of the population a year, five years, or even ten years from now. Because planning always is made ahead of time, long-term plans are necessarily made five or ten years before hand. If we are to formulate long-term plans, we must, at least, roughly fix the ratio between population and all the other aspects of the national economy; otherwise, there will be problems when the time comes, and the situation will be even more troublesome. For this reason, we cannot avoid but endeavour to undertake research on the size and composition of the current population and, on this basis, determine the concrete trend of demographic growth as well as make projections of this trend. In order to have correct projections, there must be thorough research.[95]

There is ample justification for Chuan's case for an expansion of demographic research; no planning, short- or long-term, can be founded on a total demographic void. And, demography is also an important scientific discipline in its own right. However, in China as elsewhere in the world, demographic research does not proceed in a political vacuum;[96] nor is it unincumbered with the problem of personnel and personalities.   And, there were such complications in China in 1957. The *Wen Hui Daily* (Shanghai) made this clear on 27 April of that year:

The population problem as an area for scientific research has just today begun to attract the attention of the academic world, and there were no penetrating criticisms

95. Ibid.

96. As a case in point, consider the recent Congressional clamor over the types and number of questions that may and can be included in the 1970 census of the United States.

of the Malthusian population principle in the past. Some people have in their minds only the memories of some abstract ideas of the superiority of our society. They do not know that under our superior socialist system, new problems nevertheless occur continually, one of which is the population problem. If we do not carefully investigate and resolve it, it will inevitably affect somewhat the progress of socialist construction. Some say, there are difficulties in initiating research on the population problem because in the past few specialists did research in this area. Is this saying correct? It is both correct and incorrect. It is true that in the past few studied the population principle of Marx and Lenin. But, this is not equivalent of saying that a certain condition for research does not exist at present. It is also true that some comrades do not understand these matters. It must not be forgotten that we still have quite a few seasoned specialists, and that they had once devoted all their hearts and soul to this specialty. [Admittedly], their perspectives were different, their opinions were in mutual disagreement, and many changed their callings after the liberation. They have achieved, though, differing degrees of progress and ascent under the educational influence of Marxism and Leninism during the last seven or eight years. Today as we take a further step to carry out the directive of "Let a Hundred Schools Contend," it is absolutely imperative that they be mobilized to "readjust banners and drums" and quickly march out of retirement. We believe that if these old experts participate actively in the discussion, they will have much to contribute. . . . This newspaper has decided to help expand the discussion of the population problem, and hopes that experts and scholars of all disciplines will join in the discussion. . . . Of course, this newspaper-forum is only a starting point. As regards the institution of a full investigation of our nation's current demographic circumstances [and through which to establish the proletariat demography], comparatively long-term efforts on the part of those in the academic world will be required.[97]

However, this pointed reminder of the availability of population experts from another period did not constitute a prelude to hoped-for developments. It was actually a sequel to a seminar that the *Wen Hui Daily* had sponsored four

97. *Wen Hui Daily* (Shanghai), 27 Apr. 1957.

weeks earlier. This seminar was held in Shanghai on 30
March, and at least fourteen scholars and medical experts
and officials spoke their minds during the gathering in the
newspaper's conference room. An account of what they said
was subsequently published, in two parts, in the *Wen Hui
Daily* on 8 and 9 April. The second part of the report was
devoted mainly to opinions concerning the acceptability and
effectiveness of specific means of birth and conception limitation, and is not germane to the issue at hand. What is of
interest here is the fact that among those listed in attendance,
during the first part, the old experts predominated. And apparently, they had already been at work prior to their seminar
participation.[98]

For example, Hu Huan-yun, a professor at the East China
Teachers' College, who taught human geography for more
than twenty years and compiled various population distribution and density maps of China and its provinces before 1949,
was working on similar projects based on the 1953 Census
data. One paper of this series was published in the *Wen Hui
Daily* on 21 March in which Hu assessed China's population
problem in the perspective of the population density of Kiangsu Province. Hu, and most other participants, favored a reduction in the rate of population growth either as a chief or as
a supplementary measure to accelerate the speed of economic
development. However, there was at least one statement
of critical neutrality at this seminar; Wu Fei-tan, a professor
at Fu Tan University, maintained that he disagreed with all

98. These were: Hu Huan-yun, Yeh Yuan-lan (professors, East
China Teachers' College); Hsu Shih-chin (professor, the First Medical
College of Shanghai); Yin Cheng-i (professor, Shanghai College of
Finance and Economics); Hsieh Chih-chen (head of the Welfare Sec-
tion of Shanghai Municipal Women's Federation); Hu Chih-yuan
(chief, Obstetrics Department, Shanghai People's Hospital No. 6); Li
Mu-shan (deputy-chief, Shanghai Municipal Bureau of Health); Yin
Pei-ming, Wu Hi-tan, Chiang Hsueh-ma, Soong Cheng-hsien, and Chi-
Chi-shen (all of Fu Tan University); Yang Ssu-ping (lecturer, East
China College of Government and Law); and Chen Chang-hen (staff
member of Shanghai Museum of Literature and History).

three schools of population thought that had emerged in modern China:

> 1. "Population surplus," theorists such as Chen Chang-hen, Chen Ta, Wu Ching-chao, Yen Yang-chu, and others, who asserted that China has too many people, and that neither industrial development or border population settlement can solve this.
> 2. "Nationalistic" population theorists, namely, Sun Yat-sen who argued that if other nations increase their populations while China does not, the destruction of the nation and the extinction of the Chinese race will follow.
> 3. Optimist population theorists who espouse the view that given China's vast territory and rich resources, it can support additional people.[99]

Of special significance was the participation of Chen Chang-hen in the colloquium. Chen, whose involvement with demography and politics dates from the mid-1910s, was a high official in the Kuomintang regime. He took part in the discussion simply as a staff member of Shanghai Museum of Literature and History, and was both reminiscent and remonstrative in his exposition:

> [During the last reign] of the Ching dynasty, the Ministry of Civil Affairs conducted a census [1910]. Later, Rockwell, the American minister to China, sent his counselor to get this set of preliminary figures from the Department of Interior of the Peking Government, and placed the number of households at about 70,000,000 in the nation as a whole. . . . Rockwell thereupon arbitrarily multiplied this by 4, which he assumed to be the average size of the Chinese household, to obtain a total national population of 280,000,000. But, Walter Wilcox, Professor of Population Statistics of Cornell University, United States of America, borrowed the result of the 1920 U.S. Census that showed the average household size to be 4.8 in Amer-

---

99. As reported in *Wen Hui Daily* (Shanghai), 8 Apr. 1957. Wu also stated that pessimistic population views have a historical background in China, citing the earlier writings of Hung Liang-chi.

ica and multiplied this by the number of households in China to place China's population at 300,000,000 at the end of the Ching. Actually, both Rockwell and Wilcox deliberately underestimated the total size of the Chinese population. The reason for this was that the United States was much opposed to Japanese immigration to Hawaii and mainland America: they therefore deliberately underestimated the total size of China's population in the hope that Japan would redirect its immigrants and aggression toward China. The year before the 18 September 1930 Incident, the Japanese Imperial Government invited the International Statistical Association to hold its annual conference in Tokyo. Wilcox attended the conference. At the meetings, various Japanese population statisticians presented papers of a more or less same vein to indicate how serious the Japanese population problem was. I was selected by the Kuomintang Government as a representative to the conference. For several tens of days, I was at the Department of Interior of the Kuomintang Government in Nanking, and used a calculator myself to recount the household data collected by the Ministry of Civil Affairs at the end of the Ching. I found that at that time, there were 71,268,651 households in the nation, and that the total population was 368,146,520. The average size of the household thus was 5.17 persons. Also an independent analysis by Mr. Wang Shih-ta of Tsing Hua University of the same household data gave a household total of 70,430,432 and a population total of 372,563,555, or an average of 5.29 persons per household. Mr. Wang's findings and those of mine were very close to each other as well as considerably greater than the estimates made by Rockwell and Wilcox. Our findings thus repudiated their malicious estimates. During the annual conference of the International Statistical Association, I sharply criticized Wilcox's estimate and stunned him into silence. (I faulted him for basing his estimate of China's population at the end of the Ching on the average household size calculated from the 1920 Census of a highly industrialized United States. Because China then was only an agricultural nation, the average size of its household was naturally one person greater than that of the United States. Thus, in a letter to Professor John S. Buck of the Nanking University in 1931, he [Wilcox] indirectly acknowledged his error. But, he then stubbornly employed instead the average figure of 4.9 persons per household obtained from a census of India. Thereupon, he amended his original estimate to 343,000,000. This shows how strongly he was wedded to an [erroneous] opinion.) [100]

Chen's recollection of past events diverts attention momentarily from the main concern here. But, it is inserted here on account of its possible place in the annals of Chinese demography. More importantly, it illustrates both his stand on China's population problem and, again, the affinity between population analysis and politics. And, Chen's telling of this anecdote, in part, stemmed from his then immediate disagreement with Wang Ya-nan:

> Of the past population census data of our nation, I also once carefully investigated and analyzed myself. Such statistics are necessarily not very reliable, but I cannot fully agree with some scholars' opinions—such as Wang Ya-nan's—that they are nothing but a muddled account. Actually, the early population data of any country in the world are, as a rule, very primitive and full of defects. [101]

Here, at the beginning of April, Chen publically chided Wang Ya-nan for his apparent, total discount of the available, albeit defective, demographic statistics of China. This rebuke was, nevertheless, phrased in rather mild terms in comparison to what he later said of Wang, in May.

While Chen Chang-hen and others were expressing their vows and misgivings in the pages of the *Wen Hui Daily* in Shanghai, Chen Ta, Fei Hsiao-tung and their fellow exponents had their replies to Wang and other recommendations published in *New Construction* and in other publications in Peking. Under the rubric of "Establishing Demography of the Proletariat Class," Tung Chieh, a university professor, gave an itemized account of the variety of empirical data that demographic research can produce and bring to bear on policy moves on all fronts of the population question. [102]

100. *Wen Hui Daily* (Shanghai), 8 Apr. 1957. For references to Chen's earlier publications, see footnotes 8, 9, and 15.

101. Ibid.

102. Tung Chieh, "To Establish the Demography of the Proletariat Class," pp. 1–3.

However, this useful inventory was sandwiched between two statements that throw less light on demographic research than on the then evolving confrontation:

We know that Marx and Lenin bequethed not much in the way of population theory and were patricularly short on the explanation of the principles of population of the transitional period and socialist society. This makes it necessary for us, their heirs, to redouble our research efforts to supplement and develop it. But, in a number of recently published papers on China's population problem and the Marxist population theory, it seems that there are still people who assert that neither the current size of our nation's population nor its high rate of increase presents any problems at all, and that if only social productive power is enhanced and the contradiction between the people's need for rapid economic and cultural expansion and the inability of the present economic and cultural circumstances to satisfy their need is resolved, a still greater population growth and a still larger population will not be any problem. At the same time, doubts still persist in regard to our current extensive dissemination of birth control information. Some assert, "This still is in need of further scientific research" and are worried that birth control propaganda may enable Neo-Malthusianism to "resurrect itself in a borrowed corpse." If such opinions and anxieties were correct, then expanding demographic research would be like "arrow-shooting in search of a target," or "much ado about nothing." As the demography of the proletariat would be void of research aims, it would be very difficult to develop into a special science! Then, we ought to "exercise caution over the matter" of spreading propaganda about conception avoidance and of practicing birth limitation. But, are these views and anxieties really correct and necessary?[103]

In sum [on the basis of what demographic research can contribute to policy], we can clearly recognize that our nation's population does not at all portent no problems and that these are not merely problems of numbers and growth. For this reason, to widen the scientific analysis of China's population problem, of course, is not "arrow-shooting in search of a target" or "much ado about nothing." . . .

103. Ibid., p. 1.

Admittedly, the law of population of each society is determined and limited by the basic economic law of that society.   To study a society's population law apart from its
basic economic law, of course, is eternally stupid and
fallacious.   But, conversely, the law of population can also
have an impact on the pattern of society's economic law.
To deny the objective existence of the law of population
and to attempt to substitute society's basic economic law
for the law of population are also one-sided viewpoints, as
are the denial of the influence of population change and
expansion on society's economic change and expansion and
the thesis of automatic disappearance of the population
problem in the wake of a solution of the economic problem.[104]

In the same issue of *New Construction,* Fei Hsiao-tung
also took exception to the proposition that there is no need
to limit population increase because one's labor can produce
more than one can consume or that one person more is better
than one fewer.   Simultaneously, he complimented the
Academy of Labor (Political) Cadres for sponsoring a population seminar of its own in March 1957, which Fei and Chen
Ta both attended, but was quick to point out that the scope
of this seminar, the first ever held since liberation, was in-
congrous with the nation's need.   In other words, he joined
in the call for an expansion of demographic research; for, in
his view, "the important matter of population that is intimately tied to [the management of] national affairs is a far
heavier task than what a small number of scholars can
shoulder if they are able only to undertake research behind
closed doors in one or two rooms and have to trek everywhere
to beg for information."[105]
Implicit in this apparently justified appeal to the government for more assistance in demographic research were the
charges that a suitable medium for an exchange of ideas was
not available to persons engaged in population analysis and
that demographic statistics were hard to come by.   To an

104. Ibid., p. 3.

105. Fei Hsiao-tung, "What Does Population Research Entail?" pp.
5 ff.

extent, both were probably not ill-founded, on the one hand. On the other hand, signs of relative improvement also abounded: to wit, the flow of demographic and related articles increased substantially after the publication of the results of the 1953 Census.[106]   At least two formal papers by demographers were presented at international conferences outside of China.   Tai Shih-kuang read his paper before the Indian Statistical Institute in Calcutta in December 1956,[107] and Chen Ta's paper was part of the proceedings of the International Statistical Institute in Stockholm in August 1957.[108] Chen Ta was also listed as a participant of the 1954 World Population Conference in Rome, but did not actually attend the meetings.[109]

Chen Ta also had occasion to recall his involvement with family-limitation activities in the 1920s and 1930s and to again proffer relevant insights publicly in March 1957.[110] These ideas were later repeated by him in a long, scholarly discourse on birth limitation and marital postponement that *New Construction* published in its May 1957 issue.   In it, Chen articulated his total opposition to aborticide and artifically induced abortion as methods of limiting births and made cogent arguments in favor of marital postponement.[111] But, the significance of the paper lies, not in merely how Chen verbalized what he desired to explicate, but also in the fact that he evidently had free access to current studies and data of foreign and domestic origins.   Apart from his own earlier studies, his citations included, among other dated items, a number of the then recent sources: *Population Bulletin*

106.   Cf. the articles in newspapers during this period and in such journals as *Statistical Work* (Peking).

107.   Tai Shi-kuang, "1953 Population Census of China."

108.   Chen Ta, "New China's Population Census of 1953 and Its Relations to National Reconstruction and Demographic Research."

109.   United Nations, *Proceedings of the 1954 World Population Conference (Rome)*.

110.   *Brilliance Daily* (Peking), 14 Mar. 1957.

111.   Chen Ta, "Birth Limitation, Marital Postponement, and New China's Population Problem," pp. 1–15.

(Washington, D.C. [November], 1956); *Proceedings of the World Population Conference, 1954* (United Nations, New York, 1954); *Demographic Yearbook, 1955,* (United Nations); Yoshio Koya, "A Study of Induced Abortion and Its Significance," *Milbank Memorial Fund Quarterly* 32 (New York [July], 1954; R. L. Meek, ed., *Marx and Engels on Malthus* (London, 1953); John Hajnal, "The Marriage Boom," *Population Index* (Princeton, New Jersey [April], 1953); *Bulletin of the International Statistical Institute* (India, 1951); Frank Lorimer, *The Population of Soviet Union* (Geneva, 1946); P. H. Landis, *Population Problems* (American Book Co., 1943); and various reports of the Scripps Foundation for Research in Population Problems (Oxford, Ohio, 1939).

Thus, the evidence does not uphold the charge of book-burning and book-banning in China. An inevitable question is: How can this be reconciled with Fei's registered complaint about isolation of scholars and data scarcity? There is no proof that Fei himself suffered directly from such deprivations, as he was then actively engaged in research, teaching, and national politics.[112] Thus, he must have spoken out either on behalf of deposed or disadvantaged scholars (e.g., Chen Chang-hen) or in the interest of other causes, or both. And, there is ample evidence that his complaint was part of a coordinated effort to expand demographic research and to reestablish sociology in China, which Fei and his associates sought to shape and lead.

The abolition of sociology departments and sociology courses took place in China in 1952, when a reorganization of the curricula of institutions of higher learning was made. In January 1957, Wu published in *New Construction* an article "Does Sociology Still Have a Place in New China?" Fei followed with a statement in the *Wen Hui Daily* on 20 February and also formally requested a change in the official attitude towards sociology at a conference on propaganda activities called by the Central Committee of the Chinese

---

112. Fei Hsiao-tung was a delegate to both the People's Political Consultative Conference and the National People's Congress.

Communist Party (24 March). On 10 April, *New Construction* organized a symposium on sociology, which was chaired
by Fei. Less than two weeks later (23 April), Fei, Wu, and
six others were elected at a meeting of the Department of
Philosophy and Social Sciences of the Academy of Sciences
to form an "organization subcommittee." Its functions were,
at a suitable opportunity, to assist in establishing (within
the department) a committee of research in "social problems."
    Simultaneously, Chen Ta, Wu, and others were also en-
gaged in a number of other activities: in a petition to the
National Committee of the Chinese People's Political Consultative Conference (7 March), they urged the establishment of a population research organization and the reintro-
duction of courses in demography at the university level. In
an interview published in the *Wen Hui Daily* on 16 April
1957, Chen reiterated his view about the restoration of
sociology. In May, Chen and others wrote a letter to the
Ministry of Higher Education, voicing their opposition to the
previous elimination of sociology departments. And, there
was a private meeting in June that was held in Chen's home
and was attended by Chen, Fei, Wu and others. The name
of the research committee on social problems was changed
to "Sociology Work Committee," and Chen was elected the
committee chairman. The resolutions of that meeting included: (1) a systematic recruitment of those academic
colleagues trained in sociology; (2) the reestablishment of the
Chinese Sociological Society; (3) the restoration of sociology
departments in universities, first in Peking and Shanghai,
then in Canton and Chengtu; and (4) the tentative appointment of Wu Ching-chao as the director of a sociological research center at the People's University in Peking.[113]
    Quite apart from the issues of the restoration of sociology
and of the expansion of demographic research, the clash over
the question of population numbers itself was building up
to a climax toward the end of April 1957. In its statement
on the need to expand the discussion, the *Wen Hui Daily*

113. *New China Bi-Monthly,* 1 Aug. 1957.

(Shanghai) stated that all viewpoints would be welcome, but, interestingly enough, voiced the hope that participants would refrain from "putting hats on people's heads indiscriminately" (i.e., name-calling) and assuming a dogmatic and bully stance.[114]

Yang Ssu-ying, who, in 1955, took up the issue of birth control in the Party's chief journal (before there were open moves in this regard) published another article in the same magazine in April 1957. Unless there were strong reservations about birth control within the Party ranks, it would be hard to conjecture a reason for this reiteration of its necessity on grounds of China's economic difficulties during the transitional period and of maternal and infant welfare.[115] Reading this paper, however, also gives a close-up of the impasse between Wang Ya-nan and others on the one side, and Wu Ching-chao and associates, on the other side. As Yang put it:

> Under socialist system arises a new socialist law of population. The socialist system of public ownership of productive resources gives rise to the highest likelihood of the elimination of unemployment and poverty. Under a socialist system, the laboring masses gain a tremendously wide employment opportunity. All in all, the situation is: on the one hand, population increases at a rapid rate; on the other hand, the level of material well-being of the people is being raised continuously. . . . There are people who believe that Malthusianism is especially applicable to the states that, in the past, for a long time were the colonies [of imperialism]. For example, the backwardness and poverty of such countries as India is allegedly a result of an excessive population growth. Is this, in fact, true? It is entirely not so. During the last three hundred years, India's population increased to 389 million from about 100 million or 3.8 times. But, what about its "affluent" mother country—England? Between 1700 and now, its population of 5,100,000 has grown to 41,800,000, or eight folds. If we compare India to other European countries, the rates of

114. *Wen Hui Daily* (Shanghai) 27 Apr. 1957.

115. Yang Ssu-ying, "The Premise of Birth Control Advocacy Is not Malthusianism," pp. 172–75.

population increase during the years 1870–1910 in Germany, Belgium, the Netherlands, and Russia were 3.2, 2.53, 3.28, and 3.91 times, respectively, greater than that of India. What is the situation with respect to population density? In 1941, India's population density was 246 persons per square kilometer, but those of England, Belgium, the Netherlands and Germany were 703, 702, 639, and 348 persons per s/km, respectively. [Of course, population density figures themselves do not adequately explain the problem because population distribution is uneven in countries of large or small sizes and in different regions. But, making rough comparisons of this kind still is necessary.] This makes clear that Malthusianism has no factual basis in the history of human societies. This also explains that to attempt to use Malthusianism to account for the poverty and backwardness of the colonies is to whitewash colonialism and is without scientific meaning.

In the past, many Malthusian scholars once displayed a "scientific" facade and concluded that the territory of China could supply consumption materials to maintain at most 200 million to 280 million persons. This fallacious thesis has been shattered by actual events. Because of the revolutionary victory and the expansion of production, we have within a short period of time abolished hunger for the first time in the history of our nation as well as solved, step by step, the unemployment problem and appreciably raised the level of living of the entire people, though our nation's population has passed 600 million. Moreover, since national liberation, under comparatively backward technological circumstances, we have rapidly made large strides in the national economy. This would have been inconceivable had there not been such a massive source of manpower.

Since liberation, owing to the improvement and stability in the livelihood of the people and an extension of medical and sanitary facilities, our nation's birthrate has gone up, death rate declined, and the rate of natural increase has risen considerably. [The average rate of natural increase is over 2 percent per year.] Even though the technical basis of our agricultural production has, nevertheless, greatly exceeded the rate of population increase [since liberation, our nation's total output of good grain has been: 220 billion catties in 1949; 335 billion catties in 1952; 339 billion in 1954; 365 billion catties in 1955; and about 385 billion catties in 1956]. Industrial production has been increasing about 10 percent per year. During the fifteen years between 1952 and 1967, on the basis of the present rate, our nation's population will increase by one-third [giving a total population of 800 million], but, according to the figures in the *1956–1967 National Agricultural Programme (Draft)*, food grain output can increase one and one-half times [from 335 billion to 838.5 billion catties]. During these fifteen years, it is estimated that industrial production will increase around tenfold. This proves beyond doubt that, for our people, the only correct path to wealth, power, health, and happiness is to undertake democratic revolution, and socialist revolution and construction thereafter, and not by reducing the population to 280 million or 200 million.[116]

Thus, what divided Wang Ya-nan, Yang Ssu-ying, and associates and Wu Ching-chao, Fei Hsiao-tung, Chen Ta, and others was their respective extrapolations, into both the immediate and distant future, of post-1949 trends in agricultural and industrial developments in China. This difference impinged directly on the question of the capability of the Chinese government to meet the demographic and related challenges of the day:

Wang Ya-nan: Because the socialist system absorbs and mobilizes a great many more people in production, and because it can stimulate all those joining in production to exhibit selfless enthusiasm and to activate all hidden potentials, [it] can steadily increase the social wealth. . . . After the high tide in agricultural cooperativization in August 1955, the attainment of the increases in agricultural production as envisaged in the First Five-Year Plan has been secured. According to the proposals for expanding the national agriculture from 1956 to 1967, agricultural production will be very greatly increased on the basis of cooperativized agriculture. . . . After the [1955] high tide in agricultural cooperativization, only about three years will be needed to bring to full maturity a new form of the socialist revolution. The elimination of unemployment and the total utilization of surplus manpower obviously need not wait until the Second and Third Five-Year Plans.[117]

116. Ibid., pp. 172–73.
117. Wang Ya-nan, *Marxist Population Theory*, pp. 41–42.

Wu Ching-chao: The employment of an additional 1.5
million workers each year is not a small number according
to the experience of other countries. . . . In 1900, there
were 28.3 million jobholders in the United States, and in
1956, there were 68.8 million.   During these 56 years, the
increase amounted to a total of 40.5 million, or an annual
average of 0.7 million. . . . At the beginning of her First
Five-Year Plan [1928–32], a total of 10.8 million persons
were employed in the Soviet Union, but by 1955 48.4
million were employed.   The total gain of 37.6 million jobholders in 27 years meant an annual average of only 1.4
million.   In our own country, the increase in the number
of employed persons reached an annual average of 1.1
million during the period of the First Five-Year Plan
[1953–57]. . . . The Second Five-Year Plan [1958–62]
. . . calls for an increase of an additional 6 to 7 million
persons, . . . [or] at most, an annual average of 1.4 million. . . . But if our rate of natural increase were still
to be 20 per 1,000, then by 1967 [the end of the Third
Five-Year Plan] there will possibly be more than 6 million
people who will demand new jobs each year![118]

The gap between these estimations of future trends could
not have been wider, by all known standards.   And, the difference also reflects their differential appraisal of the role of
population size and growth in society's material and non-
material well-being.

Even though Wu Ching-chao and fellow writers anchored
their expressions in the concept of optimum population, they
implicitly subscribed to Malthus in that a constant rate of
reproduction was assumed throughout their analyses.   This
assumption is as provocative against the backdrop of the
infamy of Malthus in China as it is untenable.   Its unten-
ability stems from the fact that it makes no allowance for
possible fertility reduction in the course of social and economic transformation.

As a final note to his most comprehensive and stimulating

118. Wu Ching-chao, "A Treatise on the Problem of China's Population," p. 6.   It should be noted that not all social scientists trained
in the West agreed with Wu and his associates.   For example, Sun
pen-Wen, a sociologist trained in America, argued that a population
of 800 million is the best for China (see *Wen Hui Daily*, 11 May 1957).

treatment of the development of conflicting population theories up to 1900, E. P. Hutchinson cogently stated:

> Inquiry into the influence of nondemographic factors on population raised reasonable doubt whether population is really a primary force or an ultimate variable in social and economic affairs. Early nineteenth-century theorists treated population as an independent variable, a cause of various consequences, good and bad. In the course of time, however, it became increasingly clear that population is not an ultimate cause, but is itself affected in size and trend by many factors in the social and economic environment. In this respect it is a dependent variable, a product of prior influences, a link rather than the origin of a chain of cause and effect.[119]

This admits of the distinct likelihood and actuality of change in reproductive behavior in response to social and economic changes.

Also, as Hutchinson aptly characterized, the optimum population concept was a *partial* solution to the centuries-old controversy of population numbers. He added, "but hopes of determining in practice the optimal size [for greatest returns] for an actual population were not fulfilled. The real value of the concept proved to be not empirical but theoretical and conceptual. . . . Implicit in the new theory was the lesson that the significance of a given change in population does not depend only upon the direction of the change, but also upon the conditions under which the change occurs, for an increase in numbers, for example, may be beneficial in some circumstances, detrimental in others."[120] But, even in terms of the development of intellectual thought only, whether this optimal view represents a "well-balanced judgement, striking a middle position between Malthusian pessimism and anti-Malthusian optimism, neither exaggerating nor underestimating the influence of the population variable

119. E. P. Hutchinson, *The Population Debate: The Development of Conflicting Theories up to 1900* (New York: Houghton Mifflin Company, 1967), p. 406. Reprinted by permission of the publisher.

120. Ibid., pp. 392–93.

in human affairs, is not a question that can be answered once and for all." And, in the twentieth century, Hutchinson noted, the subject of population has been continually debated, and that "the debate on overpopulation versus underproduction and maldistribution has continued, sometimes personified in terms of Malthus versus Marx."[121]

As other Chinese writers not directly involved in the debate during the first quarter of 1957, reasoned later in the year,

the population of various nations can be grouped into three categories: (1) colonial, semi-colonial countries, or countries whose productive power is low, or whose development is at the early stage of capitalism. Fertility and mortality are both high, but the rate of natural increase is small. Countries included in this group are Old China, India and Egypt before Independence, Chile, Imperial Russia before the Revolution, England, France, and Germany in the nineteenth century; (2) countries that have a relatively high productive capacity or that have already reached the last stage of capitalistic expansion. Even though mortality has declined, fertility has decreased even further; therefore, the rate of natural increase is also not very high. England, France, West Germany, the United States, Australia, and New Zealand belong to this second group; and (3) the third group includes all socialist countries. Apart from the USSR, the other socialist nations are still in the early stages of socialist construction. In these nations, the rate of natural increase tends to go up because of the improved standard of living, a rapid decline in the death rate, and little-changed fertility. And, in response to further advancement in socialist construction and a still higher standard of living, the practice of late marriage and birth control will emerge. There will be a gradual drop in the birth rate, but the speed of the decline in the death rate [which has already approached the minimum] will also slow down. A reduction in the rate of natural increase will, in turn, become evident. In short, in the course of socialist construction, population numbers will proceed, step by step, from an initial rapid increase to a stable growth.[122]

121. Ibid., p. 407.

122. Chang Pai-kun, et al., "A Socialist Theory of Population and China's Population Problem," pp. 36–63.

Presumably, family-planning programs and other forms of direct interference with marriage and reproductive practices would be capable of initiating or accelerating fertility decline as society's circumstances undergo change. This was explicit in the epic campaign to promote family limitation in China. But, whether or not family-planning programs and propaganda are more decisive modifiers of fertility behavior than social and economic changes is still being hotly debated among demographers, sociologists, and others. Nonetheless, quite apart from the question of their potential impact on fertility, an immediate tactical issue is: what is the best line of appeal that can facilitate the dissemination and acceptance of contraceptive knowledge and paraphernalia?

Throughout the ages people everywhere have been called upon (implicitly or otherwise) by society to be fruitful or to cease and desist, as the case may be. "Fertility control" may be used to denote this type of appeal to regulate population numbers in the interest of the society as a whole, which may involve such impersonal calculations as the size of the military-manpower pool, the maximization of national wealth, the conservation of natural resources, the promotion of material well-being, the survival of the people, and the like. Yet, in the modern era, the number and timing of births increasingly reflect the desire and decision of individual couples. In other words, "family limitation" refers to the regulation of childbearing in accordance with personal circumstances and inclination. This distinction, of course, is largely an analytical construct, though of considerable policy import.

First, societal and individual interests may not necessarily parallel one another with respect to reproduction. Various schemes of family allowances and symbolic inducements are known to have not brought about desired fertility increases in the interest of the society as a whole in France, Germany, Italy, Australia, and the Soviet Union. It can also be readily demonstrated that a substantial growth of population is inevitable, but may not be compatible with the interest of society, even if individual couples have no more than the 3 or 4 children that they themselves consider ideal in times of extremely low mortality. Second, as is generally known, discrepancies between verbalized ideal family sizes and actual fertility are prevalent in many countries and areas. Where the latter exceeds the stated family size preferences, the discrepancy has been presumed by some to reflect either ignorance or inability to make effective use of contraception, on the one hand. On the other hand, the lag may only be a gap between changed collective preference for smaller families at the societal level and unchanged familial circumstances favoring large families. Or, it may be simply indicative of the overt acceptance of the small family ideal on the part of individual couples but covert acquiescence or conformity to existing social patterns of fertility.

Thus, in reality, actual fertility is, so to speak, *un*regulated, to a small or large extent, from the standpoint of either societal or individual interest or both. In terms of tactics, of course, it is impossible to emphasize both societal and individual interests in appeals to secure hoped-for modifications in actual fertility. But, in reality also, not all lines of appeal are politically expeditious in a given situation; thus, choosing a line of appeal involves political calculation as do policy decisions on such a controversial matter as the control of population numbers.

To encourage the adoption of family-planning practices, China chose during 1954–1957, as previously documented, to phrase the appeal *mainly* in terms of maternal and infant welfare.[123] In terms of population control, this line of appeal was indirect, and indirection would seem preferable to inaction. And, there had been plenty of actions before Chung Hui-nan, Wu Ching-chao, Chuan Wen-tien, and others directly or indirectly invoked the Malthusian threat which transferred the issue of population numbers to the ancient, and an immensely more controversial, context. In the name of a viable program designed to promote fertility control, however, might it not

---

123. The appeal was not exclusively in these terms; for writers on both sides acknowledged that planned births are also consistent with the requirements during the transitional period. They differed as to whether planned reproduction was permanently necessary.

be a plausible proposition that they had unncessarily broached and resurrected the Malthusian controversy?

In December 1955, as previously indicated, there appeared in *New Construction* a lengthy article in which Wu, Chen and others were vociferously assaulted for their pre-1949 reactionary population views.[124] This attack represents another manifestation of the contradiction between two equally plausible, but opposing, views of the quantitative problem of population. This, in turn, to borrow again from Hutchinson, is related to man's dual role. "People are both producers and consumers, so it is understandable that at times population growth should have been regarded primarily as an addition to manpower and productive capacity, at other times as an increase in the number of mouths to be fed."[125] Thus, in terms of intellectual freedom and academic discussion, a staunch defense should and can be made on behalf of Wu, Chen, Fei, and associates. However, had they been simply involved in the pursuit of an academic objective, this would not be an entirely misplaced effort in their defense. In fact, their demographic enterprise was not isolated, and probably not insulable, from the politics of population.

Apropos of both the auspicious days of 1957 and the intimate relationship between population and politics were the circumstances surrounding the visit to China by Josué de Castro in May of that year. A former director of the Food and Agriculture Organization of the United Nations and a Catholic by birth, de Castro lectured during his trip to an audience consisting mainly of members of the Chinese Academy of Sciences. The *Wen Hui Daily* (Shanghai) gave a brief account of his advocacy of fertility reduction through improved diet (i.e., according to his formula, an increase in protein intake) rather than contraception, but specifically noted the following exchange:

Professor Lo Kai-fu asked if it would be all right to adopt contraceptive measures if it was not possible to presently

124. See footnote 33.
125. E. P. Hutchinson, *The Population Debate,* pp. 6–7.

improve the food situation. He [de Castro] said, "If the food situation cannot be changed, then the government ought to be changed." This evoked a loud laughter in the audience.[126]

This anecdote coincided, perhaps, quite accidently with the turning of the political tide that had carried family-planning programs to the zenith of national priorities. The utterance also may have been a purely innocent, albeit imprudent, remark on de Castro's part. The episode, in any event, seems to have been rather remotely, if at all, connected with the ensuing deflection of the epic campaign to encourage planned reproduction in China. But, the politics of population was doubly evident in the *Wen Hui Daily*'s direct quotation of de Castro's words, which could not have been a matter of non-premeditation. Thus, not only was the issue of population numbers joined, but its political ramifications were also unambiguously brought to the fore.

There were other additional complications. During the Hundred Flowers, criticisms of the state of affairs generally came from members of a number of minority political parties. This led to the exposure of Chang Nai-chi, Lo Lung-chi, Chang Pai-chun, Huang Shao-hung, Wang Kun-lun, and Tan Pin-shan who were accused of being anti-Party, antipeople, antisocialist, and anti–democratic dictatorship, and of harboring political ambitions. All six were members of the State Council when it first acted on birth control revisions in 1953, and belonged to either the China Democratic League or some other minority political party. Chang Po-chun and Lo Lung-chi were identified as the leaders of this "Chang-Lo Alliance." They and Chang Nai-chi consequently were removed from their ministerial posts in the Departments of Communications, Forest Industry, and Food, respectively.[127]

A member of the China Democratic League, Fei Hsiao-tung was also involved in various activities in which the Chang-Lo

126. *Wen Hui Daily (Shanghai)*, 17 May 1957. Josué de Castro's approach to fertility reduction is stated in his book, *The Geography of Hunger*.

127. See *People's Handbook* for 1956 and 1957.

Alliance had an interest.[128]   Wu Ching-chao was also a member of the Democratic League.   And, the connections between the *Wen Hui Daily* and members of the League were extensive, and dated from pre-1949 years.

Thus, it seems that the issue of birth control was implicated in a situation where ideology, politics, and personalities were poignantly entangled and where the climate of opinions once again turned steadily inauspicious with respect to public exhortations to advance family-planning practices.   Notwithstanding Shao Li-tzu's efforts at the National People's Congress in July 1957, open birth control activities diminished in volume amid the charge that Fei, Wu, Chen, and others sought to use the huge population of China to prove "the transformation of China into a socialist country is impossible; it is like the building of palaces on a sand beach, a totally wasteful effort."[129]

But, the deflation of the birth control campaign was gradual rather than abrupt, given the need to work out and implement other policy substitutes.   Therefore, it does not seem merely a coincidence that the Great Leap Forward and the People's Commune followed closely, though somewhat overlapped with, the all-out national attempt at mass contraceptive education.   Nevertheless, the basic decision on population that was made in 1956 has not been supplanted. Fertility control remains a national policy, though there have been fluctuations in public emphasis and direct action.

128.   Fei Hsiao-tung, "Admission of Crimes," in *The Complete Report,* pp. 1334–40.

129.   Li P'u, "Do Not Allow the Rightists to Use the Population Question to Advance Their Political Conspiracy."

The Control of Population Numbers: Means and Preferences

Chapter six

Quite obviously, subject to and in accordance with the controlling viewpoint, the stated meaning of policy decisions affecting population numbers can vary over time. The formulation and implementation of China's national fertility policy has been, in part, contingent upon the calculation that the effect of its possible success would be to lessen current demands for consumption goods and to aid economic development in the long run. But, also quite clearly, the acceptance of this policy has been and still is principally in terms of maternal and infant well-being. This policy, coupled with social and economic changes in Chinese society, presumably will lead to a greater and greater overall reduction in the fertility rate. There can be no dispute that intensive efforts were made in China in the mid-1950s to foster "planned reproduction," to use the Chinese term for fertility limitation. The campaign was, however, punctuated by disputes over its terms of reference.

In the preceding chapter, the interplay of the forces that produced the short-term fluctuations in birth control activities in China in the recent past has been re-created. The focus has been deliberately on relevant and relatively discernible political and ideological factors. The chief reason for this is that they are part of the fundamental forces affecting the definition and direction of policy regarding population. This emphasis should not blind us to the fact that in China misgivings about the birth control campaign have not been rooted only in such considerations. There were, for instance, allegations that the promotion of birth control required complete abstinence or a total cessation of childbearing. Expressions of this kind could not be and were not ignored in the course of the birth control campaign.[1] In addition, efforts had to be made to allay the fear of those who stated that moral deterioration and social decay were likely to issue from an open dissemination of contraceptive information and devices. Concern for the possible spread of sexual promiscuity also had to be assuaged.[2] But, documentation of the extent of such reservations and anxieties is far more difficult than that of the politics and ideology of population policy. The fact is that only minimal and scattered traces of clues to the former aspect of the birth control campaign appeared in print. Because of this, anything more than this minimal reference to the existence of opposition to birth control on social and moral grounds must be postponed to a time when a more adequate supply of data is established.

As the issues of definition and the acceptability of birth control as a public function are closely tied to national objectives, taboos, hopes, and fears, their resolution is terms of whether or not population size and growth ought to be regulated in *any* way. The circumstances affecting decisions of this character should and can be distinguished from those having to do directly with *how* or by what *means* a particular policy goal is to be fulfilled. The separate treatment of the two sets of issues thus is analytically advantageous. The fact is that the propriety and sufficiency of specific means of fertility control themselves can be and often are matters of

1. See, for example, *China's Women,* 1 May 1957, p. 8. Also, cf., *Brilliance Daily* (Peking), 7 May 1957.

2. A brief reference to expressions of this type can be found in *Kwangchow Daily* (Canton), 20 Jan. 1957.

controversy. The recent acrimonious exchange on the contraceptive pill in the United States is a case in point.

With reference to the means, the control of fertility can be conveniently and logically examined in terms of: (1) conception and birth prevention within marriage, and (2) delayed matrimony. Within marriage, temporary or permanent prevention of conception and birth may be accomplished by a single application of or repeated resort to one or more of a variety of techniques and methods. Classifiable roughly into five categories ("ascetic," chemical, mechanical, physiological, and surgical), these methods vary a great deal in the degree of effectiveness, use-difficulty, and acceptability on aesthetic, moral, and religious grounds, as well as in reversibility and side- and after-effects. Rudimentary knowledge and forms of these methods have been remarkably ancient and diffused, though their modern counterparts are more numerous and highly sophisticated. A good many of them (e.g., diaphragms, condoms, jellies, creams, foams, foam-tablets, and so on, plus the rhythm method and coitus interruptus) have, for some time, been labeled conventional in the literature and in public usage.

In China in recent years, all these aforementioned methods have been explicitly prescribed for use by the general public. Not even implicit exceptions to them have been registered by any party involved in the issue of fertility control. Nor have there been known objections to a modern verision of another old technique of limiting fertility, which entails the insertion of a foreign substance into the womb, that is presently in vogue under the name of intra-uterine device (the IUD). Consequently, none of these above named methods will be considered here.

This leaves three major methods of conception and birth prevention within marriage to be considered: sterilization, oral contraception, and abortion. Sterilization has been systematically propagated in India in recent years, oral contraception has gained wide publicity and acceptance inside and outside of the United States, and the legalization of induced abortion has cut fertility substantially in Japan, as well as in several countries in eastern Europe, during the last two decades. All three methods have also been seriously promoted in China since 1949, amid rather divergent views regarding their safety, contraceptive value, and moral, social, and personal costs. In the following pages, these three methods of conception and birth prevention will be taken up individually.

Thereafter, attention will be shifted to delayed marriage, which has also become an integral component of China's population policy. But, unlike the other means of family limitation, marital postponement has had an unique career in China in recent years. Not only was encouragement to delay marriage an integral part of the social and family reform spelled out immediately after 1949, long before the decision to promote planned reproduction, but also following an interlude of quiet contraceptive efforts of some three years, the renewed exhortations encouraging later marriage, in 1962, constituted the prologue to a continuing phase of fertility control activities in China. The issue of marital postponement will be the focus of the final section of the present chapter.

Sterilization

In relation to fertility control by way of *conception* prevention, sterilization is the only purely surgical method of proven value. Abortion is considered either as a physiological or a surgical method of *birth* prevention as it may and can be induced by various abortifacients. Of all the methods of family limitation available at present, moreover, sterilization is also the only method that requires no more than one application, is practically irreversible, and is not linked to one of the sexes. These circumstances and other considerations make it (vasectomy or salpingectomy) a both highly effective as well as controversial instrument of fertility control. Sterilization provides a genuine relief from additional pregnancies; it also generates fears of possible loss of manhood (or womanhood) in fact and in appearance.

So far as post-1949 discussions of surgical methods of conception prevention in China are concerned, however, they were not limited to sterilization only. They also included positive assertions and apparently public trials of the effectiveness of acupuncture and cauterization as a combined method of fertility control. An enthusiastic endorsement of this method appeared even before the intensification of birth control activities in China that occurred in March 1957. The endorsement was in the form of an interview printed in a major newspaper of nationwide circulation:

As soon as we learned of the possible contraceptive value of acupuncture and cauterization, another comrade and I immediately went to see Mr. Sun Hui-ming who is a specialist in acupuncture and cauterization. Other people told us that Mr. Sun has already applied these methods and helped a number of mothers avoid pregnancies.

After learning the purpose of [our] visit, Mr. Sun smiled and . . . said, "Twenty years ago, when I first mastered acupuncture and cauterization, we already had four children. My wife then did not wish to have another child. Thereupon, I tried them on her. . . . Indeed, she had no additional births! Several years later she changed her mind and wanted to have another child. I applied the needle to a different sinus in her body. She soon became pregnant with our fifth child. . . . After the liberation, many women comrades with letters of introduction from their organizations came to see me for contraceptive assistance. My own eyes have also seen that the health, work, study, and family life of many women comrades have been adversely affected because of too many children. I therefore acceded to their requests. Since then, I have treated a total of ten comrades with acupuncture and cauterization. In eight cases, the result has been excellent. The other two comrades came to talk to me when they again became pregnant. From what they said, it seems that their pregnancies may have been due to a failure on their part to follow post-surgical precautions as instructed. According to my experience, contraception by acupuncture and cauterization is relatively reliable and does not have any side effects. As a matter of fact, these methods were described long ago in *Encyclopaedia of Acupuncture and Cauterization* by Yang Chi-chou of the Ming dynasty (1368–1644 A.D.). Ordinarily, these methods should guarantee women freedom from pregnancy for three to five years."[3]

3. *China Youths Daily* (Peking), 10 Aug. 1956.

The interview ended with an appeal to the health departments of all places to speedily organize all practitioners of acupuncture and cauterization in their own localities for the purpose of exchanging relevant experience. Furthermore, practitioners of traditional medicine and doctors trained in Western medicine were urged to make a united effort to ascertain and appraise, through research, the scientific basis of acupuncture and cauterization in order to make possible their application to contraceptive work.[4] The extent to which these appeals were heeded in China cannot be ascertained. Fragmentary reports indicate that one experiment was carried out in a hospital for railroad workers and their dependents in the Hangchow region of Chekiang Province. It involved some fifty women employees and wives, all of whom had at least three children. They underwent the operation between November 1956 and March 1957 and reportedly experienced neither menstrual disturbance nor physiological discomfort. The plan was to keep a close observation of them and an additional fifty women for a period of two years before the results of the study would be announced.[5]

However, even though it is known that acupuncture flourishes in China, since 1957 there has been no known reference to it in discussions on population control and contraceptive methods. Insofar as surgical methods of the prevention of conception are concerned, sterilization thus appears to have been the chief concern. When the question of birth control was publicly raised for the first time in China in 1954, little systematic consideration seems to have been given to the ways in which individual couples are to prevent conception and birth. Only gradually did the examination and evaluation of the various known contraceptive approaches and methods attain a degree of specificity. Sterilization was no exception.

Both before and after the formal approval of sterilization, there was an attempt to promote its general acceptance in China. The period of intensive promotion was in the months

4. Ibid.
5. *Chekiang Daily* (Hangchow), 24 Apr. 1957.

of March and April in 1957, though occasional references to sterilization continued to appear for some time thereafter. Initially restricted to couples with six or more children, vasectomy and salpingectomy were permitted to couples with four or more children, and, since May 1957, have been allowed without reference to family size.[6] At the height of the 1957 campaign, descriptions of the clinical details involved in the operation and accounts of personal experiences were printed in newspapers in metropolitan centers as well as in cities with as few as 200,000 inhabitants. Apart from the caution that sterilization probably means the permanent termination of reproduction and is more suitable for couples with several living children, these published statements were largely consolatory. They were obviously designed to dispel common fears and misgivings about sterilization among doubters and potential users, particularly those relating to possible loss of sexuality and other adverse physiological changes in the male.[7]

In this latter context, and given the fact that knowledge of castration permeates all levels of Chinese society, one of the problems involved in the popularization of vasectomy thus pertained to the necessity for differentiating these two types of surgery and the clarification of their respective effects. Premier Chou En-lai recently remarked:

Sterilization is simple and harmless for men while more complicated for women. In China, however, which has just freed itself from semifeudalism, there is great resistance among men to the practice of sterilization to curtail exces-

6. The first relaxation was made in March 1956. *Daily Worker* (Peking), 13 Jan. 1957; and *People's Daily* (Peking), 23 May 1957.

7. See *Peking Daily* (Peking), 15 Mar. 1957; *New Hunan Daily* (Changsha) 21 Mar. 1957; *Harbin Daily* (Heilungkiang), 26 Mar. 1957; *Kueilin Daily* (Kwangsi), 9 Apr. 1957; *Daily Worker* (Changchow, Kiangsu), 9 Apr. 1957; *New China Daily* (Nanking), 23 Dec. 1957; *Great Impartiality Daily* (Peking), 18 Mar. 1957; *Wuchow Daily* (Kwangsi), 13 Apr. 1957; *Labor Daily* (Yentsi, Shantung), 28 May 1957; *Tsingtao Daily* (Shantung), 1 Sept. 1957; *New China Daily* (Nanking), 27 Dec. 1957; *Canton Daily* (Canton), 12 Apr. 1957; and *Liuchow Daily* (Kwangsi), 11 Jan. 1958.

sive reproduction. Others are likely to say that such a man has been castrated; he has become a eunuch![8]

Similar reflections were also voiced in the 1957 campaign.[9]

In November 1963, the *People's Daily* carried the announcement of the publication of a number of handbooks by the People's Health Publishing House in Peking. These covered a variety of topics ranging from internal medicine, blood transfusion, and heart diseases to the prevention and treatment of scarlet fever, typhoid, malaria, poliomyelitis, food poisoning, and so forth. The surgical procedures for salpingectomy and vasectomy were detailed in two separate volumes in this series of handbooks, which had been prepared especially for use by medical and health workers in towns and villages.[10]

Thus, there can be little doubt that sterilization remains a major method of fertility control within the scheme of population control in China. It should be made clear, however, that both in recent years and during the 1957 campaign, vasectomy has been favored. It continues to receive a greater emphasis in the various mass media in China. Accounts of personal knowledge of sterilization again were printed in women's magazines and other publications.[11] Apart from its simplicity, the cost of vasectomy also is far less than either salpingectomy or abortion; according to one schedule published by the Municipal Bureau of Health of Kwangchow in 1957, the charges were ¥40, ¥20, and ¥8 for salpingectomy, abortion, and vasectomy, respectively.[12]

8. This quotation is from Edgar Snow's account of his interview with Chou En-lai in Africa in January 1964, as printed in the *New York Times*, 3 Feb. 1964. Copyright 1964 by The New York Times Company. Reprinted by permission. Permission also granted by the estate of Edgar Snow, Robert P. Mills, literary agent.

9. See, for instance, *Great Impartiality Daily* (Peking), 2 Aug. 1957.

10. *People's Daily* (Peking) 27 Nov. 1963. None of the pamphlets are available, however.

11. See *China's Women* (April 1963):10–11; ibid. (January 1964): 30.

12. *Kwangchow Daily* (Kwangchow), 12 Apr. 1957.

One well-publicized story concerning vasectomy was that of an interview between Premier Chou and a couple in August 1963, when the former was touring the latter's factory in China's northeast at the time. It was originally reported in *China Youths Daily* on 1 September 1963. Because of a number of salient points in this story, it deserves some space here:

Premier Chou talked with a female comrade, who has two children—aged four and ten. . . . [He] asked her sympathetically her age and when she was married. Li Ying said that she is 32 and was married at the age of 20. It would seem that she married rather early; but comparatively speaking, since she had two children in the twelve years of her marriage, it cannot be said that she had children too close together. The Premier expressed his approval.

Li Ying then told the premier, "This is because we are practicing planned parenthood. Two years ago, the father of these children had a vasectomy so that there would not be any more births." . . . The premier asked, "Was that what you two were willing to do?" Said Li Ying, "This was our wish." The premier seemed pleased; he praised them for doing the right thing, especially the husband.

. . . The premier invited him [Sun Yen-wen] to participate in the conversation. Communist Party member Sun told the premier that he is 41; he enlisted in 1945 and was an officer in the People's Liberation Army.

The premier further inquired about the economic circumstances of their family as well as his physical condition after the surgery. Sun replied that he is now the vice director of the factory. . . . He and Li Ying earn a combined income of a little over ¥200 monthly, and so their family financial situation is not bad. They practiced planned parenthood not because of economic considerations. What is more important is that this is in the interests of their work and the health of the mother and children. As to whether vasectomy would affect health, Sun told the premier that there have been no inimical effects on his health or on their marital life.

The premier was pleased to hear this . . . and also said that in this matter of planned parenthood, the Sun Yen-wen couple have set a good example, especially the husband who voluntarily assumed the burden of planned parenthood and deserved emulation by other people.[13]

Suffice it to note that, both implicitly and explicitly, this account studiously reflects the official position on fertility control in general and sterilization in particular. It salutes the postponement of marriage as well as the regulation of family size and child-spacing in marriage. It stresses the responsibility of the male with respect to planned parenthood and strikes at popular fears of adverse consequences of vasectomy.

On the other hand, note the occupational status of the husband, and what this may imply in terms of his educational attainment. Note also the respective ages of the husband and wife at the time of the vasectomy. Note still further the combined income of this couple and their family size. These circumstances make it obvious that this pair is not representative of Chinese couples at large.

Yet, in any attempt to promote, and in any assessment of, vasectomy as a means of fertility control, a large number of questions that this story stimulates obviously must be answered. They include: What are the characteristics of all sterilized males and females up to now in China with respect to occupation, education, and income? What are the most frequent ages at sterilization for them, and what is their distribution by their own ages and those of their spouses at the time of sterilization? What is the average family size of the couples involved? Yet, these and other questions obviously cannot be answered for the time being because of the absence of information.

What can and will be attempted here, therefore, relates only to the probable range of sterilization that may be required to produce some material effect on the rate of population growth. Given the greater official endorsement of vasectomy in China, the present exploration is in terms of the number of vasectomies required to bring about various rates of growth lower than the reported rate of 2 percent per annum.

13. *China Youths Daily* (Peking), 1 Sept. 1963. Chou En-lai also alluded to the story in his talk with Snow in 1964 (see footnote 8).

Although both the Japanese and Puerto Rican records of sterilization show the predominance of women among those sterilized, it matters little as to whether the number of male sterilizations or the number of female sterilizations is used as the basis for discussion here.[14] The principal concern is the volume of sterilization needed to reduce fertility, not the factors affecting male or female acceptance or rejection of sterilization as a method of fertility control. The reproduction of a married couple can be terminated by the sterilization of either partner.

In China, as elsewhere, the suitability of sterilization as a means of fertility control is repeatedly stated to be contingent upon the presence of several living children. Quite coincidentally, married men and women who differ in culture and are separated by geography seem to have followed this dictum. In Puerto Rico, for instance, the contraceptive history of a sample of women indicates that sterilization followed the fourth pregnancy in about two-thirds of the cases and was performed only after the seventh pregnancy in nearly 29 percent of the cases.[15] Among a group of sterilized men in a district of the State of Maharashtra, India, the average number of living children exceeded five.[16] In Japan, information from persons sterilized since the Eugenic Protection Law went into effect shows that more than three-quarters of the mothers had three or more children at the time of sterilization of either themselves or their husbands, and that over a third had four or more living children when sterilized. Only an insignificant proportion of the Japanese sampled had one or no living children, though a little more than one-fifth of them had only two living children at the time of sterilization. This latter fact may be indicative of an emergence of a pattern of small families in Japan.[17] Nevertheless, it is clear that sterilization

14. See Yoshio Koya, *Pioneering in Family Planning,* chapter 8, table 2, p. 111; and Reuben Hill, et al., *The Family and Population Control,* pp. 126–28.

15. Hill, et. al, *The Family and Population Control,* p. 176.

16. Kumudini Dandekar, "Vasectomy Camps in Maharashtra," pp. 147–54.

17. Koya, *Pioneering in Family Planning,* pp. 113–15.

occurs fairly late in the fertility histories of the Puerto Ricans, Indians, and Japanese for whom relevant information is available.

The tardiness in the employment of sterilization to control birth may be variously explained. Given popular notions about it, many a couple may have been unwilling to submit themselves to sterilization until after several "failures" at ascetic, chemical, or mechanical contraception. Others may have been totally ignorant of any contraceptive methods and undergone sterilization out of desperation. For still others sterilization may have been a decision deliberately taken after the birth of a desired number of children. Or, the late resort to sterilization may partly be "a function of the recency of its popularity. If large scale facilities are relatively recent or if knowledge of these facilities and acceptance of the method are recent, then the pattern of late sterilization might be [a temporary] one soon to disappear."[18] Solid data in support of this last point are still scarce, but seem to be emerging. Of the sterilized Indian males of Maharashtra, the average age gradually dropped from 40.2 to 38.9 during the period 1959 to 1962, and the average number of children per sterilized male followed a similar trend falling from 5.73 to 5.08 during the same period.[19]

Of course, even if further declines in the average age and average number of children at sterilization could be presumed, it is obviously impossible to predict, as of now, the rapidity with which they may occur. But, it can be said that, assuming the stability of prevailing age-specific fertility rates, the shorter the interval between marriage and sterilization, the greater the effect of sterilization on fertility. Of crucial importance to the question of population control is the empirical relationship between the timing of sterilization within marriage, which curtails individual reproduction, and the conse-

18. Hill, et al., *The Family and Population Control,* p. 177.

19. Dandehar, "Vasectomy Camps in Maharashtra," pp. 150–51. It should be noted that the changes in the average age and average number of children may have been due to the cessation of cash bonus to those who volunteered to be sterilized after their forty-fifth birthdays.

quent impact on the national fertility. In this connection, reliable estimates of the number of sterilizations required to reduce fertility to specific levels within specified time-periods presuppose the availability of good data on age at marriage, proportions of those ever married by age, the age distribution of the population, and, of course, age-specific fertility rates. In the case of China, unfortunately, published demographic statistics provide only a very rough outline of its gigantic population pyramid.

In the case of Japan:

> Assuming that the average age at the time of sterilization was approximately 30 and that the future fertility would have followed the current trends among Japanese women, the loss of future births from [a reported total of] 72 thousand [sterilized] women would be about 140 thousand. If we assume that actual sterilizations are five times the reported number, the loss of fertile women by 1960 would amount to about 560 thousand, and the loss of anticipated births 700 thousand. . . . These, it should be noted, are the anticipated consequences only of the sterilizations that . . . occurred between 1949 and 1953.[20]

Between 1954 and 1959, some additional 240,000 female sterilizations were performed by doctors designated by the Japan Medical Association in accordance with the Eugenic Protection Law of 1948. Thus, from 1949 to 1959, according to official statistics, there was a total of 320,000 female sterilizations in Japan. Actual operations during these eleven years may have been at least three times this official tabulation, possibly reaching a grand total of nearly one million female sterilizations.[21] If, as has been maintained, female sterilizations in Japan have already reached a magnitude sufficient to markedly depress fertility in future years at a ratio of about one sterilization to two births, the anticipated loss of births would be two million. In other words, there would be an annual reduction of about 140,000 births over a period of fifteen

20. Koya, *Pioneering in Family Planning,* pp. 85–86.
21. Ibid.

years (the presumed average number of years during which the sterilized women would have been capable of childbearing) even if no additional sterilizations took place. This anticipated annual loss would amount to not quite 9 percent of the number of births that occurred each year in Japan from 1953 to 1959.[22]

In Japan, according to a United Nations estimate, the number of females aged 20 to 44 years was 16.5 million in 1955, of whom 80 percent were ever married.[23] Thus, so far as the Japanese experience is concerned, a 9 percent reduction in the annual number of births would seem to require the sterilization of one of every 13 ever-married women between 20 to 44 years of age.

There is good reason to believe that an equivalent number of sterilizations would have a larger impact on fertility in China. The decrease in the Japanese birth rate was already marked in the late 1950s, being about 20 per 1,000 in 1954 and 17.6 per 1,000 in 1959; and this decline reflects, in particular, the prevention of births by couples in the relatively older age groups. The extent of fertility control among Chinese couples aged 30 and older is unlikely to be of a similar magnitude. Thus, in China, the potential benefit of sterilization would be greater than that of the 1-to-2 ratio shown for Japan, even if the average age at sterilization is also about 30. One sterilization might prevent three or even four births; one sterilization out of every 13 persons might mean a 15 to 20 percent reduction of births annually over a period of fifteen years, even if no other contraceptive measures were used.

On the other hand, a greater proportion of Chinese marriages than Japanese marriages probably take place at ages below 20. In the absence of effective contraception, early marriage in China means a relatively longer period of exposure to the risk of pregnancy and, therefore, is likely to exert an

22. The number of births per year was in the neighborhood of 1.65 million in Japan.

23. United Nations, *The Population of Asia and the Far East, 1950–1980*, p. 104; and Irene B. Taeuber, *The Population of Japan*, p. 211.

influence in the direction of increased fertility. Thus, use is made of the ratio of one sterilization to two births in the present discussion.

According to one estimate, there were 114.8 million males aged 20 to 44 years in China in 1958.[24] If 80 percent of them are married, the sterilization of one of every thirteen married males would amount to a total of some 7 million operations. This would mean the prevention of some 14 million births over a fifteen-year period, or not quite one million births per year. Although this is an impressive figure, it falls far short of the number of births that must be eliminated in order to realize a 10 percent reduction in annual births. To achieve such a reduction, an estimated total of some 19 million sterilizations would have to be performed within a year if the Chinese birth rate is assumed to be 40 per 1,000. At a daily rate of 52,000 operations, it would be possible to accomplish this objective. According to the most recent report, most of China's 2,000 *hsien* have, as of March 1963, established one to two general hospitals, and most of these *hsien* hospitals have a department of surgery.[25] Taking this to mean a minimum of 2,000 *hsien* hospitals in existence in China, and assuming only 50 percent of them to be capable of performing the necessary surgery, the daily quota for each hospital would be 52 sterilizations.

If realized, this would also mean that the rate of population growth in China would be reduced from the reported 2 percent per annum to about 1.5 percent per annum. On the other hand, to depress the rate of population growth to 1 percent per annum, it would require a total of about 43 million sterilizations or the sterilization of about one-half of the married males aged 20 to 44 years. For India as a whole, K. Dandekar estimated that to achieve a 47 percent reduction in the Indian birthrate, sterilization would have to be performed on some

24. John S. Aird, *The Size, Composition, and Growth of the Population of Mainland China,* p. 81, table 13.

25. NCNA (Peking), 26 Mar. 1963.

44.8 million married males having two living children.[26] Given the fact that China's population is much larger, the present estimate thus appears to be on the conservative side. Nevertheless, even if only the smaller goal of 19 million sterilizations could be considered possible, the elimination of some 2.5 million births per year would certainly seem well worthwhile in terms of population control in China. And, even if this limited aim could not be entirely realized, partial accomplishments would still be preferable to no accomplishment.

This notwithstanding, a scheme of population control in China probably could not be based on a single method of fertility control. Thus, it should not be overlooked that sterilization is being sanctioned in China along with *all* other contraceptive techniques and methods.

Oral Contraception

Up to the end of 1969, as far as can be ascertained, only scattered mention was made of oral contraception in China since the renewal of public birth control activities in 1962, in contrast to the recent advocacy of sterilization. During the campaign in the 1950s, however, there were numerous open discussions of "oral contraceptives" in China, particularly in 1956 and 1957. As is well known, in 1956 the first clinical trials of oral contraceptive pills began in places outside of China. The results of these and additional field tests eventually led to the approval of Enovid (in 1960) and, later, others (e.g., Ortho-Novum) as oral contraceptives in the United States.

Both Enovid and Ortho-Novum are made of synthetic chemicals known as the 19-nor steroids, which have a molecular structure similar to the naturally occurring hormone, progesterone. According to one account of the developments in pharmacology between 1949 and 1959 in China, several plants of the dioscorea group are reported to have been found

---

26. The married male population in 1959 was estimated to be 94.6 million. See Kumudini Dandekar, "Sterilization Programme: Its Size and Effects on Birth Rate," pp. 220–32.

to possess a high content of drosgenin, the starting material for the synthesis of steroid hormones.   Progesterone is specifically stated to have been one of the several steroids then being studied for large-scale production at the Institute of Organic Chemistry, the Chinese Academy of Science.[27]   There was also a report of initial success in the production of what were reportedly oral contraceptives in China in May 1957. They represented the result of research carried out at the Institute of Pharmaceutical Research in Shanghai, and the first batch of the compound was shipped to the Union Medical College in Peking for testing on animals.   The drug was stated to have been made of a substance extracted from an unnamed plant of Indian origin.[28]   It was asserted that two pills before ovulation would prevent conception during the following two or three months.   In August 1957, it was further claimed that the basic ingredients for another contraceptive compound could be derived, as a by-product, from either the process of coke production or a chemical process of unspecified kind; these are 3,5-diniethy phenol and p-amino benzene sulfonic acid, from which the compound m-hydroxyquinone is produced.   The latter reportedly was an oral contraceptive.[29]   It is, of course, difficult to evaluate these and similar reports. One could discount them entirely as having no validity, particularly in view of another report printed in the *People's Daily* that, as of October 1957, no definite conclusions had

27.   E. Leong Way, "Pharmacology," p. 378.   The other steroids were testosterone, methyltestosterone, and cortisone.

28.   *Wen Hui Daily* (Shanghai), 28 May 1957.   Additional references to this drug can be found in *Tienmen Daily* (Hopeh), 16 June 1957; *Daily News* (Shanghai), 24 June 1957; and *Great Impartiality Daily* (Peking), 2 Aug. 1957.   The unnamed Indian plant presumably was garden peas.   In their article on "Ecologic Determinants of Population Growth," pp. 107–25, Carl Taylor, John B. Wyon, and John E. Gordon gave the following citations: S. N. Sanyal, "Sterility Effect of the Oil of Pisum sativum Linn and Its Relations with Vitamin E," which appeared in five issues of the *Calcutta Medical Journal* (47 [September 1950]:313; 48 [1951]:53; 49 [1952]:399; 50 [1953]:409; 51 [1954]:101) and in two issues of *International Medical Abstracts and Reviews* (17 [1955]:13; 18 [1955]:31).

29.   *Great Impartiality Daily* (Peking), 2 Aug. 1957.

emerged from laboratory and other tests of the contraceptive effectiveness of the various compounds then in existence in China.[30]   Nevertheless, a beginning appears to have been made on the possible manufacture of oral contraceptives in China. The Chinese pharmaceutical industry is certainly capable of preparing the necessary ingredients for oral contraceptive drugs.   Therefore, the relative absence of discussion on the question of oral contraception from 1962 to 1969 in China cannot be explained in terms of technical ineptitude or ignorance.

Oral contraception, as just noted, received attention in China in 1957.   The examination of the issue appears to have started earlier in the summer of 1956.   At the third session of the First National People's Congress then in progress, Shao Li-tzu applauded the attempt by the Ministry of Health to collect contraceptive recipes from among practitioners of traditional medicine.   Specifically, he related and recommended for study one oral contraceptive formula:

> Fresh tadpoles coming out in the spring should be washed clean in cold boiled-water, and swallowed whole three or four days after menstruation.   If a woman swallows fourteen live tadpoles on the first day and ten more on the following day, she will not conceive for five years.   If contraception is still required after that, she can repeat the formula twice, and be forever sterile.[31]

This particular formula originated with Yeh Hsi-chun, whom Shao Li-tzu lauded as a progressive herbalist and who was also a member of the National People's Congress.   Either concurrently or subsequently, Yeh also served as the deputy director of the Department of Health of Chekiang Province. Available reports indicate that under his direction, tests of the formula on women were being planned by persons in his department in March 1957.   It was stated that should the women who volunteered for the experiment become pregnant, the

30. *People's Daily* (Peking), 20 Oct. 1957.

31. The recipe was contained in Shao's speech in *The Complete Report*, p. 375.   See also Irene B. Taeuber, "Population Policies in Communist China," pp. 261–274.

Health Department would permit abortion and assume the responsibility for terminating the unwanted pregnancies. Meantime, tests on cats and white mice were reportedly carried out by a team of embryologists and histologists at the Medical College of Kwangsi Province and at the Research Institute of Traditional Medicine in Chekiang Province.[32] These experiments were undertaken in spite of (or, perhaps, because of) the fact that, in September 1956, Yeh himself professed ignorance of the effectiveness of tadpoles as oral contraceptives.[33]

Details of some of the experiments were subsequently published. For instance, one study made by the Research Institute in Chekiang involved a group of some sixty-five women volunteers. All of them had given birth to at least three children and were between 25 and 40 years of age. Of the sixty-five who participated in the experiment from April to August 1957, 42 were workers in a textile factory in Hangchow, Chekiang. Starting on the third, fourth, or fifth day after the menses, these women were instructed to swallow 24 and 20 live tadpoles, respectively, on two successive days. Notwithstanding the somewhat heavier dosage than Yehs original prescription, 43 percent of the women became pregnant within four months.[34] Thus, in addition to the real and imagined exposure to tape-worms, schistosomisasis, and other parasites when live tadpoles are swallowed (as some critics in China warned in 1956[35]), the risk of pregnancy evidently was not lessened. In fact, it may have been increased; for, some of the women could have employed another contraceptive method of proved effectiveness in place of tadpoles. It was not until April 1958 that tadpoles were officially declared to have no contraceptive value.[36]

32. *Wen Hui Daily* (Shanghai), 30 Mar. 1957; and *Health News* (Peking), 7 May 1957.

33. *Great Impartiality Daily* (Tientsin), 5 Sept. 1956.

34. *Liberation Daily* (Shanghai), 15 Apr. 1958.

35. For instance, *Daily News* (Shanghai), 1 Sept. 1956, and *Great Impartiality Daily* (Tientsin), 5 Sept. 1956.

36. *Liberation Daily* (Shanghai), 15 Apr. 1958.

Thus, there was a lapse of nearly two years between the first publicity given to tadpoles as oral contraceptives and the official disclaimer in 1958. During this interval, as can be seen in table 13, a plethora of other oral contraceptive recipes was published in China. Because of gaps in information, the list should probably not be regarded as exhaustive. Nonetheless, it is evident that, except in a few instances, the dissemination of specific recipes (either singly or severally) was extensive. They were published in periodicals of nationwide circulation and, simultaneously or successively, in provincial and municipal newspapers. As would be expected, these oral contraceptive recipes were offered to the public and the health authorities by herbalists or some organizations of practitioners of traditional medicine. A conspicuous exception is that the Municipal Bureau of Health of Shanghai, the largest metropolis in China, was cited as the source of information for the first two recipes in the table. The probable circumstances of this development will be touched upon later.

Presumably, all these oral contraceptives recipes have been in circulation for generations; and, in some cases, the recipes were handed down from one generation to another among herbalists in the same family. For instance, the belief that silkworm eggs (recipe no. 11) could serve as an oral contraceptive dates from the seventh century. Sun Ssu-mao, who died in 695 A.D., included this among what he called his "prescriptions worth a thousand pieces of gold."

In his *Medical History of Contraception,* Norman Himes made specific reference to Sun Ssu-mao in his review of Chinese contraceptive texts, but referred to neither silkworm eggs nor to any of the other recipes listed in the table. Himes related what is known as the *Ssu wu tang,* "Four ingredients broth," which is the decoction of the same last four ingredients as in recipe number 1, and to which two pinches of rape seeds are added before consumption.[37] It appears that, in 1956–57, most of these recipes presumably were printed and, thereby, made part of public discourse for the first time in the history of traditional medicine in China. Their publica-

37. Norman Himes, *Medical History of Contraception,* pp. 108–12.

TABLE 13

Oral Contraceptive Recipes

Ingredients	Preparation and Dosage	Presumed Potency	Promoting Agent or Agency and Source of Information
1 Brassica rapa, L. (4 mace*) Angelica polymorpha, Vas. (3 mace) Conioselinum univitatum, Turcz. (½ mace) Rohmannis Lutea, Maxim. (3 mace) Paeonia albiflora (1 mace)	Place all ingredients in an earthen pot. Add about 2 cups of water, and simmer 30 minutes. Strain to obtain a first decoction of about ½ cup. Add another 2 cups of water to the ingredients. Repeat the process to obtain another ½ cup of decoction. Combine both decoctions. On the day of cessation of the menstrual flow, drink ½ cup each after lunch and dinner. Prepare and take two additional recipes in the same manner on the two following days. Repeat the whole process at the end of the menstrual flow during the next two months.	Permanent	Shanghai's Municipal Bureau of Health. *Great Impartiality Daily* (Tientsin), 22 July 1956. Reprinted in *Chungking Daily* (Chungking), 26 July 1956, *Hupeh Daily* (Wuhan), 2 August 1956, *New China Daily* (Nanking), 23 August 1956, and *China's Women*, no. 9, 1 September 1956. *Harbin Daily* (Harbin), 3 August 1956.
2 Adenophora verticillate, Fisch. (3 mace) Dioscorea Japonica, Thurb. (3 mace) Alisma plantago (3 mace) Barks of Paeony (3 mace) Cornus officinalis, S. et Z. (3 mace) Pschyma cocos (3 mace) Cinnamon (3 mace) Tze Yu Kuai† (3 mace)	An antidote to recipe no. 1		*Great Impartiality Daily* (Tientsin), 22 July 1956.

TABLE 13 (continued)

Ingredients	Preparation and Dosage	Presumed Potency	Promoting Agent or Agency and Source of Information
3 Mung beans	Pulverize 10 to 20 fresh beans. Swallow one preparation each day for 3 days after the termination of the menstrual flow.	1 month	*Chekiang Daily* (Hangchow) 12 August 1956. Recommended by Kao Teh-ming of the Chekiang Institute of Women's Health.
4 Canarium album (Linese olive)	Soak in Kaoliang spirit for 10–15 days. At the end of menstruation, take 7 of the prepared olives each day for 3 days.	1 month	Ibid.
5 Agaric (20 mace) Fresh *Tilü* (40 mace) Steatite (20 mace)	Add water to the ingredients and simmer. Drink the decoction on three successive days immediately after the menses.	1 month	Ibid.
6 Persimmon stalks	Place 7 stalks on an earthen tile. Bake dry on fire. No metal utensils should be used to touch them. Do not burn stalks. Pulverize. Swallow one whole preparation with yellow wine (millet wine) after the menses. Do not drink yellow wine excessively. (Antidote: persimmon)	1 year	*Hengyang News* (Hunan), 25 August 1956. This and the following three recipes were presented in the name of the Editor of *Hengyang News*. In all cases, an endorsement was given by the Hospital of Traditional Chinese Medicine, Peking.
7 Melilotus officinalis, Lam. (2 mace)	Place the leaves in water. Boil. Drink 1 cup on the first day after the cessation of the menses	1 month	Ibid. Reprinted in *Chungking Daily*, 29 August 1956. *China's Women*, 1 September 1956.

TABLE 13 (continued)

Ingredients	Preparation and Dosage	Presumed Potency	Promoting Agent or Agency and Source of Information
8 Zanthoxylum piperitum, L. (10 mace)	Boil in water. Cool. Wash feet in the solution after the cessation of the menses.	1 month	*Hengyang News* (Hunan), 25 August 1956. Reprinted in *China's Women*, 1 September 1956.
9 Solanum melongena, L.	Take 14 flowers just before blossoming, sun dry and then place on an earthen tile. Bake on fire. No metal instruments should be used. Pulverize. Swallow with yellow wine after the first menstrual flow following childbirth. (Antidote: eggplant)	Indefinite	*Hengyang News* (Hunan), 25 August 1956. Reprinted in *Chungking Daily*, 29 August 1956. (Side effects: menstrual irregularities during the 3 following months, and a tendency to gain weight.)
10 Brassica rapa, L. (3 mace) Artemisia keiskeana, Mig. (3 mace) Vaccaria vulgaris, Host. (3 mace) Angelica polymorpha, Vas. (3 mace) Carthamus tinctorius, L. (8/10 mace) Gypsum (3 mace)	Place all ingredients in an earthen pot. Add 2 cups of water. Follow the instructions for recipe no. 1. Starting on the third day after the menses, drink ½ cup each time after lunch and dinner. Repeat on the next 2 days.	1 month	*Chungking Daily* (Chungking), 29 August 1956. Reprinted in *China's Women*, 1 September 1956, and *Health News* (Peking), 31 July 1956.
11 Bombyx mori (3 mace of eggs)	Roast but do not burn. Swallow with aged wine on third, fifth, and seventh days following delivery.	Permanent	From Sun Sau-mao's "Thousand of Gold Prescriptions." Sun lived in the Tang dynasty and died in 695 A.D. This and the preceding and following recipes (nos. 9, 10, 12)

TABLE 13 (continued)

Ingredients	Preparation and Dosage	Presumed Potency	Promoting Agent or Agency and Source of Information
			were formally introduced at the First Symposium on the Treatment of Women's Diseases, sponsored by the Traditional Chinese Medical Society of Hopei Province.
12 Semen plantagiuis, L. (2 mace) Lotus stemens, L. (2 mace) Zanthoxylum piperitum, L. (½ mace) Calcareous spar (1½ mace) Melilotus officinalis, Lam. (1½ mace)	Mix and grind the ingredients into fine powder. After menstruation, take 1 mace each, 3 times a day until the supply is gone. Or, divide the preparation into two equal portions, take one portion immediately after the menses, and the other 15 days later.	1 year	Introduced by an herbalist in Hopei. *China's Women*, 1 September 1956.
13 Verbena officinalis, L. (5 mace) Caprifolium, L. (5 mace)	Cook in water. Drink the broth all at once as soon as the menses cease. Repeat for several days.	Unknown	*Hangchow Daily* (Hangchow), 18 October 1956. Introduced by an herbalist at a symposium attended by some 25 doctors of both Western medicine and traditional Chinese medicine.
14 Angelica polymorpha, Vas. (10 mace) Conioselinum univitatum, Turcz. (5 mace) Rohmannia lutea, Maxim (6 mace) Paeonia albiflora (3 mace) Pachyma cocos, L. (3 mace)	Wrap calomel in very thin paper, and burn into ashes. Combine all ingredients. Pulverize and sift with fine cloth. Add honey. Roll into small balls of about 3 mace each. From the day after the cessation of the menses, take one pill each time before sleep until the supply is	10 months to 1 year	Recommended by an herbalist in Hopeh province. *Hopeh Daily* (Pao-ting), 4 December 1956.

TABLE 13 (continued)

Ingredients	Preparation and Dosage	Presumed Potency	Promoting Agent or Agency and Source of Information
Alisma plantago, L. (3 mace) Radix liquiritae, L. (3 mace) Bignonia chinensis, Lam. (5 mace) Verbena officinalis, L. (5 mace) Hydrargyri sulphidum rubrum (1½ mace) Calcareous spar (3 mace) Atractylis orata (5 mace) Calomel (1 mace) Semen areca (2 nuts) Su Hsiang† (3 mace) Ts'un Hsiang‡ (1/10 mace)	exhausted. (For women who have just given birth to a child, wait until 30 days after the delivery.) No other drugs should be ingested at the same time; otherwise, the effect of the pills will be nullified.		
15 Arsenic monosulphide (½ to 3 mace) Calcareous spar (3 mace)	Pulverize. Swallow with water. One preparation should suffice. To assure success, take two additional doses. The three preparations may be taken separately; starting on the day after the menses, take one dose a day. No intercourse within a week after the last dose.	9 months	*Anhwei Daily* (Anching), 30 August 1958.

Note: *1.33 lbs. = 1 catty; 1 catty has 16 *liang* (ounces) or 160 *chien* (mace).
†English translation of the Chinese name of the ingredient, the identity of which has not been established.

tion obviously resulted from the attempts to change a nation (e.g., the spread of contraceptive knowledge) and to cherish her heritage (e.g., the promotion of traditional medicine) simultaneously.

Traditional medicine gained renewed prominence in China in 1955 and the following years. Consistent with this was the official policy statement that the key to the successful perpetuation and promotion of China's medical heritage lies in its being studied by doctors trained in Western medicine. Instructions to that effect were issued in 1955 by the Ministry of Health. Not only were physicians trained in Western medicine directed to cooperate with the traditional herbalists and to take more note of their methods of therapy, but pharmacologists and other medical scientists were also urged to study the *material medica* of China.[38] Li Teh-chun, the minister of health, reported that special programs of study were instituted for physicians, professors, lecturers, and teaching assistants in medical schools at the end of 1955. It was planned that some 5,000 similarly situated persons would be given an opportunity in 1956 to become acquainted with various aspects of traditional medicine. In order to strengthen the work on traditional drugs of plant, animal, and mineral origin in China, a research institute was established and began its work in December 1955. Furthermore, Li Teh-chun announced that up to the end of May 1956, approximately 10,000 practitioners of traditional medicine were absorbed into, or placed on the staffs of, public hospitals and clinics throughout China. In addition, some 67 hospitals for traditional medicine were opened, and more than 1,200 clinics for traditional medicine were created during the same period.[39]

In 1955, there were reportedly some 500,000 practitioners of traditional medicine in China. They outnumbered, by a

---

38. E. Leong Way, "Pharmacology," p. 365. Of interest was an effort by the late Prime Minister Lal Bahadur Shastri to strike a compromise in a similar battle that continues to rage between the advocates of Western medicine and the defenders of the traditional system of medical practices in India (see *New York Times*, 20 July 1965).

39. Li Teh-chun, speech, *The Complete Report*, p. 147.

very wide margin, doctors trained in Western medicine; the latter numbered only between 50,000 and 75,000 in China in 1958. Thus, the influence of the traditional medical practitioners should not be underestimated. As an organized group, and given their numerical strength and indigenous character, traditional medicine and its personnel would and clearly did acquire and wield power consistent, if not commensurate, with their numbers and status in post-1949 Chinese society. As previously indicated, Yeh Hsi-chun, who spoke of tadpoles as oral contraceptives, was the deputy-director of the Department of Health of Chekiang Province. That two of the recipes were promoted in the name of the Municipal Health Bureau of Shanghai could not simply have been a fortuitous coincidence; it must have been one of the consequences of the conscious elevation of traditional medicine.

One could deplore or deprecate the recent dissemination of the various oral contraceptive recipes in China. One could sneer at the use of rape seeds (recipe no. 1), olives (5), stalks of persimmon (6), buds of eggplant flowers (9), safflower blossoms (10), or honeysuckle (13) as possible oral contraceptives. Moreover, as is well-known, gypsum ([hydrous calcium sulphate] 10) is used for making plaster of Paris and as a dressing for soils; calomel ([mercurous chloride] 14) as either an anthelmintic or a purgative agent in medicine; and realgar ([arsenic monosulphide] 15) is employed as a pigment and in pyrotechny. Therefore, one could also abhor what amounted to an endorsement of these substances as oral contraceptives. However, little would be gained and much would be lost by this stance. Beyond the question of the contraceptive effectiveness of these recipes and, in some cases, possible harm to health, their printed circulation in 1956–57 and the accompanying developments have policy implications and significance in several ways.[40]

---

40. Of relevance is the fact that the pill being marketed in the United States and elsewhere has also generated wide concern among both users and medical practitioners. Yet, in spite of many uncertainties in regard to its side- and long-term effects, it still enjoys official sanctions for its sales. The politics of drugs is not nation-bound.

It is sufficient here to note some of the immediate reactions in China to the publication and popularization of these oral contraceptive recipes. These pertained to their contraceptive effectiveness and possible health hazards, and are probably the questions that invariably arise in the minds of all who see them for the first time. In China itself, initial expressions ranged from caution to incredulity over these recipes, particularly the official and medical sanctions implicit in their publication. However, it should be pointed out that the acceptance of these materials as possible contraceptives evidently was never unanimous even among practitioners of traditional medicine themselves in China. Some were ambivalent in their attitudes and commented that they had no opinion at all because they never used them in practice to determine their contraceptive effectiveness, if any. Nor, for this reason, would they discredit them completely as being without any contraceptive efficacy. On the other hand, others warned against their ingestion, not because of a lack of proved contraceptive potency, but because of what they termed "regrettable consequences" (e.g., permanent serility) that were likely to follow from their consumption.[41] Views on the utility of the various contraceptive recipes, thus, were not entirely consistent even among practitioners of traditional medicine, though they all seem to have supported the request that these recipes be scientifically and systematically analyzed.

Also urging careful analysis and testing were those who were much less hesitant and less reluctant in questioning the contraceptive and hazardous potential of the various recipes, in print and in private circulation. Nevertheless, open opposition apparently was slow to develop and to declare itself. Two quotations from Chinese papers may adequately illustrate the situation that prevailed in the early fall of 1956:

As regards the use of rape seeds and so forth as oral contraceptives, . . . precisely because of their publication in

41. *New China Daily* (Nanking), 10 Sept. 1956; *China Youths Daily* (Peking), 7 Aug. 1956; and *Chekiang Daily* (Hangchow), 12 Aug. 1956.

Party newspapers, the consequence is likely to be far-reaching. We who hold a different view wish to bring it forth for discussion by all. Traditional practitioners in general dare not express their opinions because they do not wish to be wrong; they profess that "their talents are inferior and their learning superficial." This is understandable. However, it is very strange to see that gynecologists and other medical experts in provincial and public hospitals of traditional medicine [where there is no lack of them] have uttered not a single word concerning the contraceptive value of this recipe.[42]

Recently, it seems that we are a little infatuated with simple prescriptions. So long as they are recipes introduced by some practitioners of traditional medicine or secret family formulas now disclosed for the first time, they are all decorated with the label "science" and given extravagant propaganda and extensive promotion. Such a treatment is granted whatever their ingredients and therapeutic value are, whether or not there is any scientific base, and irrespective of possible side effects or dangers. Furthermore, those [who are responsible for introducing these recipes] do not welcome a discussion of them. Nor does a person dare voice an opinion, fearful of being stigmatized as "anti–traditional medicine" or "harboring decadent bourgeois thought".[43]

Thus amid, or despite, sporadic caution and dissent, oral contraceptive recipes continued to appear in print and to enjoy relatively favorable publicity toward the end of 1956. However, criticisms also became more direct, more frequent, and more forceful both just before and just after the beginning of 1957. From various parts of the country came reports of deaths and disabilities arising from the ingestion of both specified and unnamed preparations.[44] As previously

42. *New China Daily* (Nanking), 10 Sept. 1956.

43. *People's Daily* (Peking), 8 Sept. 1956.

44. A few or some of the preparations may have been abortifacients. For reports of various unfortunate incidents, see *Harbin Daily* (Heilunkiang), 11 Nov. 1956; *Brilliance Daily* (Peking), 9 Dec. 1956; *New Hunan Daily* (Changsha, Hunan), 8 Dec. 1956; *Sian Daily* (Sian), 17 Jan. 1957; *Liberation Daily* (Shanghai), 13 Feb. 1957; and *Wen Hui Daily* (Shanghai), 1 Mar. 1957.

noted, the official disavowal of tadpoles as contraceptives belatedly came in April 1958. Available documents indicate that it was probably not until late in 1957 that attacks on the use of other contraceptive recipes attained any degree of specificity. In one instance, for example, recipe number 4 and the herbalist who introduced it were roundly criticized: in one locality in North China, some 265 women purchased pills prepared according to this recipe. Five to ten months later, 97 of these women were reached by the local maternal- and infant-health clinic via interview and questionnaire, which revealed that 36 of them either never actually consumed any pills or stopped taking them after a short while. Of the remaining 61 women who took the pills as instructed, 24 were pregnant at the time of the follow-up study. After eliminating another 22 women because of age, lactation, and simultaneous employment of other contraceptives, only 15 women reportedly could have benefited from the pills. The significance of the latter fact should probably not be stressed, in view of the short time that lapsed between the purchase of the pills and the probe into their effect.[45]

Even if it could be argued that a *total* lack of contraceptive effectiveness of these pills was not conclusively established, the inquiry produced definite information concerning their side effects. In addition to stomach and abdominal pains and bodily aches, nausea, vomiting, diarrhea, and menstrual irregularities were said to be the most prevalent aftereffects.[46] In another report, a local clinic of traditional medicine in Honan Province was accused of selling what in effect was a poisonous contraceptive powder made of calomel, leeches, and two other ingredients. The purported toxic symtoms varied from person to person among more than twenty cultural cadres of a particular school, including swelling of the body, blistering of the tongue, urination of blood, and swelling of the vagina.[47]

45. *Hopeh Daily* (Paoting), 12 Nov. 1957.

46. Ibid.

47. *Brilliance Daily* (Peking), 7 Dec. 1956; and *Chungking Daily* (Chungking), 5 Feb. 1958.

It is relevant to note that criticisms of oral contraceptive recipes did not go unanswered. Insisting that the value of condoms could not be depreciated should a lack of care lead to their rupture during use, it was argued that oral contraceptive recipes ought not to be rejected indiscriminately because incorrect or unsupervised use could have been responsible for the reported ill-effects or pregnancies.[48] Attempts to evaluate various herbs were also reported to be actually under way in 1957, one of which was carried out by two doctors at the internationally-known Union Medical College in Peking.[49] A formal request for additional study of Chinese herbs was also repeated by a practitioner at the Kwangtung Provincial Political Consultative Conference in the summer of 1957.[50]

What became of these studies and how intensive and numerous they were cannot be ascertained. There have been no reports of research findings, positive or negative, on the contraceptive value of any of the herbs. Nevertheless, although, as late as 1958, new descriptions of oral contraceptive recipes continued to appear along with public warnings against their reckless use,[51] there has been no revival of the cult of traditional contraceptive recipes in China in recent years. In this connection, it may be well to take cognizance of the remarks about the situation in 1956:

> After the publication of Chinese oral contraceptive recipes, many people placed their hope [to avoid pregnancies] in them. Irrespective of possible effects, and in the absence of medical consultation, they wantonly accepted and experimented with them. The result has been that they not only failed to achieve their aim but also ruined their health. Their search for an effective oral contraceptive is easy to comprehend. [But], the various agencies and their personnel responsible for contraceptive propaganda work and

48. *Harbin Daily* (Heilungkiang), 26 Mar. 1957.

49. *Brilliance Daily* (Peking), 28 Mar. 1957.

50. *Southern Daily* (Canton), 14 May 1957; and *Health News* (Peking), 2 Apr. 1957.

51. *Chungking Daily* (Chungking), 5 Feb. 1958.

instructions must make it clear [to these people] that no
oral contraceptives of proved value exist at present, and
advise them not to adopt carelessly drugs of presumed contraceptive effectiveness.[52]

Whether the relative lack of reference to oral contraceptive
recipes constitutes an intentional avoidance of repetition of
what were clearly unfortunate incidents in 1956–57 can only
be surmised. Some of the oral contraceptives promoted in
the name of preserving the heritage of traditional medicine
evidently were in public opprobrium. However, the issue does
not seem to have been resolved with finality; there is neither
direct nor circumstantial evidence in support of this.[53] On
the one hand, the influence of traditional medicine and its
personnel still must be reckoned with in China today. On
the other hand, at least since 1969 or possibly earlier, oral
contraceptive compounds have become available in large quantities to women in China. Two types of the oral pill are being
distributed: one combines norethindrone and ethynyloestradiol; the other megestral acetate and ethynyloestradiol. In
addition, injectable contraception (i.e., steroidal compounds)
is also being experimented with at present (see below, page
273). Thus, actual developments in fertility control by physiological means may well have relegated the controversy over
traditional contraceptive recipes to history.

Induced Abortion

Also, in contrast to the circumstances surrounding the
earlier drive, birth control activities in China are now being

---

52. *Brilliance Daily* (Peking) 3 Dec. 1956.

53. See *Great Impartiality Daily* (Tientsin), 22 July 1956; *Chungking Daily* (Chungking), 3 Aug. 1956; and *Labor News* (Shanghai), 7
Sept. 1956. It is well known that systematic investigation of native
plant medicines continues to be important outside China. For instance,
a symposium on medicinal plants was held in Kandy, in December 1964,
under the joint sponsorship of the government of Ceylon and the
UNESCO South Asia Science Cooperation Office. Also, for a recent
assessment of the role of plants in modern medicine, cf. Margaret B.
Kreig, *Green Medicine: The Search for Plants that Heal.*

carried on by qualified medical personnel in a low key (see below) and with minimal reference to larger political and ideological issues of past years. In this connection, note should be taken of some pertinent remarks by Premier Chou in 1964:

> We do believe in planned parenthood, but it is not easy to introduce all at once in China, and it is more difficult to achieve in rural areas, where most of our people live, than in the cities. . . .
> Since the Second World War Japan has achieved a remarkable decline [in her rate of annual population increase] to about 1 percent. We have sent people to Japan to study means and results there. Our present target is to reduce population growth to below 2 percent; for the future we aim at an even lower rate.
> However, I do not believe it will be possible for us to equal the Japanese rate as early as 1970—for some of the reasons mentioned. For example, with improved living conditions over the past two years our rate of increase *again* rose to 2.5 percent! Therefore, our emphasis on planned parenthood is entirely positive; planned parenthood, where there is increased production of goods and services, is conducive to raising the people's standard of living. That is why we have been very carefully studying it during the past two years.[54]

Fertility control in China is a monumental task. Though Premier Chou's statement carries an implication that there had been a short recession in the rate of population growth in China because of increased mortality probably between 1960 and 1962, the erosion of China's population pyramid will have to begin at the base and will be slow. The disclosure of the dispatch of a Chinese study mission to Japan is of special interest here, though its arrival and itineraries in Japan have yet to be verified and traced. Might this mean that abortions on a massive scale could not and should not be ruled out as a component, perhaps a major one, of China's fertility policy? Induced abortion has proved effective in a short span of time in Japan—a country whose cultural and

54. As printed in the *New York Times,* 3 Feb. 1964.

social ties with China are many and extensive. This circumstance has fostered a belief in its possible adoption in China.

With respect to the Japanese achievement in fertility control, induced abortions have been responsible for nearly all of the decrease in the birthrate in a decade. The Japanese birth rate stood at 34.3 per 1,000 population in 1947 and has shown a steady decline since then, falling below 17 per 1,000 in 1961. In absolute terms, the annual number of births fell from over 2,680,000 to about 1,650,000 during the same period, which amounts to a reduction of over one million births per year. In the meantime, the number of induced abortions averaged over 1,100,000 from 1953 onward, giving an annual abortion rate of nearly 13 per 1,000.[55] There can be, therefore, no dispute that induced abortion has proved effective in the decline of the Japanese birthrate.

It would be an extreme distortion to claim that all knowledge of the Japanese achievement has been denied admission in China, but references to it in China have been very infrequent in the years since 1949. In fact, the desirability of induced abortion as a means of fertility control received only scattered comment in China prior to the intense campaign to promote birth control in 1957. When Shao Li-tzu first broached the subject of birth control in 1954, he purposefully down-played the place of abortion in his argument:

> The provisions of the Constitution [Article 96] to place mothers and children under the protection of the state is encouraging enough. But if a child continues to be born to a mother every year even if she is no longer medically fit or when her burden has already proved to be too heavy for her [even if we disregard the suffering of the mother], it is no easy job for the state to place all such mothers under its protection. . . . *In China, the question of abortion can be left alone,* but [as a matter of urgency], medical theories on contraception must be propagated while contra-

55. Irene B. Taeuber, *The Population of Japan,* pp. 275–76. Also Christopher Tietze, "The Current Status of Fertility Control," pp. 426–44.

ceptives should be supplied and practical guidance on contraception given.[56]

Shao's avoidance of induced abortion must have been intentional; the keynote of the various discussions[57] in the next two years or so was its *un*desirability, a fact that may have accounted for his initial reluctance to discuss the issue. Specifically, the therapeutic benefits of induced abortion were recognized in cases where the health or life of the mother was at stake, but its general use in the termination of unwanted pregnancies was considered inappropriate and ill-advised. The exhortation stressed the idea that induced abortion is unnatural and violates the normal physiological process, and that it is likely to lead to internal inflammations and hemorrhage, menstrual irregularities, or even death.[58] In addition, it was emphasized that induced abortion is an ineffective method of fertility control as pregnancies can recur in the future, and that the liberalization of its use is likely to result in greater carelessness in the employment of other relatively effective means, such as diaphragms, condoms, and the like.

On the other hand, in 1956 the government apparently was also under pressure to relax the conditions under which abortions had been and were presently allowed. Instead of restricting abortion to couples with from four to six children, it was urged that it be permitted after the birth of two children if both the husband and wife agreed. There was also a suggestion that abortion be allowed in cases where the mother was in very poor health and if there were other difficult circumstances. In the face of these popular demands, the vice-minister of the Department of Health stated, in August 1956, that he was personnally in agreement with such suggestions

56. *People's Daily,* 18 Sept. 1954.

57. See *Brilliance Daily* (Peking), 7 May 1956; *China's Women,* no. 6 (1 June 1956): *New Hunan Journal* (Changsha, Hunan), 8 Dec. 1956; and *Shenyang Daily,* 17 Nov. 1956.

58. There is evidence that is consistent with this claim, but it is difficult to evaluate the effects of induced abortion on maternal mortality and maternal health (see Taeuber, *The Population of Japan,* p. 277).

and that the Department was reviewing the whole question of induced abortion. Meantime, he expressed the hope that local health branches and medical officials would show leniency and flexibility in the application of the existing regulations, so as not to defeat their original purpose, i.e., the protection of maternal health.[59]

Formal changes in the regulations were announced on 15 May 1957, whereby abortions would be allowed without reference to family size, provided: (1) the operation was to take place within three months of gestation; (2) there were no other health impediments; and (3) there had been no abortion during the preceding twelve months. These relaxations were introduced, it was stated, in order to prevent dangers to health arising from clandestine abortions.[60]

In practice, however, a more liberal interpretation of the former regulations seems to have taken place almost as soon as the vice-minister of the Health Department publicly voiced his hope. At the 1957 National People's Consultative Conference (in March), a deputy, who is also a doctor, strongly deplored the wastefulness of resources involved in abortions and their accompanying crowding of hospital beds and doctors' work schedules, which she had observed in the municipal hospitals in Peking. She said, "Since the relaxation of regulations governing abortion by the Health Department last year, the number of abortions in Peking's municipal hospitals went up in a straight line," and she reported that a total of 1,593 abortions were performed in the 24 municipal hospitals during the second half of 1956.[61]

A similar though much less specific objection to abortion was also registered at a symposium under the auspices of the China Medical Association[62] in Peking on 20 February 1957. Of the 30 or more specialists in gynecology, neurology, physiology, urology, endocrinology, biochemistry, and pharma-

59. *Great Impartiality Daily* (Tientsin), 22 Aug. 1956.

60. *People's Daily,* 23 May 1957.

61. Ibid., 9 Mar. 1957.

62. Ibid., 23 Feb. 1957; and *Brilliance Daily* (Peking), 22 Feb. 1957.

cology, all were of the opinion that induced abortion was not a suitable method of fertility control, pointing again to its health hazards.[63]   This view was apparently shared by many of their medical colleagues throughout the nation.[64]

Thus, it was hardly surprising that the announcement of the new measure on 15 May drew a prompt rebuttal from the China Medical Association. In a resolution carried unanimously, the Standing Committee of the Association declared on 24 May that "the new directive on induced abortion was, from the medical point of view, unsound."   Prior to this, on 17 April, a Committee of Experts appointed by the Association forwarded to the Ministry of Health of the Central Government, a list of specific objections to induced abortion:[65]

1. Induced abortion is an hazardous operation and can subsequently lead to various physical discomforts and physiological irregularities.

2. Induced abortion is contrary to the principle of "Prevention First."   Nor does it constitute a solution to the problem of repeated pregnancies.

3. The great majority of our population is rural, and it is in the rural villages where the population problem is most serious.   But, under the present medical conditions in rural areas, it is impossible to institute an abortion program.   It is also no small task if we were to train, within a short period of time, a large number of medical personnel for the job and to provide the necessary medical facilities.   If we have this power, it would be better to devote it to promoting contraception.

4. A large-scale abortion program is also difficult even in urban centers, and, if attempted, will interfere with performance of routine medical treatment.

5. To liberalize the restrictions on abortion at a time when contraception is being promoted, is self-defeating because it opens the "back door" to those who are negligent

63. This observation is based on information in a large number of provincial newspapers, which are too numerous to be cited here (see *Wen Hui Daily* [Shanghai] 20 Apr. 1957; *Chungking Daily,* 9 Apr. 1957; and *Kianghsi Daily,* 23 Feb. 1957.)

64. This is the association of doctors trained in Western medicine rather than in traditional medicine.

65. *Great Impartiality Daily* (Peking), 30 May 1957.

in the use of contraceptives. In case of those whose medical bills are paid for from public funds, certain abuses are likely to occur; for, abortion means also a vacation.

6. Induced abortion contravenes the principle of the equality of the sexes. Childbearing is a joint responsibility, but abortion places the burden and risk on the women only. It also encourages the men to adopt a negative and irresponsible attitude toward contraception.

These constitute the most articulate opposition to induced abortion as a method of fertility control in China. The usual medical arguments against abortion were, in this instance, buttressed by objections based on practical difficulties and sociopsychological considerations. Coming as it did from the China Medical Association, this opposition assumes an added significance; for the cooperation of the Association is of fundamental importance in any viable abortion program. The number of Chinese doctors trained in Western medicine is estimated, as previously indicated, to have been between 50,000 and 75,000 in 1958. Though some of them received their training in Japan, the majority of them were educated either in the missionary medical schools in China or in a Western country. This background partially explains the opposition of the China Medical Association to induced abortion.

The opposition to induced abortion, however, does not seem to have been limited to the medical profession alone. None of the demographers and sociologists (e.g., Chen Ta, Fei Hsiao-tung, and Wu Ching-chao) favored its use in their discussions of fertility control during the period of the Hundred Flowers. Chen Ta attacked abortion on humanitarian grounds.[66] Ma Yin-chu, the most vocal and persistent advocate of population control in China, was opposed to induced abortion.[67] In at least one instance, the All-China Women's Federation was urged to protest against its use because abortion ran counter to the principle of the equality of the sexes.

66. Chen Ta, "Deferred Marriage, Birth Control, and Population Problems of New China," pp. 1–16.

67. *Wen Hui Daily* (Shanghai), 27 Apr. 1957.

It is, perhaps, not without significance that the Federation is known to have neither protested nor endorsed the use of abortion.[68]

Indeed, it is hard to find any prominent Chinese figure inside or outside the Communist Party who entered a plea for the adoption of mass abortions as a national policy. As previously noted, Shao Li-tzu was initially unwilling to discuss the issue because of his "lack of courage at that time." Later in 1957, when he did speak out on the subject, his view still showed restraint: "I do not deny the harmful effects of artificial abortion, and I am also in agreement with the staging of a major campaign to publicize these harms along with a massive propaganda campaign on contraception. I only disagree with the prohibition or restriction of induced abortion by decree or coercion," and "my disapproval of legal or coercive prohibition or restriction of induced abortion should not be construed as approval of abortion. I think that there cannot be anyone who approves or promotes abortion."[69]

Notwithstanding the changes in the regulations governing abortion in May 1957, the official attitude remained cautious. Li Teh-chun, the health minister, for instance, declared that the ease of restrictions was to let individuals decide for themselves whether or not to undergo the operation and that the Ministry neither favored unhampered abortions nor encouraged the practice of induced abortion.[70]

Indeed, as has been reported, some cadres of the Chinese Communist Party underwent abortions before and since 1949.[71] But, these appear to have been abortions performed as a matter of personal convenience rather than the result of Party policy. It is likely that the Party has tacitly allowed the practice in the past. But, there is no evidence that the Party is likely to alter this position with respect to abortion:

68. *Tsingtao Daily,* 6 June 1957; and *Brilliance Daily* (Peking), 4 June 1957.

69. *People's Daily,* 20 Mar. 1957; and *Brilliance Daily* (Peking), 4 May 1957.

70. Ibid., 3 June 1956.

71. *Great Impartiality Daily* (Peking), 30 May 1957.

"We absolutely will not follow the Japanese approach. Our present attitude toward induced abortion is sound: induced abortions are allowed when, owing to certain difficulties, the women are unwilling to continue their pregnancies, in order to prevent hazards to health arising from clandestine operations, on the one hand. On the other hand, it must be made clear to the masses that induced abortion is detrimental to the health of women, and that, if contraceptives are not used after the operation, they will again become pregnant and will not realize the goal of planned reproduction."[72]

It may be recalled that the performance of some 1,600 abortions during the second half of 1956 is reported to have constituted an extra burden on the hospital facilities and doctors in Peking. Granted that there was some exaggeration in this complaint, there remains much validity to the objection cited by the China Medical Association, that the shortage of medical personnel renders impossible the introduction of induced abortion as an effective means of birth control. The announced Chinese birth rate was 37 per 1,000, and the death rate 17 per 1,000. On the basis of these rates, if China were to duplicate the Japanese record (i.e., to cut the rate of natural increase to about 1 percent per year) in twice the length of time (i.e., twenty years) beginning now, it would mean roughly over 18 million operations a year towards the end of the period, or a cumulative total of over 250 million abortions between 1962 and 1982. In 1956, the cost of an induced abortion in China was reported to be a little over U. S. $10; a minimum of $2.5 billion would be required to realize this goal, not including the costs involved in hospital construction and the training of physicians.

There is also as yet no way to estimate, even in the most general terms, what it will take to convince enough people in China to willingly submit themselves to induced abortion. There is no evidence that even remotely suggests that the Medical Association has modified its stated opposition to induced abortion. On the contrary, at a meeting on planned

72. Tien, Feng-Tao, "China's Planned Reproduction and Population Increase," pp. 458-68.

births called by the Kwangchow (Canton) Municipal People's Congress in August 1964, Dr. Chang Hsing-hui, chief of the Department of Obstetrics of the Kwangtung Provincial People's Hospital, reiterated that induced abortion is a negative approach to fertility control.[73] Similarly, Dr. Wang Tawan, director, Department of Gynecology, Tientan Hospital, Peking, argued that planned reproduction must not depend on induced abortion. To support her argument, Wang offered a both graphic and statistical account of its hazards:

> Since, for instance, the scraping of the uterus is done inside the mouth of the womb, it cannot be seen with the eye. The surgeon carries out the operation by the feeling of the hand. In the early period of pregnancy, the uterus expands and the uterine wall is very soft, but the instrument used for scraping is made of metal. If the scraping is heavy, it may cause damage to the muscular structure of the uterus or even tiny perforations. When the scraping is gentle, the uterus may not be fully emptied and part of the fetus may still be left in the womb, causing continuous bleeding, inflammation, and pain in the abdomen. . . . Judging by the conditions after the operation, induced abortion has an unfavorable impact on the human body since it is a kind of forced interruption of pregnancy. . . . Of the 200 women who underwent induced abortion at the gynecological department of a certain hospital in the city, 42.5 percent experienced menstrual irregularities, 28.6 percent leucorrhoea, 56 percent headache, dizziness, insomnia, and palpitation, 17.6 percent loss of sexual desire, and 6.5 percent inflammation of the pelvis.[74]

The issue of induced abortion is further complicated by the lack of strong spokesmen in China to promote its adoption. Induced abortion is likely to remain legal in China as it has been for some time. However, the immediate past, coupled with some real practical difficulties, should leave no doubt about the slim prospects for the employment of induced abortion on a truly massive scale in the control of population numbers in China. Consistent with this conclusion

73. *Southern Daily* (Kwangchow), 24 Aug. 1962.
74. *Daily Worker* (Peking), 27 Sept. 1962.

is a report by Tameyoshi Katagiri (regional director, International Planned Parenthood Federation, Western Pacific Region) and Takuma Terao, professor of demography, Keio University, that although vacuum aspiration equipment is to be seen in most of the 70,000 commune hospitals, the actual number of abortions seems to have been on the low side. According to these two Japanese who visited China in April 1972, in Ton Wan People's Commune near Shanghai (population: 23,000), "the cumulative total for tubal ligations is 1,156 and for vasectomies 681, and there are 453 pill users, 270 women with IUD's, 17 experimenting with injectables, and many people using condoms and traditional methods of birth control." Abortion received no specific mention in this instance. In another case, among the 3,000 women in the fertile age group in the Shao Yun Shang urban area of Hangchow, "the cumulative total of pill users in 1971 was 727, of IUD acceptors 157, of condom users 553, and 19 women were on injectable contraceptives. 584 women had been sterilised, and 49 men had had vasectomies. About 550 women were lactating or their husbands were temporarily absent. During 1971, 186 legal abortions were performed."[75]

Marital Postponement

In sharp contrast, delayed matrimony has been enthusiastically supported by many in China since 1949. Formal reference to it first appeared in the text of China's Marriage Law of 1950.[76] Within a specified period of time, say, one hundred years, average age at first marriage is a chief determinant of the length between, and the number of, generations. Demographically, therefore, postponement of marriage is a potentially powerful mechanism for fertility control, because it can eliminate one or more generations within a century if the age at marriage is increased from 20 to 30. However, it would do

75. International Planned Parenthood Federation, "Wide Range of Family Planning," pp. 5–6.

76. *The Marriage Law of the People's Republic of China* (Peking: Foreign Languages Press, 1959).

great violence to the spirit of the Marriage Law to insist that demographic considerations were at all responsible for their inclusion in the code.

Nor would it be correct to read population calculation into the Law's two major provisions limiting the issuance of marriage certificates to duly registered couples-to-be of legal age. Neither the requirement (as stipulated in Article 4 of the Marriage Law) that marriages be registered with civil authorities nor the stipulation that the minimum age be 18 for girls and 20 for men is a demographically deliberate act. What is involved here amounts to a redefinition of marriage as a social contract rather than a pact between two families, and to a formal ban on youthful marriages as such.

In short, the Marriage Law was conceived as nothing other than an instrument of family change. The *People's Daily* gave a confirmation of this when it published its first editorial on fertility control in March 1957. In answer to the question of how to restrict reproduction, it stated:

> First [of all], the custom of early marriage must be changed. The earlier the marriage, the higher is the fertility, and this also creates greater difficulties for the young couple. In order to limit reproduction, later marriage must necessarily be promoted. In our country in the past, the evil custom of early marriage prevailed, which once inflicted much pain on young men and women. *In order to change this custom, the Marriage Law established the minimum age for marriage.* But, this stipulation does not mean that a person must marry once the minimum age is attained. In fact, marrying after the age of 25 is beneficial and does no harm. At present, many young people were married not only before age 25, but also prior to the age 20; this has consequently created many problems for those involved. In many villages, the phenomenon of early marriages, even below the minimum age stipulated in the Marriage Law, still exists. Therefore, we must make every effort to conduct educational propaganda among the masses to break down the evil custom of early marriage and to promote the practice of marrying a little later.[77]

77. *People's Daily,* 5 Mar. 1957. Italics added.

Here, postponement of marriage was formally, but belatedly, endorsed also as a means of fertility control, however circumscribed the original intent was at the time of the adoption of the Marriage Law. This endorsement was preceded by other purposeful references to this effect some months before 1957. Shao Li-tzu, for instance, raised the question at the 1956 session of the People's Political Consultative Conference.[78] Both at the outset and since then, the application of marital postponement to China's population problem has been accepted in principle by persons of every political hue. For example, all of the participants in the fertility debate of the 1950s enthusiastically subscribed to it, even though they were divided on such other means as sterilization, oral contraception, and abortion.[79]

Thus, unlike other means of fertility reduction, delayed marriage occupies a unique place in the contexts of both China's social policy in general and antinatal decisions in particular. China's Marriage Law of 1950 was a convincing testimony to a national decision to rid the country of the suffocating constraints of age-old family and marriage customs and to release men and women into the societal stream. From this standpoint, also unlike other means of fertility limitation, delayed marriage more directly serves to channel the energies of young men and women into study and work. It can also profoundly restructure the Chinese family itself. Therefore, it would seem very plausible to maintain that whatever its demographic and economic benefits, the consensus shown in postponement of marriage among persons of diverse ideologies and political affiliations in China stemmed from their prior commitment to reducing the hold of the family on the individual. To declare unaimously for delayed marriage as a means of fertility limitation, as was done in the course of the birth control campaign, was very much in keeping with this basic and far-reaching objective.

---

78. Shao Li-tzu, *People's Daily,* 20 Mar. 1957. In this speech, Shao recalled what he had said a year earlier (see footnote 80, below).

79. For individual citations, see the various footnotes in this chapter where their names are given.

This common stand on postponement of marriage was also solid enough to withstand the divisive fertility debate in China. As previously indicated, public acclamations of delayed marriage constituted the prologue to birth control activities in the 1960s. However, it should be added that there were at least two small, but tactically meaningful, disagreements behind the united front. Both pertained to the means of securing the acceptance of marital postponement among the young people. Shao Li-tzu outlined the differences in his speech before the third session of the Second People's Political Consultative Conference:

> To appropriately revise Article 4 of the Marriage Law: Delayed marriage must be encouraged as we promote fertility limitation. . . . But, is it necessary to revise Article 4 of the Marriage Law and to raise the legal minimum age for marriage in order to promote delayed marriage? There are divergent views in this regard. Many people maintain that to promote delayed marriage, we should only employ propaganda and education, and that there is no need to amend the Marriage Law. The stipulation in the Law that "marriage can be contracted only after the attainment of the 20th birthday in the case of a man and the 18th birthday in the case of a woman" was based on the dual consideration of reasonableness and social custom. In adopting it, special heed was paid to the circumstances in the vast countryside; any move to revise it and to raise the legal minimum age for marriage now would be likely to cause many to come into conflict with the Law. The consequences would prove difficult to handle. This is a considered opinion that is also very judicious.
>
> Another opinion is: as nearly seven years have elapsed since the promulgation and enforcement of the Marriage Law, impressive progress has been made everywhere in society during this period. For this reason, no bad results would follow an upward revision of the legal minimum age for marriage. Moreover, to promote delayed marriage, the Marriage Law must be revised; for, only then will it be possible to double the returns with half the effort. It is not enough to rely only on propaganda and education.
>
> Last year I myself recommended that the whole committee be polled to see if it would accept a change in the age requirement for marriage to 23 years for males and 20 years for females. The result of the survey was that a

great majority of the members favored it.   At this conference, there are a total of six draft resolutions all of which
urge that the Law be amended to provide a higher legal
minimum age for marriage. . . . As to whether a recommendation will be made to amend Article 4 of the Marriage
Law at the fourth session of the First National People's
Congress, and as to how the legal minimum age for marriage for both sexes will be modified [the six draft resolutions differ with one another in this regard], suitable solutions will be forthcoming [from the Standing Committee].[80]

In short, the proponents of delayed marriage as a means of
reducing fertility were divided on the question of how to secure
its general acceptance.   One issue dividing them was whether
or not the Marriage Law should be amended in order to achieve
it.   Many thought not, whereas others attached a great deal
of importance to this legal approach.   Among those who favored elevating the age requirement, moreover, there was disagreement over the details of the presumably needed change.
With respect to the latter issue, various medical experts in
China made diverse suggestions as to the age at which young
men and women should or should not marry.   Lin Chiao-chi,
a gynecologist, and Hsu Yin-kui, a neurologist, reiterated that
the legal age for marriage is the minimum, but not the best
age for marriage.   Li Tsun-en, an internist and head of Peking
Medical College, and Yen Jen-yin, another gynecologist, asserted that students should not get married during their college years.   Fu Lien-chang, president of China Medical Association, stated that the suitable ages for marriage were about
25 years and 30 years for women and men respectively.   Chang
Hsi-chun, a physiologist, argued that it would not be too late
for females to marry between 20 and 25 and for males to marry
between 30 and 35.[81]   And, Shao Li-tzu himself sounded an
uncertain note on the subject:

80. *People's Daily,* 20 Mar. 1957.
81. *Brilliance Daily* (Peking), 22 Feb. 1957; and *People's Daily,*
23 Feb. 1957.   These views were expressed at a symposium organized
by the China Medical Association.   It was held on 20 February 1957,
and more than 40 medical experts (among whom are some traditional
medical practitioners) attended it together with Shao Li-tzu and the
representatives of Peking Municipal Women's Federation.

A clarification must be made here: Malthus's advocacy of marital postponement and our current promotion of delayed marriage have absolutely nothing in common. Malthus maintained that men should not marry before 38 [sic] years of age. Because his position is utterly against human nature, it, of course, cannot win adherence. The aim of our current promotion of delayed marriage is to persuade people, in the light of their concrete circumstances, to voluntarily postpone marriage for a little while, but not to rigidly require marriage to be delayed until this or that age. As regards a possible revision of the age requirement in the Marriage Law, I am only in favor of the age 23 for males and 20 for females. Should we want to make it still higher, I would accept 28 for men and 25 for women at most.[82]

The six draft resolutions, which Shao Li-tzu referred to earlier in 1957, were sponsored individually and collectively by twenty-five deputies to the third session of the Second National Political Consultative Conference. So far as can be ascertained, all save one of them were medical and public health experts. They all wanted to see a higher age requirement for both sexes written into the Marriage Law.[83]

Thus, there is enough evidence to suggest that medical personnel (principally those trained in Western medicine) were the chief proponents of compulsory postponement of marriage in China. At the third session of the Second National People's Political Consultative Conference in 1957, Dr. Li Chien-sheng, in fact, urged that middle-school students be forbidden from marrying.[84] Wang Chung-chiao, president of Chekiang Medical College, was even more categorical and recommended also that married youths be refused admission to senior middle schools and middle technical schools.[85]

In the early 1960s Fu Lien-chang reiterated his 1957 suggestion as to when men and women may suitably marry; and, in

82. *Daily Worker* (Peking), 21 May 1957.

83. The recommendations were as follows: 20 (female), 22 (male); 22 (female), 25 (male); 22–23 (female), 25–26 (male); and 25 (female), 30 (male). *People's Daily,* 14, 15, 17, 19, and 24 Mar. 1957.

84. *People's Daily,* 9 Mar. 1957.

85. *Chekiang Daily,* 5 May 1957.

their parallel discussions of this issue, Drs. Yeh Kung-chao and Wang Wen-pin also made specific but similar recommendations.[86] However, all these were then proffered as the ideal or suitable age for marriage rather than possible amendments to the Marriage Law. Perhaps the lack of definitive criteria for revising the minimum age for marriage was an inherent weakness in the case for postponement of marriage through coercive legislation. In any event, the issue of what constitutes the suitable age for marriage lost its relevance once it was decided that the possibility of extending the practice of delayed marriage could be best enhanced by such other means as propaganda and education rather than legal proscription.

In 1962, Chou Hsin-ming, deputy head of the Institute of Law of the Chinese Academy of Sciences, made a plea against achieving marital postponement by legislation:

> Article 4 of the Marriage Law . . . is primarily directed against the practice of early marriage in the old society. . . . The minimum age for marriage stipulated in the Law is based on the degree of the consciousness of the broad masses. . . . After liberation, we must gradually change the bad habit of early marriage with a view to the final elimination of this evil. But the bad custom formed over several thousand years cannot be eliminated in short order. To do a thorough job toward this end, we must go through a long period of propaganda and education. . . . The statutory age for marriage is the minimum and not the maximum age for marriage, . . . [and was] worked out by the government in accordance with the principle of opposing early marriage and with due regard to the degree of consciousness of the masses. . . . Since the advantages of a delay after reaching the statutory age are numerous, we should encourage suitable postponement among the broad masses of youth. . . . In the course of discussion, some young people held that encouragement of marital postponement calls for revising the Marriage Law and raising the statutory marriage age at a higher level. Such a view is wrong because a law is established on the basis of facts.

86. See footnotes 92, 94, and 95. Their suggestions were : 23–27–28 (female), 25–30 (male); 23–27 (female), 25–29 (male); and 25 (female), 30 (male).

At present, the custom of early marriage still exists in our society. Its elimination can by no means be achieved through upward revision of the statutory age. . . . The arbitrary elevation of the statutory age for marriage would be ill-advised. We believe that with the political-ideological level of the broad masses of youths rising to an increasingly higher level, they will surely devote their energy in pursuit of great ideals in socialist construction and consciously postpone their wedding date. Thus the custom of early marriage will be no doubt on the way to its extinction.[87]

Previously, in 1957, Chen Ta adopted a similar stance on the question of delayed marriage. Though, like the China Medical Association, Chen was unequivocally opposed to induced abortion, he implored people in and out of the government *not* to raise the legal minimum age for marriage. At the end of a lengthy article in *New Construction*, Chen Ta summed up in these words:

In order to raise the age at which people marry, we should establish a system of marriage registration in the nation, particularly in the villages. Statistics on age at marriage should be extensively and continually collected. Only on this basis can we then gradually elevate the actual age at marriage. If we wish to raise people's age at marriage, we cannot follow our subjective opinions. Nor can we adopt coercive decrees. We can only gradually accomplish it through the [eradication] of the old custom of early marriage and the initiation of appropriate arrangements to increase the age of entry into the labor force [i.e., the gradual abolition of child labor] and to expand educational facilities to enable more students to enroll and stay in schools longer. In determining such practical measures, we should specially emphasize delayed matrimony for women.[88]

The Marriage Law was not amended in 1957. Though some renewed the call to revise it in the early 1960s, nothing was changed at the time. Nor have there been any modifica-

---

87. *Daily Worker* (Peking), 7 Nov. 1962.

88. Chen Ta, "Deferred Marriage, Birth Control, and Population Problems of New China."

tions in Article 4 since then. There is little likelihood that future support for similar moves will be any greater. Thus, suffice it to say that the government once more rejected the advice of a number of prominent doctors of medicine in the matter of delayed marriage as it did in the case of induced abortion. But, although the medical opposition to induced abortion was not entirely without merit (e.g., the known shortage of trained personnel to perform the operation), the belief that postponement of marriage can be brought about by legal coercion can hardly be so characterized. The government was obviously wise in rejecting it, and in so doing, agreed with Chen Ta and others who sought to stimulate marital moratorium through the institution of appropriate social and economic measures.

As repeatedly noted, the rationale of China's fertility-control policy has been, and still is, that planned reproduction enhances the health and welfare of mothers and children, and enables husbands and wives in general to devote greater amounts of time and energy to study and work. In the 1950s, the advantages of marital postponement were itemized in almost identical terms. Thus the unanimous endorsement of marital delay was not accidental at the time. Two statements from the mid-1950s illustrate the point:

. . . Early marriage adversely affects physical and mental development: for girls who have not attained physical maturity, their internal secretions will undergo change following marriage, and this will hinder further bodily growth. There are many skinny and short women whose growth has stopped and who cannot grow in size. This will also affect their own children who likewise cannot develop properly. If early marriage persists from generation to generation, it may even adversely affect the whole people in a certain way. A very young mother is herself only a "big" child, lacks experience and knowledge of child-rearing, and can only bear but not bring up children. Therefore, in terms of both health and education, the quality of her children cannot but be poor. A woman who is married early is sometimes the mother of three or four children before the age of 22 or 23. The development of her own intelligence is naturally impeded because she lacks any opportunity to study, and her thought also cannot develop soundly. Apart from her work, she cannot but devote most of her time and energy to rearing and teaching her children. Thus, a maiden of still innocent years becomes "maternalized" ahead of time. Some women turn anxious and despondent emotionally and have only a fugacious maidenhood. A flower bud that bears fruit before it is yet in full blossom is not a normal kind of physiological development. Early marriage may also stimulate other social problems. Young couples are generally not sound financially; the arrival of children means added economic burden. The many social problems to which this gives rise are easy to imagine. Beyond this, the fact that women who get married early become decrepit prematurely can cause many men to pursue improper sexual activities, which is also a common social problem.[89]

Early marriage is harmful. The suitable ages for marriage are between 25 and 30. Early marriage is harmful from any standpoint, be it of physiology, procreation, occupational career, or the health and welfare of the next generation. Before the age of 30, young people ordinarily are comparatively short of knowledge, experience, skill, and finances. They should not be involved in love affairs or get married too early. They should concentrate energies, study with one mind, labor energetically, secrete themselves in strenuous efforts, perfect self-discipline, and lay the foundation for their lifelong careers. It has been said, "To plan for the year is in the spring; to plan for one's life is during youth," and "One who does not exert himself in youth will mourn in vain in advanced years."[90]

The unanimity in regard to marital postponement also differed qualitatively from the approval given to several conventional methods of contraception in China. Expressions of preference for condoms, diaphragms, jellies, and such, explicitly accented their contraceptive value. But, as is shown above, statements in favor of postponement of marriage laid stress upon its individual, conjugal, and social benefits. Thus, is it not also fortuitous that in the early 1960s renewed publicity was initially given to postponement of marriage follow-

89. Wang Pao-yin, "What Kinds of Harm Does Early Marriage Bring to Young Men and Women."

90. Chung Hui-nan, "Birth Control and Later Marriage."

ing the ebb in the nationwide campaign to promote planned reproduction during the late 1950s. On 4 April 1962, the *People's Daily* published a letter from a reader who repented of her early entry into marriage:

> I am an apprentice in Shichingshan Steel Company, Peking. I am 20 years old. . . . I came to this company at 17, . . . not long after that, I got married and became pregnant very shortly thereafter. . . . Although the leadership took every care of me, my health became worse during my pregnancy. . . . My first child is now one year old, but I am pregnant again. One child has already upset me. . . . What should I do if I have another child in the future? . . . I envy very much some of my female comrades who have dealt with their marriages properly. Take teacher Hao Tien-fen for example. She . . . got married at 27. She is good in her work, study, and physical health and is an advanced producer and leader of a production unit in the factory. She can also take good care of her child. Now, I have really learned a lesson that it is not good to get married and give birth to a child too early.[91]

Immediately after, and within a year of, the publication of this letter, four other extended discussions of the medical, legal, personal, marital, and societal aspects of marital postponement appeared elsewhere. In the order of appearance, their respective authors were: Yeh Kung-shao, dean, School of Public Health, Peking Medical College;[92] Chow Hsin-min, deputy head, Institute of Law, the Chinese Academy of Science;[93] Wang Wen-pin, assistant professor, China Medical University;[94] and Fu Lien-chang, president, China Medical Association.[95] And elaborations and reinforcements of the

91. *People's Daily,* 4 Apr. 1962.

92. Yeh Kung-shao, "What is the Most Suitable Age for Marriage?" *China Youths Daily,* 12 Apr. 1962. Yeh subsequently reiterated his view in *China Youths Daily,* 9 May 1963.

93. Chow Hsin-min, "On the Encouragement of Late Marriage and the Statutory Marriage Age."

94. Wang Wen-pin, "A Talk About the Question of Age for Marriage from the Physiological Angle."

95. Fu Lien-chang, "A Talk with Young Comrades About the Question of Marriage."

major themes articulated by these persons soon followed in still other places.[96]

As three of the four feature articles were authored by persons in the medical profession, they can be combined for discussion here. And, because both the point of departure and the focus of their analyses were indistinguishable from those of similar expositions in the 1950s, only a concise reference to their contents is warranted. In short, one purpose of these articles, studded with physiological details, seems to have been to provide an elementary course in sex education. The essence of the message is that various physiologically unfortunate consequences will follow from early marriage, including interference with normal physical and mental development and symptoms associated with "excessive sexual activity." The health, study, and work of the individuals involved thus will be adversely and deeply affected by early marriage. In addition, from the standpoint of procreation and the health and upbringing of children, early marriage will prove harmful to mothers and children alike. The positive significance of delayed marriage was also reiterated as in the following brief quotation:

> Tall buildings are erected from the ground. Without the solid foundations laid in an earlier stage of construction and without the efforts of the bricklayers, magnificent mansions cannot subsequently rise from the ground. This is also true in the case of our careers; that is, if we do not make energetic efforts when we are young, to regret in our advanced years will be of no avail.[97]

In the subsequent secondary publications wherein these central themes were amplified, the amplifications consisted of: (1) condemnations of early marriage in the form of confessions of personal miseries or self-blame, and (2) commendations of marriage at suitable ages in terms of individual

96. For example, *China Youths Daily,* 10 May 1962, 17 July 1962, 22 Nov. 1962.

97. Wang Wen-pin, "A Talk About the Question of Age for Marriage from the Physiological Angle."

well-being or self-enrichment and personal achievement. To fully preserve and communicate the flavor of the campaign to discredit early marriage, one such account entitled "I Do not Want to Get Married Early" is reproduced in full below:

Comrade Editor:

I am the woman chief of the Ta-miao brigade, K'ung-ts'un commune, Ch'u'fu *hsien*, Shantung province. I am now 24 years old. Very seldom one sees a girl of my age not yet married in our village. When I was 18, people already began to look for a husband for me. Mother told me: "Since you were a child I had been consulting the fortune tellers who said that you should get married at 18. When a girl is due for marriage it is better for her to do so and if she should remain unmarried, there would probably be trouble." I was nearly dumfounded when I heard this. I did not want to get married early for the simple reason that it would impede my progress. So I told my mother that I was still young, did not know much about the world yet, and that this problem should be left alone until after a couple of years. It took me some time to convince my mother. Finally she consented to postpone the marriage question till I reached 20.

Two years later, I was 20. Twelve girls of my age all got married. Matchmakers again came to our house. My mother was excited again. I still managed to get over this. I said: "Mother, I am a woman cadre. I must do a good job of Party work, labor, and study. I have not yet made any contribution, and if I get married in such a hurry, I certainly won't feel happy. Early marriage brings children early and that would be a handicap to my career. Do you want to see me live a miserable life, young as I am." I kept on repeating this, and my mother was moved. Then I told her about the conditions of those of my age who have been married early. Each of them has several children. Some of them, after running down their own health, could not keep their children healthy either. They could not participate in labor and could not do any work. K'ung Hsien-lan, one year my junior, who got married when she was 19, is now a mother of 3 children and cannot do any work. Prior to her marriage, she was known as "Hua Mu-lan" [a heroine in Chinese history] on the production front. She regretted very much and often said: "It was my own mistake to have made a wrong decision then." After mother was convinced by these facts she agreed with me. She said:

"What worries me is this. You are already a grown-up girl of 20! 'When a boy or girl reaches the marriageable age, he or she should get married.' If I should still keep you home, people would criticize me of being muddleheaded. If you have already made up your mind, then it would not make you much older if you wait for another couple of years."

Although I overcame the impediment of my family I still have to deal with people around me. A distant relative, an aunt, living in our neighborhood kept on nagging at me: "In our K'ung family we have been none like you who is so capable and popular among the people. I feel proud of you. But you cannot neglect your marriage problem. An old saying goes: 'As time goes on, you grow old. If you do not make up your mind quick, you will not be able to marry a good husband when you are over 20.' Since you are no longer young, you should not delay any further." By the end of last year, someone gave my mother this grand idea: It is for the parents to make a decision; find a nice young man and introduce him to her, and if "luck would have it," then things will be settled. So since March this year, people came to my house one after another: cadre, worker, commune member, and college graduate. Some promised me a big dowry, others said that they would take me out to have a good time. Still others said that they could find me a nice job in the city, if I would accept their proposals. But, I have made up my mind not to get married early. People then began to criticize me and said: "These are promising young men. Any of them is better than she. She really does not know how to enjoy life and prefers to live in misery." "Don't worry about her. When such a day comes she will run into the 'bridal sedan chair' herself." "Let her be an old maid 80 years old!" After hearing all these gossips, I began to waver. I thought then that I was already over 20 and might as well get married, so that I would not hear any more rubbish like this. But, on second thought, I wondered if it is happiness to marry a husband and depend on him. I would rather not enjoy that kind of "happiness." I prefer to live on my own labor. I recollect that our family in the old society had nothing to eat and wear, and it was after liberation that we stood up. Ever since the establishment of lower cooperatives in 1955, I have in the past eight years been actively participating in labor production. In 1959 I was honored with membership of the Communist Party. Owing to the cultivation of the organization, "a little girl with yellow hair" has now become a woman chief of a production team. In the course of the eight years, I have on twelve occasions received awards from the province, special district, *hsien*, and the commune. I am now still young and strong and should devote my whole energy to production and work, in order not to disappoint the Party and the commune members. The delay in my marriage can do me only good and no harm.

Recently, the young people of our village and I studied at a symposium articles in *China's Women* and other newspapers regarding the advantages of getting married late. Every one realized there were many advantages in getting married late: (1) It is good to one's health, study, work, and labor, and, above all, it is beneficial to the socialist construction. (2) It proves better for the young people to get married after they have physically fully developed, for it would insure the health of the next generation. After people understood fully these points, they showed a greater production ardor. They all said to me: "Your decision in getting married late is good." Young Communist League member Wu Cheng-chun, who is now 18, originally decided to get married after summer. After discussing the matter with her boy friend, she has now decided not to get married until she is 24. Her boy friend, being a national cadreman, has written her several times and agreed with her on this point. Their affection for each other is increasing as time goes on. They frequently write each other, encouraging themselves to make progress. There are still other girls who are now consulting their parents to allow them to get married late. In this connection, even the old people said: "These young people are right. We should back them up." Now getting married late has become a standard practice in our village.[98]

In this and other similar narrations, the circumstances and crosscurrents confronting the individual at the ill-defined threshold of marriage in China are vividly demonstrated. Also, the sociological and policy significance of the words of this writer and similarly situated Chinese females is placed in sharp definition. Lest unwarranted conjectures be read into the situation, however, the above statement should be

98. Kung Shao-chun, "I Am Not Willing to Get Married Early," *China's Women*, no. 8 (1 August 1963): 1 ff.

read with the jubilant account of an American girl entitled "Why I Am Glad I Didn't Marry While in College" that follows:

Personal, professional, economic reasons all lead to one answer—I am glad I didn't marry while in college! In retrospect it seems one of my wisest decisions.

When I look back at my college experience I feel I gained immeasurably from a full social and academic life. My independent status allowed complete freedom to explore my interests. I enjoyed memberships in social, academic, and political groups. I participated in extra class projects. Living and working in close contact with a large group of girls was an unscheduled course in human relations. If I had been married, many of these activities would have necessarily been curtailed. A married student must assume additional responsibilities that do not face the unmarried undergraduate: primarily the establishment and maintenance of a home and adjustment to married life in a college atmosphere. The axiom that "two can live as cheaply as one" often does not meet the test, and married students find they must seek outside work. The fortunate student may find work that relates to her college major. Usually, the job is just a source of income that requires time away from studies. A girl enters a college marriage realistically when she can see beyond mere physical attraction. Marriage in college requires a degree of maturity that many people do not attain at that age.

We all agree that college is not an end in itself. College is only a foundation towards a satisfying career and a purposeful life. In college we have the opportunity to develop and expand this foundation. The college atmosphere is primed for learning—book learning and, more important, learning about oneself. It is the one prolonged space in our lives when we are expected to explore our minds and personalities. There is time to find that individual known as self. I feel that in order to take advantage of all that may be attained in college a student benefits from freedom from the responsibilities of marriage.

.   .   .   .

The experiences obtained through leading a full and diversified college life proved the most helpful when I was working as a home economist. I had to rely on my own initiative, imagination, and judgment in many situations. Most jobs today require more than book knowledge.

Every employer seeks the person who can command himself and the many unexpected situations that arise on the job.

The store of personal and professional experiences obtained by pursuing my chosen career enriched and continued my self-development; I met the public, worked with people of different ages whose opinions conflicted, worked with men as well as women—single and married. I was able to exchange ideas with veterans and newcomers in the professional world. Through radio work and public demonstrations before large groups of people I developed poise and confidence.

Unmarried, I was free to choose the job I wanted in a city I liked. When assignments needed extra work, I was able to stay overtime at the office. If a trip came up, I could leave on short notice. I believe that my promotions came more quickly because I was able to arrange my life as the job required.

As a career girl living within my own fixed income I learned to budget money. This financial independence later made management of family finances an easier task.

Although most of these experiences are eventually gained through marriage or can be acquired simultaneously with marriage, the opportunities for meeting such situations do not arise as often in married life. Also there is not the pressure that exists in business to meet the challenge and acquire the knowledge as quickly. After marriage, the time necessary for complete professional advancement is usually not available.

After marriage when it seemed necessary to gain employment I found that the name I had established from my few years of professional work practically wrote the contract for a job. The jobs open to me were both professionally inspiring and financially rewarding.

When one is weighing the merits of marriage over a career, one should realize that if the marriage in question is the right one it will wait. Mine did and I believe we are a happier couple.

Gaining confidence and maturity in the professional world have made me a more successful wife and mother. Family respect and admiration are always important in a satisfying family situation. My husband takes pride in my accomplishments. I also feel that I had fewer adjustments to make in marriage than had my friends who married while in college or immediately after college, perhaps because some of my personal and economic adjustments had already been made. These adjustments often turn that romantic so called "rosy glow" into grey depression. The decision to marry while in college is a personal one. My independent college days better prepared me for a satisfying career and a happy marriage.[99]

The similarities and differences between the two accounts are strikingly obvious. In both instances, the advantages of delayed marriage are defined in personal as well as in social terms; they relate to self-reliance and career development, as well as to the emergence of a richer personality, marital life, and motherhood. But, two extra benefits are recognized in the Chinese script, delayed marriage also serves to prevent ill health of women and the arrival of children too early in life. Given their material affluence and contraceptive exposure, American women may still enjoy relative health and remain childless even if marriage is not postponed. Second, both accounts disclose the ever-present pressure to marry; the decision not to marry early is taken in defiance of the views of those around the individual in question. But, the identity of the presumably "significant others" is different. Parents (mothers in particular), relatives, and other concerned adults are the prominent figures on the Chinese scene. Such kin and neighborly folks assume a lesser role in marriage decisions in America where the opinion of one's peers is more keenly felt. Third, in either case, the contrast is between the behavior of the majority and that of the minority; delayed marriage thus also contravenes a social norm. But, the act is unmistakably a direct breach of long-established tradition in Chinese society. Seen in the context of the secular trend of age of first marriage in the United States,[100] postponement of marriage has been essentially a resistance to "current" fad

99. Marion Bunting, "Why I Am Glad I Didn't Marry While in College," *Journal of Home Economics* 47 (December 1955): 757–58. Copyright by the American Home Economics Association, Washington, D.C. Reprinted by permission. Reprinted in *Marriage and Family in the Modern World: A Book of Readings,* ed Ruth Shonle Cavan (New York: Thomas Y. Crowell, 1963).

100. Cf. Thomas Monahan. *The Pattern of Age at Marriage in the United States;* and Paul Glick, *American Families,* chap. 3.

in the mating game. More importantly, seen in comparative perspective, decisions to delay matrimony in different socio-cultural settings are not necessarily identical sociological phenomena. In one society, they may amount to no more than a course of action that enables the individuals involved to realize or develop alternate goals in life. In another society, they are literally acts of rebellion.

Of course, advocacy of marital postponement has not al-ways occurred in revolutionary situations. In the nineteenth century Malthus advocated postponement of marriage partly because it would "tend in the most marked manner to stimu-late industry." In other words, to use Petersen's translation, "A man who postpones marriage until he is able to support his family is driven by his sexual urge to work hard."[101] Other writers of the nineteenth century, for both similar and other reasons, also urged that early marriage be discouraged. Walker, for instance, stressed the incompatibility between early marriage and labor mobility as the latter may be hin-dered by the former at a time of life when the workers, if mobile, are able to obtain the most advantageous employment and wages.[102] Postponement of marriage was also recom-mended by an earlier theorist who took an optimistic stance on the population question, "as the preferred means of pre-venting overrapid growth of numbers, with age twenty-five for marriage suggested as perhaps the most beneficial to so-ciety."[103]

However, Malthus's[104] various other contemporaries were in disagreement with him over the desirability of marital post-ponement. Some maintained that the practice would be pro-ductive of immorality, social irresponsibility, and orphans.[105]

---

101. William Petersen, *Population,* pp. 615–17.

102. E. P. Hutchinson, *The Population Debate,* p. 304.

103. Ibid., p. 345. The theorist in question is Thomas Edmonds.

104. Ibid., pp. 325, 329, 333, 335.

105. Part II of Charles G. Cock, *English Law* (London, 1951), p. 49, as quoted in Hutchinson, *The Population Debate,* p. 43. Hutchinson pointed out, Cock may have been overcritical of the state of affairs under the Stuarts.

Calling the Malthusian principle of population a "manifest truth," Thomas Cooper nevertheless defended early marriage:

Obeying the urgency of the calls of nature common to the whole animal creation, men marry and beget children, and then strive to provide for them. Population therefore is the great stimulus to exertion, and the great check to parental extravagance and expensive indulgence. Marriage and its concomitant offspring, produce kind and social feelings, feelings of duty founded on natural associations, prompting to industry, regularity, and self denial.

Moreover, early marriages are productive of a better state of society than late ones. This is manifest in our own country; and it must of course happen, that the earlier, vicious, and selfish propensities and indulgencies are repressed and counteracted, the more virtuous will society be. Not merely more chaste, but more regular, more self-denying, and social in its general tone and feeling. The earlier we are accustomed to give up our own wants and wishes for the sake of those we love, the sooner and more habitual will every social feeling be formed and become.

The governing principle of voluntary celibacy, however prudent or even commendable it may be and sometimes is, rests upon an exclusive carefulness of a man's self, and a carelessness of the common good. Hence, although early marriages may produce poverty, and incessant exertion, it seems to me a less evil to society, that superfluous population should be gradually thinned by infantile diseases attendant on scanty subsistence, than that the first and most imperious precept of nature should be disobeyed, or subjected to every species of vicious substitute.[106]

Thus, conflicting assessments existed of the real and conjectured effects of postponement of marriage. But, it remains indisputable that formal controls on marriage were in force during the Elizabethan period. The situation, as Cock described it, then was as follows:

They who could not maintain a wife, might not marry; for a License they could not have, the Bishops taking care enough with their Officers that the poor might not have lawful favor of a License, lest their Hospitality might be

106. Ibid., pp. 279–80.

chared, or impaired by their maintenance, and their pub-
like denouncing the bands of Marriage the first time; the
Parish for the like cause hindered it the second, if any
cause were; and usually none were permitted marriage till
the man were thirty five at least, and the women thirty.[107]

And, in time, postponement of marriage has been identified
as having been a significant check on fertility in various European populations before the advent of mass contraception and
just prior to, and in the course of, economic development.
Hajnal went a step further and speculated:

> The traditional argument, that late marriage retards popu-
> lation growth, has already been mentioned but other pos-
> sible effects need to be explored. In the European pattern
> a person would usually have some years of adult life be-
> fore marriage; for women especially this period would be
> much larger than outside Europe. It is a period of max-
> imum productive capacity without responsibility for chil-
> dren, a period during which saving would be very easy.
> These savings [e.g., by means of the accumulation of house-
> hold goods in preparation of marriage] might add sub-
> stantially to the demand for goods other than the food,
> etc., required for immediate survival. In this respect de-
> layed marriage may be similar to income inequality in
> stimulating the diversion of resources to ends other than
> those of minimum subsistence; but when later marriage is
> the norm the total volume of demand generated might be
> much larger than that which can be caused by a small class
> of wealthy families in a population at subsistence level.
> Could this effect, which was uniquely European, help ex-
> plain how the groundwork was laid for the unique European
> "take-off" into modern economic growth.[108]

The evidence that Hajnal marshalled in support of his depiction of Europe's pattern of delayed marriage is impressive.
What is of special interest is his observation that the emergence of this pattern may have been partially consequent upon

107. Ibid., p. 26.

108. J. Hajnal, "European Marriage Patterns in Perspective," in
Population in History, D. R. Glass and D. E. C. Eversley, eds. (Chicago:
Aldine Publishing Co., 1965), p. 132. Reprinted by permission of Ed-
ward Arnold Publishers Ltd., London.

the institution of parish registration (licensing) of marriages in the areas examined in the sixteenth century. Age requirements for marriage were spelled out in the decree,[109] as exemplified in the case of Elizabethan England. As a matter of hindsight, the demographic significance of this measure seems obvious. But, whether or not it was so apprehended at the time of its formulation is, at best, uncertain. As Hutchinson remarked, "It would be too much to assume that these and other measures affecting population were purely or primarily population measures, for other purposes were no doubt served, but considerations of population were at least present."[110]

As to whether the rise in the average age at first marriage in China in response to the institution of civil-marriage registration will be as high as that which occurred in Europe, it is difficult to say. Given the fact that family-planning programs are being carried on in China, postponement of parenthood within marriage is now a well-known alternative to extended delay of marriage. Nevertheless, relative to China's past, a pattern of somewhat delayed matrimony can be expected to emerge. If this comes to pass, it can have a cumulative effect on economic development, *provided* that a reduction in expenditure is simultaneously exercised at the time of actual marriage.[111] But, even if Hajnal's reading of Europe's marital revolution proves to be correct, his generalization presumably sums up an assumed outcome of hundreds of millions of decisions to defer sexual and related gratifications over two centuries or more. Thus, immediate economic gains would be unlikely to be large enough to generate the support for delayed marriage that actually came to pass in China in recent years. The impetus lies elsewhere and in the national determination to overthrow the old family institution.

In policy terms, therefore, although delayed marriage has been and still is the least controversial means of fertility limitation in China, revolutionary changes in the family institu-

109. Ibid., p. 127.

110. Hutchinson, *The Population Debate*, p. 26.

111. See *People's Daily*, 6 Apr. 1964, for examples of the discussion of the issue of marital frugality in China.

tion and society are most immediately involved in its diffusion. Its relative noncontroversial status is largely a function of the fact that persons in influential quarters inside and outside the government have previously committed themselves to restructuring the family and its place in society. Its impact on fertility therefore cannot be overestimated.

The focus of this chapter is the various open discussions and disputes over the question of means that arose in the course of the birth control campaign in China. Although they were controversial issues, the pertinency of this account lies also in the fact that the outcome of a fertility policy cannot help but be affected by the "tools" adopted to achieve the objective in question. More importantly, this review serves to point up the risk of incompleteness of any analysis of developments in China (e.g., the decision to encourage planned reproduction) if it is confined to the narrow perspective of politics and ideology. Furthermore, it also throws some light on what other elements are involved in the making of a nation's fertility policy, and indirectly compensates somewhat for the present scarcity of information about the extent of dissensus over birth control on social and moral grounds. The present analysis makes it clear that there are a large number of both old and new forces operating at different levels in China that are helping to shape population policies in general and fertility policy in particular.

It should also be noted that, in contrast to the issues of abortion, sterilization, and oral contraception, a distinctly different set of assumptions were followed in the decision against revising the Marriage Law. Beside their acceptability and practicality, the dissemination of the former means of fertility control was based, in large part, on the premise that ignorance and general unavailability of them was the primary source of high fertility. With respect to marital postponement, the course of action (or, nonaction) was partially dictated by an awareness of the limits of legal coercion, but owed mainly to the recognition of the dependence of the desired change in marital behavior upon the implementation of measures making marriages less attractive or rewarding socially and economically. The approach to delayed marriage thus was of an indirect—probably a far more effective—character.

This choice in favor of indirect stimulation of marital postponement has other implications for the present discussion of China's fertility policy. Like almost all other assessments of China's demographic future during the last two decades, this review has been chiefly in terms of the inception, evolution, and content of the Chinese family-planning programs. But, whether or not fertility reduction can be induced by efforts of this kind remains a controversial issue itself.[112] Admittedly, family-planning programs have an undeniable role in China's demographic transition. But, it seems imperative that the issue of fertility control be also placed in the broader context of social and economic transformation. After all, and of foremost importance, Chinese society *is* a changing society.

Some of the salient developments of this kind will be specified, together with their role in the emergence of a new fertility pattern, in the next chapter of this volume.

112. Cf. Kingsley Davis, "Population Policy: Will Current Programs Succeed?" pp. 730–39; Judith Blake Davis, "Demographic Science and the Redivertion of Population Policy," pp. 62–67.

Societal Reorganization and Population Change

Chapter seven

In the preceding five chapters, China's demographic decisions have been analyzed in detail. The discussion has also been extensive in that a large variety of specific measures are examined in each chapter. However, the scope of the analysis has been narrower than initially projected. Almost without exception, the particular measures referred to in the text have been explicitly demographic in intent, even though they may have served other purposes at the same time. This is at variance with the broader definition of population policy stated in chapter 1. This initial conceptualization is, in the words of Alva Myrdal, that "a population policy can be nothing less than the social policy at large." Accordingly, it is imperative that the present analysis be expanded to take into account such other developments as may be consistent with this comprehensive view.

It is appropriate to observe here that a United Nations assessment of China's demographic future (see chapter 8, pp. 339–40) mentioned its policy of encouraging contraceptive practices only *after* it had identified and related various salient social and economic measures to fertility change there. This order of itemization of developments affecting fertility is of interest as well as in keeping with a substantial consensus among demographers of diverse ideologies and nationalities on the relationship between demographic change and social and economic measures at large. With reference to fertility change, for example, Kingsley Davis recently reiterated that family planning programs are not likely to succeed in the absence of a restructuring of the occupational and domestic institutions of societies desiring to reduce fertility.[1] At the last World Population Conference in 1965, the thrust of a number of volunteered and solicited written contributions also followed an identical line of reasoning. These had to do with both actual and anticipated fertility changes in such widely scattered places as Pakistan, Japan, the Armenian Soviet Socialist Republic, and India:

> In this predominantly Muslim country [Pakistan], religion as such does not bar family limitation. The main reason for high fertility seems to be social traditions concerning the status of women, early and universal marriage with motherhood. . . .[2]

> In all spheres of the economic, cultural and scientific life of the Armenian Republic, women are actively at work side by side with men. As its productive focus develops, the Socialist State allocates increasing funds for the improvement of cultural levels. In individual families, one of the conditions for improving the standard of living is to raise the working skills of the family members. . . . [The] data for the Armenian Soviet Socialist Republic confirm the existence of an inverse correlation between the fertility and the cultural level of women. However, the importance of this correlation is sometimes exaggerated. Some authors represent it as the major influence on fertility levels. In our view this is a fallacious theory. As has been pointed out above, cultural levels, while they do have an important influence on female fertility, are a secondary and derivate in-

1. Kingsley Davis, "Population Policy: Will Current Programs Succeed?" p. 738.

2.. Envir Adil, "The Use of Statistical Guides and Measures of Effectiveness in Determining Government policy for Influencing Fertility —Pakistan," pp. 63–67.

fluence, depending on the level of development of productive forces and on the structure of society.[3]

To state differently, in postwar Japan, the government in general was not in a position to tell the people what to do but rather to follow the people, and to help them accomplish their desire. A big question then is what factors were most conducive to the creation of such a high motivation towards family planning among the Japanese. The question is, all in all, a very complex one. But in answering this, one may possibly count such factors as: a high degree of literacy, universal education system, great interest of parents to give even better education to their children, effect of prolonged years of compulsory education after the war, enormous influence of newspapers and magazines and other reading materials, impact of the new Constitution which prescribed, among other things, equal inheritance by all children, rising status of women. . . .[4]

In Japan a variety of birth-control measures have been legalized in recent years [there is widespread resort to artificial abortion and contraceptive methods, even including the sterilization of the parents after the birth of a given number of children]. . . . However, it would be wrong to believe that the birth-rate in Japan has fallen solely as a result of the above-mentioned measures to reduce it artificially. On the contrary, these measures have been merely the accompaniment of such basic factors as the growth of the urban population caused by the development of industry, the rise in the cultural level of the Japanese people, the influx of women into social production in the expansion of women's participation in the national cultural life. . . .[5]

The immediate aim [in India] is to reduce the birth rate to 25 per 1,000 as soon as possible. The means advocated to achieve this goal are as follows: (a) popularizing adoption of family limitation methods . . . ; (b) stimulating social changes which affect fertility, such as raising the age

3. L. M. Davtyan, "The Influence of Socio-economic Factors on Natality (as exemplified in the Armenian Soviet Socialist Republic)," pp. 73–77.

4. Mihoru Murainatsu, "Policy Measures and Social Changes for Fertility Decline in Japan," pp. 96–99.

5. E. A. Sadvoksasova, "Birth Control Measures and Their Influence on Population Replacement," pp. 110–14.

of marriage for women, improving the women's status, education, and employment opportunities.[6]

Notwithstanding this widely shared knowledge, China's demographic future has, for two decades, been appraised, with a few exceptions, primarily in terms of the range and intensity of its family-planning programs. The changing pitch of China's national campaign to promote fertility limitation proved overwhelming and almost hypnotizing to eager ears. Dire predictions and zealous applause have thus alternated with one another in quick succession within a short span of time. Rarely have there been glimpses in other directions. As a consequence, only a partial awareness exists of the many salient developments that, in the long run, will be of critical importance in relation to the emergence of new demographic patterns in China. For this and other reasons stated above, an assessment of China's demographic future in the context of social and economic transformation is in order.

The focus here will be the constellation of social and economic change affecting fertility, given the fact that fertility change is the foremost, though not necessarily chronologically the first, component of demographic transition.

Fertility reduction has now been widely accepted as a desirable goal in the course of economic development. China has also committed itself to achieve this end; and, presumably, the flow of personnel and funds into family-planning programs there is in accord with this commitment. Whether the current allocation of manpower and money (which is not known) is sufficient is not a concern in the following pages. Nor is it the immediate aim to assess the prospect for fertility reduction in terms of improved techniques of contraception. Whatever contraceptive innovations may be forthcoming inside and outside of China, the impact of known methods of family limitation has been remarkably visible in a large number of countries for quite a long time. These are relevant issues, but will not be discussed for the simple reason that to do so

6. B. L. Raina, "Possible Effects of Public Policy Measures on Fertility in India," pp. 100–104.

would be to re-enter the conceptual closure from which all but explicitly demographic measures have been excluded.

Quite obviously, social and economic changes that can affect fertility are too numerous to include them all in one brief analysis. Only selected items can be treated here. Specifically, the extent of the emancipation of women in China and the dispatch of educated urban youths to the countryside will be described, and their implications for fertility change will be depicted in the following pages. Both the changed status of women and mobility have long been accepted, in theories of fertility change, as two leading determinants of reduced fertility in the modern era.

Employment and Education of Women

Unlike the two other demographic processes (i.e., mortality and migration), fertility behavior is conditional upon the cooperation of two individuals of different sexes. That is, whatever the form this coming together of a man and a woman assumes in a society, human reproduction is a joint affair. As such, a modification in fertility can follow even if only one of the conjugal pair undergoes, for whatever reasons, a change of mind and behavior. Whether the man or his wife is the key person in this regard remains an unsettled question. In family-planning literature, for instance, women are often thought of as more easily remolded to follow contraceptive advice because childbearing is a direct burden for them. An opposite view is that where the male has a dominant role in the family setting, approaching the wife alone is unlikely to result in a successful family limitation. In either case, a restructuring of the family is a prerequisite for fertility change. The present analysis examines: (1) the extent of the growth of female employment in offices, factories, shops, and other extra-familial occupations and activities; and (2) the changing rewards for women on the basis of personal achievements. The assumption is that both types of development constitute prima facie evidence of the emergence of conditions conducive to relatively rapid fertility decline. The analytical framework is that fertility behavior is a component part of family phe-

nomena.   Its change is an inevitable consequence of family
and societal reorganization.

On the Urban Scene

On account of policy decisions and sharply increased investment in national enterprises, nonagricultural employment
has considerably expanded in recent years in China.   Between 1949 and 1958, the number of persons employed in this
sector of the economy increased from 26,267,000 to 56,867,000.
A substantial portion of this growth occurred during the
Great Leap Forward in 1958, the increase being from 39,-
667,000 in 1957.   Because of a change in the classification of
persons previously excluded from nonagricultural employment statistics, the reported gain in 1957–58 was noncom-
parable to the expansion of the earlier years.   On the whole,
the state component of the nonagricultural sector swelled
through the addition of new workers and employees and the
reclassification of persons formerly employed in private establishments.   Of the 56,867,000 persons in nonagricultural
occupations in 1958, only 1,538,000 remained in private employment.   An additional 2,196,000 persons in service occupations and in traditional medicine were included, for the
first time, in the 1958 count.   Undoubtedly, some women
were engaged in these three types of work.   However, no
breakdown of any of them by sex is possible.   Consequently,
as is shown in table 14, the known number of females in
nonagricultural employment probably is somewhat below the
real figure.   Of the 45,323,000 workers and employees (i.e.,
wage earners) in 1958, 7,000,000 were women.[7]   These are
exclusive of persons in such traditional nonagricultural occupations as handicrafts, salt extraction, fishing, and certain
types of trade and services, and do not include women in
urban communal workshops and service establishments.

7. On the other hand, because of the inclusion of an unspecified
number of persons employed in state farms and forestry in the statistics
on workers and employees, the number of female workers and employees in nonagricultural occupations may not have been too different from
the 1958 figure shown in table 14.

However, irrespective of the question of statistical comparability, the large jump in the number of workers and employees between 1957 and 1958 is of substantive import. Since 1958, the term "workers and employees" has been used to denote "persons working for the enterprises owned by all the people and for government agencies and receiving wages from the state."[8] Between 1957 and 1958, the number of female workers and employees more than doubled, compared with an 80 percent increase in the case of male wage earners. The net effect is that wage has now a great deal more *formal* meaning to a great many more persons in the labor force, particularly women.[9]

The number of female workers and employees also had been growing at a higher rate before 1958. In the eight-year period between 1949 and 1957, male workers and employees tripled, whereas, the increase was more than five times for women wage earners, who reached a total of 3,286,000 in 1957. A significant share of the increase has been in the modern industrial branch of the economy. By 1959, some 60% of the female workers and employees were engaged in such industries as textiles, machine-building, chemical and pharmaceutical products, and so forth, and they constituted 16 percent of the total industrial workers and employees.[10]

Concomitant with the rising number of employed women in recent years have been other both subtle and profound changes. These dovetail well with one another and give cause for optimism in regard to the emancipation of women.

First of all, the matter of employment in relation to fertility

8. N. R. Chen, *Chinese Economic Statistics*, p. 110.

9. As is also shown in table 14, another one million women workers and employees were added to the state payroll during 1959. As of now, the 1966 statement merely reiterated the known gains between 1949 and 1957. (See note at the bottom of the table.) The number of female workers and employees a present is unknown.

10. Quite a number of women in industry were engineers, designers, and technicians, and more have become qualified in recent years (see footnotes 15 and 17 below). Most of the women technicians in these places attended college or technical school after 1959. NCNA (Shenyang), 1 Mar. 1965.

TABLE 14

WORKERS AND EMPLOYEES BY SEX AND TYPES OF OCCUPATIONS OF FEMALES, 1949–1965

(In Thousands Unless Otherwise Indicated)

YEAR	TOTAL*		FEMALE WORKERS AND EMPLOYEES		
	Male	Female	Professional, technical	Industrial	Service
1949	7,404	600			
1950	......	......			
1951	......	......			
1952	13,956	1,848		990,000 (74% increase since 1950)†	
1953	16,124	2,132		‡	
1954	16,374	2,435		1,300,000 (128% increase since 1950)§	
1955	16,603	2,475		"over 2,000,000"‖	
1956	20,964	3,266#			
1957	21,220	3,286**			"12% of the 8,440,000 commercial workers are women"††
1958	38,323	7,000			
1959	......	(100%)‡‡	11% (Culture &public health workers)‡‡	60% (Textile, machine-building, chemical, pharmaceutical)‡‡	11% (Trade & social services)‡‡
1959	......	8,000†‡‡§§		‖‖	
1965	......				##

*1949–1958: N. R. Chen, *Chinese Economic Statistics*, pp. 422–23. Data pertain to workers and employees in industry, state farms, forestry, water conservancy, capital, construction, transport, posts, telecommunications, trade, the food and drink industry, finance, banking, insurance, state education, medicine and public health, cultural affairs, government administration, mass organizations, urban public utilities, and meteorology. The 1958 figure includes those employed in newly opened industrial establishments at the *hsien* (county) level and below and the workers and employees in the various industrial and other enterprises, agencies and organizations that the state transferred to the communes.

†*People's China*, no. 23, December 1952.
‡Women workers and employees in the railway system increased by 20% between 1952 and 1953. C. C. Lei, "The Rights of Women in New China," *Law in the Service of Peace* 1–2:102.
§*China Reconstructs*, no. 2 (March-April 1953-54).
‖*People's Daily*, 8 March 1956.
#"Women work in factories, commercial enterprises, schools and government offices," NCNA 3 March 1957. Another source reported that at the end of 1956, there were "over 2,800,000 women workers and employees," who constituted 13% of the nation's total number of workers and employees. Also, 60% of the textile workers were women; and 50,156 or about one-fourth of railway workers were women (*Current Events Handbook*, no. 5 [6 March 1957]).
**447.7% over that of 1949. *People's Daily*, 8 March 1960.
††*Daily Worker*, 23 October 1958.
‡‡NCNA (Peking), 30 April 1959. For reasons unknown, these percentages do not add up to 100. As of this date, women constituted 16% of the total industrial workers and employees, and they numbered 14 times that of ten years ago.
§§Year-end figure; including women workers in industry, commerce, education, and other spheres, but not including the 40% to 60% of city housewives in community workshops and social services (NCNA [Peking], 2 March 1960).
‖‖Women technical and engineering personnel in industry have increased 7 times compared with 1952, the year before the first five-year plan (Ibid.).
##"The number of women workers in industry is now more than double what it was in 1957 at the end of China's First Five-Year Plan. It is more than 10 times the number at the time of liberation" (NCNA [Peking] 6 March 1966). No precise figures are given in this report.

change has to do with the *opportunity* to enter chosen occupations as much as with the level of actual employment. With the exception of certain kinds of work unsuited for women, for health reasons, every branch of *industry* is now open to women in China. And, the barriers to professional, technical, cultural, and administrative occupations also have come down, as the following reports show:

> In the past, it was very rare to find a woman researcher in the mathematics circles of China. But, now, one-seventh of the researchers in the mathematics research institute are women.[11]

> Women now account for one-fifth of the research workers at the Chinese Academy of Sciences today, a 42 percent increase since 1957.[12]

> Women technical and engineering personnel in industry have increased seven times since 1952, the year before the First Five-Year Plan.[13]

> The women intellectuals of the national capital are scattered not only in the medical, teachers' training, and arts circles, . . . but are also engaged in teaching or re-

11. NCNA (Peking) 3 Mar. 1957.

12. Ibid., 6 Mar. 1962.

13. Ibid., 2 Mar. 1960.

search in the scientific fields of physics, geology, paleontology, entomology, the study of heredity, cytology and embryology, plant protection, horticulture and arboriculture, economics, and philosophy. Women researchers can also be found in the new scientific fields such as aerodynamics, semi-conductor, nuclear physics, computer techniques, and plastics.[14]

More than 600 women engineers, designers, and technicians, all of whom are young, post-liberation graduates, are working in the metallurgical, steel-rolling, power generation, machine-building, and mining departments of Anshan, China's leading steel center.[15]

More than five thousand women are teaching in Peking's universities and colleges. The number is more than double the figure in 1958. Over 120 of them are professors and associate professors. Women are teaching diverse subjects ranging from geology, water conservancy, iron and steel, petroleum, aeronautical engineering, and agriculture to medicine, literature, and the arts. One out of every 4 faculty members in Peking, Tsinghua, and other leading universities in the capital is now a woman. The Peking Geological Institute has two hundred women faculty members as against only ten when it was set up in 1952. Many young women lecturers and assistants are graduates of the Institute.[16]

Women account for 9 percent of the technicians in the locomotive industry in Dairen. . . . The Dairen Shipyards . . . now has 20 women designers . . . most of the women technicians in Liaoning attended college or technical school after liberation.[17]

In Peking, in 1965, 24.3 percent of college teachers, 44 percent of secondary school teachers, and 62 percent of primary school teachers were women.[18]

Second, equal pay for same work is an established right and has been in force since 1949. Women are also entitled to paid

14. Ibid., 3 Mar. 1957.
15. NCNA (Shenyang), 1 Mar. 1962.
16. NCNA (Peking), 5 Mar. 1962.
17. NCNA (Shenyang), 1 Mar. 1965.
18. NCNA (Peking), 6 Mar. 1966.

maternity leaves and other benefits.[19] In economic terms, therefore, it is more expensive to employ females than males. Notwithstanding this differential cost, China as a whole has been and still is moving in the direction of employing more females. That women have been increasingly recruited into China's industrial, professional, and cultural work force thus is not the result of a deliberate policy to exploit them economically. It stemmed directly from the decision to promote their emancipation.

Third, not only are almost all occupations open to females, but positions of responsibility within them are also accessible to women.[20] That advancement to supervisory and leadership ranks has become visible in China is commensurate with women's changing place in the labor force. It constitutes the most convincing evidence of recognition and reward for achievements among employed women, which, in turn, can only serve to attract others to enter the occupational world.

Fourth, along with the elevation of their economic and occupational status, women have also made salient political gains at all levels in the country.[21] The inclusion of a growing num-

19. All women workers have 56 days maternity leave on full pay, with medical expenses borne by the enterprise. And, women factory workers may retire with pensions at the age of fifty, and women office workers at the age of fifty-five. In addition, factories run their own nurseries and kindergartens.

20. "More than five hundred women are working as managers or holding other top executive posts in the factories in Shanghai, China's largest manufacturing center" (NCNA [Shanghai], 26 Feb. 1962).

"There are today . . . 167 directors and deputy-directors in the Shanghai textile industry. . . . Both the director and deputy-director of [the] Central Laboratory [at the Anshan Iron and Steel Complex] are women. . . . Some 500 women are working as factory directors, section leaders, or workshop heads in the country's machine-building industries" (NCNA [Peking] 6 Mar. 1966).

"New China has trained a considerable number of women hospital superintendents, department heads, and medical professors and experts. In Shanghai . . . *two-thirds* of the *medical workers* are women" (NCNA [Peking] 6 Mar. 1966).

21. According to a 1966 report, "there are 542 elected women deputies in the (then) current Third National People's Congress, the su-

ber of women in the political and administrative structures of the country extends the scope of their emancipation far beyond the immediate and direct enhancement of the status of the few in the short run. In a longer-term perspective, their political participation will almost certainly be to fortify their equality with men in all spheres of social life. The penetration by women into formerly men's political territory can mean only greater and greater participation in decision-making rather than merely passive employment and involvement.

Fifth, in all likelihood, the current lag in female employment, in relation to their number in the total population, is probably only transitory in China. The extent to which women have actually been given employment in the modern nonagricultural sector has inevitably been limited by the circumstances at the start of a program of economic development and social transformation. Orleans estimated that, of all living college graduates in 1960 who had received their training prior to 1949, 18 percent (or, 23,000) were women. This is about the proportion of students enrolled in institutions of higher education who were females in each of the ten years between 1937 and 1946. In other words, there was virtually no change in the enrollment of women in higher education during this period. Nor was there any change in the proportion of girls in the total enrollment in the secondary schools; in 1939, it amounted to 19 percent, and in 1946, 20.2 percent. The combined total of women with *completed* higher and secondary education was approximately 149,000

-----

preme organ of state power. This is a 17.83 percent of the total. Nineteen have seats on the Standing Committee of the National People's Congress. [And,] no fewer than that at various levels in the country. They constitute 22 percent of the total membership of these congresses. . . . The country [also] has more than 300 women heads of provincial, city, *hsien,* and district governments." Ibid. "More than 117,000 women are deputies at all levels of the local people's congress as in the East China Province of Shantung. . . . Workers, peasants, shop assistants, educators, doctors, nurses, and scientists who have displayed high working enthusiasm and creativeness and made contributions to the socialist cause are in the ranks of the women deputies" (NCNA [Tsinan] 1 Mar. 1965).

in 1949.[22] Women qualified for professional, technical, and other nonmanual employment thus were in short supply.

Since 1949, as is shown in table 15, the absolute number and the proportion of female students in the total enrollment in institutions of higher education have both increased. Probably, on account of female graduates of secondary schools as well as of the capacity to accommodate and train students at the college level, the expansion apparently reached a plateau in 1957–58. There seems to be no clear reason for this pause in the increase of female students. However, the other important feature of post-1949 educational expansion is that the lower the level of the institutions, the higher the increase, particularly in the more recent years. It takes some time (a decade or so) before the impact of such increments is felt (i.e. about 1968) at the higher level. Whatever the rate of university admissions at the present time, this greatly enlarged enrollment at the base of the educational system presages a further change not only in the employability of China's women, but also in their general educational status. And, the influence of increased education on fertility is well known.

Thus, so far as women in the cities are concerned, preliminary, albeit fragmentary, data demonstrate that they have made notable breakthroughs in the short time span of a decade.

TABLE 15

Number of Female Students in Educational Institutions, Various Levels. and Percentage of Enrollment, 1949–1958

Year	Higher Educational Institutions		Secondary Specialized Schools		Secondary General Schools		Primary Schools	
	N	%	N	%	N	%	N	%
1949 ..	23,000	19.8	158,000	....	....	....	....	....
1952 ..	45,000	23.4	158,000	24.9	585,000	23.5	16,812,000	32.9
1957 ..	103,000	23.3	206,000	26.5	1,935,000	30.8	22,176,000	34.5
1958 ..	154,000	23.3	397,000	27.0	2,667,000	31.3	33,264,000	38.5

Source: Adapted from *Ten Great Years* (Peking, Statistical Bureau, 1960) as quoted in Leo Orleans, *Professional Manpower and Education in Communist China*, p. 145.

22. Leo Orleans, *Professional Manpower and Education in Communist China*, pp. 143–46, 172.

Educational ascendancy, occupational advancement, economic independence, and political involvement have unbridled women in Chinese society; a resumption of a passive and subordinate existence on their part is inconceivable. Nonfamilial careers unheard of in traditional China now are not only possible but also satisfying, and apparently secure. The energy of an ever-growing number of urban females thus will be so diverted and absorbed in ventures outside the home.

This constellation of developments in urban China thus encourages a sense of demographic optimism. However, the gains on the urban scene could be less generously characterized, and their impact on China's fertility largely discounted. The 1953 Census of China gave the total urban population as 77,670,000, or 13.2 percent of the total population of 587,960,-000.[23] The rate of urbanization in China has been low in recent years, reflecting, in part, deliberate efforts to stablize urban growth. Although the net gain in the urban population amounted to an estimated total of 35 million in 1957 (the last date for which statistics are available), the upward shift in percentage points is unimpressive. The urban population of the total population was little more than 14 percent in that year. Thus, like their male counterparts, the great majority of Chinese women live and work in the countryside. It is *their* schooling and job situations, not those of the urban minority, that may make a material difference in the Chinese fertility rate.

In the Rural Setting

By the time agricultural reorganization was stabilized in the mid-1960s, three types of administrative and production units emerged in the countryside: people's communes, production brigades, and production teams. The production team is also the basic accounting unit in Chinese agriculture and is responsible for its own profits and losses. Production brigades are made up of production teams, which numbered 3,000,000

23. No absolute figures by sex were given. The overall sex ratio was 107.7 males per 100 females.

in 1959. Some 12 to 24 brigades make up a people's commune, each brigade consists of about 10 production teams, and some 30 to 40 neighboring families are ordinarily included within a production team. In all, there are approximately 80,000 production brigades. Women constituted "30 to 40 percent of the labor force of *many* production brigades" in 1966.[24] On this basis, women would have comprised *less* than 40 or 30 percent of the *total* agricultural labor force. Unless the adjective "many" is in error, this would mean that female participation in the labor appears to have been somewhat below the estimate frequently quoted in the literature in the mid-1950s. The agricultural labor force in 1955 reportedly included 262 million persons, of which some 46 percent (119 million) were female.[25]

Whether the higher or the lower figure is accepted as an approximation of the actual magnitude of female participation in the rural labor force, woman remained a minority, albeit substantial, component of it. The fact that the proportion of women in the labor force is smaller than their proportion in the total population reflects, in a large measure, the requirements of childbearing and homemaking. (Obviously, obstacles to full labor participation still exist). But, the more crucial question is: What are the specific types and nature of work in which *working* women in the rural area are engaged?

In their study of cottage industries and fertility in Japan, Jaffe and Azumi reported that married women engaged in agriculture had a higher fertility than those not in the labor force, and that there was very little difference between the latter's fertility and that of those who are self-employed or unpaid family workers (workers in home industries). One

24. NCNA (Peking), 6 Mar. 1966. Italics added.

25. See N. R. Chen, *Chinese Economic Statistics,* p. 109. However, as of 1957, another source reported "women members of agricultural, herdsmen, and fishermen's cooperatives totaled 110 million, and those of handicraft cooperatives numbered 1.5 million" (NCNA [Peking], 7 Mar. 1957). Another report dated 2 March 1960, however, stated that "in the countryside, over 90 percent of all the able-bodied women are working."

implication is that participation in productive work under conditions in which a woman can combine home and work duties is not related to reduced fertility. Cottage industries serve to maintain traditional forms of social and family relationships, which is one major element involved in sustaining traditionally high fertility.[26]

That participation in the labor force per se is not related to fertility has also been reported in other recent studies. Fertility differences by work status, for instance, have been shown to be nil among a group of married women in selected Turkish villages. The absence of role incompatibility in the rural setting again is cited as the chief explanation.[27] Gendell is also of the view that in the traditional sector of developing societies, "economic activity is largely agricultural or consists of handicrafts, both of which are conducted at home, and women economically active at home seem to be no less fertile than women not economically active."[28]

Statistics on females by types of work within China's agricultural sector are nonexistent. But, in a proposal for realizing China's 1956–67 National Agricultural Program, the All China Democratic Women's Federation provided a most comprehensive list of productive and related activities that rural women were encouraged to undertake.

> 1. Rural women should enthusiastically join the agricultural producers cooperatives. . . . Women saltmakers, fisherwomen, and boatwomen should actively join the cooperatives of salt workers, fishermen, and boatmen. Herdswomen should, together with herdsmen, join pastoral cooperatives. . . .
>
> 2. Efforts should be made to enable within the next seven years every able-bodied woman in the countryside to give at least 120 working days a year to productive work. Women who can give 120 working days and more to pro-

---

26. A. J. Jaffe and Koya Azumi, "The Birth Rate and Cottage Industries in Underdeveloped Countries," pp. 52–63.

27. J. Mayone Stycos and Robert H. Weller, "Female Working Roles and Fertility," pp. 210–17.

28. Murray Gendell, "The Influence of Family-building Activity on Women's Rate of Economic Activity," p. 285.

ductive work at present should, where possible, strive to give more working days to productive work. Women who cannot give 120 working days to productive work at present should strive to give 120 working days and more within seven years. To this end, women of the countryside should systematically organize their household work so that they can give more time to productive work where possible.

3. Learn how to cultivate and manage with the aid of new technique, cotton, tobacco, tea, hemp, and oil-bearing crops that can better be managed by women. Learn how to select seeds, prepare seeds by soaking, mix seeds with insecticides, do proper thick planting, thin out the shoots, protect the plants, practice artificial pollination, apply fertilizer, weed, kill insects with insecticides, and lop off superfluous branches of plants. Learn the horticultural art of growing fruit trees and vegetables.

Take part in work that women are suited to do in building water-conservancy projects, conserving water and soil, improving the soil, and enlarging the acreage of arable land.

Open the sources of manure in multiple ways; accumulate manure, human excrements and urine, fowl and swine dung, firewood and grass ashes; devise ways of accumulating miscellaneous manures; learn how to make green manure and make manures by high temperature.

Learn how to use the new type of farm tools suitable for women such as double-wheel and double-blade plows, seeders, shellers, and ensilage cutters.

4. Rural women are to contribute more strength and create more wealth in subsidiary production and livestock-breeding in which they are engaged. Rural women should keep more swine and take swine-breeding as one of their main sideline occupations [Islamic women are exceptions] in order to step up supply of meat, increase earnings for peasant families and cooperatives, and open up a source of manure. They should learn how to keep swine and accumulate feeding experience. They should try to find diverse kinds of substitute feeds and keep more swine with less grain consumed. Attention should be given to protecting female animals and taking good care of young animals. More chickens, ducks, and geese should be kept. They should learn the methods of preventing animal and fowl diseases and simple ways of curing swine and fowl diseases. Rural women should take an active part in keeping bees, tending silkworms, making sugar, vermicelli and beancurds, knitting mats and baskets, and other sideline occupations.

5. . . . Rural women should bring into full play such good points of theirs as patience and carefulness and make themselves an active force for eliminating insect pests and plant diseases. . . . Rural women are to take an active part in afforestation work. According to the special features and possible conditions of women, they should cast seeds in denuded mountains, grow saplings, protect tree nurseries, plant trees, build forests, protect forests, and prevent forest fires.

6. At the time of harvesting, all rural women should gather, thrash, and keep the crops carefully and . . . setting up creches in the cooperatives during the busy farming season is an indispensable work to free the labor power of women and protect the safety and health of children.

7. Women working in state farms, livestock-breeding farms, technical stations, tractor stations, and health centers should love their jobs, study their business, improve their working ability, and contribute more to the building of the new rural areas of socialism.[29]

The range and variety of female working activities remain the same agricultural and related pursuits that have been followed in Chinese villages for centuries. Coupled with the explicit appeals for better organization of household chores, for greater numbers of creches during harvests, and for appropriate recognition of "special features and possible conditions of women" in work arrangements, this clearly means that rural women take part in productive work in and near their homes. For the great majority of them, they also do so on part-time basis; 120 working days a year apparently constitute an acceptable, if not the regular, share of female participation in the labor force.

Thus, in view of the types of productive work detailed in the proposal of the All China's Democratic Women's Federation, the significance of rural women's participation in the labor force in relation to fertility would seem minimal. It would seem premature, therefore, to predict a reduction in fertility in rural China where, for the great majority of women, the female working role apparently still is subsumed under their conjugal and material roles, and their productive work

29. NCNA (Peking), 8 Mar. 1956.

evidently remains an integral part of familial rather than non-familial activity.

Furthermore, describing some recent developments in women's education in rural China, Tsai Chang, president of the All China Women's Federation, stated in 1960:

> Women illiterates still make up the majority of illiterates at present. In view of this, our women's federation must place on their order of the day the mobilization and organization of women to study culture and science. The Central Government has instructed us to fulfill the target of the anti-illiteracy campaign among young people basically before the end of 1962. We must assist the departments concerned in mobilizing and organizing young women illiterates and exert tireless efforts to accomplish this objective ahead of the schedule. Those women who have shaken off illiteracy should be encouraged to "hurry on without stop" by attending primary, secondary, and even higher spare-time schools, raising their cultural level step by step.[30]

Thus, educational efforts appear to have been mainly to eliminate mass illiteracy among adults, though younger persons now have every educational opportunity from primary school to college. In relation to fertility change, however, a rise in educational attainment probably would have only limited impact in the short run, especially when it is brought about by a rapid extension of adult education.[31] As educational attainment can occur subsequent to childbearing or employment or both, it may serve only to modify reproductive ideals, but it cannot erase fertility realities. The simultaneous

30. Ibid., 2 Mar. 1960.

31. As Stycos and Weller reported, working women in Turkish villages were considerably better educated (i.e., a greater proportion of them attended schools) than nonworking women. In this instance, the former also seem to have been more sympathetic to family-planning and to desire fewer children than the latter, though neither schooling itself nor employment appears related to actual fertility. This, they reasoned, might possibly denote a "precontrol" period in which behavior has not yet caught up with stated attitudes and desires ("Female Working Roles and Fertility," p. 214).

emergence of significantly altered family ideals and sizes in response to a general elevation of the level of education will likely become visible only in the long run after new generations come of age.

Thus, unlike the urban case, the prospect for fertility reduction of considerable magnitude would seem highly problematic so far as China's rural sector is concerned. Given the fact that only a minority of women are city residents, China's demographic future thus appears to be in great jeopardy.

Changing Rewards for Rural Women

However, this note of pessimism would induce despair only if one were to ignore other developments in the villages and to dismiss some obvious, but salient, qualifications surrounding existing analyses of fertility and employment in other countries. In their study, for instance, Jaffe and Azumi suggested that "perhaps the most desirable industries to be introduced into an underdeveloped country would be those using large quantities of female labor away from home, in modern factories, stores, offices, etc." Implementation of this suggestion would encounter as well as create immensely difficult problems.[32] Aside from its practicality, the suggestion also seems to be only partially supported by their own findings. The fact that Jaffe and Azumi focused on *unpaid* family workers in cottage industries and women engaged in agriculture, presumably also unpaid, raises the possibility that the absence of payment for such work might have been an unnamed intervening variable of no small consequence. Stated positively, a system of compensation for women traditionally engaged in unpaid work might be a most practical alternative, under the circumstances, to enforced departure from home to take up paid employment in competition with men for presently scarce jobs.

Details of the evolving system of income distribution (i.e.,

32. Jaffe and Azumi, "The Birth Rate and Cottage Industries in Underdeveloped Countries," p. 62. They remarked that rapid placement of females in such jobs would be at the expense of male workers and give rise to social and political unrest.

payment in kind and cash for participation in productive work) in the Chinese countryside have now become sufficiently clear to allow some tentative observations regarding their probable effect on fertility.   In the days before the introduction of the advanced agricultural producers' cooperatives in 1955, compensation for women who joined the mutual-aid teams and agricultural producers' cooperatives was calculated on the basis of "workdays." This method of computation was retained until the formation of the people's communes in 1958.[33]   A special editorial of *China's Women* described distributive aspects of the innovation in these words:

After the liberation, . . . and particularly after the co-operativization of agriculture, the feudal patriarchal system began to shake from its very root. However, there were still many families that relied mainly on their male labor power to earn their income, and that recorded their female members' work-points under the name of the heads of the families. In these families, therefore, the economic power was entirely in the hands of the patriarchs, and women were still in a dependent position. Following the introduction of the people's commune system, a new system of distribution has been enforced that combines the wage system with the supply system. The people began to rely on the commune and their own labor for basic means of living, but not on their patriarchs any more. As the wage is issued directly to the laborer, women can receive compensation for their labor as long as they are willing to work. They can thus depend on themselves for food and clothing, and do not have to rely on their husbands or parents-in-law. In this way, the women's status in the family has been changed and the patriarchal system has been abolished everywhere; the manager of economic affairs in the

33. Basically, according to the Model Regulations for Advanced Agricultural Producers' Cooperatives (30 June 1956), "What is left of the total income [after subtracting costs of production and reserve and welfare funds] shall then be distributed according to the total number of workdays credited to members, including workdays for agricultural production, subsidiary occupations, managerial work of the cooperative, and bonus workdays awarded to production brigades or individual members."

family should be the ablest member of the family but no longer necessarily the patriarch.[34]

Along with, or subsequent to, the shift to direct payment to individual workers, the method of calculating their remuneration was also adjusted and made more favorable to women. Providing some 80 percent of commune members' income, the production team makes three distributions a year, largely in the form of grain, on the basis of the number of work-points each member has accumulated during the year. The value of each work-point is the fraction of the total income to be distributed, divided by the total number of work-points of all team members. *In general,* work-points are tied to agricultural and closely allied "tasks" themselves. Each task is worth a standard number of work-points, which is fixed by trial and error according to the performance of an average agricultural worker and with reference to other relevant criteria.[35] Regardless of the sex of the person, the same number of work-points will be given to whoever performs a particular job.

The implementation of the work-point system has expectedly given rise to numerous problems. Some of these are of a technical nature, pertaining to bookkeeping and related matters, which need not concern us here. It also has apparently

34. *China's Women,* 16 May 1959.

35. Chen Mae Fun, "Paying the Peasants," pp. 263–64. Other criteria involved in the computation of task-based work points include the tools used, the technical qualifications necessary, the degree of physical effort required, the climatic conditions, time needed to complete the task, importance of the task toward agricultural production, and whether it is carried out during the slack or busy agricultural season, and so forth. Where it is impossible to fix the number of work points, the alternate method of computing work points is as follows: for every 10 hours of work, a member can receive a specified number of work points. They are alloted to each worker according to physical strength, political consciousness, technical qualifications, attitude toward work, and so forth. Thus, an average male agricultural worker may receive 10 points, a more able one 11 points, a lesser man 9 points; whereas, a woman will receive 8, an above-average female worker 9, and a poor woman 7.

had tremendous repercussions in the intersex and intrafamilial spheres, though ages-old patterns and attitudes remain to slow the arrival of the day when the wife will be "the equal half" in the marriage. In the words of *China's Women,* "the complete emancipation of women still needs considerable time":

> At present, as certain kinds of labor remain heavy and clumsy, women are still limited to certain fields of production and thus cannot develop their still larger function. Besides, women's technical and cultural levels are still too low to catch up with the needs of the development of the state and production; . . . the residues of the "prefer-male-to-female" thinking still exist in various degrees in society; and some women still indulge themselves in ideas of conservatism, self-abasement, and dependency. [But], because conditions are different from place to place and development is extremely uneven, problems of women are not the same throughout the country.[36]

However, as work-points have now been specified, to a not insignificant extent, in terms of tasks rather than individual workers, women are the major beneficiaries. This task-oriented method of alloting work-points has transferred the principle of same pay for same work to a clearly more institutionalized foundation. The impact of this transition is pointed up in a description of what occurred in one village: a greater rate of participation of women in production and in more varied types of work, and a greater efficiency in completing jobs.[37]

More importantly, the overall potential significance of direct payment to each worker and the institutionalization of same pay for same work in agriculture and associated pursuits lies in the direction of far-reaching changes in the Chinese family structure:

36. "On the New Stage of the Women's Movement," *China's Women,* 16 May 1959.

37. "Same Pay for Same Work to Men and Women in Chinghsi Production Brigade," *China's Women,* no. 11 (November 1961).

The people's communes practice a wage system based on the principle of "to each according to work" and at the same time practice a supply system that to some extent embodies the rudiments of the principle of "to each according to needs." . . . With wages paid directly to each worker, women can completely free themselves from their subordinate status and achieve economic independence. . . . In this way the feudal patriarchal system is being further demolished. Many capable women are now entrusted with the major share of family responsibility.[38]

In conjunction with all other changes,[39] the work-point system may well be the first step towards the restructuring of the occupational and the domestic institutions that for centuries held women in subordination in Chinese society in general, and in the rural area in particular.[40]   The conditions thus generaged may well turn out to be the correct "mix" that is conductive to relatively swift modifications in reproductive ideals and behavior.

To put it in another way, what can be said of the work-point system and its influence on fertility is as follows: recent research findings in other societies have shown, as just noted, that women's participation in productive work is related to family limitation.   But, this relationship seems to be contingent upon a relatively specific set of circumstances that make it impossible or inconvenient for married women

38. Tsai Chang, "The Party's General Line Illuminates the Path of Emancipation for our Women." It should be noted that more work and no food for the idle also have been stressed in connection with the work-point system.

39. Of particular importance is the fact that encouragement to delay marriage has become both a matter of law and of continuing social engineering in China since 1950. Though its progress there can only be surmised, it may be noted that delayed matrimony has become visible in widely scattered Chinese communities in Singapore, Malaysia, and Hong Kong. There is reason to suspect that the impetus behind this convergence in behavior outside China seems to have come, at least in part, from within Chinese culture. See also chapter 4 above.

40. Cf. Kingsley Davis, "Population Policy: Will Current Programs Succeed?" p. 738. Also, Judith Blake Davis, "Demographic Science and the Redirection of Population Policy," pp. 62–67.

to combine their work with domestic responsibilities. In short, one intervening variable is the separation of place of work from the place of residence. However, extrafamilial employment and activities obviously entail far more than merely physical separation from home. And, the findings of the negative role of the latter in fertility behavior should not be equated with a presumed drop in the frequency of sexual intercourse. That would be a sensational but misplaced inference concerning the importance of extrafamilial employment and activities in relation to fertility change. Rather, they should be read as a definitive break from tradition in that, for women so engaged, individual status and worth is no longer by ascription only. For them recognition and reward for achievements can have both an immediate and a cumulative meaning, and can provide a powerful incentive to limit family size. In old China, women always worked, especially in agricultural and related rural pursuits, but exclusively as unpaid family workers. In this perspective, therefore, a system of individual rewards fundamentally alters the structure of the family and the place of women in the family. It denotes a break from tradition that may be of equal, if not greater, crucial importance than employment outside the home in and by itself.

In demographic research, a great deal of reliance can be and is placed on an electronic computer where statistical data are abundant. Where they are scarce or imperfect, computer simulations may be resorted to in order to gain, among other things, some appreciation of the direction and range of the phenomena under examination. Neither of these is feasible here, given the fact that knowledge of the level of reproduction in China (i.e., the dependent variable in question) is singularly imprecise. This appraisal of some of the developments affecting women has been predicated on the assumed modifications in reproductive ideals and behavior in the direction of reduced fertility. It is, in a manner of speaking, a simulated mensuration of the potential impact of known developments affecting women's place in Chinese society. But, it is a simulative exploration that is anchored in research findings in other societies. Needless to say, the diversion of women from their traditional occupation of child-bearing, which is confidently surmised here, awaits confirmation.

Educated Youths on the Move (Hsia Hsiang)

An upshot of the preceding appraisal is that social and economic measures designed to serve nondemographic ends frequently can influence demographic trends and patterns in a number of significant ways. But, it should be made clear that the developments affecting women also simultaneously or eventually affect men. After all, the consequences of societal and familial transformation cannot but permeate the fabric of the whole society. The status of women has undergone change in China on account of their occupational diversification, educational ascendancy, and related gains, as has the structure of interdependence of men and women in the familial setting. Thus, it would be neither fair nor correct to conclude that women and their changing role in Chinese society are the only key elements in China's demographic transition.

There, in fact, have been a number of measures that have directly affected young men *and* women. Of these, some are deep- and far-reaching efforts having to do with the education, employment, and mobility of youths in the course of China's industrial construction. None of them has initially been explicitly demographic in intent, but all of them are actual or potential determinants of population developments. Defining the range of their demographic impact therefore is in order, and as necessary as the preceding assessment of the changing rewards for women in China.

Along with other nations on the road to industrialization, China is often said to enjoy many advantages, particularly in the areas of technology and innovations, that were not available wholesale to industrialized nations at the initial stages of their development. These advantages are undoubtedly real. What is generally not stressed in this situation, however, is the fact that use of techniques and equipment introduced from outside a nation is partly dependent upon a rise in the

TABLE 16

NUMBER OF STUDENTS ENROLLED IN AND GRADUATED FROM PRIMARY
SCHOOLS, SECONDARY SCHOOLS, AND INSTITUTIONS OF HIGHER EDUCATION,

1949–1960

(In Thousands)

		LEVEL OF SCHOOL				
	Primary	Secondary			University	
YEAR	Graduates	Junior	Senior	Graduates	Entrants	Graduates
49 – 50	2,829	832	207	296	....	18
50 – 51	4,232	1,067	238	284	35	19
51 – 52	5,942	1,384	184	221	35	32
52 – 53	9,945	2,231	260	454	66	48
53 – 54	10,136	2,572	360	644	71	47
54 – 55	10,254	3,109	478	969	94	55
55 – 56	12,287	3,320	582	939	96	63
56 – 57	12,307	3,830	366	1,299	166	56
57 – 58	16,225	4,340	780	1,313	107	72
58 – 59	....	7,340	1,180	....	152	62
59 – 60	....	....	....	....	270	....
Total	84,157	....	....	6,419	1,092	472

SOURCE: Adapted from Leo Orleans, *Professional Manpower and Education in Communist China,* p. 32, table 2, p. 35, table 3, and p. 61, table 1.

general level of literacy. The importance of education and
the role of the educated thus are indicated. These considerations notwithstanding, an effort has been made to enlarge
educational facilities of all descriptions in the country. The
result of this expansion is partially reflected in table 16.

The number of students enrolled in all schools has also continually reached new heights in the years since 1960, though
the magnitude of the rate of increase (which has not been disclosed) may have been somewhat smaller than most of those
shown in table 16. With respect to the years for which relatively reliable data are available, the salient feature of the
educational expansion in China is that the greatest growth
has occurred at the primary level. The number of students
who have completed primary school increased nearly six times
between 1949 and the end of the 1957-58 academic year. At
the secondary level, during the same period, the number of
graduates increased a little more than four times. There was
also a threefold increase in the number of students who graduated from institutions of higher learning between 1951 and
1958.

This pattern of differential growth probably owed much to the circumstance that a more rapid expansion at the higher levels was precluded by available personnel, physical plant, and funds. The maintenance of high academic criteria for admission to middle schools, colleges and universities undoubtedly contributed to it. Whatever the specific reasons, the effect is that, over the years, there has been an increasingly greater discrepancy between the number of graduates of primary schools and the number of students enrolled in junior secondary (high) schools. Likewise, the number of students admitted into institutions of higher learning has been small relative to the number of students who graduated from senior secondary schools. Thus, in 1957, for instance, for every student in the university, there were 4 in senior secondary schools, 11 in junior secondary schools, and 150 in primary schools. Cumulatively, therefore, of the students who finished the primary school, an estimated total of 77.7 million were either unqualified or barred by reason of space from further schooling at the secondary level. Another 5.5 million graduates of senior secondary schools failed to gain entrance into universities.

It should be stressed that the extension of education to include greater and greater numbers of persons is in itself an intrinsic component of development. However, although education adds to the impetus of economic development, it is also a potent stimulus socially and demographically. Its role in fertility reduction in places outside of China has been empirically confirmed, and is of a significant magnitude. Presumably, increased education can be expected to produce a similar effect in China in the long run. But, in the short run, the influence of education on the overall fertility is unlikely to be large, given the fact that only a minority of the educated persons have been able to continue beyond the primary school. Nevertheless, from the swelling ranks of relatively educated persons there has been other instantaneous fallout. Of particular relevance here are the various moves both to cushion the impact of this circumstance on the occupational structure and to relate such personnel to the ongoing economic and social transformation. Yet, it is precisely these conspicuously nondemographic measures that are likely to exert a more immediate depressing influence on the Chinese birth rate.

In terms of the manual-nonmanual dichotomy, individuals can be placed along a verticle scale based on differential prestige conventionally attached to the various occupational pursuits. But, there is also a horizontal (geographical) dimension to the question of manpower utilization: persons in the labor force can be employed either in urban places or rural areas. Roughly speaking, therefore, according to current or anticipated needs, China's manpower can be distributed in four different sectors: urban nonmanual, urban manual, rural nonmanual, and rural manual. The urban nonmanual sector is the smallest, and the urban manual and rural nonmanual sectors fall somewhere between it and the rural manual sector. That is, the bulk of the economically active population is employed in the last sector, as has been the case for centuries; economic development of China thus far has allowed only a limited change in its occupational structure. For instance, the Second Five-Year Plan (1958–62) projected an annual average increase of 1.4 million persons in the nonagricultural sector. That is, for the time being and in the foreseeable future, the great majority of educated persons can only be employed in the rural manual and nonmanual sectors. As previously noted, this expansion, especially at the primary and secondary levels, has evidently occurred at a much faster rate than employment opportunities in the nonmanual sector. The lag probably is as unavoidable under the circumstances as the enforced termination of formal education for a considerable number of students at the conclusion of their precollege schooling. However, whatever qualifications may be in order regarding the aforementioned statistics on school enrollment, ways must be found to provide suitable occupational outlets for the tens of millions of graduates of primary and secondary schools. But, had the suitability of employment outlets for this large number of students been simply an issue to be resolved by students themselves, the matter of occupational placement would have been a lesser problem.   There are other complicating factors, however.

In this connection, and to give a partial list of other complicating factors, it is of interest to quote a passage from Martin C. Yang's *A Chinese Village:* "A member of the Yang clan, for example, had a very good reputation as a student when he was in the market-town school.   He was praised by the teachers, the community leaders of the whole market-town area, and also by the senior members of the P'an clan, so that great hope was roused among all the people of the clan. . . . The young man was *very unconventional.*   Even after he became a college student, he still came home to work on his father's farm during the summer vacations.   He dressed like an ordinary farmer.   This gave the kinsmen and the villagers the impression that he was not going to be a scholar or a gentleman or an official, and they became indifferent to him."[41]   This is indicative of not only what an educated person cannot or should not do but also what he must or ought to do.   It shows the extent to which immediate and distant family members and neighbors influenced or attempted to proscribe and prescribe occupational choice.   In the process of undergoing what is socially viewed as personal transmogrification through learning (the age-old term for education), pressures are built up against an individual's maintaining the occupational status of his family or orientation and, at the same time, for him to be upwardly mobile in the occupational world (and beyond the village in the case of a rural youth).   For him and those similarly situated, therefore, the social expectation is that they leave or avoid jobs that amount to only "the manipulation of things" and follow pursuits in "the manipulation of people."

One consequence of post-1949 expansion in education is that a large number of people became aware of occupational alternatives that had been unknown or unreachable for them and that had been denied to their parents and older relatives. Given this downward extension of the ladder of opportunity,

41. C. Martin Yang, *A Chinese Village,* pp. 140–41 (italics added).

and in the social context of occupational decision-making, relatively educated in significant numbers have come to entertain aspirations for further education or employment that is both currently and potentially more rewarding than any type of work in rural areas.

Of course, the question concerning the suitable employment of educated persons would have constituted a problem of lesser magnitude, were material incentives amply available to be extensively applied to induce their voluntary relocation to places where they are needed. The fact is that where differential rewards exist in China, they tend to draw people, educated and otherwise, in the opposite direction. Wages and other amenities are more favorable in urban places, particularly in industrial and commercial centers, than in rural areas.[42] To the extent that persons with some education or literacy are more likely to stay in or migrate to the cities, therefore, social erosion of the rural communities analogous to the process of mining natural resources becomes inevitable in the wake of expanded educational opportunities. Moreover, its dysfunctional impact is compounded by the fact that the urban nonmanual sector (which is the traditional outlet for educated) is unlikely to be able to absorb any appreciable number of the growing educated population from within the cities themselves. Nor is it likely that the urban manual sector can absorb any substantial in-migration from rural areas.

Quite apart from its demographic implications, the suitable placement of educated persons in relation to economic development and social reorganization becomes what may be a problem of diverting them from their traditional occupational goals. And, since 1950 or 1951, this redirection of the educated has been repeatedly discussed in numerous publications. A more systematic espousal of the many points that were raised and subsequently formed the basis of extensive programs of occupational diversification between then and now, reads like this:

42. See chapter 3, table 7.

1. At present, an incorrect view that is widely prevalent in our society asserts that all graduates of primary and secondary schools must be promoted to secondary schools and institutions of higher learning, respectively. Those who cannot continue their studies and who must find employment in industry, agriculture, and other lines of labor thus are considered *shih-hsueh* [a term that has no English equivalent and describes a person who is willing and able but is denied an opportunity to continue formal education]. Because of this, they become pessimistic and disappointed, and are resentful of the people's government. This is an extremely unhealthy and erroneous thought. The real substance of this view is the low esteem for manual labor and manual workers, and it considers manual work menial. This is both a feudalistic and bourgeois point of view. In the last four years, our educational leadership failed to recognize the dangerous character of this kind of thought. It was a fundamental error that they did not undertake a penetrating and systematic criticism of it.

2. New China's educational endeavor is to foster the younger generation to become mature elements in the over-all expansion of socialist society, and to enable them to participate in the effort to develop a great socialist country. . . . The aim of New China's education therefore is to increase the productviity of the people. This means, first of all, that the people must be educated to develop the socialist attitude toward manual labor, to view it as a glorious task, and to accept it as the duty of all who are capable of performing manual labor.

3. Our primary education is of a compulsory nature. That is, within a certain number of years, we must gradually make it possible for all children who reach school age to receive a primary education. The purpose of universal education [at the primary level] is to raise the cultural standard of the laboring masses, and to help promote among future factory workers, peasants, and other laboring poeple a certain degree of political awareness and cultural attainment. . . . [They] can thus assume a more correct attitude toward labor, better grasp techniques, and become productively able persons in industry and agriculture. Before the secondary education is [also] made universal, it is natural that only a small portion of graduates of primary schools can proceed to secondary schools. At the present stage, the objectives of our secondary education are, apart from furnishing a certain number of freshmen for institutions of higher learning, also to increase the

cultural level of the people and to supply to various development enterprises of the nation workers whose political level and cultural accomplishment are somewhat higher than graduates of primary schools. . . .

4. The people's government has adopted a policy of opening school doors to workers and peasants, and has also taken various measures to establish conditions favorable to workers and peasants and their children taking up studies [such as scholarships and special schools]. . . . At present, not only do children of workers, peasants, and other laboring people constitute an absolute majority of the student population of primary schools, but also their share in secondary schools and universities has been steadily growing year after year. According to estimates in 1952, of the total student population of primary schools, over 80 percent were children of workers and peasants. At the secondary level, their proportion was more than 57 percent. In 1953, about 22 percent of the students in institutions of higher learning came from families of workers and peasants. It is certain that the proportion of such students . . . will step by step continue to increase in schools at all levels.

5. There are a number of students who are unwilling to become workers and peasants, and who regard manual work and land cultivation as being "too dirty," "too exhausting," and "too disgraceful." Many heads of households of the students are also loth to have their children and siblings become workers and peasants. They feel that, if [their children and siblings] are going to "suffer" anyway, what would then be the reason for having an education. There are teachers who also think that it is both "unpropitious" and "unfortunate" for students to work in factories and on the land. . . . In feudal days, one of the mistaken views in China was that "all pursuits are inferior; only booklearning is superior." This view still influences, in no small measure, teachers and heads of households of our time and, thereby, is poisoning the great mass of students.[43]

From, or along with, this and similar statements, two principal types of programs have emerged on the national scene. With varying degrees of specificity in goals and coordination in organization, direct participation in manual activities has been made either a part of the curriculum during the regular

43. *People's Daily,* 26 Aug. 1963.

school year or the focus of work projects in the summer or some other irregular times. Also, both on an annual basis and on special occasions, appeals and assistance have been continually forthcoming to mobilize students to go to the countryside. This latter effort, known generally as *hsia hsiang* (go down to the villages), has been broadened to include regularly employed persons in what has been designated as *hsia fang* (transfer down to the countryside). The purposes of these programs have been variously stated, as follows: to build a socialist countryside; to contribute to agricultural production; to temper and remold the attitudes and thought of youths for the purpose of turning them into true successors to the revolution; and to eliminate three major differences inherited from bourgeoise past, i.e., between mental and manual labor, between urban and rural areas, and between theory and practice.

In the best of circumstances, the needed impetus for the successful attainment of these objectives probably will accelerate only slowly. In this context, it is of interest to note that about a decade later in 1963:

There are some people who believe that [Chinese] villages have no need for knowledge, and that it is "too bad" for educated youths to become peasants. This is an old-fashioned viewpoint. Is it really "too bad" for high school students to become peasants? Does this mean that this constitutes "the use of large material for small purposes [the employment of talented men in inferior capacities]? Comarade Mao Tse-tung told us, "after having studied from the primary school to the university, a person still cannot be accepted as a fully developed intellectual. To transform such persons who have only book-knowledge into intellectuals in name as well as in fact, the only way is to make them take part in practical work. . . . For high school students to go to the countryside to experience real life, it is but the necessary way to gain complete knowledge. How could it be termed a waste of talents? Ours is a socialist country. The great majority of the people must participate directly in productive work. The aim of learning is not to separate 'mental workers' from 'manual workers,' but is to enable a person to become a worker equipped with both knowledge and a socialist consciousness. That educated youths go to the villages and join the practical struggle, is only to consolidate their proletariat point of view, . . . and to infuse step by step 'mental work' with 'manual work.' . . . Only thus can we guarantee that our youths will be able to shoulder the great responsibility of revolution."[44]

In another article entitled "The Responsibility of Parents and Household Heads," parents and household heads were again, as in the 1950s, enjoined from "erecting barriers" to make it difficult for their children to take up employment on the farm, in the factories, or in the shops:

Fundamentally, even if schools in our country were more numerous and bigger in size, it would not be possible for every junior secondary-school graduate to go to senior secondary school, or for every senior secondary-school graduate to go to the university. Therefore, many youths must either remain in the village to cultivate the land, or work in factories, or become sales clerks in shops. Only thus will it be possible to organize our society based on the division of labor. That [these] several youths are enthusiastic about their participation in such various lines of work is a clear indication of their understanding of this easily comprehended principle.

On the whole, children have trust in and respect for the opinions of their parents and household heads. . . . [Therefore], should parents encourage their children and add to their forward-looking faith [in what they are going to do], or should they place an extra burden on their children [by trying to dissuade them from entering into such occupations]? . . . Those parents who "erect barriers" for their children may say that their action reflects their concern for the future of their children. These parents have, in various ways, taught their children that they study to become famous and to gain personal advancement. . . . These are the thought remnants from the old society. . . . Even if we view the time when children are about to leave school and to go to work as a "gateway" in the life journey of the youths, parents must help their children pass through it in the least painful manner.[45]

44. Ibid.
45. Ibid., 17 Aug. 1963.

However, what can be deduced from the above complaints is far more than the mere existence of social inertia against change. The opposition obviously was of a considerable magnitude—a fact that is altogther expected. The significance of China's programs to redirect its educated youths into diverse occupational pursuits and away from the urban centers lies precisely in the kinds of changes envisioned. With respect to agricultural and village development, for instance, it would be unsound to follow a course of action that simply increases the supply of fertilizer, farm machinery, improved seeds, and the like. Educated persons are also needed in the rural areas to act as change catalysts and to contribute to rural improvement in matters relating to education, health, cultural activities, and administrative functions. These efforts are imperative steps in planned economic development.

Of course, a great deal could be said of the effectiveness of the exhortations and related efforts to deploy educated youths to places where they are needed. But, this would be beyond the immediate purpose of the present discussion, which is to indicate some of the possible or probable effect on fertility of specific social and economic measures.

There can be no question that the number of youths involved in the two types of programs referred to above is very large. No systematic reports have been issued on the volume of participation; but from 1955 to 1964, a total of some 40 million youths have reportedly responded to the appeal to go to the countryside and to take part in physical labor. In 1964 alone, some 300,000 youths are stated to have left towns and cities for rural areas in the entire nation. (In 1953, the number of youths of both sexes between 10 and 24 years of age is estimated to be 156.9 million.) This purposefully assisted and village-bound migration of youths seems to have continued even between 1966 and 1968, when Chinese youths were on the move to and from the urban centers during the Cultural Revolution. Since then, their deployment to the countryside has been resumed, and is still making news.

On the basis of such fragments of relevant statistics as have been found in official pronouncements, speeches, and similar sources, and nonstatistical data, mostly in the form of descriptions of emerging patterns, these programs have been neither a disastrous failure nor, instantly, an outstanding success. (It is exceedingly difficult to evaluate these or any other programs of similar sort—e.g., the Peace Corps of the United States—because of the diffused character of their impact.) In the immediate context, and relative to Chinese society of pre-1949 years, the efforts to increase occupational diversification among educated persons probably have greatly undermined the monolithic scale with which success was measured in the past. No longer is the occupational hierarchy an unidimensional structure; recognition and rewards for achievement are now possible in occupations that were formerly deemed beneath the dignity of the educated. Youths are serving as accountants in the communes, tractor operators on the farm, and workers in menial jobs throughout the nation. To the extent that educated youths in China have become diversified occupationally, they deserve to be classified, metaphorically speaking, as migrants in time. They have leaped forward and out of the past in one brief spell, jettisoning traditional occupational norms. Further, and more importantly, their temporary or permanent sojourn in rural districts has also made them migrants in fact.

Taken together, it seems that these programs have wrought changes of a basic kind in the social structure and processes. The individual on the move no longer lives in the ancestor's shadow and becomes at least once removed from the pervasive influence of traditional familism. In the absence of direct evidence, the salience of this changing constellation of the forces affecting him cannot be firmly underscored. Nevertheless, it does not seem imprudent to conclude that this and similar developments cannot but enhance the possibility of a meaningful reduction in fertility.

Ideally, data for the present analysis should have included rates of participation in these programs by age, sex, and marital status. However, such statistics are not available. Nor are the related employment data by length of stay in the countryside. Thus, the impact of these programs on fertility can only be inferred. The conclusions therefore are, as in the

case of the changing role of and rewards for women, sugges-
tive rather than definitive. Their validity can only be tested
as events unfold and as the needed data become available.

Appraisal and Conclusions

Chapter eight

The twenty years, 1949–69, saw the adoption and implementation of more explicit demographic measures than any other similar time-interval during China's past millennia. The great variety of measures put into effect are by no means lasting solutions to China's population problem. In fact, some were merely short-lived programs, and only time can yield the necessary evidence of the effect of some other decisions. Nevertheless, and summarily speaking, they are significant steps toward a more conscious management of demographic affairs at both the individual and societal levels. The measures tried or still in force have reflected a progressively more discriminate awareness of the consequences and determinants of patterns and trends in population distribution and redistribution, land use and reclamation, and planned parenthood as well as of the limits of demographic measures. There is unmistakable evidence, however, that the basic attitude toward population size and growth has undergone a fundamental revision during this brief period of twenty years.

In 1964, as previously indicated, there was the statement by a high official in China, which reads: "China has sufficient space. We could easily feed an additional 200 million people or more in this gigantic country. And even if some day we should have reached the 800 million or one billion mark, the country would still be big enough for them. We have rich mineral resources, and we have gigantic quantities of land that can be cultivated."[1] However, this pronouncement is far from an endorsement of unlimited population growth; rather, it should be taken only as an official estimation of what China is capable of doing if necessary.

Indicative of this far-reaching change are the many discursive reports published since early 1965 on the relative and absolute advantages of mechanical implements over human hands in a variety of circumstances. In one way or another, these statements reflected the view that too many hands may and can be dysfunctional. Some of the variants of this emerging theme of the dysfunctionality of too many people in certain situations are: "labor productivity doubles amid a 50 percent reduction in personnel and improvements in the management of the enterprise"; "with efficient use of equipment, one shift can do the work of two"; "too many people do not necessarily facilitate the accomplishment of a task"; and "many people produce clumsy work; fewer hands turn out ingenious product." A first systematic espousal of this thesis was published in the *People's Daily* on 27 April 1965. Entitled "Do Not Be Superstitious About 'Many People Expedite Work,'" portions of it read:

> The adage "many people expedite work" is very much in vogue. Is this a correct maxim or not? It is both correct and incorrect.
> A very large population is our nation's one major unique characteristic, and, from the standpoint of pressing the revolution and construction, also a great advantage. People are the first most precious of all things in the world. Only through the full mobilization of the positivism on the part of all people in the whole nation, will it be possible to fully develop their wisdom, intelligence, and creativity. Only then, will it be possible to accomplish many tasks of which a small population is incapable, and to achieve many spectacular wonders that are beyond the reach of small

1. See chapter 4, footnote 33. This statement was made sometime *before* 24 July 1964.

populations. Comrade Mao Tse-tung said, "For our nation to catch up to the capitalist countries and agricultural countries in agricultural and industrial production, the time may not be as long as had been once imagined. Apart from the Party's leadership, the 600 million people are a determining factor. When there are many people, discussions are numerous, enthusiasm is high, and work zeal great." In the national context, and from the viewpoint of a broad framework, many people do indeed expedite work, i.e., the task of building socialism.

But, it must not be said that in all circumstances, the saying "many people expedite work" will always hold true. For example, in the case of an enterprise or a trade unit, we cannot maintain that "many people expedite work." However, there are at present still some people who are addicted to this superstition of "many people expedite work." They believe that the more numerous the people the higher the production, and that the more the people the easier it is to accomplish a job. Therefore, in order to increase production or to improve job efficiency, they invariably think, first of all, in terms of personnel expansion or organizational growth. In their view, to increase production without additional personnel, or to increase production and reduce personnel simultaneously, is like "to want horse to run, but, at the same time, to want horse not to eat grass."

Comrades who adhere to the superstition "many people expedite work" may not be able to comprehend that many people can, on the contrary, impede work, hinder an expansion of production, and adversely affect an improvement in efficiency. The fact of the matter is that this is not hard to understand. This is because the phrase "many people" here pertains to an excess of personnel from the objective standpoint of actual need. Who would be interested in technical innovations, or in improvement in work efficiency, or how would it be possible to develop positivism and creativity, when a task that one person can obviously fulfill is brazenly assigned to two persons, and when a matter that one unit can obviously discharge is unvaryingly given to several departments to handle? . . . Furthermore, how can productivity and work efficiency be increased under the conditions of a myriad organizational layers, excessive personnel, extreme specialization, extensive work duplications, and mutual obstruction and nullification of each other's efforts.

On the other hand, with fewer people on hand when there are many things to do, they all will consequently de-

velop a sense of positivism. They will give thought to, and
devise ways of making, technical innovations and improving
work efficiency. How can productivity and work efficiency
not but be increased? Under certain circumstances, therefore, we say that fewer people facilitate job completion.
Here lies the reason why many people, on the contrary, do
not expedite work.
Dialectical materialism emphasizes the concrete analysis
of concrete phenomena. In order that manpower is fitting-
ly in line with the actual requirements of production, not
only must we undertake a concrete analysis of the existing
structure of an enterprise, we must also concretely study
its division of labor, the form of labor organization, and so
forth, to see what aspects of the arrangements are suitable
and what aspects are not suitable. In regard to any kind
of experience, we must use our brain to evaluate it. We
should not be in blind opposition to it. Nor should we
accept it blindly. If one does not believe that [the quan-
tity] of people is the leading factor [affecting productivity
and work efficiency], and if one also blindly follows others'
footsteps, one will not be able to break out the encirclement
of the superstition that "many people expedite work."[2]

The process of decision-making obviously is a dynamic one:
time and circumstances have allowed the experimentation of
variously designed programs relating to population in recent
years in China. However, the mere invocation of the common
saying "nothing ventured, nothing gained" would fail to
adequately reflect the essence of the evolution of China's
demographic decisions. The majority of the measures have
been coordinated steps rather than make-shift prescriptions.
Taken as a whole, the past twenty years should go down in
history as the watershed in the management of China's
demographic affairs. Concomitant with, or consequent upon,
learning what is possible and what is not possible, policy
assumptions have been subject to redefinition in deeds and
words. The gains have been subtle, and salient changes in
perspective and in the dimensions of the overall framework
within which demographic decisions have been or are being
made. Neither a rapid increase of the population nor an

2. *People's Daily*, 27 Apr. 1965.

infinite multiplication of the Chinese people is now accepted in China, in fundamental contrast to the expressions of the earlier years.

However, though China's demographic decisions have won wide publicity and been extensively scrutinized, their direct effects on population growth and distribution still remain very much undefined statistically. Presumably, the rate of urbanization has been slow or slower than it would have been, had no efforts been made to regulate the growth of large metropolitan centers and to retain rural population. And there is credible, albeit indirect, evidence that fertility is now falling in China. In the latter connection, one report of the evolving fertility situation reads: "From personal observations and chance conversations with recently confined mothers and with members of hospital staffs, it appears that the once threatening high birth rate has been brought under control, at least in Shanghai and probably in most other industrial cities. In the villages, however, family planning is still in the early stages. Maternity wards in Shanghai hospitals are conspicuously less busy than they were in the past, and a fair portion of beds are vacant."[3] Presumably also, therefore, the demographic momentum has been arrested, at least to an extent. Apropos of this, a recent United Nations prognosis of the Chinese population trend to the year 2000, explicitly forecast a pending decease in fertility and stated:

> While the timing, rapidity and extent of such a decline cannot be predicted, the probability of its occurrence within the next few decades appears high. It is related to economic and social changes which will almost certainly occur in a country where the government has taken strong initiatives to overcome long standing obstacles to progress. The communal organization of agriculture, the diversifica-

3. *Far Eastern Economic Review,* 14 October 1965, pp. 47–50. Katagiri and Tearo also reported that in 1971, in Ton Wan People's Commune, the birthrate has fallen to 13.6 per 1,000 from 46 per 1,000 in 1963 ("Wide Range of Family Planning," p. 6). Based on birth registration for the first three months of 1972, metropolitan Shanghai, with a population of 10.5 million, reported a birthrate of 11 per 1,000 (*New York Times,* 19 October 1972, p. 34).

tion of the role of women, the emphasis given to education and acquisition of industrial skills, and other social changes to which (China) is committed are apt to favor an eventual reduction in the average size of families. . . . Eventually, decreasing mortality as well as continuing changes in the social and economic structure of the country would be likely to strengthen motivation for keeping families small. Furthermore, the Government has adopted a policy of encouraging the limitation of births.[4]

The twentieth anniversary of the founding of the People's Republic of China has been celebrated. In temporal perspective, these two decades are an insignificantly emphemeral moment in Chinese history. Yet, perhaps, in no other comparable period, has there ever been a more bountiful crop of paradoxical predictions of the government's imminent collapse, on the one hand, and of the immediacy of its embarkation upon territorial conquests, on the other hand. The quality of such gazes into the crystal ball, however, is uniformly poor; they have been made through politically tinted glasses, based on the simplistic causal postulate of population and war. Such wayward prophecies have characteristically not withstood the test of the actual events during the score of years that have just lapsed.

Likewise, many other contradictory accounts of recent social and economic events in China have been no more than merely sensational annotations of surface phenomena. Following the sighting of women and men wearing outwardly identical clothing, for instance, the desexualization of women in China has been repeatedly asserted. The management of China's economic affairs, particularly in the agricultural sector, has also been repeatedly vilified for its alleged low efficiency and inability to provide more than the bare sustenance of life. Almost in the same breath, however, the growth of China's population has been said to continue only unabated. None of these has been borne out by the information that is available. Both a total cessation of reproduction and a quick solution to China's population problem are as fictitious as

4. United Nations, *World Population Prospects,* pp. 56–77.

the notion that China is a nation with a mammoth population headed in the direction of demographic bankruptcy.

Nothwithstanding this dismal record of past predictions, neither the inclination nor the temptation to speculate about things to come has diminished. China's ability both to care for its existing population and to affect population growth remains a very lively and irresistible issue. Let any inaccuracies in the present account of China's demographic decisions be corrected should additional facts warrant it. But, let this volume be a contribution to the continuing dialogue and prognosis on China's demographic future.

Appendixes

Appendix A

Regulations Governing Urban Population*
(Ministry of Public Security, with the Approval of the
State Administrative Council, 16 July 1951)

ARTICLE 1. The present regulations were formulated with a view to maintaining social peace and order, safeguarding the people's security, and protecting their freedom of residence and of movement.

ARTICLE 2. Except for the troops, organs, and barracks of the People's Liberation Army, the people's public security forces, and the people's police, and so forth, together with the diplomatic personnel of foreign diplomatic missions in China, these regulations are applicable to all urban population.

ARTICLE 3. All those living under one principal, living together, and eating and sleeping at the same place, whatever their number or their relationship, shall be counted as one "household." In the case that one family is divided up to live separately, to eat separately, and to live apart at some distance from one another; or in the case that a number of families, though living at the same place, are to be financially independent of one another, they may be counted as separate

*Survey of China Mainland Press (hereafter cited as SCMP), no. 137, July 1951.

"households." The classification of households is as follows:

1. Residential households: For ordinary residential households, the principal is considered the head of the household. When the household is made up of separate individuals, he who has lived there longest or who holds a steady job shall be considered the head of the household.

2. Industrial and commercial households: All public or private enterprises, factories, companies, shops, workshops, cooperatives, warehouses, hospitals, and places of amusement shall be considered households with their respective manager, factory superintendant, or other kind of supervisors considered to be the head of the household.

3. Public residence households: In the case of hotels, inns, traders' hostels, and guilds, the manager or the principal shall be considered the head of the household. If a traveler should reside there for more than 3 months or set up a business therein, he should be considered a separate household by himself.

4. Floating households: All those who have no place of abode on land but live in ships or boats, or those who though possessed of places of abode on land, yet eat and live for long periods in ships or boats, shall have the principal of the ship as head of the household.

5. Temple households: All temples and churches belong to this category. The principal of the place of worship concerned shall be considered the head of the household.

6. Alien households: All foreign nationals living on Chinese territory (except for those covered by special governmental decrees) shall be considered alien households with the responsible person considered to be the head of the household.

ARTICLE 4. The control over residents shall be uniformly carried out by the people's public security organs. All the registration records, forms, and documents needed should be reduced to the simplest form for the convenience of the people. These records and forms, uniformly designed by the Ministry of Public Security, may be reprinted by people's security organs of the provincial level. People may not refuse to admit public security personnel when engaged in their work.

ARTICLE 5. Any change in the members of the household should be properly reported by the head of the household concerned who shall proceed to the local public security organ with his census record:

1. *To move out:*

All those who move out should first notify the local public security organ of change of residence, cancel the census record of the old place of abode, and apply for change-of-residence permit (change of residence within the jurisdictional area of the same public security organ does not require a permit).

2. *To move in:*

A. All those who have moved in should report to the local public security organ to enter his name in the census record within 3 days of arrival. When available, the change-of-residence permit should be submitted; if not, other documents of a suitable nature should be submitted instead.

B. Released bogus civil and military functionaries together with released criminals should submit documentary evidence provided by the military, judicial, or public security organs concerned for registration in the census record.

3. *Birth:*

Registration for birth should be carried out one month within the date of birth, either by the head of household or by the parents concerned.

Abondoned babies should be immediately reported to the public security organ concerned by the discoverer for its disposal.

4. *Death:*

A. Death should be reported within 24 hours of the event and before being encoffined, by the head of the household, or a family member, or by the neighbor concerned.

B. Sudden death, or when the cause has not been made clear, or by contagious disease, should be reported immediately by the head of the household, a family member, or the discoverer.

C. Stillbirth should be reported, first within the category of birth and subsequently within the category of death.

A burial certificate is necessary for the burial of all of the above-mentioned cases of death.

5. All cases of: marriage, divorce, separation, merging of households, disappearance, return (of the missing one), fostering of child, adoption, employment, discharge, starting business, closing down business, change of head of household, change of job, and so forth should be reported.

ARTICLE 6. Visitors staying for 3 days and more should be reported to the public security sub-station.

ARTICLE 7. Census records should be kept by all households and faithfully entered for checking. Hospitals should have census records as well as records of in-patients, and arrival and departure of patients should be regularly reported. All hotels should have hotel registers, which are to be turned over at bed time to the local public security organ concerned for examination.

ARTICLE 8. Violation of these Regulations shall be punished according to the severity of the case.

ARTICLE 9. All organs of the People's Government, people's organizations, schools, munitions factories and so forth are considered to be public households. Such public households are also subject to control by public security organs according to regulations that shall be separately formulated.

ARTICLE 10. The present Provisional Regulations shall come into force on the date of their promulgation. All previous measures and regulations on the control of urban population shall be annulled to make way for the implementation of these Regulations.

ARTICLE 11. Concrete detailed measures or supplementary measures for these Provisional Regulations may be formulated by the public security organs of various administrative regions, provinces (or municipalities), on the basis of the spirit of these Regulations.

ARTICLE 12. These Provisional Regulations are approved by the BAC and promulgated by the Ministry of Public Security.

Appendix B

Decision on Labor Employment Problem*
(State Council, 3 August 1952)

Unemployed Personnel Left Over from the Old Order

The long-term aggression of imperialism and the long-term reactionary rule of Kuomingtang (Nationalists) have combined to create a serious situation of unemployment and left behind a tremendous number of jobless people to New China. During the past three years, much has been done and accomplished by the People's Government in the way of solving the unemployment problem and of giving relief to those unemployed living in hardship. First of all, the public functionaries left by the Kuomingtang reactionary regime were retained in toto by the People's Government at the time of take-over, and then large numbers of unemployed workers and unemployed intellectuals left over by the reactionary rule were mostly given jobs as economic restoration and development as well as construction work advanced during the past three years.

*Adapted from SCMP, no. 388, August 1952.

Up to December 1951, over 1,200,000 unemployed workers found work, of whom 600,000 workers and employees were absorbed into state industries and mines. About 1,000,000 unemployed intellectuals have been given jobs, through training recruitment, or by individual appointment, since the time of liberation. In rural village, where agrarian reform has been completed in areas covering an agricultural population of 400 million, the loafers, the army officers of the old regime returning to the countryside, and the ever nonproductive landlords have, like the peasants, received their own share of land to till. At present, whether in urban districts or rural villages, the number of employed is the largest, as compared with any period in history, and, at the same time, the number of people with labor power but remaining unemployed is the smallest in history.

Situation Now Is Different from Pre-liberation Days

However, there is still a part of unemployed intellectuals and former army officers and government officials left over by the old regime, whose problem of employment remains yet unsolved, due to their lack of technical knowledge or ability and due to the nation's construction work being not yet fully developed. At the same time, in the face of incessant reform of social economy in the past three years toward the direction of New Democracy, many nonproductive trades not beneficial to the people's livelihood or engaged in profiteering by speculations and hoarding or catering to the decadent and extravagant life of landlords, compradores, and bureaucrats, have been eliminated, which naturally has given rise to new unemployment or semi-unemployment. Other factors that contribute to the state of unemployment are: (1) as a result of production reforms, the reform of labor organizations, and the promotion of advanced production methods, working efficiency in our industrial, mining, and communications enterprises has been rationally raised, and there leaves a surplus in the workers and employees originally employed; (2) a large number of housewives who under the old order either could find no employment or were looked down upon, or depended on their husbands with no desire of finding work to do, now come out to ask for employment and, therefore, constitute quite a large surplus labor force in the cities; and (3) despite the agrarian reform, the insufficiency of arable land space remains basically unchanged, which, coupled with the mutual-aid movement and improved farming tools, will increase the surplus labor force in rural villages unless subsidiary production is actively undertaken. As the surplus labor is now flowing from rural villages to urban districts in an unplanned or nonorganized manner, it will precipitate the gravity of unemployment or semi-unemployment in the city. It must be recognized, however, that the unemployment or semi-unemployment in cities that accompanies the economic reform and the surplus labor in urban and rural districts attendant upon the production, social, agrarian, and organizational reforms, are only temporary difficulties inevitable in our march forward, and the whole situation is basically different from the unemployment problem encountered under the reactionary rule.

To find work for all unemployed people and to fully utilize the surplus labor available in urban and rural districts is a problem that must be solved in the course of the large-scale national construction, and also is one that can be gradually solved as production develops.

With a view to meeting the large-scale national construction, solving the employment problem for all jobless people in an overall manner, gradually eliminating the state of unemployment or semi-unemployment, systematically directing the abundant surplus labor in urban and rural districts to production and social enterprises, and gradually effecting a centralized distribution of labor, the State Council in July called a special conference on the labor employment problem. The following stipulations are hereby made as based upon the conclusions derived from the discussion and study made at the conference.

Severance To Be Made According to Law

1. All public and private enterprises must observe the Common Program and the policy and laws of the People's Government and actively develop production and business. In the impending large-scale national construction, all public and private enterprises that meet the needs of the nation and the people have a bright future. Even if temporary difficulties may be encountered by certain enterprises, they should be overcome by active development of production and business, and not by cutting their staff, so as to safeguard the interests of the employees and workers and to avoid increasing unemployment. Any severance of workers and employees must be effected according to the Labor Union Law and other relevant regulations.

All public and private enterprises, when becoming overstaffed due to practice of production reform and raise in working efficiency, must adopt the policy of keeping all the surplus personnel and paying them their original wages (to be included in the cost of production). Severance shall not be permitted. Under such conditions, training should be given them by rotation so as to raise their technical, business, and political levels in preparation for use as the enterprises are enlarged or for unified distribution by the state. This will encourage the initiative of the workers and employees in making inventions and rationalization proposals.

Labor to Go with Capital at Change of Trade

If, due to reorganization of economy, certain private enterprises become devoid of a future and have to change into another trade, labor should, by principle, be transferred to the new line as in the case of capital. If, after securing the approval of the industrial and commercial administrative organs for the change of trade and upon consultation between capital and labor to arrange for the transfer of the workers into the new trade, there still remains a portion of the workers who cannot be placed in the new trade, a request may be filed by capital in accordance with the Labor Union Law and other relevant regulations with the labor department for the termination of employment of such personnel, and severance may be effected upon the ratification of the labor department.

When certain private enterprises, due to serious losses leading to inability to carry on, even after labor-capital consultation to promote business, have to retrench or close down, the approval of the industrial and commercial administrative organs should be obtained in the case of closure of business and approval of the labor department should be obtained in the case of severance of part or all workers and employees. Priority of restitution should be given to the workers and employees thus separated when the business is expanded or restored.

The labor department should deal with the problem of severance carefully in accordance with present conditions, with equal regard to the benefit of labor and capital. Reasonable requests for severance should be approved, and those made under pretext or the suspension of work, wages, or food before permission to close business is secured from the industrial and commercial administrative organ should be resolutely checked.

Although the industrial and commercial administrative organ should carefully deal with requests for closure or change of trade in order to stabilize economic conditions and minimize unemployment, it should fully ascertain the financial situation, the business project, and the reasons for opening the business when any application for permit is considered, so that opening or closure of business blindly, ultimately causing unemployment, may be avoided. To correctly deal with these, a consultative committee may be set up under the industrial and commercial administrative organ of large cities, with the participation of the labor department, the trade union council, the industrial and commercial association, and other relevant organs and bodies.

To Observe Eight-Hour System Where Possible

For the sake of safeguarding the health of the workers and employees, raising labor productivity, and enlarging the size of employment, the system of working eight-ten hours per day should be strictly observed in a systematic and planned manner. All comparatively larger public and private factories, mines, and communications or transportation enterprises should practice the eight-hour system where possible. The one-shift-a-day system can be changed into two- or three-shift system where circumstances as to raw materials, marketing, and technical conditions allow. State-operated shops or cooperatives in industrial or mining districts or large or medium cities should also follow the eight-hour system. The working hours for those engaged in work harmful to health should even be shortened to less than eight hours. Extra-hour and extra-shift practices should be strictly prohibited in all private and public enterprises.

All unemployed workers should be registered and given training for change of trade or introduced to new employment. Those who cannot get employment immediately or participate in training and who have difficulty in living, should be placed through "work relief," "land reclamation," or "self-salvation through production projects," or given temporary or long-term relief.

The women workers who are family members of the unemployed workers and other women workers (housewives) should be organized to do processing work or engage in handicraft production, when raw materials and marketing conditions permit, or be absorbed into other types of work according to needs and possibilities.

Intellectuals and Educated Housewives

2. Concerning the problem of intellectuals, the fundamental situation is that there are too few intellectuals to meet the nation's large-scale construction. However, of the unemployed intellectuals at present, an utter majority have no technical knowledge or ability, as the result of the colonial

economic and educational systems of the old order. Ideologically their progress is rather slow. Some of them have begun to become politically awakened while others are still comparatively backward, while yet others have truly complicated political backgrounds. Most of them are middle aged and harassed by family burdens. They are unwilling to go to rural villages, much less to remote regions, and most of them have actual difficulties in doing so. All this constitutes the reason why they have not been able to get employment earlier. Part of them have never had any employment, especially the educated housewives, due to various reasons.

On the other hand, certain enterprises and organizations have, in the past, accepted only students and cadres and had misgivings about absorbing the unemployed intellectuals to participate in work. These scruples must be removed. We must face reality and take an overall view. The policy of wide absorption, education, reform, and use of all unemployed intellectuals must be adopted, otherwise the urgent needs of national construction will not be met. More especially, the educational, health, trade, and cooperative departments must do all they can to absorb them for training, reform, and use. At the same time, the unemployed intellectuals should realize their own shortcomings and endeavor to reform themselves ideologically. Those with dubious political backgrounds should be taken in just the same when they have made honest and frank confessions. A few of the unemployed intellectuals who have the qualifications to enroll in institutes of higher learning or technical schools, should be helped to receive further training to meet the further development of national construction.

Among the unemployed intellectuals one finds a number of learned people of local repute, but as they are aged and physically weak, they are unable to stand heavy work. Steps should be taken to give them proper work and adequate care. To the aged intellectuals who have completely lost their working ability and who are experiencing difficulties in living, suitable relief should be given.

To the housewives who are intellectuals now asking for employment, special consideration should be given as they mostly have to look after household work. Therefore they can only be gradually organized into part-time work, with certain amount or remuneration paid them as living subsidy.

Concerning Army Officers and Government Officials of the Old Regime

3. The large numbers of army officers and government

officials left behind by the Kuomingtang reactionary rule, who
in former days generally gave support to the reactionary rule
and some of whom may still be opposed to the People's Government, have mostly been influenced by the great victory of
the people during the past three years and now pledge support to the people in an attempt to redeem themselves by
merit.

The majority of these officers and officials have returned to
their countryside and received their shares of land to engage
in agricultural production. Part of them upon their return
have been placed under surveillance by the local people who
were dissatisfied with them, which is only correct and necessary. But for those who are honestly engaged in production,
abide by the law of the government, and show no reactionary
acts of any kind, they should have their old status changed,
three years after the liberation of the place, through the
agreement of the *hsiang* people's representatives meeting and
with the ratification of the *hsien* people's government. Their
new status should be determined by the nature of their
present labor and profession (except that if they were landlords, the change of their status should be governed by the
stipulations relative thereto). Some of these officers and
officials remaining in the cities have already found work or
some means of living, but others are engaged in irregular
business, and still others experience serious difficulties of living. The latter two kinds of people should be registered,
trained, and helped to change trade, so as to become further
reformed through work. Those whose previous political background is not particularly questionable and who have honestly
cleared up their problems, should still be trained and reformed
for employment. Those senior officers and officials who cannot participate in training for change of trade and who actually experience difficulties in living but whose past history was
not particularly bad and who had not aroused too great an
indignation of the people, should also be given proper care.

Those who have done their part in the 1911 Revolution, in
the Northern Expedition, in the anti-Japanese war, or in up-
rising during the liberation war (and then sent back to the
countryside), and who do not have a particularly bad record,
should receive priority consideration in disposal.

Surplus Labor in Rural Villages

4. The large amount of surplus labor available in rural
villages is different from the unemployed or semi-unemployed
in urban districts. They have land to till and means of living,
but in them reside great labor potentialities that must be

given full play and diverted to production. As arable land is already not sufficient under present technical conditions, there would be more surplus labor available as further progress is made. As a fundemental solution, it is therefore necessary to start immigration to the northeast, the northwest and the southwest, so that land reclamation to enlarge the tilling area without affecting the development of animal husbandry and the conservation of soil can be carried out, that small-scale water irrigation to change dry land into paddies can be developed, and that improvement of seedling and farming techniques to raise unit production can be promoted. In densely populated areas there still are large tracts of wasteland (such as sandy land, alkaline land, and red earth land) that, as shown by experience, can be utilized and therefore should be reclaimed with the surplus labor of rural villages organized. Soil conservation, improvement of soil, dredging of rivers and lakes for the reservation of water, and the soil and water conservation of upland should all be conducted in a planned manner.

Apart from the above, planned development of subsidiary production, handicrafts and the processing of agricultural by-products, afforestation, fishery, river conservancy, road repairs, and the construction of large-scale hydraulic works will absorb a tremendous amount of surplus labor. All responsible departments should draw up plans and implement them according to local needs. Handicraft cooperatives, especially, should be set up wherever possible to promote the handicrafts suitable for both export and home consumption.

Active efforts must be made to get things organized to launch a movement of mutual assistance and cooperation, on which to base our work of immigration, land reclamation, water conservancy and the like.

Urban and industrial developments and the progress of national construction will absorb the necessary labor from rural villages, but this must be done gradually, and cannot be accomplished all at once. It is therefore necassary to prevail upon the peasants and check their blind desire to flow into the cities.

National Minorities and Returned Overseas Refugees

5. The unemployment problem of national minorities scattered in cities now mainly involves the Muslims and merits careful attention. Due to the differencese in habits and customs, the sphere for them to find work is narrow. Apart from giving them help in individual cases, it is best to get them organized and absorbed into industrial and mining en-

terprises, with particular consideration given to their habits and customs.

6. Adequate care must be taken of the returned overseas refugees and poor overseas Chinese. The overseas Chinese-affairs organs and the civil-affairs organs must look into the problem carefully. No stone should be left unturned to find them work or to place them in production work so that none of them will be left jobless or without schooling or displaced. Help should be given to those without labor power, being helpless and living in difficulties.

7. There also exists a number of indigent aged, invalid, or disabled people and homeless children. They should be either housed for education or given relief. For those among them who still have labor power, they should be organized into production to help maintain their living. The able-bodied loafers and beggars should be given forced labor. Where possible, they should be concentrated and given reform through labor.

Unified Registration and Separate Training

8. All urban unemployed should be registered in a unified way, including the following types: All workers and employees of brain and brawn of public and private industrial and commercial enterprises, communications and transport units, handicraft workshops, organizations, bodies, or schools, as well as building and transport workers, who have no definite work after severance; seasonal workers and workers unable to find work after the decline of their line of trade; unemployed intellectuals with the cultural level of junior middle school; independent producers after suspension of business; traveling merchants, hawkers, agents of capital, and small industrial and commercial operators, having no income to maintain a living after suspension of business and requesting to get employed; and unemployed army officers and government officials (of the former regime) experiencing difficulties of living and asking for employment.

Following registration, they should be disposed of in accordance with their respective conditions. Training should be given in general by groups and in different periods, and work should be given step by step as required by the development of national construction and according to the conditions of the individual. In accordance with needs, political training and training for employment and for change of trade should be conducted generally by the departments that will employ them later. If the unemployed after registration are found to be in actual living difficulties, they should be given proper relief.

To effect a unified solution of the labor employment problem and to gradually achieve the centralized distribution of labor, employment committees should be set up in the Central People's Government, the administrative regions, the provinces and all large cities who will have offices with exclusive personnel to direct labor departments and other relative organs to undertake registration and disposal of all unemployed. Municipalities under provinces may also set up employment committees upon the ratification of the provincial people's government.

To Bring Labor Potentialities into Full Play

To deal with the employment problem for the unemployed and the semi-unemployed of urban districts and to tackle the problem of utilizing the tremendous amount of surplus labor in both urban and rural districts, we must first, based upon the needs of national construction, view the problem as a whole, take a long-range view, and do what should and can be done at present so that we can gradually eliminate the state of unemployment and give full play to the labor potentialities of the urban and rural districts, so that more wealth can be created for the state and society, and great strides can be made in the nation's economic and other constructions.

Appendix C

Directive on Dissuasion of Peasants From Blind Influx into Cities*
(State Council, 17 April 1953)

According to recent reports, since the spring season numerous peasants desirous of taking part in industrial construction have entered cities to look for jobs. These peasants numbered over 20,000 according to returns from Shenyang and Anshan alone. In view of the fact that urban construction has just started and the demand for labor is limited at present, blind influx of peasants into cities increases unemployment in cities, making it difficult to deal with the problem, and greatly affects spring plowing and sowing in the countryside by the decrease of manpower, causing loss to agricultural production.

In order to curb further development of this chaotic condi-

*SCMP, no. 554, April 1953.

tion, the following directive is hereby issued. It is desired that all provincial and municipal people's governments will supervise the concerned units in fully carrying out, at their responsibility, the following measures:

1. All provincial and municipal people's governments should immediately notify the *hsien, chu,* and *hsiang* governments as well as peasants' associations to patiently dissuade the peasants who prepare or ask to enter cities from so doing by explaining to them: that industrial construction in cities is only at its start and the existing number of building workers exceeds demand; that if they go to cities freely they will be unable to find jobs and will not only incur traveling expenses but will also hinder rural production; and that if in the future additional workers are needed for urban construction, the *chu* and *hsiang* governments will be officially notified to recruit labor in a planned and organized manner.

2. Except those in possession of official documents issued by factories, mines, and building construction companies, confirming that they are contract workers, all peasants desirous of entering cities to find employment shall not be issued certificates of introduction by the *hsien, chu,* and *hsiang* governments.

3. Except those needed by the work units, all peasants who have entered cities should be persuaded by the labor and civil-affairs departments of the people's governments, in conjunction with trade unions and other relevant organs in the districts of their residence, to go home. In the course of disposal of the cases, a careful attitude should be taken. Those actually lacking traveling expenses may be given an allowance by the civil-affairs department and persuaded to go home. Those actually experiencing difficulties in livelihood should be given appropriate relief.

4. All peasants freely recruited by building-construction units from the countryside or contracted workers who are not needed at the present moment should be uniformly dealt with by the building-construction units themselves in persuading them to go home and in issuing them traveling expenses.

5. *Hsien, chu,* and *hsiang* people's governments that indiscriminately furnish letters of introduction should take the responsibility of mobilizing those peasants whom they recommended to the cities to find employment and who are unable to find employment, to return home.

6. Rural cadres and militiamen who have freely gone to cities to find employment should uniformly return home to lead peasants in spring ploughing and sowing. Disabled servicemen and retired servicemen who had already been

settled down in the countryside but who later went to cities to find jobs should also return home to take an active part in production in order to ensure fullfillment of agricultural production plans of the state.

7. All building-construction units in cities should notify the local building-construction bureaus and labor departments of their plans, date of start of work, number of workers required, and precise plans of projects, in order that manpower can be distributed and regulated in a planned and organized manner. Without the permission and introduction of the labor departments, workers may not be arbitararily recruited in the countryside, still less can notices be posted up for indiscriminate recruitment or workers.

Appendix D

Criteria for the Demarcation between Urban and Rural Areas
(State Council, 11 November 1955)

Because economic circumstances and living arrangements are not at all alike between urban and rural populations, the various functions of the government accordingly must be carried out differently in urban and rural areas. Urban and rural populations must also be computed separately. In order that uniform steps are followed by various departments and bureaus when they undertake planning tasks, statistical work, and other activities in accordance with different urban and rural characteristics, the criteria for the demarcation between urban and rural areas are now established as follows:

1. Places that meet one of the following criteria are urban areas (*Chen* and *Cheng*):

A. Areas where municipal people's committees are set up and sites of *hsien* (or *chi**) people's committees or higher are located (except the administrative and executive organizations in the pastoral nomadic areas).

B. Places that have a permanent resident population of 2,000 or more, of which more than 50 percent are nonagricultural population.

2. Sites of mining and industrial enterprises, railroad stations, industrial and commercial centers, transportation hubs, middle-level schools and above, scientific research organiza-

---

* *Chi* (Banner) pertains to civil subdivisions in the Inner Mongolian Autonomous Region.

tions, and the residential areas of their employees and workers
(of the above) are classified as urbanized residential areas
whose population is more than 75 percent nonagricultural,
even if the permanent resident population is short of 2,000 but
over 1,000. Also classified as urbanized residential areas
are treatment and recuperation areas where the annual number of people who came to obtain treatment and rest exceeds 50 percent of the permanent resident population.

3. All areas other than the urban and urbanized residential areas designated above are classified as villages.

4. In order to meet the functional requirements of certain
administrative departments and bureaus, *chen* and *cheng* may
be further differentiated as cities and market towns. All municipalities under the direct jurisdiction of the central government and provincial municipalities are classified as cities.
Also classified as cities are the seats of *hsien* people's committees and above as well as industrial and commercial places that
have a permanent resident population of 20,000 or more. All
other places are classified as market towns. When individual
departments and bureaus must adopt other criteria for differentiating cities and market towns because of work requirements, they should report them to State Council for approval.

5. Within the suburban area of the municipality, all the
closely adjacent suburban residential areas that are continuous with the municipal proper are all classified as urban
areas regardless of the proportion of the agricultural population. Other places within the suburban areas may, in accordance with the criteria stated in Articles 1, 2, and 3, be
separately classified as urban areas, urbanized residential
areas, or villages. The boundaries of closely adjacent suburban areas are to be determined by municipal people's committees on the basis of concrete circumstances.

The above criteria for the demarcation of urban and rural
areas are adopted to facilitate planning, statistical work, and
budgeting of the enterprises. Administrative status of various
areas and their organizational set up are not altered on the
basis of these criteria.

The determination of urban and urbanized residential areas
other than those specified in Section A of Article 1 must be
approved (by the State Council). The Department of Interior will accordingly formulate "Procedures for Requesting
Approval to Establish Urban Areas and Urbanized Residential Areas" and forward them to the State Council for approval before publicizing and implementing them.

In order to facilitate the progress of various tasks, the Ministry of Interior is given the responsibility to make immediately

a uniform determination of all urban areas and urbanized residential areas in the nation in 1956. It should also compile a "Summary Chart of the Nation's Urban Areas and Urbanized Residential Areas" and forward it to the State Council for approval for general use. Thereafter, any increase, decrease, and change in urban areas and urbanized residential areas should be made known generally by the Ministry of Interior at a fixed date.

APPENDIX E

POPULATION AND RANKING OF 102 MUNICIPALITIES
FOR 1938, 1948, 1953, and 1958

	POPULATION (In Thousands)				RANKING (According to Population)			
	1938	1948	1953	1958	1938	1948	1953	1958
Shanghai	3,595	4,423	6,204	6,977	1	1	1	1
Peking	1,574	1,603	2,768	4,148	2	3	2	2
Tientsin	1,223	1,686	2,694	3,278	4	2	3	3
Shenyang	772	1,121	2,300	2,423	6	6	4	4
Chungking	528	1,000	1,772	2,165	9	7	5	6
Kwangchow	1,022	1,414	1,599	1,867	5	4	6	7
Wuhan	1,242	910	1,427	2,226	3	8	7	5
Harbin	468	760	1,163	1,595	12	10	8	8
Nanking	440	1,230	1,092	1,455	15	5	9	10
Tsingtao	592	788	917	1,144	7	9	10	12
Chengtu	458	727	857	1,135	14	11	11	13
Changchun	360	630	855	988	17	12	12	16
Sian	218	503	787	1,368	24	17	13	11
Dairen	504	544	766	1,590	10	15	14	9
Taiyuan	177	200	721	1,053	35	42	15	14
Kunming	184	300	699	900	33	24	16	16
Hangchow	575	570	697	794	8	14	17	20
Tangshan	146	137	693	812	45	59	18	19
Tsinan	472	575	680	882	11	13	19	17
Fushun	215	513	679	1,019	26	16	20	15
Changsha	464	396	651	709	13	18	21	24
Chengchou	197	150	595	785	30	56	22	21
Wuhsi	272	273	582	616	20	25	23	29
Foochow	343	331	553	623	18	21	24	27
Anshan	120	166	549	833	55	50	25	18
Soochow	388	381	474	651	16	19	26	26
Penchi	66	321	449	449	79	22	27	36
Kirin	132	247	435	583	50	29	28	30
Nanchang	275	267	398	520	19	28	29	32
Lanchow	122	204	397	732	54	38	30	22
Shihchiachuang	194	198	373	623	32	43	31	28
Suchow	205	340	373	710	29	20	32	23
Antung	211	271	360	370	28	26	33	39
Chinchow	105	148	352	400	59	57	34	38
Chichihaerh	97	175	345	704	63	48	35	25
Kaifeng	303	300	299	318	17	23	36	44
Changchu	125	239	296	300	52	31	37	46

	POPULATION (In Thousands)				RANKING (According to Population)			
	1938	1948	1953	1958	1938	1948	1953	1958
Tzukung	176	223	291	280	36	34	38	50
Luchou	68	50	289	130	78	89	39	88
Huainan	......	......	287	280	....	....	40	48
Swatow	196	215	280	250	31	35	41	54
Kueiyang	145	240	271	530	46	30	42	31
Nantung	155	226	260	240	41	33	43	57
Pangfou	136	201	253	330	47	40	44	41
Wuhu	168	204	242	240	37	39	45	58
Ningpo	247	210	238	280	21	36	46	49
Hengyang	122	184	235	240	53	45	47	56
Kalgan	146	151	229	480	44	55	48	35
Tatung	70	80	228	243	77	80	49	54
Amoy	177	158	224	308	34	52	50	45
Hsinhailien	......	125	208	210	....	66	51	59
Wenchow	237	157	202	210	23	53	52	60
Chenchiang	213	179	201	190	27	47	53	66
Wutungchian	......	......	199	140	....	....	54	86
Paoting	216	130	197	250	25	64	55	53
Nanning	101	200	195	260	60	41	56	51
Neichiang	......	32	190	180	....	90	57	73
Fouhsin	160	180	189	290	39	46	58	47
Chinhuangtao	47	100	187	210	83	73	59	61
Hofei	94	153	184	360	66	54	60	40
Hsiangtan	103	133	184	247	57	61	61	55
Tzupo	......	......	184	......	....	....	62	....
Yangchou	127	127	180	160	51	65	63	82
Ipin	78	80	178	190	72	78	64	68
Yangchuan	......	......	177	200	....	....	65	65
Loyang	73	60	171	500	73	85	66	33
Hsinhsiang	......	......	170	203	....	....	67	63
Chanchiang	245	271	166	170	22	27	68	75
Nanchung	55	60	165	206	82	86	69	62
Kochin	......	16	160	180	....	93	70	71
Taichou	81	131	160	200	71	63	71	64
Liuchou	......	194	159	190	....	44	72	69
Mutanchiang	100	200	151	251	61	40	73	52
Paotow	70	82	149	490	76	77	74	34
Weifang	98	134	149	190	62	60	75	70
Huhehot	94	104	148	320	65	72	76	42
Liaoyang	90	110	147	169	68	69	77	78
Chiamussu	71	168	146	232	75	49	78	58
Kueilin	88	131	145	170	69	62	79	76
Urumchi	45	88	141	320	....	76	80	43
Haikou	......	60	135	402	....	87	81	37
Shangchiu	73	70	134	165	74	82	82	79
Shaohsing	149	92	131	160	43	75	83	81
Yingkou	160	159	131	161	40	51	84	80
Paochi	......	56	130	180	....	88	85	72
Tunghua	42	80	129	158	84	79	86	83
Chuchou	......	7	127	190	....	94	87	67
Lushun	133	25	126	......	49	92	88	....
Ssuping	56	76	126	130	81	87	89	88

APPENDIX E (*continued*)

	POPULATION (In Thousands)				RANKING (According to Population)			
	1938	1948	1953	1958	1938	1948	1953	1958
Anyang	94	115	125	153	64	68	90	84
Foshan	135	96	122	120	48	74	91	90
Liaoyuan	32	185	120	177	85	44	92	74
Shaoyang	83	106	118	170	70	71	93	77
Chefoo	166	227	116	140	38	32	94	85
Hsuanhua	......	......	114	......	....	....	95	....
Wuchou	103	207	111	120	58	37	96	91
Huangshih	......	28	110	135	....	91	97	87
Chuanchou	57	121	108	110	80	67	98	92
Ining	......	......	108	85	....	....	99	95
Anching	117	109	105	129	56	70	100	89
Changshu	94	64	101	101	67	83	101	93
Chaochou	152	60	101	101	42	84	102	94

SOURCE: Adapted from Morris B. Ullman, *Cities of Mainland China: 1953 and 1958*, pp. 35–36, table 3.

Appendix F

Joint Directive Concerning Implementation of Directive Advising Against Blind Influx of Peasants into Cities*
(Ministry of Interior and Ministry of Labor, 12 March 1954)

As a result of the issue of the directive advising against the blind influx of peasants into the cities by the State Council last April, the confused phenomenon of the blind influx of the peasants into the cities was for a time checked. However, because no endeavor was made to implement the State Council directive thoroughly by some places and our publicity given to the work was inadequate, some peasants were unable to comprehend the spirit of the directive. Added to this, certain *hsien, chu,* and *hsiang* cadres failed to carry out the directive seriously, and letters of introduction were issued by them in an irresponsible manner. At the same time, private arrangements were made by certain units to recruit labor in the rural villages without following the proper procedure. Moreover, because the work of production for self-salvation and other relief work were not timely carried out in certain famine-stricken areas, the phenomenon of the blind influx of

*Adapted from *SCMP*, no. 774, March 1954.

the peasants into the cities has continued with no abatement. In some places, the situation has become even more serious. Now that the Spring Festival is over and the season is the usual time for the influx of the peasants into the cities to take place, if no measure is taken to advise against it, the blind movement of large numbers of peasants will take place to the detriment of the spring sowing and the social order in the cities. In view of this, the following directive is hereby issued:

1. The various places should, in coordination with the spring sowing work, take immediate steps to adopt various methods to publicize and explain extensively to the peasants the State Council directive advising against the blind influx of peasants into the cities. The peasants should be made to understand that because city construction is at the beginning stage, the number of men needed to carry out the work cannot be too large and the building-construction workers there are already more than sufficient to cope with the need. If they head blindly for the cities, they are simply throwing away their money and time for nothing to the detriment of their production. If additional labor is needed for city construction work, the *chu* and *hsiang* governments will be duly notified and the workers will be recruited in a planned and organized manner. Without going through this organized procedure, the peasants who head for the cities on their own have no way to find work there. At the same time, we must align our publicity with the spirit of the general line of the nation. When publicizing the future development of the agricultural economy to the peasants we must explain to them the importance of agricultural production to national construction. The peasants must be made to adopt a more positive attitude toward agricultural production and to play a positive part in agricultural production and the mutual-aid and cooperation movement. In the case of the *tsun* cadres who are restless in rural work, ideological education should be strengthened so that they may be made to adopt the correct viewpoint of developing an ardor for agricultural labor and to lead the broad masses of the peasants to play a positive part in agricultural production.

2. The various places must lead the peasants to engage themselves positively in agricultural production. They must devise ways and means to increase production, to practice intensive farming, to improve production technique, to trim land, and to improve the soil. They must promote water conservancy, afforestation work, and other work that would solve the problem of surplus labor in the rural villages. Dur-

ing the slack season, they should lead the peasants to make use of every locally available facility to develop different kinds of sideline production that have a ready market. In the famine-stricken areas, the famine-stricken people should be organized to engage in production for self-salvation, and relief work should be satisfactorily carried out to solve the difficulties of the famine-stricken people in a practical manner so that they may have adequate assurance to make a living.

3. If the construction units of the various factories and mines are really in need of recruiting workers in the rural villages, they must apply to the local labor administrations for organized and planned recommendation and assignment, but must in no case make private arrangements to recruit workers in the rural villages themselves. If the recruitment of workers is still made at random in the villages, the local governments should take rigid steps to stop it. At the same time, the management and the trade unions of the construction units of the various factories and mines should concretely instruct their workers not to send for peasants of their villages to come into the cities. Letters of introduction must not be issued at random to the peasants by the *hsien, chu,* and *hsiang* governments.

4. The work to mobilize the peasants who have entered the cities to return to their villages should be handled by the civil and labor administrations in conjunction with other relevant organs. The traveling expenses should in principle be borne by the peasants themselves, but if they are in real difficulty, the local government may make them an adequate grant or provide them with free transportation. If these peasants are in real difficulty when they get back to their own villages, the local governments should give them adequate help to enable them to make a living and make another start in production.

Appendix G

Organic Regulations of Public Security Substations*
(Standing Committee of the National People's Congress, 31 December 1954)

ARTICLE 1. For the purpose of strengthening social secu-

*Adapted from *Current Background* (hereafter cited as *CB*), no. 310, January 1955.

rity, maintaining public order, protecting public property, and safeguarding civil rights, municipal and *hsien* public security bureaus may set up public security substations in areas under their jurisdiction.

Public security substations are the deputed organs of municipal and *hsien* public security bureaus to take charge of security work.

ARTICLE 2. Public security substations shall carry out the following tasks:

1. Ensure enforcement of laws on public security and social order;

2. Suppress sabotage activities flagrante delicto of counter-revolutionaries;

3. Prevent and curb activities of bandits and other criminals;

4. Place counterrevolutionaries and other criminals under surveillance according to law;

5. Handle household registration;

6. Exercise control over theaters, cinemas, hotels, seal carvers, and radio suppliers as well as explosives, inflammable articles, and other dangerous articles;

7. Guard the scene of important criminal cases and assist the relevant department in breaking the cases;

8. Direct the work of security committees;

9. Conduct propaganda among inhabitants concerning elevation of revolutionary vigilance, observance of law, observance of public order, and respect to public morality;

10. Take an active part and assist in welfare work for inhabitants.

ARTICLE 3. Public security substations should be set up according to the size of area, number of population, social conditions, and work requirements.

ARTICLE 4. A public security substation shall have one chief, one or two deputy chiefs, and several people's policemen.

Public security substations shall work under direct leadership of municipal and *hsien* public security bureaus or of public security subbureaus.

ARTICLE 5. Public security substations must maintain close contact with the masses, deal with letters from the public seriously, receive people's calls and make reports, and hear people's criticism and proposals at meetings of inhabitants or sessions of inhabitants' committees.

ARTICLE 6. Persons working in public security substations must fully observe laws, observe work discipline, and refrain from breaching laws and discipline and from encroachment upon civil rights.

ARTICLE 7. Railway and water public security substations shall also be governed according to these Regulations in general.

Organic Regulations of Urban Residents' Committee*

(Standing Committee of the National People's Congress, 31 December 1956)

ARTICLE 1. For the purpose of strengthening the organization of street residents in cities and their work and furthering the public welfare of residents, residents' committees may be set up according to residential areas under the guidance of people's councils of municipal *chu* and municipalities without *chu* divisions or of their deputies' organs.

Residents' committees are mass and autonomous organizations of residents.

ARTICLE 2. The tasks of residents' committees are as follows:

1. Undertake public welfare work for residents;
2. Reflect views and demands of residents to local people's councils or their deputed organs;
3. Mobilize residents to respond to government calls and observe laws;
4. Direct mass security work;
5. Mediate over disputes among residents;

ARTICLE 3. Residents' committees shall be organized as follows:

1. Residents' committees should be set up according to the conditions of residence of residents with consideration given to the area demarcation under the jurisdiction of the population section of public security office and, in general, should each cover 100 to 600 households of residents.

Under residents' committees are set up residents' teams composed generally of 15 to 40 households each. The number of teams set up by each residents' committee may not exceed 17.

2. A residents' committee shall have 7 to 17 members, with one to be elected by each residents' team; one chairman and

*Adapted from *CB*, no. 310, January 1955.

one to three vice-chairmen shall be co-opted from among the members; among them there should be one to take charge of women's work.

A residents' team shall have one head and in general the member of the residents' committee should act as the head of the team concurrently; one to two deputy heads may be elected if necessary. In case a member of the residents' committee is elected committee chairman or vice-chairman, the team that elected him may elect another team head.

3. A residents' committee representing a small number of residents shall in general not set up a work committee and its work shall be undertaken by its members with labor divided. A residents' committee representing a large number of residents may, according to requirements and with approval of the people's council, set up permanent or provisional work committees to work under the unified leadership of the residents' committee. Permanent work committees may be set up not exceeding five, in such fields as social welfare (including care for dependents of martyrs and servicemen), security, culture-education-health, mediation, and women's work. Temporary work committees should be abolished upon conclusion of their work.

Work committees should enlist activists among residents in their work, but where possible one person should assume one duty only so that they are not overburdened with work.

4. Elements subject to mass surveillance and elements disfranchised among residents should be incorporated into residents' teams but not be allowed to act as members of residents' committees, heads of residents' teams, or members of the work committees; when necessary, the head of an inhabitants' team has the power to stop their participation in certain meetings of the residents' team.

ARTICLE 4. A residents' committee shall be elected for a term of one year.

In case a member of a residents' committee cannot assume the post for some reason, another member may be elected to replace him or fill up the vacancy.

ARTICLE 5. In general, organs, schools, and large enterprises shall not participate in residents' committees but should send their representatives to the conferences relevant to them called by the residents' committees and should observe the resolutions and compacts of the residents' committees concerning public interests of residents.

In workers' residential areas in which office employees and workers of enterprises live together and in large collective living quarters, either a residents' committee should be set up under the unified guidance of the people's councils of municipal *chu* and municipalities without *chu* divisions or of their deputed organs, or else the committee of workers' dependents organized by trade unions may take up the work of the residents' committee.

ARTICLE 6. In city areas where minority nationals live together, a residents' committee may be set up separately; where the households are small in number, a residents' team may be formed.

ARTICLE 7. In case of necessity to assign tasks to residents' committees or their work committees, the work departments of the people's councils of municipalities and municipal *chu* and other organs should make unified arrangements subject to approval by the people's councils of municipalities and municipal *chu*. The work departments of the municipal and municipal *chu* people's councils may exercise professional guidance over the relevant work committees of the residents' committees.

ARTICLE 8. Residents should observe the resolutions and compacts of residents' committees concerning public interests. In carrying out their work, residents' committees should, on the basis of democratic centralism and voluntariness of the mass, fully manifest democracy and may not resort to coercion.

ARTICLE 9. Public and miscellaneous expense for residents' committees and living allowance for members of residents' committees shall be allocated under centralized plans by the people's councils of provinces and municipalities directly under the Central People's Government according to scales to be separately fixed by the Ministry of the Interior.

ARTICLE 10. Expenses defrayed by residents' committees for public welfare work may be collected from residents on a voluntary basis and subject to concurrence of residents and approval of the people's councils of municipal *chu* and municipalities without *chu* divisions. Apart from this, no donations may be collected and no funds may be raised among residents.

Appendix I

Organic Regulations of Urban Street Office*

*(Standing Committee of the National
People's Congress, 31 December 1954)*

ARTICLE 1. For the purpose of strengthening the work among inhabitants and maintaining close contact between the government and residents, the people's councils of municipal *chu* and municipalities without *chu* divisions may set up street offices according to work requirements as their deputed organs.

ARTICLE 2. Street offices may be set up in municipal *chu* and municipalities without *chu* divisions having 100,000 population and more and may also be set up in municipal *chu* and municipalities without *chu* divisions having less than 100,000 population and more than 50,000 population if work requirements actually need street offices, and shall not be set up generally in municipal *chu* and municipalities without *chu* divisions having less than 50,000 population.

Establishment of street offices shall be subject to approval by the people's council of the next higher level.

ARTICLE 3. The area under the jurisdiction of street offices should generally correspond to the area under the jurisdiction of public security substations.

ARTICLE 4. Street offices shall carry out the following tasks:

1. Undertake matters assigned by the people's councils concerning work among residents;
2. Direct the work of residents' committees;
3. Reflect the views and demands of residents.

ARTICLE 5. A street office shall have one director, several secretaries, according to the amount of work and size of area under jurisdiction, and one deputy director if necessary.

A street office shall have 3 to 7 full-time cadres including one to take care of work among women.

Directors, secretaries, deputy directors, and cadres of street offices shall be appointed by the people's council's of municipal *chu* and municipalities without *chu* divisions.

ARTICLE 6. Without approval of municipal and municipal *chu* people's councils, the work departments of municipal and municipal *chu* people's councils may not directly assign tasks to street offices.

ARTICLE 7. Running expenses for street offices and wages for working personnel shall be allocated by the people's coun-

*NCNA (Peking) 31 December 1954.

cils of provinces or municipalities directly under the Central People's Government under centralized plans.

Appendix J
Directive Concerning Establishment of Permanent System for Registration of Persons*
(State Council, 9 June 1955)

Following is the text of a directive of the State Council of the People's Republic of China concerning the establishment of a permanent system for the registration of persons as adopted by the eleventh meeting of the plenary session of the State Council of 9 June 1955.

The census-taking and registration of persons work carried out in 1953 has laid down a foundation for the establishment of a permanent system for the registration of persons. At present, steps have been taken to establish or to arrange for the establishment of this system in the greater part of the country. In order to make a good job of this work, the following instructions are hereby issued:

1. The administration of the registration of persons throughout the country is to be handled by the Ministry of Internal Affairs and the civil affairs department of the people's councils of the *hsien* level and above. The work is to be handled by public security stations in cities and towns, and by *hsiang* and *cheng* people's councils in villages and in towns where there are no public security stations.

2. In places where the registration of persons was formerly handled by the public security stations, the work is still to be handled in accordance with the provisional regulations governing the registration of persons in cities promulgated by the Ministry of Public Security on 16 July 1951. In villages and towns where there are no public security stations, the *hsiang* and *cheng* people's councils should maintain a register of persons, registers of birth and death, and registers of new arrivals and departures. The *hsiang* and *cheng* registers of persons should record all the permanent residents in the *hsiang* and *cheng*, and names should be added or removed all the time in accordance with the actual changes taking place to show the actual number of residents in these *hsiang* and *cheng*. The registers of birth and death as well as of arrivals and depar-

*Adapted from *SCMP*, no. 1082, July 1955.

tures should record all changes in population so that all changes can be traced. Particulars and measures governing the registration are stipulated as follows:

A. Birth: Within one month of the birth of a child, the father, mother, or other party concerned should report the parents of the child to the *hsiang* or *cheng* people's council of his/her place of domicile, or to the party responsible for the administrative organization under the *hsiang* or *cheng* people's council who will undertake to transmit the report to the *hsiang* or *cheng* people's council for registration in the register of birth.

B. Death: In the case of natural death, the head of family or other party concerned should report the death within one month of its occurrence to the *hsiang* or *cheng* people's council of his/her place of domicile, or to the party responsible for the administrative organization under the *hsiang* or *cheng* people's council who will undertake to transmit the report to the *hsiang* or *cheng* people's council for registration in the register of death. In the case of unnatural death (like suicide, homicide, and death of an unaccountable nature) and death from infectious diseases, the head of family or other party concerned should report immediately the death to the party responsible for the administrative organization under the *hsiang* or *cheng* people's council of his/her place of domicile, or direct to the *hsiang* or *cheng* people's council for registration so that an inquest into the death may be made.

C. Departures (including departure on account of marriage): When the whole family or an individual changes its or his/her permanent address, the head of family or the individual concerned should comply with the following stipulations prior to the departure taking place. In case of a change of permanent address inside the same *hsiang* or *cheng* being reported to the *hsiang* or *cheng* people's council, the change will be registered as a change of address only, and no emigration procedure need be taken. In the case of departure from a *hsiang* or *cheng* to another place inside the same *hsien*, the emigrant should apply to the *hsiang* or *cheng* people's council for a removal permit, and his departure should be recorded accordingly in the register of departures by the *hsiang* or *cheng* people's council. In the case of departure for another *hsien*, the *hsiang* or *cheng* people's council should issue or arrange with the competent organ of a higher rank to issue, to the person a removal permit and record his departure in the register. When a person is away from his place of domicile for over six months, he should complete the departure procedure. The departure of a landlord whose class status has not been changed must have the approval of a *chu* office or a *hsien* people's council. The departure of a party who has been deprived of his political rights or is on parole, under conditional condemnation, or is placed under surveillance must first have the approval of a *hsien* municipal judicial organ or public secretary organ before the emigration procedure can be completed in accordance with the above-mentioned stipulations. All removal permits are centrally printed and prepared by the public security organizations.

D. New arrivals (including new arrivals on account of marriage):   When the whole family or an individual removes to a new place, the head of family or the individual concerned should within five days after arrival report its or his/her arrival to the party responsible for the administrative organization under the *hsiang* or *cheng* people's council of its or his/her new place of domicile, and produce its or his/her removal permit and other documents for inspection.   The *hsiang* or *cheng* people's council should, on the basis of the report of the party responsible for the administrative organization, record the immigration into the register of arrivals after the documents are inspected.

In the case of changes in the makeup of households caused by a divorce, separation, co-tenancy, lost and found, adoption and taking over of children, taking on and dismissal of servants, the heads of families or the individuals concerned should report the changes to the *hsiang* and/or *cheng* people's councils or to the parties responsible for the administrative organizations under the *hsiang* and/or *cheng* people's councils who will transmit these reports to the *hsiang* and/or *cheng* people's council's to complete the registration or cancellation procedures in accordance with the regulations governing departures and arrivals.

3. Registration of persons for organs, organizations, schools, and enterprises: In places where there are public security stations, the registration is to be handled by the public security stations.   In villages and towns where there are no public security stations, the registration is to be handled by the *hsiang* or *cheng* people's councils.   The organs, organizations, schools, and enterprises concerned should also designate special personnel to assist in the registration.

4. Statistics on persons registered are to be prepared once a year for the time being.   Places of *hsiang* and *cheng* level should submit their changes in population figures for the previous year to *hsien* every February.   The *hsien* should report their changes in population figures to the province every March, and the provinces should report their changes in popu-

lation figures to the Ministry of the Interior every April.
In the case of places under the jurisdiction of *hsien* where
the registration of persons is handled by public security stations, at the time when places of *hsiang* and *cheng* level hand
in their reports, the public security stations should report the
changes in population figures in places under their jurisdiction to the *hsien* public security bureau, which will in turn
transmit same to the *hsien* civil affairs section. At the time
when the *hsien* hand in their reports to the province, the
municipal public security bureau should report the changes
in population figures in their municipalities to the municipal
bureau of civil affairs, which will in turn transmit same to
the provincial department of civil affairs. In the case of
municipalities under the direct control of the State Council,
the public security bureau should report the changes in population figures to the bureau of civil affairs for transmission to
the Ministry of Internal Affairs before the end of April every
year.

5. The provincial people's councils and the autonomous
organs of the autonomous areas may formulate flexible measures compatible with the local conditions and customs for the
national minority areas under their jurisdiction and base on
these flexible measures to report on population figures. The
formulation of flexible measures by different places should
be reported to the Ministry of the Internal Affairs for record-
ing.

6. Because the permanent system for the registration of
persons is at the initial stage of introduction and working experience in this connection is lacking, in carrying out the work,
the people's councils of all levels must put the work of publicity, inculcation, and organization into successful implementation and should subject their subordinate organs concerned
to intensified checkup and supervision and strengthen their
concrete guidance. The people's councils of *hsien* and autonomous *hsien* should call together, at the opportune moment,
the personnel handling the registration of persons (*hsiang*
clerks and members of civil affairs and public security committees) in the various *hsiang* and *cheng*, with one or more *chu*
as unit, and give them short courses of training. The spirit of
this directive should be explained in detail to and discussed
thoroughly with these personnel and should be constantly
publicized through them for the inculcation of the broad
masses of the people. In this way, we will be able to build
up and strengthen the permanent system for the registration
of persons step by step in the course of several years.
It is hoped that the people's councils of the various

provinces, autonomous areas, and municipalities under the direct control of the State Council will report the experience gained and the problems come across in the enforcement of this directive to the Ministry of the Interior as the occasion arises.

Appendix K

Provisional Measures Governing Grain-rationing in Cities and Towns*
(State Council, 25 August 1955)

Chapter 1: General Principles

ARTICLE 1. The provisional measures governing grain-rationing in cities and towns are formulated with a view to implementing the policy of the planned supply of grain, putting on a sound basis the system of grain supply in cities and towns, promoting grain conservation, and insuring the reasonable distribution of grain to facilitate national economic construction.

ARTICLE 2. Except for those localities that have not carried out unified purchasing and unified distribution of grain, cities and towns, including county seats and industrial and mining areas, will implement these measures.

These measures also apply to those government organizations, enterprises, schools, and capital construction sites that are not in cities and towns but have been decided by the provincial and autonomous district people's councils.

ARTICLE 3. All cities and towns enforcing these measures will implement the system of rationing by mouths (persons) and grades on the nonagricultural population, rationing by households on industrial and commercial trades, and rationing by classes on animal feed.

ARTICLE 4. Mouth rations for the residents, grain for use by industrial and commercial trades, and grain for animal feed will be distributed with verified supply and on presentation of cards. These cards are divided into seven groups: city and town resident grain-supply card; grain-supply card for industrial and commercial trades; city and town animal-feed–supply card; city and town resident grain-supply transfer card; grain ticket for nationwide use; local area grain ticket; and local area animal-feed ticket: The printing of

*NCNA (Peking) 25 August 1955.

these cards and measures governing their utilization will be separately fixed by the Ministry of Food.

Chapter 2: Rations for Residents

ARTICLE 5. The people's councils of provinces, autonomous districts, and municipalities under the direct jurisdiction of the Central People's Government will guide the work differentiation of the city and town residents, their ages, and grain-consumption habits in various localities, and follow the stipulations listed below to determine the concrete supply classification of city and town residents and the standards of the monthly rations of processed grain and unit catties to be implemented in provinces, autonomous districts, and municipalities under the direct jurisdiction of the Central People's Government.

1. Localities with rice as the staple food:

A. Workers engaged in special heavy manual work—45 to 55 catties, with the average not to exceed 50 catties.

B. Workers engaged in heavy manual work—35 to 44 catties, with the average not to exceed 40 catties.

C. Workers engaged in light manual work—26 to 34 catties, with the average not to exceed 32 catties.

D. Work personnel of government and people's organizations, staffs of public and private enterprises, shop assistants, and other office workers—24 to 29 catties, with the average not to exceed 28 catties.

E. College and middle-school students—26 to 33 catties, with the average not to exceed 25 catties.

F. Residents in general and children of 10 full years and above—22 to 26 catties, with the average not to exceed 25 catties.

G. Children above 6 full years and under 10 full years—16 to 21 catties, with the average not to exceed 20 catties.

H. Children above 3 full years and under 6 full years—11 to 15 catties, with the average not to exceed 13 catties.

I. Children less than 3 full years—5 to 10 catties, with the average not to exceed 7 catties.

2. Localities with miscellaneous grain and flour as the staple food:

A. Workers engaged in special heavy manual labor—50 to 60 catties, with the average not to exceed 55 catties.

B. Workers engaged in heavy manual labor—40 to 49 catties, with the average not to exceed 44 catties.

C. Workers engaged in light manual labor—29 to 39 catties, with the average not to exceed 35 catties.

D. Work personnel of government and people's organizations, staffs of public and private enterprises, shop assistants, and other office workers—27 to 32 catties, with the average not to exceed 31 catties.

E. College and middle-school students—29 to 36 catties, with the average not to exceed 35 catties.

F. Residents in general and children of and above 10 full years—18 to 23 catties, with the average not to exceed 22 catties.

G. Children above 6 full years and under 10 full years—18 to 23 catties, with average not to exceed 22 catties.

H. Children above 3 full years and under 6 full years—12 to 17 catties, with the average not to exceed 14 catties.

I. Children under 3 full years—6 to 11 catties, with the average not to exceed 8 catties.

ARTICLE 6. Households will be designated as units for city and town residents; the persons living in the family will be appraised into supply categories by the resident committees, resident groups, or other organizations. Staff and workers, government and people's organizations, enterprises, and schools, and college and middle-school students will be appraised to fall into various supply categories by the units to which they are subordinate. All will come under their households. Name lists will be compiled and together with census cards, they will be sent to the local people's councils or other designated organizations for verification and issuance of city and town resident grain-supply cards. Those staff and workers of government and people's organizations, enterprises, and schools, and college and middle-school students, whose families are not in the cities and towns will have their grain supply handled by the units to which they are subordinate.

Those personnel of government and people's organizations, enterprises, schools, and capital construction sites that are not located in cities and towns will be verified by their respective units, and appraised into supply categories. Name lists will be compiled to send to the organizations designated by the people's councils of the provinces and autonomous districts in which they are located for verification and issuance of (city and town) grain-supply cards.

ARTICLE 7. City and town residents having meals outside or traveling may bring their own food or they may present city and town resident grain-supply cards to draw local area grain tickets or grain tickets good for nationwide use within the amount of their rations.

ARTICLE 8. City and town residents where there are marriages, births, deaths, separations, and unions should, after going through census registration procedures, present their census cards to arrange for additions, reductions, or transfers in grain supply.

ARTICLE 9. City and town residents who change their residence should present their grain-supply cards to the original issuing organizations to draw grain-supply transfer cards. They will present the transfer cards to the new area to make arrangements for securing grain supply. During their change of residence, should they have surplus grain, they may bring it along or sell it to state food stores to draw local area grain tickets or grain tickets good for nationwide use.

Residents of localities that have not enforced unified purchasing and unified distribution of grain who move into cities and towns that have enforced grain-rationing will present papers issued by the people's councils of their former localities or from the organizations designated by them together with the census cards of the newly moved in localities to make arrangements for grain supply in accordance with Article 6 of these measures.

ARTICLE 10. Regarding the special food needed by the national minorities during festivals, the people's councils of the provinces, autonomous districts, and municipalities direcently under the direct supervision of the Central People's Government will stipulate measures to give consideration, based on the principle of conservation and national customs. For returned overseas Chinese and residents of localities that have not enforced unified purchasing and unified distribution of grain-rationing, the people's councils of their original areas or the newly arrived localities, or the overseas Chinese affairs organizations will issue them the documents needed to purchase grain. For those who are guests of state organs, the receiving units will prepare estimates for grain purchasing.

ARTICLE 11. For the personnel of the embassies and the consulates of the various countries in China, foreign diplomatic missions, foreign guests, experts, advisers, and professors, and their families, grain will be supplied in accordance with their actual needs on presentation of papers from foreign affairs organizations or organizations of jurisdiction.

For foreign nationals in general, the foreign affairs organizations will issue papers, and the local people's councils or their designated organizations will verify and issue city and town grain-supply cards, based on Article 6 of these measures.

Foreign vessels entering the ports will be supplied with grain on presentation of papers from the organizations of jurisdiction.

ARTICLE 12. City and town residents having surplus from

the rations they bought in accordance with rationing standards may resell them, give them away as presents, and carry out mutual accommodation; or they may sell them to the state grain stores, but they will not speculate in grain.

ARTICLE 13. Inhabitants of rural districts traveling to and fro in cities and towns may bring their own grain or they may follow the provisional measures governing unified purchasing and unified distribution of grain in rural districts to exchange for local area grain tickets or grain tickets good for nationwide use. City and town residents supplied with rations by the state will not duplicate again the computations of rations during the unified purchasing and unified distribution of grain in the rural districts.

Chapter 3: Grain for Use by Industrial and Commercial Trades and Products Made of Grain

ARTICLE 14. Grains required by industry and handicraft industry to be used as raw materials or subsidiary material. Each production unit, in accordance with its consumption rate, shall formulate a grain-consumption plan and it shall be submitted to the local people's committee or other appointed organizations for approval and issuance of a grain-supply card for industrial and commercial trades. As for grains required for making wine, a grain-consumption plan shall be formulated by the provincial, autonomous region, or municipality monopoly company, and it shall be submitted to the people's committees of provinces, autonomous regions, or municipalities, or other appointed organizations for approval and issuance of a grain-supply card for industrial and commercial trades.

ARTICLE 15. Grain required by restaurants, food-product businesses, confectionery businesses, and subsidiary food-product businesses in cities and towns. Each business unit shall formulate a grain-consumption plan, and this plan shall be submitted to the local people's committee or other appointed organizations for approval and issuance of a grain-supply card for industrial and commercial trades.

ARTICLE 16. Sales of prepared rice by restaurants and noodles, vermicelli, and other wheat food by food-product businesses to residents and people in transit shall be made only upon presentation of local area grain ticket or grain ticket for nationwide use. With these tickets restaurants and food-product concerns may buy back equal amounts of grain from any food store specially appointed by the state. A grain ticket shall not be required for the purchase of confections, huntun (7412 7388), and gruel. Concrete items of products made of grains that require the presentation of grain tickets will be stipulated by the people's committees of provinces, autonomous regions, and municipalities in accordance with the local conditions.

Chapter 4: Grain for Use as Feed Material

ARTICLE 17. In accordance with the following rules and in coordination with local conditions, the people's committees of provinces, autonomous regions, and municipalities shall set up standards of feed consumption for livestock to be enforced within areas under their control.

1. For horses and mules, 4 to 7 catties of raw grain per head per day;
2. For donkeys and camels, 2 to 4 catties of raw grain per head per day;
3. For milk cows, 4 to 6 catties of raw grain per head per day; and
4. For swine, the amount of feed shall not exceed the standard set up in the rural and nearby areas.

Each individual case will be considered separately. Feed supplies shall include bran, chaff, and bean cakes. The percentage to be added in the feed mix will be determined by the people's committees of provinces, autonomous regions, and municipalities in accordance with general conditions.

ARTICLE 18. Feed supplies required by government organizations, fraternities, enterprises, schools, and residents of cities and towns for feeding livestock that engage in production and transportation work. Each unit shall formulate a consumption plan in accordance with the set standards and submit it to the people's committee of the locality or other designated organizations for approval and issuance of a city and town animal-feed–supply card. As for feed supplies required by livestock and animals for scientific research, exhibition, demonstration, and insemination, the responsible unit shall formulate a feed-consumption plan and submit it to the local people's committee or other designated organizations for approval and issuance of a city and town animal-feed–supply card. Whenever changes occur in the number and variety of livestock and animals, the responsible unit shall conduct negotiations with the organization that issued the original feed-supply card for additional amounts of feed or have the supply reduced.

ARTICLE 19. When livestock or animals shall be shipped to other localities, the responsible units shall obtain a local feed-supply ticket for the amount of feed fixed by the city and town animal-feed–supply card. With this local feed-supply ticket, feed supplies may be purchased from animal-drawn cart stations, (stables?), and state-operated food stores. Upon presentation of local feed-supply tickets collected by animal-drawn cart stations and stables an equal amount of feed shall be reimbursed by food stores appointed by the state.

ARTICLE 20. Feed supplies required for livestock and animals rented by government organizations, fraternities, enterprises, and schools from nearby rural areas for transport purposes. The necessary amount of feed for such livestock and animals may be obtained by filing a request with the local people's committee or other designated organizations for approval.

Chapter 5: Addenda

ARTICLE 21. All people's committees of provinces, autonomous regions, and municipalities must base their activity on the detailed regulations of these provisional measures, put them into effect, and report to the State Council.

ARTICLE 22. Households engaging in agricultural production in cities and towns in short grain supply and feed supply for livestock. The supply of mouth grain and feed to these households will be handled in accordance with the stipulations prescribed in the provisional measures governing the unified purchase and distribution of grain in rural districts.

ARTICLE 23. Measures governing the supply of grain to military units will be formulated separately.

ARTICLE 24. These measures will be enforced as promulgated by the State Council.

Appendix L

Regulations Governing Household Registration*

(Standing Committee, National People's Congress, 9 January 1958)

ARTICLE 1. These regulations are enacted to maintain social order, protect the rights and interests of the citizens, and serve socialist construction.

ARTICLE 2. The household registration of servicemen in

*Adapted from *SCMP*, no. 1695, January 1958.

active service shall be handled by the military organs in accordance with the relevant regulations governing control of servicemen in active service.

Except separately provided for by law, these Regulations shall apply to the household registration of foreigners and stateless persons residing in the territory of the People's Republic of China.

ARTICLE 3. Household registration shall be under the charge of the public security organs.

In cities and *chen* where public security stations are established, the areas under the jurisdiction of the public security stations shall be their household control areas; in *hsiang* and *chen* where no public security stations are established, the areas under the jurisdiction of the *hsiang* and *chen* governments shall be their household control areas. The *hsiang* and *chen* people's councils and the public security stations shall be household registration organs.

In respect to persons living in organs, organizations, schools, enterprises and business units, and in public dormitories, the units concerned shall appoint special persons to assist the household registration organs in household registration. In respect to persons living in scattered places, the household registration organs shall directly handle the household registration.

In respect to servicemen who are not on the active list living in military organs and servicemen's dormitories, the units concerned shall appoint special persons to assist the household registration organs in household registration.

In respect to the households of agricultural, fishery, salt, forestry, livestock-breeding, and handicraft cooperatives, the cooperatives concerned shall appoint special persons to assist the household registration organs in registering the households. In respect to households outside the cooperatives, the household registration organs shall directly handle the registration.

ARTICLE 4. A household registration organ shall keep a register of households.

In cities, water-dwelling areas, and *chen* with public security stations, a household (registration) book shall be issued to each household.

In the countryside, a household (registration) book shall be issued to each cooperative; and no household (registration) book shall be issued to outside households. The household (registration) books and the items entered therein shall be valid to prove the identity of citizens.

ARTICLE 5. Households shall be taken as units of household registration. Persons living with the person in charge shall form one household with the person in charge as the household head. A person living alone shall form a household with himself or herself as the household head. Persons living in organs, organizations, schools, enterprises and business units, and in public dormitories shall form one or several households. The household heads shall be responsible for registering households according to these Regulations.

ARTICLE 6. Citizens should register themselves as permanent residents in localities where they regularly reside. A citizen can only register himself or herself as a permanent resident in one locality.

ARTICLE 7. Within one month of the birth of an infant, the household head, relative, foster parent, or neighbor shall report to and register the birth with the household registration organ in the locality in which the infant permanently resides.

In the case of a foundling, the person who receives and fosters it or the foundling institution shall report to and register the birth with the household registration organ.

ARTICLE 8. Upon the death of a citizen, the household head, relative, foster parent, or neighbor shall report to and register the death with the household registration organ before the funeral in the case of a city and within one month in the case of the countryside. In the case of the death of a citizen in his or her temporary place of residence, the household registration organ in the temporary place of residence shall notify the household registration organ of his or her permanent place of residence to record the death and have the original registration annulled.

If a citizen dies of accident or of unknown causes, the household head and finder should immediately report to the local public security station or the *hsiang* and *chen* people's council.

ARTICLE 9. In case an infant dies before registration of its birth, both birth and death should be reported to and registered with the household organ at the same time.

ARTICLE 10. Before moving from his household control area, the citizen concerned or the household head shall report to the household registration organ for registration of removal, receive a removal certificate, and have his or her original registration annulled.

A citizen who wants to move from the countryside to a city must possess a certificate of employment issued by the labor department of the city, a certificate of selection issued by a school, or a certificate issued by the household registration organ of the city permitting the removal to the city, and apply to the household registration organ in his or her permanent place of residence for permission for removal and fulfill the procedures of removal.

The removal of a citizen to a frontier defense area must be subjected to approval by the public security organs of the *hsien*, municipality and municipal *chu* in which he or she permanently resides.

ARTICLE 11. Before enlistment, a citizen called up for active service or the household head shall, bringing with him the call-up notice, report to the household registration organ in the locality of his or her permanent residence for registration of removal, and have his or her registration annulled, but no removal certificate shall be issued.

ARTICLE 12. In case of arrest of a criminal for trial, the organ that makes the arrest shall notify the household registration organ in the locality of his or her permanent residence to have his or her registration annulled and, at the same time, notify his or her dependents of the arrest.

ARTICLE 13. A citizen who moves to another locality or the household head shall, within three days of arrival in the case of the countryside, report to the household registration organ for registration, bringing with him the removal certificate, and surrender the removal certificate for cancellation.

Citizens who have no removal certificates may report to the household registration organs in the localities of new residence for registration on the production of the following certificates:

1. Certificates issued by the *hsien* and municipal military service organs or organs at regimental level or above in the case of demobilized servicemen and retired servicemen;

2. Passports or entry permits issued by the People's Republic of China in the case of overseas Chinese and students returned from abroad; and

3. Certificates issued by the release organs in the case of persons set free by the people's courts, people's procuratorates or the public security organs.

ARTICLE 14. Convicts who are paroled and whose sentence is suspended, elements subject to mass surveillance, and other persons deprived of political rights by law, when they move to other localities, must obtain the approval of the *hsien*, municipal, and municipal *chu* organs or people's legal affairs or public security organs through the household registration organs before they may register for removal; upon arrival at the localities to which they remove, they should immediately report to the household registration organ for registration.

ARTICLE 15. A citizen who temporarily resides for three days and more in a city outside the municipal and *hsien* areas in which he or she permanently resides, or the household head in the locality of temporary residence, shall within three days report to the household registration organ for temporary registration and for his or her registration to be annulled before departure. In respect to citizens who temporarily put up at a hotel, the hotel shall keep a guests' registration book and enter their names in the book from time to time.

Citizens who temporarily reside within the municipal and *hsien* areas of permanent residence or temporarily reside in the countryside outside the municipal and *hsien* area in which they permanently reside shall not register temporary residence except in the case of those who put up at a hotel and who shall be registered by the hotel from time to time.

ARTICLE 16. Citizens who leave their place of permanent residence for private business and stay in other localities for more than three months should apply to the household registration organs for extension of the period of stay or fulfill the procedures of removal. If they have neither the reason for extension of the period of stay nor the conditions for removal, they should return to their place of permanent residence.

ATICLE 17. When the records of the household registration need be changed or corrected, the household head or the persons concerned shall report to the household registration organ, which will change or correct the records upon verification of the case.

The household registration organ may at its discretion ask the applicant for proof required for the change or correction of records.

ARTICLE 18. Change of names of citizens shall be governed by the following provisions:

1. In case a person under 18 years of age requires change of name, he or she or his or her parent and foster parent shall apply to the household registration organ for changing the registration record;

2. In case a person of 18 years of age and over requires change of name, he or she shall apply to the household registration organ for changing the registration record.

ARTICLE 19. In case of change of household records due to marriage, divorce, adoption of children, establishment of identity, division of household, merging of households, missing persons, or other circumstances, the household or the persons concerned shall report to the household registration organs for changing the records.

ARTICLE 20. Penalties shall be imposed or criminal responsibility traced for the following, according to circumstances of each case:

1. Not reporting on households according to provisions of these regulations;
2. Making false statements on households;
3. Forging, altering, transferring, lending, or selling household certificates;
4. Taking the place of another under false pretences;
5. Failure of hotel managers to register guests according to these Regulations.

ARTICLE 21. Upon discovery of any counterrevolutionaries or other criminals in the course of household registration, the household registration organs should request the judicial organs to ascertain and prosecute those criminally responsible.

ARTICLE 22. The Ministry of Public Security shall make designs of and the public security organs of provinces, autonomous regions, and municipalities directly under the Central Government and shall print the household registration books, forms and certificates under centralized plans.

Citizens should pay cost of the household (registration) books and removal certificates received.

ARTICLE 23. The autonomous organs in nationalities autonomous districts may draw up local regulations in the spirit of these Regulations, taking into account the specific conditions in their localities.

ARTICLE 24. These Regulations shall take effect from the date of promulgation.

Appendix M

Provisional Regulations Governing Home Leaves and Wages of Workers and Employees*
(State Council, 16 November 1957)

ARTICLE 1. These provisional regulations are enacted with a view to solving, in an appropriate manner, the problem of enabling workers and staff members living apart from their families to return home for the purpose of visits.

ARTICLE 2. "To return home for the purpose of visit" within the meaning of these regulations refers to a visit made by a worker or staff member to his or her father, mother, and spouse. Any worker or staff member of state enterprises,

NCNA (Peking), 10 February 1958.

public-private joint enterprises, operation units, government agencies, or people's organizations, who lives apart from his or her father, mother, and spouse and is unable to return home for family gatherings or public holidays, will be entitled to the privileges of these regulations, provided that the worker or staff member concerned has already completed one year of uninterrupted service.

ARTICLE 3. No privileges stipulated in these regulations are to be granted to any worker or staff member who lives together with his or her father, mother, or spouse, or lives not far away from his or her home so that he or she can return home on public holidays for a family gathering. These regulations also shall not apply to any worker or staff member who is yearly entitled to another kind of paid leave for two or more weeks without interruption. One of the spouses shall be entitled to the privileges of these regulations if they work at different places and cannot meet each other on public holidays, although both may live together with their father and mother.

A worker or staff member working in the same locality as his or her father or mother shall be entitled to the privileges of these regulations if his or her spouse lives somewhere else, rendering gathering in public holidays impossible.

ARTICLE 4. In principle, a worker or staff member shall be permitted to take leave only once a year for the purpose of returning home to visit his or her family. The period of leave shall be from two to three weeks—public holidays included—depending on the time required for the journey.

When the administrative authorities cannot grant leaves to certain workers or staff members because of work requirements, approval should be obtained from the concerned basic-level trade union. Such levels shall be accumulated for the next year during which a leave from four to five weeks is to be granted to each of the concerned workers or staff members.

A worker or staff member who requires more than ten days for a round trip may be granted a leave from five to six weeks once every two years. The time required for the journey shall be counted as a part of this leave.

Bibliography

Chinese Newspapers and Journals (various dates)

Hsiamen Daily (Amoy)
Anhwei Daily (Anching)
Brilliance Daily (Peking)
Changchow Daily (Honan)
China Reconstructs
Chekiang Daily (Hangchow)
Chianghai Daily (Hsi-ning)
China's Women
China Youths
China Youths Daily (Peking)
Chungking Daily
Daily News (Shanghai)
Daily Workers (Peking)
Great Impartiality Daily (Peking and Tientsin)
Great Impartiality Daily (Hong Kong)
Harbin Daily (Heilungkiang)
Health News (Peking)
Hengyang News (Hunan)
Hopeh Daily (Paoting)
Hunan Daily (Changsha)
Hupeh Daily (Wuhan)
Kiangsi Daily (Nanchang)
Kwangchow Daily (Kwangchow)
Labor Daily (Yentsi, Shantung)

Liberation Daily (Shanghai)
Liuchou Daily (Kwangsi)
New China Daily (Chungking)
New China Monthly
New China News Agency (Peking)
New Construction
New Hunan Daily (Changsha)
Peking Review
People's Daily
People's Handbook
Shenyang Daily (Shenyang)
Sian Daily (Sian)
Southern Daily (Kwangchow)
Statistical Work
Study
Tienmen Daily (Hopeh)
Tientsin Daily (Tientsin)
Tsingtao Daily (Shangtung)
Wen Hui Daily (Hong Kong)
Wen Hui Daily (Shanghai)
Wuchow Daily (Kwangsi)
Yangtze Daily (Wuhan)

Documents, Articles, Speeches, and Monographs (in Chinese)

"Chief Tasks in the Migration Work for 1957, The." *Brilliance Daily* (Peking), 6 February 1957.

Chang, Ching-wa. "Why Must We Reduce Urban Population." *Daily Worker* (Peking), 4 January 1958.

Chang, Pai-kun, et al. "A Socialist Theory of Population and China's Population Problem." *Economic Research,* no. 4 (17 August 1957): 36–63.

Chang, Ying-lin. "Hung Liang-chi and His Principle of Population." *Eastern Miscellany* 23, no. 2 (25 January 1926):67 ff.

Chao, Ching. "A Critique of Recent Reactionary Population Theories in China." *New Construction* 5 (3 December 1955):26–32.

Chao, Hsueh. "On the Question of the Reclamation of Wasteland." *Great Impartiality Daily* (Peking), 29 April 1957.

Chen, Chang-hen. *On the Population of China.* 8th ed. Shanghai: Commercial Press, Ltd., 1928.

———. *Wen Hui Daily* (Shanghai), 8 April 1957.

Chen, Deng-yuan. *China's Land System.* Shanghai: Commercial Press, Ltd., 1932.

Chen, Ta. "Deferred Marriage, Birth Control, and Population Problems of New China." *New Construction,* no. 5 (May 1957):1–16.

Chiao, Yu. "On the Problem of Resettlement and Reclamation." *Brilliance Daily* (Peking), 15 January 1957.

Chinese People's Liberation Army's Policy on the Entry into Cities. Hsin Hua Book Co. (Central China Edition), 1949.

Chou, En-lai. Interview. *China Youths Daily* (Peking), 1 September 1963.

————. *Report on the Proposals for the Second Five-Year Plan for Development of the National Economy.* Peking: Foreign Languages Press. 1956.

Chou, Tung-chiao. "The Peitashan Incident, Sino-Mongolian Border, and the Sinkiang Question." *The Observer* 2 (5 July 1947):3–10.

Chow Hsin-min. "On the Encouragement of Late Marriage and the Statutory Marriage Age." *Daily Worker* (Peking), 7 November 1962.

Chu, An-ping. *The Manan River Reclamation District.* Peking: China Youths Publishing Co., 1956.

Chung, Hui-nan. "Birth Control and Later Marriage." *People's Daily,* 17 March 1957.

Directive on Temporary Methods of Handling Fixed Grain Supply in Cities and Towns. 1955.

Fei, Hsiao-tung. *Earth-bound Village China.* Shanghai: The Observer Weekly, 1948.

————. "What Does Population Research Entail?" *New Construction,* no. 4 (April 1957):5 ff.

————. "Admission of Crimes." In *The Complete Report,* First National People's Congress, 4th Session. Peking, 1957, pp. 1334–40.

Fu, Lien-chang. "A Talk with Young Comrades about the Question of Marriage." *China Youths Daily,* 2 February 1963.

First Five-Year Plan for Development of the National Economy of the People's Republic of China in 1953–1957. Peking: Foreign Language Press, 1956, pp. 40–42.

Ho, I-tsun. "Make Arrangements for the Establishment of the Friendship State Farm." *China's Agriculture,* no. 104, 25 December 1954.

Hsiao, Yo. "The Reclamation of Wasteland and the Increase in Arable Land." *Planned Economy,* no. 2, (9 February 1958):21–24.

Hsu Li-che. "Letter to Young Friends," *China Youths,* no. 209, 1 January 1959.

Hu, Yao-pong. "A Farewell Speech before Youth Volunteers Going to the Northeast." *China Youths Daily,* 16 August 1955.

Jung, Wen-tso. "The Removal of Shanghai's Factories into Interior." *New China Monthly* 1, no. 5 (March 1950):29–31.

Kung, Shao-chun. "I Am Not Willing to Get Married Early." *China's Women,* no. 8, 1 August 1963, p. 20.

Lan, Tien. "Urban Construction Be Undertaken in Accordance with the Principle of Economy, Utility, and Beauty." *People's Daily,* 7 January 1954.

Lei, Chieh-chiung. "The Rights of Women in New China." *Law in the Service of Peace* 1–2(1954–55):101–5.

Li P'u. "Do Not Allow the Rightists to Use the Population Question to Advance Their Political Conspiracy." *People's Daily,* 4 October 1957.

Li, Teh-chuan. Speech. In *The Complete Report.* First National People's Congress, 3d Session. 1956, pp. 143–50.

————. Speech. In *The Complete Report.* First National People's Congress. 4th Session. Peking, 1957, pp. 749–55.

Liang, Szu-cheng. "On China's Cities." Speech given at the second session of Second People's Congress. *People's Daily,* 11 April 1960.

Lo, Jui-ching. "Explanations of the Regulations Governing Household Registration." *People's Daily,* 9 January 1958.

Lung, C. F. "A Note on Hung Liang-chi, the Chinese Malthus." *Tien Hsia Monthly* (October 1935):248 ff.

Ma, Yin-chu. "New Population Theory." In *The Complete Report.* First National People's Congress, 4th Session. Peking, 1957, pp. 297–317.

————. "My Philosophy and Economic Theory." *New Construction,* no. 11 (November 1959):51–55.

————. *My Economic Theory, Philosophical Thought, and Political Standpoint.* Peking, 1958.

————. "To Repeat My Request." *New Construction,* no. 1 (January 1960):5–7.

Mao, Tse-tung. *On the Correct Handling of Contradictions among the People.* Peking: Foreign Languages Press, 1960.

————. *Selected Works of Mao Tse-tung.* Vol. 4. Peking: Foreign Languages Press, 1961.

Marriage Law of the People's Republic of China, The. Peking: Foreign Languages Press, 1959.

Ministry of Interior, the, and the Ministry of Labor, Central People's Government. *Joint Declaration on Continuing Implementation of the Directive Advising Against Blind Influx of Peasants into Cities.* 1953.

National Programme for Agricultural Development, 1956–1967. Peking: Foreign Languages Press, 1969.

"On the New Stage of the Women's Movement." *China's Women,* 16 May 1959.

Ou, Yu. "On the Question of Population Transfer and Land Reclamation." *Brilliance Daily* (Peking), 15 January 1957.

Peng, Te-Huai. "Report on Work in New Northwest During the Last Year." *Hsin Hua Monthly* 2, no. 6: 1233–36.

"Same Pay for Same Work to Men and Women in Chinghsi Production Brigade." *China's Women,* no. 11 (November 1961).

Selected Papers on the Founding of the People's Republic of China. Hong Kong: New Democracy Publishing Co., 1949, pp. 261–74.

"Shanghai: One Year after Liberation, 1949-1950." *Liberation Daily,* Shanghai, 1950.

Shao, Li-tzu. "Comments on Planned Reproduction." *Daily Worker* (Peking), 21 May 1957.

———. Speech. In *The Complete Report,* First National People's Congress, 3d Session. 1956, pp. 372-75.

———. Speech. *People's Daily,* 20 March 1957.

———. Speech delivered before the First National People's Congress, 4th Session. Peking, 1957.

"Some Questions Concerning Workers' Home Leave." *Daily Worker,* 19 December 1962.

State Council. *Prevention of Blind Exodus of Rural Population.* Joint Directive of the Central Committee of the CCP and the State Council, 18 December 1957.

"Strengthen Urban Planning Work and Reduce Urban Construction Cost." *People's Daily,* 23 November 1955.

Sun, Chin-chih. *Food Sources and Population Growth.* Peking: Science Publishing Co., 1957.

Sun, Ching-wen. "Urban Development." *People's Daily,* 12 August 1954.

Sun, Kuang. "Urban Population Must be Controlled." *People's Daily,* 27 November 1957.

Sun, Yat-sen. "Population Transfer to Mongolia and Sinkiang." In *Industrial Progress,* 1924.

———. See Chen Deng-yuan.

Tang, Chi-yu. *China's Reclamation and Cultivation.* Shanghai: Yunshun Publishing Co., 1952.

Tung, Chieh. "To Establish the Demography of the Proletariat Class." *New Construction,* no. 4 (April 1957):1-3.

Ten Great Years. Peking: Statistical Bureau, 1960.

Tien, Feng-Tao. "China's Planned Reproduction and Population Increase." *People's Health Protection,* no. 5 (1 May 1959):458-68.

Tien, Lin. "Comparison of the Last Seven Years to the Last Century." NCNA, 7 July 1957.

Tsai, Chang. "The Party's General Line Illuminates the Path of Emancipation for Our Women." *China's Women,* no. 1, 1 January 1960.

Wang, Chi-lung. "Strive to Strengthen Further the Solidarity of All Nationalities in Building a New Sinkiang." *Nationalities Unity,* 6 December 1961.

Wang, Feng-tsai. *Explanatory Statements on National Programme for Agricultural Development (Draft), 1956-1967.* Peking: China Youths Publishing Co., 1956.

Wang, Pao-yin. "What Kinds of Harm Does Early Marriage Bring to Young Men and Women." Speech at the third session of the Second

People's Political Consultative Conference. *People's Daily,* 14 March 1957.

Wang, Wen-pin. "A Talk about the Question of Age for Marriage from the Physiological Angle." *Daily Worker* (Peking), 15 November 1962.

Wang, Ya-nan. *Marxist Population Theory and China's Population Problems.* Peking: Science Publishing Co., 1956.

————. "Further Considerations of Marxist Population Theory and China's Population Problems." *New Construction,* no. 104 (3 May 1957):16.

Wei, Chuan-ching, et al. *The Economic Geography of Heilungkiang and Sungari River Valley.* Peking: Science Publishing Co, 1956.

Wu, Ching-chao. "Capital and Population During Industrialization." *The Observer* 3 (13 September 1947):10–12.

————. "Land Distribution and Population Accommodation." *Independent Commentary,* no. 1550 (1947).

————. "A New Treatise on the Problem of China's Population." *New Construction* (3 March 1957):1–8.

Wu, Fei-tan. "Optimum Population." *Wen Hui Daily* (Shanghai), 8 April 1957.

Wu, Pai-shi. "The Population Theory of Hung Liang-chi." *She Hui Yen Chiu (Sociological Research)* 91 (1935):241–43.

Yang, Ssu-ying. "On Malthusianism." *Study,* no. 10 (2 October 1955):24–25.

————. "The Premise of Birth Control Advocacy Is Not Malthusianism." *Study,* no. 109 (3 April 1957):172–75.

Yao, Sou-shih. "Smash the Enemy's Blockade and Struggle for the Development of New Shanghai." *Shanghai: One Year After Liberation* in *Liberation Daily* (Shanghai), 1950, pp. 7–11.

Yeh, Kung-shao. "What Is the Most Suitable Age for Marriage?" *China Youths Daily,* 12 April 1962.

Books and Monographs

Aird, John S. *The Size, Composition, and Growth of the Population of Mainland China.* International Population Statistics Reports, series P-90, no. 15. Washington: Bureau of the Census, 1961.

Bowman, I., ed. *Limits of Land Settlement.* New York: Council on Foreign Relations, 1937.

Chao, Kuo-chun. *Agrarian Policy of the Chinese Communist Party.* London: Asia Publishing House, 1960.

Ch'en, Jerome. *Mao and the Chinese Revolution.* New York: Oxford University Press, 1967.

Chen, N. R. *Chinese Economic Statistics.* Chicago: Aldine Publishing Co., 1967.

de Castro, Josue. *The Geography of Hunger.* Boston: Little, Brown, & Co., 1943.

Eldridge, Hope T. *Population Policies: A Survey of Recent Developments.* Washington, D.C.: International Union for the Scientific Study of Population, 1954.

Forsyth, W. D. *The Myth of Open Spaces.* Melbourne: Melbourne University Press, 1942.

Glass, David V. *Population Policies and Movements in Europe.* Oxford: Oxford University Press, 1940.

Glick, Paul. *American Families.* New York: John Wiley & Sons, 1957.

Harrington, Michael. *The Other America.* New York: Macmillan Co., 1963.

Hill, Reuben, et al. *The Family and Population Control.* Chapel Hill, N.C.: University of North Carolina Press, 1959.

Himes, Norman. *Medical History of Contraception.* Baltimore: Williams and Wilkins Co., 1936.

Hutchinson, E. P. *The Population Debate: The Development of Conflicting Theories up to 1900.* Boston: Houghton Mifflin Co., 1967.

Koya, Yoshio. *Pioneering in Family Planning.* Tokyo: Japan Medical Publishers, Inc., 1963.

Kreig, Margaret B. *Green Medicine: The Search for Plants That Heal.* Chicago: Rand McNally, 1964.

Lamb, Jefferson D. H. *The Development of the Agrarian Movement and Agrarian Legislation in China.* Shanghai: Commercial Press, Ltd., 1934.

Malthus, Thomas. *An Essay on the Principle of Population.* 1798.

Monahan, Thomas. *The Pattern of Age at Marriage in the United States.* Philadelphia: Stephenson Brothers, 1951.

Murphey, Rhoads. *Shanghai: Key to Modern China.* Cambridge: Harvard University Press, 1953.

Myrdal, Alva. *Nation and Family.* New York: Harper & Bros., 1941.

Orleans, Leo. *Professional Manpower and Education in Communist China.* Washington, D.C.: National Science Foundation, 1961.

Perkins, Dwight H. *Market Control and Planning in Communist China.* Cambridge: Harvard University Press, 1966.

Petersen, William. *Population.* New York: Macmillan, 1961.

Phelps, Harold A., and David Henderson. *Population in Its Human Aspects.* New York: Appleton-Century-Crofts, 1959.

Shabad, Theodore. *China's Changing Map.* New York: Frederick A. Praeger, 1956.

Smith, T. Lynn. *Population Analysis.* New York: McGraw-Hill, 1948.

Sun, Yat-sen. *The Three Principles of the People.* Translated by Frank W. Price. Shanghai: China Committee, Institute of Pacific Relations, 1927.

Taeuber, Irene B. *The Population of Japan.* Princeton: Princeton University Press, 1958.

Thomlinson, Ralph. *Population Dynamics.* New York: Random House, 1964.
Thompson, Warren S., and David T. Lewis. *Population Problems,* 5th ed. New York: McGraw-Hill, 1965.
Tien, H. Y. *Social Mobility and Controlled Fertility.* New Haven, Conn.: College and University Press, 1965.
Ullman, Morris B. *Cities of Mainland China: 1953 and 1958,* International Population Reports, series P-95, no. 59, Washington, D.C.: U.S. Bureau of Census, 1951.
United Nations. *The Determinants and Consequences of Population Trends.* New York: United Nations, 1953.
United Nations. *Measures for the Economic Development of Underdeveloped Countries.* New York: United Nations, 1951.
United Nations. *The Population of Asia and the Far East, 1950–1980.* Population Studies no. 3. New York: United Nations.
United Nations. *Proceedings of the 1954 World Population Conference (Rome),* New York: United Nations, 1955.
United Nations. *World Population Prospects.* St/SOA/Series A/41. New York: United Nations, 1966.
U.S. Department of State. *United States Relations with China.* Washington, D.C.: Government Printing Office, 1949.
Yang, Martin. *A Chinese Village.* New York: Columbia University Press, 1947.

Articles

Adil, Enver. "The Use of Statistical Guides and Measures of Effectiveness in Determining Government Policy for Influencing Fertility—Pakistan." In *World Population Conference, 1965.* Vol. 2. United Nations, 1967, pp. 63–67.
Bunting, Marion. "Why I am Glad I Didn't Marry While in College." *Journal of Home Economics* 47 (December 1955):757–58. Reprinted in *Marriage and Family in the Modern World: A Book of Readings,* edited by Ruth Shonle Cavan. New York: Thomas Y. Crowell, 1963.
"Central Committee Decree on Virgin and Idle Lands—I." *Current Digest of the Soviet Press* 6 (1954):1–6.
Chen Ta. "New China's Population Census of 1953 and Its Relations to National Reconstruction and Demographic Research." International Statistical Institute (Stockholm), 8–15 August 1957.
Chou, En-lai. Interviewed by Edgar Snow, as printed in the *New York Times,* 3 February 1964.
Dandekar, Kumudini. "Sterilization Programme: Its Size and Effects on Birth Rate." *Artha Vignana* (Gokhale Institute of Politics and Economics), no. 1 (September 1959):220–32.
———. "Vasectomy Camps in Maharashtra." *Population Studies* 17 (November 1963):147–54.

Davis, Judith Blake. "Demographic Science and the Redirection of Population Policy." In *Public Health and Population Change*, edited by M. C. Sheps and Jeanne C. Ridley. Pittsburgh: University of Pittsburgh Press, 1965.

Davis, Kingsley. "Malthus and Theory of Population." In *The Language of Social Research*, edited by Paul F. Lazarsfeld and Morris Rosenberg. Glencoe, Ill.: The Free Press, 1955, pp. 540–53.

———. "Population Policy: Will Curent Programs Succeed." *Science* 158 (November 1967): 730–39.

Davtyan, L. M. "The Influence of Socio-economic Factors on Natality (as exemplified in the Armenian Soviet Socialist Republic)." Translated from the Russian. In *World Population Conference, 1965*. Vol. 2. United Nations, 1967, p. 73–77.

Department of External Affairs, Australia. "Communist China—The Population Problem." *Current Notes on International Affairs* (Canberra, Australia) 29 (November 1958): 713–26.

Durand, John D. "The Population Statistics of China A.D. 2–1953." *Population Studies* 13 (March 1960): 209–57.

Eldridge, Hope T. "The Process of Urbanization." *Social Forces* 20 (March 1942): 311.

"Expanding Grain Production on Virgin and Idle Lands." *Current Digest of the Soviet Press* 6 (1954): 4–5.

Freeberne, Michael. "Changes in the Sinkiang Uighur Autonomous Region." *Population Studies* 20 (July 1966): 103–4.

Freymann, Moye W. "Population Control In India." *Marriage and Family Living* 25 (February 1963): 53–61.

Fun, Chen Mai. "Paying the Peasants." *Far Eastern Economic Review*, 3 November 1966, pp. 263–64.

Gendell, Murray. "The Influence of Family-building Activity on Women's Rate of Economic Activity." In *World Population Conference, 1965*. Vol. 4. United Nations, 1967, pp. 283–87.

Hajnal, J. "European Marriage Patterns in Perspective." In *Population in History*, edited by D. R. Glass and D. E. C. Eversley. Chicago: Aldine Publishing Co., 1965.

Ho, Franklin L. "Population Movement to the Northeastern Provinces." *Chinese Social and Political Science Review* 15 (1931–32): 346–401.

International Planned Parenthood Federation. "Wide Range of Family Planning." *China Now*, no. 24 (August/September 1972): 5–6.

Jaffe, A. J., and Koya Azumi. "The Birth Rate and Cottage Industries in Underdeveloped Countries." *Economic Development and Cultural Change* 9 (October 1960): 52–63.

"Krushchev's Speech to Young Settlers of New Lands." *Current Digest of the Soviet Press* 7 (1955): 12–13.

Lin, T. C. "Manchuria in the Ming Empire." *Nankai Social and Economic Quarterly* 8 (1935–36): 2–43.

Meadows, Paul. "Toward a Socialized Population Policy." *Psychiatry* 11 (May 1948):193–202.

Micklewright, F. H. Amphlett. "The Rise and Decline of English Neo-Malthusianism." *Population Studies* 15 (July 1961):32–33.

Moore, Wilbert. "Utilization of Human Resources Through Industrialization." In *Demographic Analysis,* edited by J. Spengler and O. D. Duncan. Glencoe, Ill.: The Free Press, 1956, pp. 518–31.

Murainatsu, Mihoru. "Policy Measures and Social Changes for Fertility Decline in Japan." In *World Population Conference, 1965.* Vol. 2. United Nations, 1967, pp. 96–99.

New York Times. Various Dates.

Notestein, Frank W. "Problems of Policy in Relation to Areas of Heavy Population Pressure." *Milbank Memorial Fund Quarterly* 22 (October 1944):424–44.

"On Procedures for Resettlement and Special Grants to Citizens Moving to Collective Farms Developing Virgin and Idle Lands." *Current Digest of the Soviet Press* 6 (1954):23.

"Party, Government Decree on Virgin and Idle Lands." *Current Digest of the Soviet Press* 6 (1954):11–14.

"Population Picture." *Far Eastern Economic Review,* 4 April 1968, p. 14.

Portisch, Hugo. Interview with a Chinese official as reported in the *New York Times,* 7 August 1964.

Raina, B. L. "Possible Effects of Public Policy Measures on Fertility in India." In *World Population Conference, 1965.* Vol. 2. United Nations, 1967, pp. 100–104.

"Reservists Go to Virgin Lands." *Pravda,* 23 October 1954, as translated in *Current Digest of the Soviet Press* 6 (1954):28.

Sadvoksasova, E. A. "Birth Control Measures and Their Influence on Population Replacement." In *World Population Conference, 1965.* Vol. 2. United Nations, 1967, pp. 110–14.

Sanyal, S. N. "Sterility Effect of the Oil of Pisum sativum Linn and Its Relations with Vitamin E." *Calcutta Medical Journal* 47 (September 1950):313.

Silberman, Leo. "Hung Liang-chi: A Chinese Malthus." *Population Studies* 13 (March 1960):262.

Spengler, Joseph J. "Socioeconomic Theory and Population Policy." *American Journal of Sociology,* 61 (September 1955):129–33.

Stycos, J. Mayone, and Robert H. Weller. "Female Working Roles and Fertility." *Demography* 4 (1967):210–17.

Taeuber, Irene B. "Population Policies in Communist China." *Population Index* 22 (October 1956):261–74.

Tai, Shi-kuang. "1953 Population Census of China." Calcutta: Indian Statistical Institute, 22 December 1956.

Taylor, Carl, John B. Wyon, and John E. Gordon. "Ecologic Determinants of Population Growth." *Milbank Memorial Fund Quarterly* 36 (April 1958):107–25.

Tietze, Christopher. "The Current Status of Fertility Control." *Law and Contemporary Problems* 25, no. 3 (Summer 1960):25.

"Tinker, Tailor . . . ," *Far Eastern Economic Review* (Hong Kong), 6 December 1962, pp. 511–12.

Walker, Kenneth. "Ideology and Economic Discussion in China: Ma Yin-chu on Development Strategy and His Critics." *Economic Development and Cultural Change* 2, no. 2 (January 1963):113–33.

Way, E. Leong. "Pharmacology." In *Sciences in Communist China,* edited by Sidney H. Gould. Washington D.C.: American Association for the Advancement of Science, 1961.

Index to Persons

General Index

Abortion: in China, 176, 177, 191, 218, 234, 235, 239, 263–73, 275; in Japan, 264–65, 271, 273. *See also* Fertility control

Acupuncture, 236–37. *See also* Fertility control; Sterilization

Agriculture: Chinese women in, 311–14; as factor in land reclamation, 124–30, 138–41, 142–62; as factor in population policy, 25, 30, 45–46, 99

Agricultural Development, National Programmes for, 132, 133 n.38, 157

Agricultural Reclamation, Department of, 145, 146–48, 154

Altai, the, 133, 135

Amoy (Hsiamen), 91, 359, App. E

Anching, 360, App. E

Anhwei, 27, 33; migration to, 36, 40, 91

Annual leaves. *See* Home leaves

Anshan, 63, 65; population information on, 55, table 4, 58, 354, App.C, 358,App.E

Antung, 358, App. E

Antzu, 39

Anyang, 360, App. E

Birth Control. *See* Fertility control

Canton, 28, 56, table 5, 143 n.60

Cauterization, 236–37. *See also* Fertility control; Sterilization

Chahar, 36, 37

Chanchiang, 359, App. E.

Changhu, 358, App. E

Changhun, 27, 358, App. E

Changsha, 358, App. E

Changshu, 360, App. E

Chaochou, 360, App. E

Chefoo, 360, App. E

Chekiang, 250

Chenchiang, 359, App. E

Chengchou, 358, App. E

Chengtu, 358, App. E

Chiamussu, 27, 55, table 4, 58, 146, 359, App. E

Chichihaerh, 27, 55, table 4, 58, 358, App. E

Child-spacing, 241

China Youths League, 142, 143 n.59

Chinchou, 27; population informa-